The Stuarts' Last Secret

THE STUARTS'
LAST SECRET

THE MISSING HEIRS
OF BONNIE PRINCE
CHARLIE

PETER PINIŃSKI

TUCKWELL PRESS

First published in Great Britain in 2002 by
Tuckwell Press Ltd
The Mill House
Phantassie
East Linton
EH40 3DG
Scotland

ISBN 1 86232 199 X

The publishers acknowledge subsidy from the Scottish Arts Council
towards the publication of this volume

British Library Cataloguing-in-Publication Data
A catalogue record for this volume is available on request from the
British Library

Typeset by Servis Filmsetting, Longsight, Manchester
Printed and bound by Bell & Bain Ltd, Glasgow

Contents

Part One: The Exile

Part Two: The Secret

List of Illustrations

Many of the portraits, documents, prints and photographs belong to the author's family to whom gratitude is expressed for permission to use them as illustrations. The author would also like to thank those intitutions mentioned below for permission to reproduce various others.

---

[1] This portrait is of particular interest. It was acquired from the Vatican in 1982. Documentation from the Vatican archives, copies of which are at the Royal Castle in Warsaw, prove that it was commissioned by the Vatican in 1740 as a copy of the 1725 original by Martin van Meytens, though with certain minor changes. It then served as the basis for the mosaic by Piero Paulo Cristofari which forms part of Clementina's tomb in St. Peter's, Rome designed by Filippo Barigioni and sculpted by Pietro Bracchi (1739–1741).

Acknowledgements

My thanks to all those in the reading room for microfilms at the National Library in Warsaw as well as Arthur Addington, Catherine Bas of the Centre Généalogique de Touraine, Anna Bezrąk, Morris Bierbrier of the British Museum, Professor Janusz Bieniak, Donald Cameron of Lochiel, Tessa Capponi-Borawska, Mellissa Dalziel of the Bodleian Library in Oxford, Dr Rainer Egger of the Austrian Kriegsarchiv, Madame Feyler of the Musée de Saverne, Alain Giraud, Anna Gordijewska, Philip Graham, Professor Barbara Grochulska, Anna Gros, Michel Guillot of the Archives Nationales in Paris, David Howard, Professor Anna Komornicka, Kasia Kraińska, Dr Wojciech Kriegseisen of the Institute of History in Warsaw, Maria Księżopolska, Piotr Księżopolski, Professor Henryk Kubiak, Dr Michał Kulecki of the Main Archive of Ancient Records (AGAD) in Warsaw, the late James Lees-Milne, Tomasz Lenczewski, Professor Bruce Lenman, Professor Waldemar Łazuga, Georges Martin, Mona McLeod, Dr. Rita Majkowska of the Polish Academy of Science in Cracow, Michel Marty, Maria Muryn of the Central State Historical Archive of the Ukraine in Lwów, Maria Niemojowska, the late Dr. Andrzej Piber of the Department of Manuscripts at the National Library in Warsaw, Roger Pierrot, Raymond Poulain of the Friends of the Musée de la Poste in Paris, Roger Powell, Josselin and Olivier de Rohan-Chabot, Professor Andrzej Rottermund of the Royal Castle in Warsaw, Hallie Rubenhold, Pierre Schulé, Desmond Seward, Michael Sharp, Mathew Sheldon of the Royal Naval Museum in Portsmouth, Maria Sierocka-Pośpiech of Main Archive of Ancient Records (AGAD) in Warsaw, Hana Slavičkova, Helena Śmiškova and Ondra Śmišek of the State Archives in Děčin in the Czech Republic, Joanne Smith of the Archives of Southampton City Council, Moritz Strachwitz of the Deutsches

Adelsarchiv, Dr. Christoph Tepperberg of the Austrian Kriegsarchiv, Robert Testot-Ferry, Tours historian Ludovic Vieira, Vicki Wells, Jerzy Wolański, Andrzej Wolański and Dr. Hubert Zenz of the Austrian State Archives in Vienna.

In particular my thanks to Agnieszka Sozavíska for suggesting I write this book and to my son, Alexander, for his great patience whilst I did so.

If I have missed out anyone, then please forgive me.

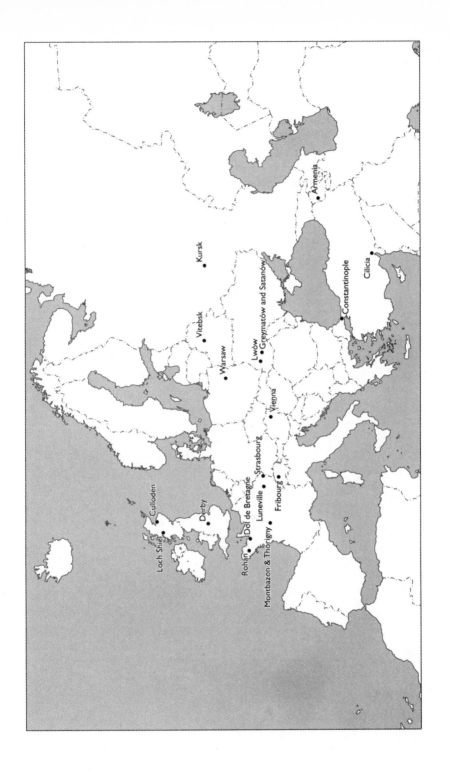

Guide to Polish Pronunciation

Polish pronunciation looks as difficult to the newcomer as Gaelic. However, it is simple, regular and stress is always on the penultimate syllable.

Vowels are pronounced:

a	(as in 'and')	e	(as in 'end')	i	(as in 'mean')
o	(as in 'hot')	u	(as in 'hook')	y	(as in 'hit')

Consonants are the same as English except for:
c   (= 'ts' like 'hits' – phonetically = 'hyc')
j   (= 'y' like 'yes')
w   (= 'v' like 'love' – or 'ff' like 'off' if at the end of a word)

There are also some groups of letters that produce a single sound:
cz   (= 'ch' like 'cheat')
ch   (= 'ch' like 'loch')
rz   (= like 'zh' or the 'je' of the French 'j'aime')
sz   (= 'sh' like 'shilling')

There are also accents:
ą   (as in 'faun')*   ę   (as in 'lent')*

(* both are pronounced nasally)

ć or ci   (like the 'ch' of 'cheat' but more delicate)
ł   (like the 'w' in 'weather' or 'pew')
ń   (like the 'ñ' in 'mañana')

ó	(like the 'oo' in 'pool')
ś	or si (like the 'sh' of 'shilling' but more delicate)
ż	(like the 'je' of 'j'aime' but harder)
ź	or zi (like the 'je' of 'j'aime' but more delicate)

(by 'delicate' it is meant that the sound is formed just behind the teeth)

<u>Examples:</u>

Lwów	: Lvooff	Nikorowicz	: Nee ko <u>ro</u> veetch
Grzymałów	: Gzhy <u>ma</u> woof	Krasicki	: Kra <u>sheet</u> ski
Przemyśl	: <u>Pzhe</u> myshl	Radziwiłł	: Rad <u>zhee</u> viw
Warszawa	: Var <u>sha</u> va	Potocki	: Po <u>tot</u> ski
Suszczyn	: <u>Soosh</u> chin	Mieczyslas	: Mye <u>chis</u> las
Świrz	: Shveezh	Dołęga	: Doh <u>wen</u> ga

Preface

There are books which do not really need a foreword and there are those where an introductory word may help. The one is no better than the other. They are, however, different.

Peter Piniński took upon himself no small task: the pursuit of history deliberately hidden. Step by step he gradually uncovered the truth and drew back the curtain obscuring old family secrets. By discovering, comparing and analysing various data and documents he unravelled a genealogical enigma with all the skill of a true detective. In his research he economised on neither time nor geography, working in archives both large and small across the breadth of Europe, hunched over documents written in a variety of languages. He made contact with people who could help him in these investigations, wrote letters, amassed material and conducted tens of interviews.

One thing I can immediately confirm is the conscientiousness, scale and precision of the research. It is impressive, though the author is not even a professional historian. No less so is his knowledge of the complexities of the epoch (or rather epochs), so essential to detailed research aimed at bringing to light new information and interpretations.

On his father's side the author is a Pole, on his mother's a Scot. From a contemporary as well as a historical perspective he probably knows both countries equally well and in addition has a command of several languages. For the task he undertook he was prepared in a way given to few.

Where the text is concerned with setting the scene and describes widely known events the author has resigned from giving sources. However, where original research work is presented each piece of information is documented with detailed footnotes.

As concerns the background of the Polish history described, the native will have few problems. However, one or two words may be justified for the benefit of the non-Polish reader. Firstly there is the court in Lorraine of the ex-King of Poland, Stanislas Leszczyński, whose daughter became the wife of Louis XV. It is no exaggeration to say that this was a place of constant meetings between the French and Polish aristocracies – a melting-pot of contacts both social and non-social. Here it was that diverse trade and political business was settled, where the freemasons of the Grand Orient met (amongst whom were many of the highest Polish nobility), together with circles of people bound by the closest of ties. About the role of Poles in French freemasonry we know quite a bit, mainly thanks to the work of Ludwik Hass. We see that Prince Adam Czartoryski was guest of honour when Philip, Duke of Orléans, was raised to the dignity of Grand Master in 1773, and that in the French and Parisian Lodges were Poles who represented all the various political camps. There the likes of the Potockis and Lubomirskis mixed with men such as the Baron de Sellonf, banker to the last king of Poland, Stanislas August.

In addition there could be found at Leszczyński's Court agents of the Bourbons' secret service (the so-called 'Secret du Roi'). Indeed, in this relatively small circle, one has the impression that everybody knew one another. No small number of them were even related by ties of blood. For example, the Stuarts were connected with many Polish families through the Sobieskis. And the Bourbons through the Leszczyńskis. Here we see only near and less near connections – cousins and aunts who stretch from Paris to the Crimea. Sometimes we know exactly the subjects of their conversations. At other times we can only guess. We know, for example, that the progress of the Enlightenment in various parts of Europe was keenly discussed, and politics not a little, alongside both family and social matters. Frequently business was also a topic. Its scope reached even to the Black Sea. For this profitable area of trade was of keen interest from at least the middle of the eighteenth century. Polish magnatial banking circles had long been associated with the region. And for France the road there was via Poland. So she started to send envoys to Warsaw and begin joint trade initiatives – companies in which participated Jean Bonneau, the correspondent of the French Government, the Warsaw bankers, and Frederick Joseph Moszyński, Grand Advocate of Lithuania (Wielki Referendarz).

Later, Franco-Polish joint ventures began to multiply, embracing both the Warsaw and Galician spheres and involving King Stanislas

August, the Radziwiłłs, the Potockis (of whom one, Anthony Protazy, was a well-known banker), as well as the greatest financiers active in Poland such as Fergusson-Tepper, Kabryt, Szulc and Łyszkiewicz. Poland, during the reign of her last king, experienced a period of considerable economic expansion. Bankers generated fortunes, supported public works and even competed amongst themselves in this regard. Ever more closely they became tied to Poland's magnatial families and began to imitate their lifestyle. They joined the Knights of Malta and, such as in the case of Nikorowicz and Prince Charles Radziwiłł, became almost intimate.

Nikorowicz and Łyszkiewicz were bankers of Armenian origin, or as was more commonly said: 'Polish Armenians'. Such families had been present in Poland since the fourteenth century, mainly inhabiting the larger towns, and remain up to the present day. From the sixteenth century onwards their customs began to become polonised, and throughout that and the next century they rapidly developed their colonisation of the eastern parts of the country. From the earliest times they enjoyed the reputation of excellent craftsmen and superb traders, linking the old Republic with Persia and Turkey. It was in large measure due to them that oriental motifs were introduced into the culture and art of Poland. Many enjoyed splendid careers in public life. Some, such as the Nikorowicz family, were granted nobility and became landowners.

Faithful to their adopted country, they remained so even after the Partitions. In autonomous Galicia, annexed by Austro-Hungary, where national liberty was at its greatest, they again played a not insignificant role. A few, like the Nikorowicz family, were outstanding in the realm of finance. Then there were those, such as David Abrahamowicz, who became eminent politicians. He was a member of the Polish Circle in the Austrian Parliament and Speaker of its House of Commons. Others, for example the Imperial Chamberlain Marian Rosco-Bogdanowicz, were eminent habitués of the salons of Lwów and Vienna. These few, for long allied with the Polish nobility, were not viewed as being 'of Armenian origin' by their German, Czech and Ukrainian counterparts, but exclusively thought of as Poles.

The Pinińskis, though originally from the province of Dobrzyń, had by the eighteenth and nineteenth centuries become one of the well-known noble families of Galicia. Whilst the old Republic still existed, the family produced chamberlains, both county and royal, founders of churches and benefactors. After the First Partition of Poland those who found themselves in Galicia were District Governors (Starosta Grodowy), and with only a few exceptions were all members of the Galician Parliament as representatives of the 'Magnatial Class'.

In 1778 Maria Theresa of Austria granted them the hereditary title of Count – earlier than other leading families such as the Gołuchowskis or Badenis. In the world of Galicia, and then progressively so in that of Austria, they gained the reputation of enlightened landlords and amateurs of the arts, were amongst the first to emancipate the peasants and both inherited and acquired a multiplicity of estates. From the times of Leonard Francis Xavier (1824–1886) the magnificent and prosperous estate of Grzymałów became associated with their name. His sons were Stanislas, Leon, Mieczyslas and Alexander – all figures well known throughout Galicia. The eldest, Stanislas, became a District Governor, a councillor of the Imperial Court as well as of the Ministry of the Interior in Vienna and a member of the Austrian Parliament. The third, Mieczyslas, also became a member of both the Galician and Austrian Parliaments whilst the ill-fated youngest, Alexander, was a poet.

However, the greatest career – and what's more in several fields simultaneously – belonged to the second oldest, Leon. He was an outstanding patron of the arts, lawyer, professor, chancellor of Lwów University (1928–29) and a member of the Parliaments of Galicia and Austria. There he occupied many high offices until 1898 when he gained the highest of all – that of Viceroy of Galicia. The full scope of his achievement will be revealed in the later pages of this book. But prior to that the reader will travel no small distance across the length, breadth and events of the old continent of Europe.

Waldemar Łazuga
Professor of Nineteenth- and Twentieth-Century History,
University of Poznań, Poland

Foreword

The tribute paid by Professor Waldemar Łazuga's Preface to the broad historical journey through Central and Eastern Europe which these pages offer us, is well-merited. The present writer need not repeat it. He is not qualified to pronounce on the history of these areas, though he finds the material fascinating and revealing. What he can without presumption do is say a word about the general field of Jacobite studies, and the contribution which Peter Piniński's painstaking researches make to it.

This book is not written as a specialised monograph for professional scholars. Rather is it family history written over a grand sweep of time about families which from the eighteenth to the twentieth centuries were involved in turbulent and dramatic events which linked my native Scotland to the Poland to which Peter Piniński so completely gives his allegiance and loyalty. It is moving that he also retains a strong interest in Scoto-Polish ties throughout history, ties which were strong centuries before the exiled royal house of Stewart married into the Sobieski family. The Stewarts have nevertheless the vital role of the point of departure for this book. Without Charlotte, Duchess of Albany, and her children, there would be no book. So this book is rooted in Jacobitism and family history.

Both areas are notoriously haunts of the pseudo-scholar and the obsessive, mentally unbalanced enthusiast. Mr Piniński is neither. Those, like myself, who have met him, as well as read his work, are doubly clear on that point. Readers can judge for themselves. This book is a great read, and the scholarship behind it is deliberately unobtrusive, but it is very extensive. Indeed, a professional scholar like myself, harassed by tidal waves of bureaucratic paper, and by the delights and time-consuming complications of teaching, blenches at the sheer volume of source material in several languages on which this book is based, not to mention the vast background reading which keeps its narrative up-to-date in tone.

There is controversy in every serious book. This one is not likely to be the exception to so general a rule. But its author cannot be accused of cutting corners or imposing wilfully improbable interpretations on the evidence. He has been careful and even-handed. Let the reader be the judge as he or she enjoys moving across the vast and exciting panorama laid out in this book.

May this extraordinary work be a harbinger of more fruitful Scoto-Polish cooperation in the peaceful decades we all pray lie ahead for western man. I wish it and its author well.

Bruce P. Lenman
Professor of Modern History,
University of St. Andrews,
Scotland

Introduction

All that radiant kingdom lies forlorn
as if it never stirred
no human voice is heard amongst its meadows
but it speaks to itself alone
alone it flowers and shines
and blossoms for itself while time runs on.

Edwin Muir

In my family we had always known that my father's great-great-great grandmother was the natural daughter of a Prince de Rohan. And that until Grzymałów, our castle in south-eastern Poland, was devastated by the Russians during the First World War there had been letters apparently from her father, though oddly not from her mother, kept in an antique desk together with the family's oldest and most valuable documents, some dating back to the fourteenth century. Even today her pastel portrait as a young, smiling woman with bright blue eyes hangs in the apartment of my aunt in southern Poland. Another is in my home in Warsaw. But no-one in the family had ever tried to find out who she really was – until the summer of 1997. Uncovering her secret involved research in twenty-two archives in seven countries.

I was born in 1956 and brought up in England not long after my mother and father came down from university at St. Andrews. Mother was from the Scottish family of Graham and it was natural enough that she should have studied there. But my father's provenance was different. In the Summer of 1939 he and my grandmother had been sent by my grandfather to England for a holiday with Scottish friends of the family. They, curiously enough, had been introduced to one another by my family whilst both were in Lwów, then the capital of Galicia – the Polish province of the Austro-Hungarian Empire until Poland regained her independence after the First World War. September the first came and war broke out. Schooling was hurriedly arranged for my father, after which he joined the Polish Air Force. When the war ended he received a place at St. Andrews. My father was an only child and by 1945 the only male of his family left. By then there was no home nor father for him to return to. One uncle had been executed in Kiev in 1940 by the Soviet NKVD (the forerunner of the KGB). Another was murdered in 1945 at the infamous Nazi concentration camp, Dora. Whilst my grandfather was killed by Tito's communists in today's Croatia.

My father's nearest relations were his paternal aunt and her husband. This uncle, however, was General Bór-Komorowski, the leader of the Warsaw Uprising, commander-in-chief of the Polish Resistance and, from 1944, of the Polish Armed Forces. Having been wanted dead or alive by Hitler for the then vast sum of £400,000, he was now wanted just dead by the Soviet-sponsored Polish communists. Had my father gone back to his country after the war, he would have been taken hostage in order to force the return of his uncle who would have been executed. It wasn't an option.

As an only son with no money and a refugee mother to support, my father urgently needed a job. But in England during the aftermath of the war there was an atmosphere of antipathy towards foreigners. However, my father had a talent for languages and, though his third, he nevertheless spoke flawless English. Uncompromised by obvious non-Englishness, he changed his name, found a good job in London and set about rebuilding some sort of security for his young family. We never spoke about matters Polish when I was young. And if there was a cultural profile, it was the Scottishness of my mother's family. The black vacuum that was my father's past was filled only by occasional visits to my Komorowski relations and from my paternal grandmother. But at the Komorowskis we left my father and great-uncle to their hushed, serious conversation and went to play in the park. My great-aunt was concerned with the present and future and was filled with infectious energy. I felt strongly drawn to her. My grandmother like-wise seldom referred to Poland and never to the past. She had a deep, pure faith and such lightness of being that it never once occurred to me what these people had been through. I had a surname with no past, chosen by my father in 1949 from a St. Andrews University Library law book for being not too ostentatious. But he was unaware of its specific identity, and its relative rarity outside Scotland contributed to the regularity with which I used to be asked where my family was from. I would answer evasively that my mother was Scottish.

When my father's mother died in 1976, her coffin was covered with carnations. The top half were white and the bottom half were red. As I stood before it, on my father's left, I asked him why those colours had been chosen. I saw the suppressed emotion on his face as he told me for the first time: 'They are Poland's colours'.

Returning home that day with my cousin, Adam Komorowski, I told him what had happened. Shortly after I changed my name back to Piniński. My father shook his head. My mother knew she couldn't change my mind. She may even have been pleased. And I started a journey into the past. After some time my father joined me. For him it was not new, but a painful return. It wasn't easy because my father was only fourteen when the war broke out. Prior to that he had lived mostly in Paris, far from his roots. My grandfather had wanted him to be educated in a cosmopolitan city and to attend a modern French agricultural college so as to be properly qualified to manage the estates he would inherit. However, all this meant that during his pre-war youth, much of his family's culture was unknown to my father. So I had to find out about it from many other sources as well. Between 1976 and 1981 I spent a large amount of time talking to distant relatives and reading whatever I could lay my hands on. Then, in the first year of the free trade union 'Solidarity', I went to Poland for what was to have been a year's research work at the National Museum in Warsaw. But when on the night of December 13th, 1981 the democratic opposition was put down, I found my visit cut short. I remember it vividly. In mid-January 1982 I was unceremoniously, and not without incident, put on a plane to Denmark. I felt furious and humiliated at being rejected as a foreigner and wanted to stay and share with my friends whatever might happen. Thereafter I continued to absorb as much information as I could, working on my Polish and visiting the country. And the private interest in my family's past developed into a fascination with Polish and Scottish history and their many parallels.

The year 1989 brought the fall of communism. In late 1990 I bought a flat in Warsaw and in March 1991 began a new life there. Today Poland has once more regained her sovereignty whilst Scotland, with her first parliament for 300 years, is perhaps beginning to regain hers. At home we speak the languages of both countries with equal frequency, whilst by day my son learns two more at his brand-new school. And no-one asks him where his father's name comes from.

My uncle and aunt Komorowski now lie side by side in a grave for the four leaders of the wartime Polish Resistance in Warsaw's military cemetary. In a magnificent state funeral they were reburied in 1994 on the fiftieth anniversary of the Warsaw Uprising. As we followed the gun carriage with my great-uncle's coffin through the streets of the capital, I found myself once again by my father and cousin's side. But this time I knew why the flowers were white and red.

And most weeks we sit down to supper with my aunt and uncle of whose existence I never knew until I came to Poland for the first time in the last semi-free days of 'Solidarity' in 1981. It was their father who in 1940 had been executed by the NKVD in Kiev. And it was their mother who remembered her father, Stanislas Piniński, showing her the letters from the antique desk in the Castle of Grzymałów from the Prince de Rohan to the smiling young woman with bright blue eyes in the portrait.

When I consider all that has changed in only twenty years, it seems strange the way in which events themselves have almost conspired to discover a secret that had remained hidden for over two hundred years. How the pieces of the jig-saw had neatly fallen into place by the Summer of 1997 when I first noticed in a biography of Bonnie Prince Charlie that his only child had borne three natural children by Prince Ferdinand de Rohan. I passed it by at first, but the thought wouldn't stop nagging at me. So I made a mental note to try and find out a little more about 'our' Prince de Rohan when I returned from holiday to Warsaw.

PART ONE

 The Exile

The Civil War of the mid-seventeenth century terminated with the restoration of the Royal family of Stuart to their thrones of Scotland, England and Ireland. Charles II's reign was followed by that of his younger brother, James VII & II. It was a time of religious antagonism. In France Louis XIV's regime was both anti-Protestant and expansionist. His bitter opponent was the Calvinist Stadtholder of Holland, William of Orange. He was both James's nephew and son-in-law. Yet James had converted to Catholicism and was set upon implementing an unpopular domestic policy of political parity for Catholics despite the majority of his English subjects being Protestant.

William feared two things – that James would be drawn into a military alliance with France, thus changing the balance of power in Europe against the Protestant bloc; and that as James was still without a male heir, the Stuart succession in favour of William and his wife would be under threat because of James's domestic policy of ecumenical egalitarianism.

William had already been interfering in domestic British politics for some time prior to mid-1688 when James's second wife, the ultra-Catholic Mary of Modena, gave birth to a legitimate male heir. The birth of James Francis Edward Stuart was the signal for William to implement a plan he had prepared earlier to keep Britain in the Protestant camp by force. Some weeks later William invaded England. His father-in-law fled into exile. There then followed repeated attempts by the Stuarts to regain their thrones. Each plagued by that family's legendary bad luck . . .

CHAPTER ONE

Power and Glory

To the Lords of Convention 'twas Claverhouse spoke
'Ere the King's crown shall fall there are crowns to be broke
So let each cavalier who loves order and me
Come follow the bonnet of Bonnie Dundee!

Sir Walter Scott

It was Spring of the year 1683. A vast Turkish army had moved out of Belgrade and was fast approaching Vienna. There in the frightened heart of Europe, Leopold, the Holy Roman Emperor, appealed throughout the continent for help. But none did he seek more than that of King John III Sobieski, King of Poland and Hammer of the Turks. To him he wrote: 'It is not so much Your Majesty's troops that we need, as Your Majesty's presence. For we are sure that your person at the head of our armies and your name alone, which is held in awe by our common foe, will mean defeat for them'.

The fearless war horse relished no prospect more. On April 1st he signed an agreement of military assistance with the Imperial ambassador, Count Waldstein, in which he would receive 1,200,000 ducats and supreme command of the allied forces of Europe if he came in person to lead the relief. The Polish King organised his forces and moved south towards Vienna which, by mid-July, was being besieged by a Turkish force of no less than 65,000 Turkish soldiers, 15,000 Tartars and thousands of other people. Inside the locked gates of the encircled city the defence, under Count Rüdiger von Starhemberg, was helpless.

The Polish Army of 21,000 arrived at Vienna on September 12th in two columns led by Field-Marshals Nicholas Sieniawski and Stanislas

Jabłonowski. En route they had stopped at the great Monastery of Częstochowa where Sobieski was given the sabre his grandfather, Field-Marshal Żółkiewski, had left there years before as a votive offering. Then, upon arrival at the siege, the king assumed supreme command of the 65,000-strong Christian army.[1] J.B.Morton, in *Sobieski, King of Poland*, lets us glimpse the opposing protagonists:

> Upon a bay horse came the Polish king, sitting in his saddle heavily, corpulent, but of majestic bearing, his moustaches still dark, his eyes full of intelligence and humour; his figure even more conspicuous by reason of the tunic of sky-blue silk which he wore. Beside him was the boy, Prince James, his son, in breast-plate and helmet. There followed the melancholy Lorraine, and the heads of all the princely Houses of the Germanies [...] The still confident Kara Mustapha reclined in his tent and took coffee. At the opening of the tent his bejewelled horses awaited him.

Battle was joined. Then came the decisive moment. Sobieski's seasoned eye surveyed the field and he summoned the commander of his elite Polish heavy cavalry. The king pointed to the very centre of the enormous, wealth-laden Turkish encampment. There stood a vast white tent comprising no less than forty-five silk-hung rooms. It was that of the grand vizier himself. As his cavalry captain peered into the distance, Sobieski told him to prepare the heavy cavalry to charge. Morton describes the sight of the 3,500 Polish winged hussars as they thundered down the small valley on the right flank led by the king himself on an Arab charger:

> As the pace quickened, and the horses broke from a trot into a gallop, the Turkish leaders saw in the forefront of the squadrons a figure that seemed to absorb into itself all the long story of Christendom in arms and the awful majesty of the Faith embattled. They saw the royal standard and the shield borne before him, and at the knowledge of his presence they lost their hope. Word spread through the ranks that the Polish King was leading the charge [...] As they drew near, there was added to the thunder of the hoofs the terrifying sound of the huge vulture and eagle wings fastened to their shoulders. In their ranks rode the high

[1] J. Wimmer, *Wiedeń 1683*, Warsaw 1983.

4

nobility of Poland, and behind them pressed the Pancernes, in shirts of mail, soldiers less splendid to the eye, but no less fierce in battle, no less tried […] There was no resistance to the shock of the charge. Everything in its way went down, whilst Lorraine and Waldeck turned the right wing of the Turks, and Jabłonowski the left. It is recorded that Kara Mustapha, in despair, said to the Khan of the Crimean Tartars: 'And cannot you help me?'; to which the Khan replied: 'I know the King of Poland. I told you that if he came, there would be nothing for us to do but retreat'.

The next day, September 13th, Sobieski wrote to his wife, Marie-Casimire:

God be blessed for ever! He has given our nation victory; He has given it such a triumph as no past century has ever seen! All the artillery, the whole Moslem camp, all its uncountable riches have fallen into our hands. The approaches to the town, the neighbouring fields, are all covered with the infidel dead and the remainder is in flight and stricken with panic […] Their tents, all their carriages are taken, *et mille d'autres galanteries fort jolies et fort riches, mais fort riches*, I have not yet seen all the booty, [*Il*] *n'y a point de comparaison avec ceux de* Chocim. Four or five quivers alone, mounted with rubies and sapphires, are worth many thousands of ducats. You will not then, my love, say to me, as the wives of the Tartars say to their lords when they return without booty: 'You are no warrior, for you have brought me nothing. It is only he who is in the forefront of the fight that can get hold of anything'.

To the Pope, Sobieski sent the green banner of the Prophet. Kara Mustapha, however, was promptly executed by strangulation on the orders of the Sultan.

The Polish historian, Professor Ladislas Konopczyński, was not exagerrating when he said that: 'On September 12th, 1683 King John III decided not only the fate of Austria, but of all Christendom'. Lord d'Abernon described it as one of the eighteen battles that changed the course of world history.

Some months later, in February 1685, in the opposite corner of Europe, King Charles II died and to his three thrones his younger brother succeeded, crowned as James VII & II. He was the twelfth in a long line of Stuart Kings of the Scots and the fourth Stuart King of

England and Ireland since his ancestor, Walter, hereditary High Steward of Scotland, had married Princess Marjorie in 1315, daughter of Scotland's legendary hero-king, Robert the Bruce, victor of Bannockburn. James was the heir of an unbroken bloodline stretching back through the great dynasties of Stuart, Bruce and Canmore to Fergus Mor MacErc, King of Dalriada, who founded the Royal House of Scotland a millennium and a half ago.

Had one known then, that in 1719, just thirty-four years after James's accession, King John III's grand-daughter, Marie-Clementina Sobieska, would marry King James VII's son, James Francis Edward Stuart, one would have been forgiven for presuming that nothing but a glorious future could possibly await this young and handsome royal couple.

Who would have dreamt that within a century the ancient royal House of Stuart would have lost their thrones of Scotland, England and Ireland to mere German electors (of Hanover); their native country would have lost its sovereignty to its old rival England; the Stuart family would become extinct; and the only member of its last generation – a duchess called Charlotte (of Albany) – would be dead?

Who would likewise have thought that during that same century the Sobieski family would have failed, after such a victory as Vienna, to place even one of their three sons on the ancient thrones of Poland and Lithuania, but lose them instead to German electors (of Saxony)[2]; their native country would have lost its sovereignty to Russia, Prussia and Austria; and the Sobieski family would become extinct with the death of its last member – a duchess called Charlotte (de Bouillon)?

For the descendants of the Stuarts and the Sobieskis the only thing that this magnificent first half of the 1680s heralded was the beginning of their decline and fall. History had prepared a multiplicity of fates with which to mock the yet unborn descendants – poisoned inheritances of preceding generations – destructive events outside their own control.

---

[2] The twin throne of the Polish-Lithuanian Commonwealth was not hereditary but elective.

CHAPTER TWO

Papa Wagner

The Church is in ruins, the State is in jars
Delusions, oppressions and murderous wars
We dare na weel say't but we ken wha's to blame
There'll never be peace till Jamie comes hame.

Robert Burns

In late 1717 the young Irish veteran of the Jacobite uprising of 1715, Charles Wogan, had been instructed to find the most eligible bride possible for the exiled Stuart king, James VIII of Scotland and III of England and Ireland – the only son of James VII & II who had gone into exile at the time of William of Orange's invasion. Finding a bride was not an easy task, for despite the donations that James regularly received from France, Spain, the Vatican and elsewhere, he was constantly short of the vast amounts needed to pay for his court with all its attendant exiles, whose pensions he granted and maintained with extraordinary generosity. His life had hitherto been exemplary, totally unstained by sordid affairs. But neither had his matrimonial plans succeeded. He had fallen passionately in love with his d'Este cousin, the eldest daughter of his uncle, the Duke of Modena, but been refused. Similarly, a political match with the daughter of the Russian tsar, Peter the Great, had been turned down. Notwithstanding the antiquity of the House of Stuart and their kinship with nearly all the major ruling families of Europe, few were prepared to cross Hanoverian England.

Finally, vetted by the Duke of Ormonde, Wogan had come up with what seemed a coup. None of the three daughters of Prince James Sobieski, son of the hero-King John III of Poland and god-child of

King Louis XIV of France, was married. With the Battle of Vienna still within living memory, that name bore the lustre of greatness, whilst the girls' mother, Hedwig Elisabeth, was a Princess of Bavaria-Neuburg, closely related to the Imperial Habsburgs and a string of reigning German princes as well as by marriage to the Kings of Portugal and Spain as well as the Grand Duke of Tuscany and the Duke of Parma.

Princess Marie-Casimire was the unloved eldest, aged twenty-four but 'astonishingly solemn' according to Wogan. She would die a spinster in 1723. The second was Princess Marie-Charlotte, but 'beyond all measure gay'. It was she who would become the last of the Sobieskis and in 1723 marry Prince Charles de la Tour d'Auvergne, Duke de Bouillon. But the youngest was the sixteen-year-old Princess Marie-Clementina, the beloved god-daughter of Pope Clement XI and considered by the Irish match-maker to be 'sweet, amiable, of an even temper and gay only when in season'.

Not without significance for King James's cash-strapped exiled court was the fact that Clementina's dowry was a huge 25 million francs together with the fabulously valuable Sobieski family jewellery which included the two famous rubies, each reputedly as large as a hen's egg. Besides this was the prospect of still greater wealth after the death of the girls' father. For Prince Sobieski had no male heir. In time most would go in support of the Jacobite cause, but for the present it seemed the perfect answer to James's problems.

The matrimonial agreement was concluded. But once it became known that the Stuart king was to marry and therefore might continue the rightful senior royal line, King George I went apoplectic with rage.[1] He put a bounty on James's head, pressurised his ally, the Holy Roman Emperor, Charles VI (notwithstanding the fact that he was a close kinsman of the young bride), to intervene and prevent the marriage, whilst simultaneously offering to add £10,000 to Clementina's dowry if she could be forced to marry any German prince at all. The

[1] The Act of Settlement of 1701 and the Bill of Rights created a situation, prior to the Act of Union of 1707, in which the English Parliament, without consulting Scotland, decided that the crowns of England, Scotland and Ireland would not pass according to the established tradition of England and law of Scotland, namely from James VII & II to James VIII & III, but that the succession would be reversed back through James VII & II, Charles II and Charles I to James VI & I, then down through his daughter's non English-speaking German grandson, Georg von Brunswick-Lüneburg, the Elector of Hanover, notwithstanding the fact that over fifty people were closer to the throne than he was. It was also determined that in future only members of the Church of England could inherit the throne of Scotland.

Habsburg ruler co-operated by firstly threatening the fifty-one-year-old Prince Sobieski with exile from his residence in Silesian Oława and then arresting Princess Clementina and her mother, together with their escorts, Murray and Hay, who had been sent by James. All were imprisoned at the Castle of Ambras near Innsbrück, together with their retinue.

Not only were James and Wogan outraged, but all Europe was scandalised, and the Pope, various princes and the relatives of the Stuarts and Sobieskis protested to the Emperor about his treatment of his own aunt and her daughter. But Charles VI's hands had been firmly tied by George I. However, the Hanoverian and Habsburg rulers had underestimated the Poles, Irish and Scots whose genius in such circumstances grows in proportion to the scale of the obstacle.

James was overworked with the preparations for Cardinal Alberoni's Spanish invasion plans aimed at a Jacobite restoration. So he entrusted the task of rescuing the situation to Wogan, with the single condition that Prince Sobieski agree to whatever plan was devised.

As an eighteen-year-old, the Irishman had escaped from Newgate Prison in a group of thirteen prisoners led by Brigadier Mackintosh after the 'Fifteen. Armed with this experience, he masterminded the ingenious escape of the royal prisoners. Travelling incognito and passing himself off as a doctor, he found his way into the cells where the prisoners were being held and quickly agreed a plan with the teenaged Polish princess. It was December 11th, 1718. Within nineteen days he was at Sobieski's residence at Oława, posing as 'Mr. Wagner', an English tourist.

At first the Polish prince agreed to Wogan's plan, but then changed his mind and, through his treasurer, offered him the present of a Turkish snuffbox taken by his father from the tent of the grand vizier at the Battle of Vienna. Frustrated by his failure, the Irishman refused to accept it. The next day Sobieski invited him for a private lunch during which the former said such a refusal was a measure of nobility and that he would, after all, place his daughter's care in Wogan's hands.

Proceeding to the headquarters of the Irish legion with Sobieski's valet, Wogan, he co-opted his uncle, Major Richard Gaydon, the gigantic Lucas O'Toole and Captain and Mrs John Misset with their French maid, Jeanneton. The latter dressed up as Princess Clementina and the group broke into the prison whilst the guards were drinking below. There they left the maid behind and escaped with Clementina through the pouring rain and into the night. However, they discovered that they had left behind not only the maid (who later rejoined her employers) but also a large package containing Clementina's Sobieski jewellery and yet more from the Stuarts which had been sent by King James to Oława. The panic-stricken O'Toole rushed back to where the package had been left but mercifully found everything as they had left it.

The Jacobite, John Walkinshaw, also appears to have helped in the preliminary marriage negotiations with Prince Sobieski. It was he who was sent to Vienna by King James to protest to the emperor about the latter's cynical detention of his bride.

The Irish team heaped praise upon the little Polish teenager for her bravery and charm and, with the man Clementina now called 'Papa Wagner', Wogan's group continued over the Brenner Pass and arrived in the safety of Bologna where the aged Cardinal Origo literally danced with joy when Wogan announced that he had brought the king's fiancée. There, on May 9th, 1719 the marriage between James and Clementina took place by proxy. In less dramatic style the journey was continued to Rome where the Irishmen were honoured by the Roman Senate and, after his return from the abortive Spanish mission, no less so by James himself.

The Pope placed at the young couple's disposal the Palazzo Muti just behind the Basilica dei Santissimi Apostoli. By coincidence it was next door to the Palazzo Odescalchi, vacated just five years before by Clementina's grandmother, Queen Marie-Casimire Sobieska, the destructive but much adored wife of King John III. James himself returned from Spain on August 28th and awaited his bride at the Cathedral of Montefiascone near the southern shore of the Lago di Bolsena to the north of Rome. At midnight on September 3rd, 1719 the marriage finally took place between the thirty-one-year-old James Francis Edward Stuart, rightful King of Scotland, England and Ireland, the only son of King James VII & II by Princess Mary d'Este, daughter of Alphonso IV, Duke of Modena, and the seventeen-year-old Princess Marie-Clementina Sobieska, daughter of Crown Prince James Louis Sobieski of Poland and Princess Hedwig Elisabeth of Bavaria-Neuburg.

In London the outwitted George I and his Hanoverian government fumed in impotent rage.

CHAPTER THREE

The Road Home

Oh there were mony beating hearts
And mony a hope and fear
And mony were the pray'rs put up
For the young Chevalier.

Anonymous

After their marriage James and Clementina held their exiled court at the Palazzo Muti. The Pope had also granted the young couple the use of the Palazzo Savelli at Albano, set in the hills to the south of the city, near a lake with wooded slopes. It was an idyllic summer residence. Outside the doors of the Palazzo Muti lay the most fashionable and gossipy capital of Europe. The Italians placed little emphasis on formal education, more on heraldry and music, and most on chivalry and appearances. They welcomed into their midst the huge numbers of visitors to Rome and were breezily free from the rigid snobbery that suffocated Paris. Here beat the heart of Catholicism at whose Papal Court reigned a relaxed and carefree attitude. Attending it were dozens of cardinals, many of whom were younger sons of Europe's foremost aristocratic families, having often started their careers in this exalted rank if they hadn't inherited much at home.

With their exiled Court, the wealthy, young, good-looking James and Clementina with their exiled Court made a strange comparison. In front of their palace stood a papal guard, one of only three in all Rome apart from the Vatican and the Quirinale, yet inside James surrounded himself with large numbers of Protestants, kept two Protestant chaplains and a Protestant chapel. Clementina was also different as she was unusually intense and devout in her worship. James's religious even-

11

handedness was echoed in his words that he didn't want to 'become an apostle, but a good king of all my subjects'. He worked hard and was meticulous in answering his vast correspondence which took him three to four hours daily. And his seriousness, reserve and patience seemed an oasis of calm amid the throng of English, Irish and Scottish exiles engaged in the bitter in-fighting typical of communities-in-exile.

Fascinated by all this was not only most of Roman society, but also the Hanoverian spies who hovered about them, led first by Baron Philip von Stosch under his pen-name, John Walton, and later by Sir Horace Mann. Their work cost the British taxpayer a large amount of money and consisted in the ruthless pursuit of every tiny detail of the lives of the Stuarts and their court, no matter how personal.

Then, just sixteen happy months after the Stuarts married, in the late afternoon of Tuesday December 31st, 1720 there occurred an event for whose discovery no spy was required. After six long days of labour during which the Pope had offered up special prayers and provided consecrated baby linen, Clementina became mother to a baby boy. One hour after his birth, witnessed by four cardinals as well as sundry princesses and ambassadors, the little Stuart Prince of Wales[1] was baptised Charles Edward Louis John Casimir Silvester Severino Maria by the Bishop of Montefiascone. His names recalled his beheaded great-grandfather, England's sainted king, the great kings of France, Spain and Poland as well as the Saint upon whose day he was born. A royal salute was fired from Castel Sant'Angelo and the Pope immediately sent greetings and presents as did the Courts of France and Spain. Rome and all Jacobite centres throughout Britain and Europe burst into unbridled celebration and even the ten-year-old Louis XV of France is said to have clapped his hands for joy. Few could imagine a better welcome for the New Year. Thus was born the child whom Giulio Cesare Cordara said was 'reared from infancy never to forego the desire or the hope of recovering the Crown' – who would become, as Sir Walter Scott later wrote:

> one of those personages who distinguish themselves during some single and extraordinarily brilliant period of their lives, like the course of a shooting star, at which men wonder, as well on account of the briefness as the brilliancy of its splendour.

---

[1] The traditional title of the heir to the British Crown.

Meanwhile, the Hanoverians began their lifelong attack on the infant which would not cease even with the victim's death, circulating satirical medals by Wermuth with inscriptions such as:

Rome offers in place of a king, one whom without witness Sobieska has brought forth, a child surviving in misery, deformed!

To his government Walton reported that the prince had been born a cripple and his mother would never be able to bear another child. And whilst letters of congratulation were flowing in from various courts and heads of state to the baby's delighted parents, Westminster was sending out diplomatic notes of protest, the pettiness of which made a laughing stock of the Hanoverian regime. It was foolish of them to try and take the moral high ground at such a time, for the South Sea Bubble was in the process of bursting – a financial fraud of huge proportions perpetrated by key members of the whig government[2] and, without doubt, by the Hanoverian royal family itself. The latter were saved from its consequences only by the brilliant handling of Sir Robert Walpole. No less unsavoury were the dreadful relationships of George I and his family. He and his son were infamous for their public fights and squabbles whilst the repeatedly unfaithful king had scandalised all Europe by hypocritically imprisoning his long-suffering wife for decades when she finally did the same to him.

It was now that Walpole commenced his long premiership, constructing a ruthlessly efficient but corrupt political system to keep the whigs in power and the Stuarts out. Yet their propaganda did not fool everyone. One Anglican minister invited to the Protestant chapel at the exiled Court was astonished to discover that 'King James is a virtuous and upright man, so distant from any form of bigotry and opposed to any religious discrimination whatsoever that never is a word spoken on that subject in his house'. Likewise, the young whig, Lord Blandford, the Duke of Marlborough's heir, noted that James 'talks with such an air of sincerity that I am apprehensive I should become half a Jacobite if I continued these discourses any longer'.

Shortly after, James became embroiled in another Jacobite conspiracy, this time centred on London itself – testimony to the deep dissatisfaction felt even in the capital of the Hanoverian whig administration. It was organised under the leadership of the London lawyer,

[2] Pro-Hanoverian political party.

Christopher Layer, and included the Duke of Norfolk, the Earl of Orrery, and Lords Bathurst, Lansdowne and Stafford, as well as Sir Henry Goring and Sir William Wyndham in England; the Earl of Mar and General Dillon in Scotland and Lord Arran in Ireland. But the long famous Stuart bad luck struck again. Just at this time the supportive Pope Clement XI died and was replaced by the hostile Innocent XIII. In desperate need of finance, James turned to the French regent, the Duke of Orléans, who promptly informed the British government, albeit on condition that no-one involved would be executed as a consequence. The Hanoverians promised, but then broke their word.

Later, on March 6th, 1725 the four-year-old Prince Charles gained a younger brother who was christened Henry Benedict Maria Clement Thomas Francis Xavier, and became the Duke of York. Yet just as the birth of two male heirs and the exemplary morality of the Stuarts had been the greatest boost to the Jacobite cause, so now occurred a disaster. James and Clementina's early marital happiness was shattered by post-natal problems, and their respective characters were ill-suited to the consequences. He was wrapped up in his work, meticulous and pedantic; she was captivating, impulsive, over-sensitive and impatient. He regarded his role as one in which he should educate his young wife; she found this patronising and felt she understood life at least as well as he did. What they did share was stubbornness.

Having taken offence at James not long after Charles's birth, Clementina left her husband and rushed off ostensibly to take the waters at Lucca. After a while she quietened down and returned, having written: 'I am trying to overcome my naughty temper, so as to appear to you the best girl in the world'. But the next time round things were worse.

Towards the end of Clementina's second pregnancy, James decided to start Charles's formal education. He dismissed the boy's nurse, the arch-Catholic Mrs Sheldon, and replaced her by the Protestant James Murray, Earl of Dunbar, and the Catholic Sir Thomas Sheridan. From then on, and especially after Henry's birth, inflamed by the destructive Mrs Sheldon, the devout Clementina worked herself up into a fury directed against the Protestants with whom James had surrounded himself. In particular she accused her husband of letting his Secretary of State, John Hay, Earl of Inverness, and his wife, Marjorie, 'come between them' – implying that James was having an affair with Lady Inverness. She furthermore protested hysterically that her son was being brought up a Protestant, despite the fact that the Pope himself had approved James's choice for their son's tutors. Matters reached a head when Clementina demanded the dismissal of all those she found offensive, stating that she would 'rather suffer death than live with people who have no religion, honour or concience'. As this was not forthcoming, she left her husband on November 15th, 1725 for the Ursuline Convent of St. Cecilia just across the Tiber.

All the courts of Europe reverberated with the scandal whilst George I and Walpole made gleeful capital of it to James' utter mortification. Eventually the exiled king partially compromised, but only after much misunderstanding and the humiliation of infuriating interferences by third parties including the Pope whose emissary-bishop James threatened to throw out of the window and whose cardinal, Alberoni, he left speechless by acidly telling him that he was forgetting himself.

Although the exasperated and bewildered James had kept up a relentless but patronising attempt to pacify his wife, he himself had been no angel. For whilst Clementina had been hurling violent and false accusations against him, he had unwisely published their private correspondence and provocatively appeared at the Opera with the flirtatious Lady Inverness. However, in January 1728, after James had taken the two boys off to distract them with a string of balls and other festivities in Bologna, the family were reunited and began to live together once more under the roof of the Palazzo Muti.

Yet the detail of their separation is not as relevant as the effect it had on those involved. For James it was a disorienting humiliation which deepened his stoicism and served only to increase the distance between him and his first born. For Clementina, whether physiological or psychological in origin, it had a devastating effect. She developed a religious fixation and isolated herself from everyone around her. She ate progressively less, prayed for ever longer periods, stopped bothering to dress properly and became duplicious and manipulative, which James interpreted as 'the finest dissimulation and hypocrisy'. Soon she became skeletal in appearance, her periods became irregular, and she began to suffer from malnutrition. It would be centuries before doctors would recognise anorexia nervosa, whilst at the time some believed her behaviour to be a form of saintly abstinence. When Clement XII became Pope in 1730 Clementina developed a spiritual passion for him and surrounded herself by priests who encouraged her asceticism. It was hardly the cure for a problem which had made her unrecognisable as the fearless teenage princess who had escaped with such élan from imprisonment at Innsbrück with Papa Wagner's team of extraordinary

Irishmen. Finally, after having spent the last four years of her life visiting hospitals, looking after the sick and distributing alms to the poor, the emaciated young woman died from scurvy caused by malnutrition in the middle of January 1735. She was only thirty-three.

Only those who have lived through the stress that anorexia imposes on a family will fully realise the scar this left on Charles and Henry. When Clementina left them in November 1725, it was already for the second time in Charles's four years of life. Henry was abandoned as a baby of only eight months. Their mother didn't return for three years and, when she did, became a waif-like religious recluse, distant and fragile, still capable of dazzling charm, but not of maternal warmth. About her hung the fear of some approaching tragedy, terrible and unfathomable. The main point of contact between mother and sons was music. Nor did the children witness anything of the love that binds a man and woman, for their parents led separate existences. And though Charles and Henry seemed happy and boisterous, throughout their childhood there had been no let-up from the traumatising atmosphere of their mother's self-destruction culminating in her death when they were aged fourteen and nine respectively. In a letter to his father, Charles promised to 'be very dutiful to Mamma, and not jump in her presence'. He was seven.

The Pope ordered that King John Sobieski's grand-daughter be buried with full state honours, and James Murray wrote that 'the Princes are almost sick with weeping', having spent hour after hour praying at their mother's bedside during her final days. Clementina's embalmed body lay in state for three days as crowds queued to pay their last respects to the person they considered holy. At last, adorned with the emblems of royalty, her body was 'temporarily' interred in the crypt of St. Peter's to await the day which would never come, when her remains could be laid to rest in the native soil of the land of her husband's ancestors. Her heart was placed by the Franciscans in an urn in the Basilica dei Santissimi Apostoli near the Palazzo Muti and for years the faithful attributed miracles to her intercession.

During James's time in Bologna one or two key things had changed. George I had died in June 1727. James had gone to Lorraine to see how the land lay, but France told him firmly to leave, peace having broken out in Europe. In addition Cardinal Fleury had taken over the reins of power in that all-important country but was ill-disposed to the Stuarts. Unfortunately for James, Fleury would live until 1743, throughout which time he maintained the Duke of Orléans' anti-Stuart policy. As a consequence George II succeeded without obstruction.

The results of the two boys' education under the cool, humourless Murray and warm, fatherly Sheridan proved very different. Henry was diligent, academic and deeply interested in learning. Charles was not. Yet this in no way annoyed the latter, indeed it encouraged him, and the brothers became close. When only two, Charles was described by John Hay as 'healthy and strong' and one who 'runs about from morning till night'. A year later Hay added that 'he is a great musician and plays on his violin continually'. At four Charles stubbornly refused to kneel when presented to the Pope. And when six and a half the Duke of Liria wrote of him: 'Besides his great beauty he was remarkable for dexterity, grace and almost supernatural address. Not only could he read fluently, he could ride, fire a gun; and, more surprisingly still, I have seen him take a cross-bow and kill birds on the roof and split a rolling ball with a bolt ten times in succession. He speaks English, French and Italian perfectly and altogether is the most perfect Prince I have ever met in my life'.

Apart from his marksmanship, horsemanship, musical talent and love of dancing, Charles's favourite sport was golf, at which he excelled. But when forced to study, Charles's vitality and exuberance became transformed into anger usually directed against his tutor. His spelling was notoriously bad and a subject for constant reproof from a father who, despite such pedantry, was not above taking his boys for midnight spins in his carriage, boating on lake Albano or visiting festivals in Rome where he would lavish them with ice cream.

Yet there was one subject about which Charles was passionate, which he not only learned to perfection but which filled him with an all-embracing inspiration he radiated to others – that he was the rightful heir to the lawful King of Scotland, England and Ireland and that it was his destiny to restore his father and family to its true position. Everything Charles did became transformed into a step towards the fulfilment of this mission. From the age of ten he had been privy to his father's secret political activities. And then, at the age of fourteen, he gained his first experience of war. Under the tutelage of his cousin, the Duke of Liria, now also the second Duke of Berwick, he was appointed General of Artillery at the siege of Gaeta which was being conducted by the Spanish to the south of Rome. He took his duties very seriously and even served in the trenches. The soldiers adored him for his vivid interest in their problems, about which he talked with the various nationalities in English, German, French, Italian and Spanish. His mentor afterwards wrote to James: 'I wish to God that some of the greatest sticklers in England against the family of Stuart had been eye witness to that siege, and I am firmly persuaded that they would soon change their way of thinking'. Even the Hanoverian spy, Walton, irritated with Charles's success, wrote to his masters that 'everyone is saying this boy will one day become a far greater adversary of the House of Hanover than his father ever was'.

Then began the frustration which would become the bane of his life. All the early marriage plans of this period came to nothing. No army would accept him for fear of Hanoverian reprisals. The Holy Roman Emperor refused him permission to serve in the Turkish wars. He was even denied a visit to Poland where his Sobieski grandfather lived and who, until his death in December 1737, kept up a regular correspondence with his grandson.

James Sobieski had specific plans for his two grandsons. In late October 1734, just three months prior to his daughter's death, he left Oława and returned to the old family seat of Żółkiew. From there he corresponded with the Russian Empress Anne in order to gain her support for his two Stuart grandchildren in his attempt to have their status formally incorporated within Poland. This parliamentary process, known as the *indygenat*, related to the recognition and acceptance of foreign nobles into the ranks of the Polish-Lithuanian nobility, giving them all the rights thereto pertaining. For Sobieski saw his grandsons' future in Poland as heirs to his massive landed estates based on Oława in Silesia, Tiegenhoff in Prussia and Żółkiew in Poland. Yet only Polish nobles could inherit land in the Polish-Lithuanian Republic. And for that the *indygenat* was essential. From the Castle of Żółkiew, on March 1st, 1735 Prince James wrote to the Empress Anne of:

> the tragic death and loss to me of Clementina, the queen of His British Royal Highness, my most beloved daughter for whom I will grieve throughout eternity, who on the 18th of January, by the will of our Lord, left this Earth. She has however left me, her desperate father, the particular consolation of her two sons, my most beloved grandsons, whom into your Imperial Majesty's protection I humbly ask you receive, that through the intervention of your all-powerful Imperial Majesty they might receive the *indygenat* at the next session of the Polish parliament.[3]

---

[3] A.Filipczak-Kocur, *Listy Jakuba Sobieskiego z 1735r.*, Miscellanea Historico-Archivistica, vol.XI, Warsaw 2000, p.248.

Terminated by his own death, nothing ever came of this plan. All other more purposeful avenues being closed, King James organised a tour of the Courts of the northern Italian states for his sons where Charles's extraordinary tact and kindness astounded his long-abused tutors. Using the title 'the Count of Albany' he met his uncle, Charles Albert, Elector of Bavaria, and impressed him with his lack of pretension regarding his role at the siege of Gaeta. Received by the highest and mightiest, Charles's triumphant tour so infuriated the Hanoverians that they expelled the Venetian Ambassador from London and issued formal protests to the Courts of Tuscany and Genoa. But it only increased the aura of fascination surrounding the handsome, young Stuart Prince.

Bursting with energy, Charles had to survive more than five years of inactivity in Rome before the international situation began to swing in favour of the Jacobite cause. Although the English Catholics and Tories[4] had been more or less squashed by the Hanoverians, disaffection in Scotland was rife. For during the late 1730s and early 1740s popular feeling had become inflamed against Westminster by the misuse of the Scottish Highland Companies which were now being sent to fight Hanover's wars on the continent despite having been promised that they would only serve at home.

Britain found herself at war with Spain from 1739 over the issue of access to Spanish-dominated American territories, and also with France from 1740 over the Austrian succession. In addition, the anti-Stuart Cardinal Fleury died in 1743 and France began to feel that a Stuart restoration might be a better alternative to the House of Hanover which kept involving Britain in European affairs.

Against this background an association of Jacobite leaders was formed in Scotland in 1738. The 'Concert of Gentlemen' comprised the Duke of Perth, Lord John Drummond, Lord Lovat, Lord Linton, John Stuart, Donald Cameron of Lochiel, Sir James Campbell of Auchinbreck and William Drummond of Balhaldy.[5] In March 1741 they signed a letter to Cardinal Fleury asking for French help and announced the readiness of Scotland to rise.

In 1743 Louis XV's emissary, John Butler, returned from England with the news that the time seemed propitious for a French invasion based on a Stuart restoration strategy. So the French King sent

---

[4] As the Whigs were pro-Hanoverian, so the Tories were pro-Stuart.
[5] Balhaldy's real name was MacGregor, but his surname had been outlawed.

Balhaldy to Rome to suggest to the fifty-five-year-old James that his eldest son come to Paris to act as nominal commander of a force under Europe's greatest stategist, the first Marshal of France, Count Maurice de Saxe, a natural son of King August II of Poland. Charles was full of enthusiasm, and after much hesitating his father agreed. The plan was to land ten thousand troops near London and announce an initiative to depose the corrupt whig regime as well as the deeply unpopular Hanoverian dynasty without making any territorial demands at all. It was assumed that one significant battle would be fought and won under de Saxe who would then be replaced by the tory Duke of Ormonde whereupon the disaffected would flock to the Stuart banner. Significantly, no diversionary attack was planned for Scotland.

Charles's journey on January 8th, 1744 from Rome to Paris was so secret that not even Henry was informed. Charles bade farewell to his father, little knowing that it would be for the last time, and set off on a 'hunting' expedition. His tutor, Sheridan, caused a distraction by falling from his mount, whereupon the prince got out of his coach, took off his wig, put on a mask and dark cloak and rode off on a black horse into the night with an attendant and two servants. Word was relayed back that he had suffered an accident and was staying at Frascati to recover. In fact, posing as a Spanish officer, he made his way via Savona and Antibes to Paris with astonishing speed and organisational efficiency. He wrote to his father upon arrival: 'Mr.Graham has been very careful of me […] Both he and the two servants have suffered by my impatience to arrive'.

By mid-February Walpole's spies already knew that Charles was in Paris and had been warmly greeted by the king. At Westminster Walpole spoke of 'the Young Pretender being in France and of the designed invasion from thence, in concert with the disaffected here'. He demanded that troops be sent for 'in the greatest haste'. Though lazy and apt to change his mind, Louis XV proceeded with the plan and sent the Marshal de Saxe to Gravelines where Charles, under the name of 'the Chevalier Douglas', was to rendezvous during the first week of March. From there he went to Dunkirk where fifteen ships, five frigates and seven thousand troops awaited him. However, a Frenchman spying for the English revealed the plans and Admiral Norris was waiting when the French ships put to sea. In addition a violent storm suddenly broke out, wreaking havoc. Twelve French vessels were lost, seven of them with all hands, and more were damaged. This was all the encouragement the French needed to give up and invade Flanders instead.

The whole thing may have been nothing more than a cynical diversion but Charles stayed on the coast until April, awaiting developments which did not come, whereupon he left for Paris. His father urged him to be patient and return to Rome. But, in his determination to press on, Charles' mood was one of growing frustration as he spent his time in the capital as well as the country houses of Northern France. It was at this period that his friendship began with his de la Tour cousins. This family comprised his highly influential courtier uncle, the Duke de Bouillon, who had been one of Louis XV's closest friends, and Charles's youthful first cousins, Godefroy-Charles, Prince de Turenne, and his sister Louise who had just married Prince Jules-Hercule de Rohan, the Duke de Montbazon and Prince de Guémené's heir. De Bouillon's wife, Charlotte Sobieska, had died in Warsaw just four years before. She had been Charles's aunt. And whereas Charles had inherited the rights to his Sobieski grandfather's Silesian estates and fabulously valuable jewellery, she had inherited the vast Żółkiew property near Lwów which she sold in 1739 to their nearest Polish-domiciled cousin, Prince Michael Radziwiłł, grandson of King John Sobieski's sister.[6]

The fateful year of 1745, known in the Highlands as *Bliadnha Thearlaich*,[7] brought with it significant change. The Prince's angry humiliation at the Stuart cause being treated as the plaything of foreigners transformed his patient obedience to his father into a determination to take fate into his own hands. Another change was his new orientation towards his mother's relations. It was now that Charles began to demonstrate that wherever his dynamic character came from, it was certainly not from his cautious father.

However, whilst his charisma, stamina, will-power and self-belief may have been pure Sobieski, the prince was just twenty-four, inexperienced and possessed of none of the military acumen and therefore authority of his heroic ancestor. Maintaining complete secrecy, even from his father, he fell in with a circle of wealthy men, mainly descended from exiled Irish families. Foremost among them was Antoine Walsh, a French naval officer, slave-trader and shipbuilder whose father had commanded the vessel that had brought Charles's grandfather, King James VII & II, to France after the Battle of the Boyne. Just as Charles was tired of the French court which refused to receive him openly, so he was impressed by these decisive businessmen.

---

[6] This sale was prompted by the fact that only Polish nobles could own land in Poland.
[7] Which in English means: Charles' Year. Phonetically *Thearlaich* is very close to 'Charlie', whence the traditional 'Bonnie Prince Charlie'.

They, in turn, fell under his persuasive charm and agreed to make large loans and organise ships and arms in support of a plan for a small invasion that would trigger a rising intended to force France to commit herself once she saw what an opportunity had presented itself.

It was a bold strategy. Initially the French turned a blind eye, knowing that even a complete flop would have a beneficial diversionary effect. The timing seemed good. In May the Marshal de Saxe had inflicted a serious defeat on the English at Fontenoy. Even Walpole was incensed by the flippancy of the Hanoverian king and Prince of Wales at his country's losses in a war he considered theirs:

> Our army in Flanders is running away and dropping to pieces by detachments taken prisoner every day; whilst the king is at Hanover, the regency at their country seats, not five thousand men in the island, and not above fourteen or fifteen ships at home! Allelujah!

Charles acquired two ships, the *Elisabeth* and *du Teillay*. The former was a 64-gunner with seven hundred and sixty troops, the latter a 44-gunner which was to carry the cash reserve of 4,000 louis d'or, and weapons comprising twenty cannon, three thousand five hundred guns and two thousand four hundred broadswords as well as ammunition. All had been paid for by loans Charles had procured and the pawning of the Sobieski jewels he had inherited. Having spent his last few days on the de Bouillons' estate at Navarre, Charles left three letters to be sent immediately upon his departure. To his father he finally revealed the secret, to the King of France he wrote in emotional terms which he hoped would encourage support, whilst the Spanish Court quickly responded to his appeal, sending four ships with arms, men and money as well as Irish troops serving in their army.

On June 21st the prince boarded the *du Teillay* at St. Nazaire. With him were the men who became known in legend as the 'Seven Men of Moidart' – two Scots, one Englishman and four Irishmen. They were the Jacobite Duke of Atholl; the Paris-based banker, Aeneas MacDonald; Francis Strickland, from an old and loyal Westmorland family; Sir Thomas Sheridan; the parson and intriguer, George Kelly; an ageing cavalry veteran of the French Army, Sir John MacDonald; and John William O'Sullivan, who had good military experience of the guerrilla variety. But though Prince Charles in his account of the Rising states: 'I landed with seven men', in fact there were more, including Abbé Butler who was a relation of the Duke of Ormonde, and also a servant of Cameron of Lochiel called Duncan Cameron from Barra who knew the Hebridean seaways perfectly.

Again fate went against the Stuarts. By chance Antoine Walsh's squadron came upon the newly refitted HMS *Lyon* off the Lizard. Already Charles's reliance upon the help of others prevented him from exercising authority. Walsh refused to assist the *Elisabeth* which took and gave a day-long pounding with the disastrous result that she had to limp back to port with over two hundred wounded or dead. Charles's ship was now on its own. The barren land of the Hebrides was sighted on July 23rd and Walsh dropped anchor off the Isle of Barra whence MacDonald returned alarmed, having learned that his brother-in-law, Roderick MacNeil of Barra, was away and the arch-Jacobite Sir Hector MacLean of Duart had just been arrested. At once the Duke of Atholl and Sheridan wanted to return, but Charles was adamant and this time Walsh backed him up. Further blows occurred. On the Isle of Eriskay Alexander MacDonald of Boisdale told the Prince to go home, to which Charles replied that he had already done precisely that by coming to Scotland. And the two key chiefs of Skye, Sir Alexander MacDonald of Sleat and Norman MacLeod, 19th Chief of Macleod, refused to rise. All three were shocked that they were expected to risk the appalling English treason laws for an expedition with no backing at all.

Charles's spirit remained unbroken and he sailed for the mainland, arriving at Loch nan Uamh[8] in the strongly Catholic and Jacobite district between Arisaig and Moidart. There Angus MacDonald of Borradale was no less horrified than the island chiefs by Charles's unsupported attempt. Nevertheless a stream of the influential came to hear the composed and confident Stuart prince over the course of the next two weeks.

On August 6th Charles wrote to Louis XV announcing his arrival and appealing for help, having told his father a couple of days earlier: 'The French Court must now necessarily take off the mask, or have eternal shame on them; for at present there is no medium'. Some support was forthcoming from the MacDonalds but the principal man who had to be won over was the strongest man in all Lochaber, Donald Cameron, Younger of Lochiel, the acting chief whose elderly father had been for years an exile in France. It was Lochiel who, in early 1745,

---

[8] English: The Lake of the Caves.

had stressed that the French must provide a minimum of six thousand troops because anything less would be suicidal and few would rise. On the way to Borradale from his great wooden house of Achnacarry, Lochiel called on his younger brother, John Cameron of Fassiefern[9], whose house stood on the north shore of Loch Eil. The latter was deeply disturbed by the answer to his question concerning how many men and arms the prince had brought with him. Doubting his elder brother's head would rule his heart he said: 'Brother, I know you better than you know yourself. If this Prince once sets his eyes upon you, he will make you do whatever he wishes.'

He was right. For Lochiel was persuaded not only by the argument that Scotland was scarcely defended and that, in the event of failure, he was guaranteed a French regiment which would bring him more income than his estate, but also by Charles's challenging words:

In a few days, with the few friends that I have, I will erect the Royal Standard and proclaim to the people of Britain that Charles Stuart is come over to claim the Crown of his ancestors, to win it, or perish in the attempt; Lochiel, who, my father has often told me, was our firmest friend, may stay at home, and learn from the newspapers the fate of his Prince.

Before he had any evidence that the Cameron clansmen would actually arrive, Charles showed his determination by sending Walsh's ship back to France. It had been his only means of escape.

Without doubt Charles had already used the argument that French help would be forthcoming, for which he had no firm evidence, but of which he was convinced. Yet having come with nothing, it was extraordinary that he should have gained even the commitment of MacDonald of Kinlochmoidart, MacDonald of Clanranald,

---

[9] The Scottish tradition of using territorial titles as well as those indicating degree of relation to a clan chief or estate owner caused problems to foreigners. 18th century records give entertaining accounts of how this confused the courtly French who had little idea how to correctly address, for example, John MacEwen Cameron, XVIII of Lochiel, Lord Lochiel in the Jacobite peerage; or his eldest son, Donald Cameron, Younger of Lochiel, acting Chief of Clan Cameron; or the latter's brothers, John Cameron, I of Fassiefern and Dr Archibald Cameron. The first might be variously referred to as 'John MacEwen', 'John Cameron', 'Cameron', 'Lochiel' or 'Lord Lochiel' (although Jacobite titles were supposed to be in abeyance awaiting a Stuart restoration); the second might be 'Donald Cameron', 'Cameron', 'Lochiel' or 'Donald, Younger of Lochiel'; the third however, would be 'John Cameron', 'Cameron', 'Fassiefern' or 'of Lochiel'; and the last 'Archibald Cameron' or 'Archibald Cameron of Lochiel'. The heir to a given title or estate might be either 'Master of ...' or 'Younger of ...'.

MacDonald of Glencoe, MacDonald of Keppoch and Stewart of Ardshiel. Also striking was the fact that, as one present at the time observed, 'We remained several days at anchor in this bay, and Highlanders were perpetually arriving to see the Prince, to whom they proved so faithful that, though all the inhabitants of the neighbourhood knew that he was there, no-one thought of going to anounce it to the English governor of Fort William'.

Then came the first real test. On Monday, August 19th, 1745 in Glenfinnan, at the head of Loch Shiel, the Royal Standard was to be unfurled. Charles arrived there mid-morning to find it deserted save for two shepherds. He went and waited in silence in a small hut. After some time one hundred and fifty clansmen of MacDonald of Morar came in with Rob Roy MacGregor's son, James Mor. They were an inconsequential band. For hours the prince waited but no more arrived. Then, at about four in the afternoon, the distant sound of the pipes began to be heard, growing steadily in volume as they came nearer. MacDonald's men stood in silence and Prince Charles came out from his hut to listen. It was Clan Cameron marching to their ancient war-pibroch: eight hundred of them, from the braes of Lochaber, Ardnamurchan and Sunart, with Young Lochiel at their head. The strongest man of Lochaber had kept his word. Behind him strode two of his younger brothers, the priest Alexander as Catholic chaplain, and the good Dr Archibald. Further back marched the various officers and gentlemen of the clan as well as the standard-bearer and so on, right down to the humblest. Finally there arrived some 350 more from MacDonald of Keppoch's clan and seventy Royal Scots.

Charles walked amongst his Highlanders and began to hear and learn the Gaelic in which he would be nearly fluent a year later. Amid his army now 1200 strong one thing was clear, Charles Stuart was indeed come home at last, and the 'Forty-Five was on. Late that afternoon, to wild hurrahs, the aged Duke William of Atholl unfurled the Jacobite Standard of white, red and blue silk which had been blessed by Bishop Hugh MacDonald, and proclaimed King James VIII, and then Charles as regent. The latter looked on, radiant, flanked by Lochiel, Keppoch, John Gordon of Glenbucket, Father Colin Campbell and the prince's new secretary and old friend, John Murray of Broughton.

Almost at once the Highland Army, raised against all the odds, marched off, stopping on August 22nd at Kinlochiel where Charles was upset by George II's baseness in announcing a bounty of £30,000 for him, dead or alive. Encouraged by his supporters, he replied in like terms. From there his army moved on along the north shore of Loch Eil, staying overnight at Fassiefern House on the 23rd, exactly one month since the *du Teillay* had dropped anchor off Barra. John Cameron of Fassiefern was no whig, as his later involvement in the Elibank Plot proved. But since 1735 he had been a burgess of Glasgow and was a shrewd businessman. Having advised his elder brother not to join the prince, he had departed for the Glenorchy home of his father-in-law, John Campbell of Achallader. It may well have been agreed between the Cameron brothers that Fassiefern should keep himself 'clean' so that in the event of the rising's failure at least one of them would be able to salvage something of the family's property – a not uncommon practice. In fact Fassiefern helped his family and clansmen considerably, both politically and financially. Notwithstanding the secrecy in which this was done, he was robbed and imprisoned by the Hanoverians in 1746, 1751 and 1753. The Governor of Fort William wrote to the Lord Justice Clerk that 'the uprooting of Fassiefern is what we ought to have chiefly in view'. Finally, on trumped-up charges, Fassiefern was sentenced to ten years' banishment, whence he returned in 1763, and died in Lochaber in 1785.

So on August 23rd, 1745 the prince was not entertained by John Cameron of Fassiefern, but by his wife, Jean. Outside, the rose bushes at the end of the house's lawns overlooking the long expance of the loch below and the hills beyond, provided the Highland army with the Stuart emblem of the white rose with which they adorned their bonnets and which became the campaign badge. The next day the Highlanders marched on with pipes playing, following their prince through hill and glen, into legend, poem and song.

CHAPTER FOUR

The Rising

Firm to his word and faithful to his trust
He bade not others go, himself to stay
As is the pretty, prudent, modern way
But like a warrior bravely drew his sword
And raised his target for his native lord.

Whig poem to Donald Cameron, XIX of Lochiel, published in
The Scotsman upon Lochiel's death in exile in 1748.

Each man who joined the Stuart Rising knew the penalty foreseen
by the barbaric English treason laws:

> They must be severally hanged by the neck, but not till they be
> dead, for they must be cut down alive; then their bowels must
> be taken out and burned before their faces; then their heads must
> be severed from their bodies, and their bodies severally divided
> into four quarters.

They also knew that the Hanoverians could muster an army of over
30,000 trained veterans, call upon the Dutch with whom they had
signed a mutual defence treaty, buy in German mercenaries and equip
them all. For they had the full resources of the Treasury as well as the
Navy to keep the French or Spanish at bay. That so many were prepared to take this risk speaks clearly of hatred of the Union as well as
disgust at the 'wee, wee German lairdie'. And although the power of
the Highland chiefs over their people was very considerable, nevertheless this cut both ways, for not all chiefs wanted their clans to rise.
Furthermore, the overall picture of Jacobite support was distorted by

complex clan rivalries. However, national honour and loyalty towards their lawful king and dynasty, the willpower and charisma of Prince Charles and, above all, the sheer bravery of the Stuart supporters are factors which it would be wrong to lightly dismiss. In emphasis of this is the fact that a full fifty seven years had elapsed since James VII & II had gone into exile and thirty eight since the 'forced' union with England. How much more pragmatic it was to back the whig regime and Hanoverian incumbents, or just stay at home. And many were the Jacobite sympathisers who took this surely reasonable latter course.

Ten days after Duke William of Atholl had proclaimed his father at Glenfinnan Charles's army had grown to two thousand men, swelled by the time they had reached the Great Glen by the Stewarts of Appin and the Glengarry MacDonnells. Ranged against it was the Hanoverian commander in Scotland, General Sir John Cope, who had twice that number and in addition held the powerful fortresses of Edinburgh, Stirling and Dumbarton. The general's aim was to concentrate his forces and, carrying extra arms for the volunteers he expected to join him, march north and take the strategic Corryarrick Pass. Little of this happened. The Jacobites beat Cope to the high pass and he was stunned to discover that even on the territories of clans whose chiefs were whig supporters, such as the Campbell Earl of Breadalbane, no Scots volunteered to join the Hanoverians. Worse, many of Cope's own troops deserted to the Jacobites, informing them of his plans. Wrong-footed, the general shied away from giving battle in the Great Glen and made first for Inverness and then Aberdeen whence his force returned to Dunbar by sea. To the south were two more Hanoverian dragoon regiments under the command of the aged General Joshua Guest. But they were not in a position to oppose the Highland army, enlarged by Ewen Macpherson of Cluny and four hundred of his clansmen, which marched rapidly to Perth, taken by Lochiel and four hundred Camerons just prior to the arrival of the main body on September 4th. Instead, Guest's dragoons retreated to the coast and awaited Cope's arrival.

It was now that Charles's two most important generals joined the Royal Standard, the fifty-one-year-old Lord George Murray, the talented but temperamental younger brother of the Duke of Atholl and a veteran of both the 'Fifteen and the 'Nineteen; and the much younger, more modest James Drummond, the Roman Catholic Jacobite Duke of Perth. They were also joined by Lord Strathallan, Lord Ogilvy and Oliphant of Gask.

Edinburgh was the next target, outside which one thousand MacDonalds and Camerons were grouped ready to force entry to the city on September 17th. At daybreak, by chance, the Netherbow Port opened and a coach came out. Seizing their chance, the Highlanders charged through with Lochiel at their head and the city of forty thousand offered no resistance. Later that day Hepburn of Keith, a veteran of the 'Fifteen, with sword drawn, led Prince Charles in Highland dress and blue sash to his rooms at Holyrood. At the Mercat Cross:

> The Heralds of Arms in their robes, the King's declarations read, all the windows of that fine street were full at every storey of men and women. When the Heralds had finished there was a continual cry of 'God Bless the King!' from both sexes and the ladies to throw themselves out of the windows with white handkerchiefs in their hands, waving about like so many colours.

In less than two months Charles was holding court and hosting balls at the ancient palace of his ancestors. The speed and scale of events seemed miraculous and underlined the absurdly passive policy of the Earl of Mar during the incomparably better opportunity in 1715. Four days later the Battle of Prestonpans was fought. O'Sullivan described the scene:

> You can't imagine what courage the Prince's activity, in setting every regiment in order, the joy that he had painted in his face, and talking some words of Gaelic to the men, inspired them all [...] He drew his sword, 'Now Gents', says he, 'the sword is drawn, it won't be my fault if I set it in the scabbard before you be a free and happy people' [...] When the Chiefs repeated to their men what the Prince said all the bonnets were in the air and such a cry that it would be wherewithal to frighten any enemy.

Though Cope's army was the same size as the enemy's and positioned well, the battle lasted only a quarter of an hour. The Highlanders outflanked Cope's forces with the help of a local guide who showed them a secret path through some marshland just before dawn. Murray then launched a ferocious infantry attack and the Hanoverians fled with one thousand two hundred killed or wounded and as many taken prisoner. Jacobite losses were minimal. Before the battle the chiefs had implored Charles not to expose himself to danger as it was 'only his presence that kept them all united and encouraged their men'. But he replied: 'Tis for that reason that they must see me. You all expose yourselves for the King and country's cause and I am as much obliged to it as any of you'. O'Sullivan observed during the fighting: 'As soon as the fire began he was in the midst of them'. Afterwards Charles arranged medical treatment for the wounded of both sides, maintaining his chivalrous attitude towards the defeated with the words: 'I can't rest until I see my own poor men taken care of, and the other wounded too, for they are the King's subjects as well, and its none of their fault if they are led on blindly'. He was now in possession of all Scotland, although the castles of Edinburgh and Stirling remained garrisoned by Hanoverian guards.

Some Mackenzies came in at this point under Lord Cromartie, as well as an Atholl Brigade formed by Duke William and Lord George Murray. So too did Lord Lewis Gordon with men from his clan, Gordon of Glenbucket with more from his, whilst David Tulloch and John Hamilton raised another four hundred and eighty. Likewise came in Gordon of Aberlour, Stewart of Tinntinnar and from the West yet more Camerons, MacDonalds of Keppoch and MacGregors of Balquhidder. Besides these were MacKinnon of MacKinnon from Skye, Lord Balmerino, Lord Elcho, Alexander Forbes, Lord Pitsligo and Lord Kilmarnock. Importantly, there appeared also the first fruit of Charles's policy towards France when three French ships brought in a number of regular French troops, four thousand guineas and some field pieces which were added to their own as well as the guns captured from Cope after Prestonpans. One of the new arrivals was Lt.Colonel James Grant who now took command of the artillery. Another was the semi-official envoy of the French Court, the Marquis d'Eguilles. But he brought no clear indication of France's policy.

After an October spent recruiting to both enlarge his army and compensate for the tendency of the Gael to wander off home after victory, the Jacobite army was approaching 6,000. Charles's inexperience now prevented him from subduing his exuberant vitality. Indeed the delay at Edinburgh essential for recruiting even narrowed the timing difference between the French preparations and the Jacobite invasion of England, the decision for which was carried by one vote. But Charles was convinced that only by further dynamic action would he force the French to commit themselves, and likewise the English Jacobites. Had he waited, or been delayed a few days, he would have been far better placed to co-ordinate his advance south with the French preparations.

For in November Lord John Drummond arrived from France with eight hundred men of the Royal Scots and some of the Irish Brigade, two squadrons of the Duke of FitzJames's cavalry and an artillery company. More importantly, Drummond brought with him two letters from Louis XV at last firmly promising more and early French military support which Voltaire later described as 'the world's greatest expedition'. Drummond also knew of the tremendous public enthusiasm in Paris which had greeted the news of the Jacobite victory at Prestonpans and, more significantly, of the Hanoverian troop withdrawals from Flanders.

Charles's strategy was working. But the French administration proceeded at a snail's pace and their military preparations were taking much longer than he realised. For this reason, the extraordinary speed of their advance worked against the Jacobites. On November 8th Prince Charles crossed the Esk into England. Carlisle surrendered on November 15th almost before the siege had begun with the total loss to the Highland army of one life. Marshal Wade's force of fourteen thousand at Newcastle failed to give fight for the combined reasons of being tactically outwitted and encountering bad weather; whilst General Sir John Ligonier's ten thousand in Staffordshire found themselves overtaken by the amazing rapidity of events. With this he fell ill and was replaced by the eighteen-stone younger son of George II, the Duke of Cumberland. It was the latter's dismal command which had been responsible for the disastrous British defeat at the Battle of Fontenoy.

Lord George Murray confused Cumberland, a day's march away at Lichfield, by a brilliant feint which had his opponent heading off in quite the wrong direction, thereby opening up the road to Derby which the Highland army reached by December 4th. They were now within 130 miles of London and strengthened by the addition of three hundred new recruits under Colonel Francis Townley which formed the Manchester Regiment. Thus recounted O'Sullivan:

We arrived the next day at Derby, where his Royal Highness was perfectly well received. Bonfires on the roads, the bells ringing. We arrived a little late. It was really a fine sight to see the illuminations of the town. The Prince's reason for striking to the left towards Derby was that he expected by that to gain two days march on Cumberland and of consequence to arrive at London before him, that was always the Prince's design, since Cumberland avoided to come to an action.

31

Wade and Cumberland's combined numbers were 24,000. However, they were behind the Jacobites, and Wade especially was painfully slow moving. Now only a mixed bag of untried men at Finchley, no more numerous than the Highland army, stood between Charles and the Palace of St. James where his father's innocent birth in 1688 as a Catholic heir had triggered William of Orange's invasion of England. With Charles in Derby, the mood in the English capital was one of utter panic and would have been still worse had the government not had some luck earlier. Just twenty-four hours before the news of the Jacobite victory at Prestonpans, 6,000 Dutch troops had landed from Flanders. This momentarily steadied a very badly shaken London. Had they landed just a day or two later 'the confusion in the city of London would not have been to be described and the King's crown, I will venture to say, in the utmost danger', according to King George's First Minister, the Duke of Newcastle. Soon after, Horace Walpole commented to the effect that had the Marshal de Saxe landed with ten thousand men he would have just walked into power, whilst 'I look upon Scotland as gone'. Conversely, morale and confidence amongst the Scots could not have been higher. One officer wrote to his wife from Derby: 'Our whole army is in top spirits and we trust in God to make a good account of them'.

Now, with Prince Charles apparently about to descend upon the capital, London believed itself caught in a co-ordinated pincer movement between the Jacobite army descending from the North, and a French landing due any day from the South. Fielding wrote that the Highland threat 'struck a terror into [London] scarce to be credited'; Wade that: 'England was for the first comer'; Walpole that: 'there never was so melancholy a town [...] I still fear the rebels beyond my reason'; the Bank of England suffered a panic run on funds and was forced to pay out in burning hot sixpences; whilst the London Jacobites swiftly put together a support fund of £10,000; pro-Stuart wall posters started appearing on walls everywhere; and the Duke of Newcastle agonised as to whether he should declare for King James instead of his Hanoverian master who, though striving to appear calm, had ordered his yachts to be laden with as many valuables as possible and kept at full alert in the Thames, ready for an eventual flight back to the Continent.

It was against such a background that Lord George Murray called Prince Charles to a meeting of the Council of War at Derby. Charles could scarcely believe his ears. All that day the chiefs and commanders argued that in the absence of material support from the English

Jacobites who had failed to match their words of support with action, Charles's army should conduct a pragmatic retreat to Scotland and join up with Lords Strathallan and John Drummond's force of nearly four thousand at Perth. They were more or less unaware of the panic in London, the readiness of the Welsh Jacobites to join them the very next day, and the precise state of the French preparations which, had the fight been taken to the English capital, would have been catapulted into action and, whatever the effect, could only have swung things further Charles's way. Consequently the majority of the Council felt isolated, exposed and deep inside hostile territory. The prince, on the other hand, was totally opposed, realising that a retreat could never be disguised as anything but a shameful moral defeat which would destroy morale and reverse the potential magnetism of the 'winning side' towards whom the London mob would probably swing. Charles' first words to Murray were: 'To retire, Lord George? Why the clans kept me quite another language and assured me they were all resolved to pierce or to die!' As Murray commented later: 'His Royal Highness had no regard for his own danger, but pressed with all the force of argument to go forward'. But Charles lacked military credibility. Nor did he possess the dictatorial powers of his adversary, being at the head of a loose alliance of often jealous and independent-minded chiefs rather than a regular, disciplined standing army. Charles failed to carry the Council with him and, according to Lord Elcho, 'fell into a passion and gave of the Gentlemen that spoke very abusive language and said they had a mind to betray him'.

According to the usually well-informed Hanoverian spy, Dudley Bradstreet, O'Sullivan was in favour of marching on London, as was the Duke of Perth. And family traditions in the Gordon and Moir families maintains that Sir William Gordon of Park and James Moir of Stoneywood were also in favour of the bolder course. Indeed Charles proved to be the one in tune with the ordinary clansmen and soldiers. For when the decision became clear to the rank and file, 'If we had been beat, the grief could not have been greater'. Of their prince, O'Sullivan commented: 'I never saw anyone so concerned as he was for this disappointment, nor ever saw him take anything after so much to heart as he did it'. And even if the men realised that the Council's decision was understandable, it was clearer still that it ran contrary to the flow of logic governing all that had gone before. The whig supporter, John Home, in his *History of the Rebellion* commented: 'There were moments when nothing seemed impossible; and, to say truth, it was not easy to forecast, or to imagine, anything more unlikely than what had already happened'. No-one better summed up the psychological transformation than the previously petrified Walpole: 'No-one is afraid of a rebellion that runs away'. His smugness was the measure of his relief.

For the French too, everything was now changed. On October 24th the Marquis d'Argenson had signed the secret Treaty of Fontainebleau between the Stuarts and France committing France to military support. Before Charles had arrived at Derby he had received a letter from his younger brother, Henry, dated November 26th, in which he had written that the French Foreign Minister had assured him of Louis XV's firm resolve to invade England and that 'you might count on it being ready towards December 20th'. This was reinforced by the Minister for the Navy who, on December 10th, wrote: 'We are at last on the eve of a mighty event. We have completed at Dunkirk and neighbouring ports all the necessary preparations for the embarkation of twelve thousand men commanded by the Duke de Richelieu [...] The disembarkation could take place before this month is out'.

Henry Stuart was one of those anxiously waiting to sail. So were his cousins and ADCs, Godefroy-Charles de Turenne and Jules-Hercule de Rohan. So too was George Keith, the Earl Marischal. But on December 29th, when the French heard the news of the retreat, Richelieu seemed surprisingly keen to halt the preparations despite his king's continued insistence on helping his Stuart cousin. Louis was reduced to ordering Richelieu to sail at any cost. But by then foul weather and an English naval blockade were preventing the French ships from leaving harbour. By February 7th it was clear that the French invasion, which earlier had seemed destined for easy success, was now doomed to failure. The French cancelled their plans and abandoned Charles and his army to their fate.

In fact the retreat from Derby was conducted brilliantly by Lord George Murray, and the Scots successfully attacked Cumberland's vanguard at Penrith. Waiting for them at Perth was the second Jacobite force of some four thousand men under Lord Strathallan and Lord John Drummond, including clansmen raised by Lord Lewis Gordon which had put to flight a whig army near Aberdeen towards the end of December. But Charles foolishly acceded to Francis Townley's suicidal request to leave him and his Manchester Regiment to garrison Carlisle, despite the fact that his men wanted to go on with the retreat to Scotland. After their inevitable surrender Cumberland began to reveal his savage nature.

On December 26th the prince arrived at Glasgow where he met Clementina, the daughter of the late John Walkinshaw of Barrowfield and Camlachie by Catherine Paterson, the daughter of Sir Hugh Paterson of Bannockburn.[1] Clementina's father had been a Jacobite agent in Rome, then James VIII's ambassador to Vienna in 1717, and finally lost his estates in 1723 because of his Stuart loyalties.

Leaving Glasgow on January 3rd, the Jacobites wasted time on a futile, misdirected siege of Stirling Castle during which the prince stayed at Paterson's Bannockburn House where he argued with the self-righteous Murray whom he bitterly resented for the decision to retreat from Derby. But when the sadistic General Henry Hawley came to relieve Stirling, Murray took only twenty minutes to lead Charles's eight thousand strong force to victory at Falkirk on January 17th. It was a significantly more impressive battle than the earlier Jacobite victory at Prestonpans. Of it O'Sullivan wrote: 'There were a great many officers killed, for gold watches were at a cheap rate. Our loss was not considerable, we had more wounded than killed'. Having fled to Linlithgow the same evening, Hawley wrote to Cumberland that his 'heart is broke'. Not that he seems to have had one. Walpole said of him: 'Frequent and sudden executions are his rare passion'. His own brigadier-major wrote that 'the troops dread his severity, hate the man and hold his military knowledge in contempt'. He was believed to be an illegitimate son of George I and therefore the natural uncle of the Duke of Cumberland who soon after assumed overall command.

Two days later, Charles was back at Bannockburn with the Patersons and Clementina Walkinshaw who was tending to the severe fever the prince had caught. Meanwhile Henry, who was still on the French coast impatiently awaiting the French fleet's sailing, had been abandoned by his cousins, de Turenne and de Rohan. Both had been itching to join the Jacobite campaign but had been ordered to rejoin their regiments in Flanders.

At the end of January Charles suffered another blow. After the victory at Falkirk which had again sent the whigs in London into despair, Charles had begun to strain at the prospect of challenging Cumberland on the legendary field of Bannockburn itself. There, on June 23rd and 24th, 1314 his ancestors, King Robert the Bruce and Walter Stewart, Governor of Scotland, had crushed King Edward II's three times

---

[1] Sir Hugh's wife was Lady Jean Erskine, daughter of Charles, 5th Earl of Mar by Lady Mary Maule, daughter of George, 2nd Earl of Panmure

greater forces of eighteen and a half thousand men in the decisive battle of the Wars of Independence. What could better inspire the Scottish army? Such a lift was badly needed. For after Falkirk a letter from General Cope had been found stating that London was no longer expecting the French to invade. And that news was damaging the Jacobite army's morale. Yet on January 29th, ostensibly worried by the number of clansmen who had gone off home and fearing the time it would take to rally them once more, Murray and the other commanders recommended throwing their heavier artillery pieces into the Forth and retreating into the mountain glens of the Highlands 'where we can be usefully employed the remainder of the Winter, by taking and mastering the forts in the north [...] And in the Spring we doubt not but an army of ten thousand effective Highlanders can be brought together'.

John Hay of Restalrig had the thankless task of delivering this message to Prince Charles, who 'struck his head against the wall till he staggered and exclaimed most violently against Lord George Murray'. Charles replied:

> Is it possible that a victory and a defeat should produce the same effects and that the conquerors should fly from an engagement, whilst the conquered are seeking it? Should we make the retreat you propose, how much more will that raise the spirits of our enemy and sink those of our own people? [...] What opinion will the French and Spaniards then have of us, or what encouragement will it be to the former to make the descent for which they have been so preparing? [...] And what will become of our Lowland friends? [...] I can foresee nothing but ruin and destruction [...] Why should we be so much afraid now of an enemy that we attacked and beat a fortnight ago when they were much more numerous I cannot conceive [...] Has the shame of their flight made them more formidable?

This time Murray did not succeed in repeating his superbly ordered retreat from Derby. He later wrote that it was 'but a flight and the men were going off like so many sheep scattered upon the side of the hill, or like a broken and fleeing army after a defeat'. He began to blame others. On February 2nd Prince Charles reviewed his regrouped forces at Crieff. He was furious. For no more than a thousand men had left his army. Relations with and within his High Command degenerated into mutual recrimination and accusations of treachery.

As Charles had foreseen, Cumberland's morale was now in the ascendant. However, the duke failed to catch the Highlanders and waited at Perth whilst on February 8th his brother-in-law, Prince Frederick von Hesse, landed at Leith with five thousand German regulars. Of Scotland Cumberland wrote that 'the greatest part of this kingdom are either openly or privately aiding the rebels and how it may be changed I don't know, at least immediately'. A little later he added: 'I am now in a country so much our enemy that there is hardly any intelligence to be got'.

Charles arrived at Inverness with his force on February 19th and installed himself at Culloden House. His aim was to reduce or neutralise Forts William and Augustus, destroy or disperse the local whig forces, take Inverness and hold as much of the coastline as possible.

Inverness was taken immediately. On March 1st Fort Augustus surrendered to a siege conducted by Brigadier Stapleton and Lochiel's Camerons, Keppoch's MacDonalds and some of Drummond's men. But they couldn't do the same at Fort William from which they retreated on April 2nd. In addition a whig army of some two thousand men under Lord Loudon was completely scattered. The balance sheet did the Jacobites credit. Then luck turned against them. At the end of March a small force under Lord Reay successfully ambushed a number of Stuart supporters who had just landed from France with £12,500 of desperately needed cash and large quantities of stores and ammunition. It all fell into the government's hands. This problem became a disaster when Lord Cromartie went with one thousand five hundred men to try and retrieve the situation. They were taken prisoner and their loss was a major blow, only partly offset by some minor successes of Murray and Drummond and the appearance of two hundred new volunteers from Argyll under Charles MacLean of Drimnin and James MacLean, Younger of Ardgour, together with some Scots who had deserted from the whig forces.

The Germans troops and three hundred English cavalry under the Prince von Hesse were already at Dunkeld. And Cumberland was ready to move his well-fed and rested army of nine thousand north from their month-long stay in Aberdeen. He left on April 8th, supported by the Navy's warships and supply ships. March had proved unkind to the Jacobites for other reasons. Charles fell ill, and so did Murray of Broughton who had been tirelessly efficient in organising all the provisions for the army. He had been replaced by the near-incompetent Hay of Restalrig and everything was now in short supply.

By April 14th the Hanoverian army reached Nairn, just ten miles from Culloden. The evening before, Charles's force had been rejoined by Lochiel who had marched from Lochaber, and some of Glengarry's men who had come from Sutherland. Now, with morale low and his troops exhausted and ill-fed, the prince blindly agreed to O'Sullivan's proposal to give battle – something which had been repeatedly refused when morale had been high and victory fresh. Charles's had been the genius which had often sensed the possible when reason appeared to indicate otherwise. But now his desperation made him oblivious to Murray's reservations concerning Drummossie Moor as a battlefield. For its flatness perfectly suited the Hanoverian artillery and lacked any slope down which the Highlanders might launch one of their devastating charges.

On the night of the 15th, MacDonald of Keppoch marched in with two hundred men. With him came one last glimmer of hope which reunited Charles and Murray – to launch a surprise night attack on the Hanoverian camp at Nairn. As Murray laid out the plan he added: 'We have another advantage that people does not think of. This is Cumberland's birthday, they'll be as drunk as beggars!' The idea was inspired. But, thanks to Hay's 'unaccountable negligence', as many as two thousand near-starving men were away searching for food. Moreover, the rear of the column could not keep up with Murray and they managed only six miles in six hours with four miles left to go at two o'clock in the morning. Finally, despite the fact that the prince sent word that he was very keen to press on, Murray took the decision to return to Culloden. Hay rode up to Murray who loudly criticised him for his failure to organise supplies. Furious, Hay rode back to Charles, accusing Murray of deliberately disobeying orders. The retreat was a mess. And the only result of the endeavour was to exhaust the army which had not slept all night.

By ten in the morning the men were barely awake and weak from hunger. Their number was down to 5,000 and the only scrap of good news was that Charles Fraser of Inverallochy had come in with three hundred men and more were on their way under the Master of Lovat. But, just as he had done the previous day, Murray insisted that in the forthcoming battle the right wing should be given to his Atholl Brigade. This was more than undiplomatic, for it outraged the MacDonald chiefs whose clan had held this honour for 450 years. Lochiel and Keppoch spoke out against giving battle that day. But Stapleton ruined any chance of good sense when he provoked the chiefs into fighting there and then by insulting them in words which Lochiel described as an 'odious and undeserved aspersion'.

About midday on the 16th the two armies were facing each other. The weather was freezing and the rain and sleet lashed by a gale. On one side stood Cumberland's 9,000 fresh and well-ordered men to the north. On the other, Prince Charles's exhausted, hungry and dejected 5,000. On the Jacobite right, as he had so stubbornly demanded, was Murray's Atholl Brigade supported by Robertsons and Menzies. Next was Clan Cameron under Lochiel, then the Stewarts of Appin, the Frasers, the Mackintoshes, the Farquharsons, the MacLachlans, the MacLeans, the MacLeods, the Chisholms and finally, on the left, the infuriated MacDonalds of Clanranald, Keppoch and Glengarry. Behind them stood the second line which included the French regulars. It was commanded by Lord Ogilvy, Lord Lewis Gordon, Gordon of Glenbucket, the Duke of Perth and Lord John Drummond with the Irish Picquets on the left wing, and the cavalry in the rear under Lords Strathallan, Pitsligo and Balmerino.

Just then a single Highlander began to walk slowly forward. The ranks watched as the lone figure reached the enemy's front line. There he gave up his weapons and asked to surrender to the Duke of Cumberland himself. He was taken through the bustle of the Hanoverian ranks where suddenly he saw Lord Bury whom he took to be King George's son. Snatching a pistol out of the hands of an English soldier, he tried to shoot the grandly dressed young man, but missed. They killed him on the spot. Yet this Scottish hero had rightly sensed that only some desperate act could save his Prince and people now.

CHAPTER FIVE

Drummossie Moor

On hills that are by right his ain
He roams a lonely stranger
On ilka hand he's press'd by want
On ilka side is danger
Yestreen I met him in the glen
My heart near bursted fairly
For sadly chang'd indeed was he
Oh! Wae's me for Prince Charlie.

William Glen

The Hanoverian artillery immediately proved its great superiority, taking full advantage of a site tailor-made for it, tearing gaping holes in the Jacobite infantry who stood, enraged at their losses, waiting for the traditional order to charge: 'Claymore! Claymore!'. The Jacobites couldn't reply. Even as the prince's horse was shot from under him and his groom killed, Charles, in his first command of a battle, revealed his ineptitude by leaving his forward troops a full half-hour in that murderous assault. Some regiments lost a third of their men. Finally, he ordered the charge after Lochiel told Murray that 'he couldn't hold his men much longer'. The order was rushed to the left and right wings of the front line by Ker of Graden, Sir Alexander MacDonald, Lachlan MacLachlan of Inchconnel and Brigadier Stapleton. Three of them made it but young MacLachlan's head was ripped from its torso by cannon fire before he reached the right.

Clan Chattan burst forward, led by MacGillivray of Dunmaglass and his standard-bearer with pipers playing. They raced through the smoke and grapeshot towards the Hanoverian line screaming: 'Loch Moy!'

and 'Dunmaglass!'. Then charged the Camerons, Murrays, Frasers and Stewarts. But the usually ferocious MacDonalds, antagonised by Murray, were so out of sorts that they never even engaged the enemy. Their attitude infected the Gordons and Farquharsons on their right. As the charge went in, an invisible piece of boggy ground forced the Jacobite centre to swerve to the right, blocking the best soldiers and squashing the Athollmen against a wall and then a dyke from which their flank was mercilessly fired upon by Wolfe's regiment. Having veered right, the centre now found it had moved into the heaviest fire of all. It was all going horribly wrong.

The Highlanders inflicted terrible damage and both Barrel's and Munro's regiments were split wide open. But the Hanoverian counterattack did greater damage still. Only three of Clan Chattan's twenty-one officers survived, whilst the Camerons' chief, Lochiel, lay helpless, his ankles smashed by grapeshot. Half of the Stewarts of Appin were either killed or wounded and eight of the chief's own family lay dead. MacLachlan of MacLachlan also fell and by him lay his son and heir. Only thirty-eight MacLeans survived. MacLean of Drimnin, learning from one son of the death of his other, attacked the Hanoverian line on his own, overcome with grief, killing one and wounding another before being hacked down. Now Charles's army was being outflanked on the left and the MacDonalds and Farquharsons began to fall back, notwithstanding the Drummond brothers cries of 'Claymore! Claymore!' Keppoch tried to rescue the honour of MacDonald, devastated that his clan should turn and run, by charging the enemy with a few lone men. He was killed in a torrent of enemy fire. Then the Hanoverian cavalry charged. But the Jacobite second line, having let the retreating MacDonalds past, closed ranks again and checked the enemy's advance with accurate volleys whilst Lord Lewis Gordon's regiment and the Royal Scots, led by the bloodstained Murray, advanced again.

The day was already lost beyond hope. The Camerons and the right retreated steadily, though terribly exposed, fighting all the way, whilst the outnumbered Scottish cavalry gave them all the protection they could from the Hanoverian dragoons, despite dreadful casualties. Ogilvy and Murray now showed their true mettle by continually turning on the enemy so as to keep them from coming close whilst the French troops coolly employed professional defensive techniques, skilfully slowing the Hanoverian advance. Old Lord Balmerino, broken, rode slowly towards the enemy and surrendered, knowing that only the scaffold awaited him. Lord Strathallan, however, charged the massed ranks of enemy dragoons in a mad rage. He was cut to shreds with forty of his men.

The retreat was now general. Twenty-five minutes after the Jacobite charge had gone in, their dead and dying lay four deep in places. Accounts disagree with regard to Prince Charles's reaction. They vary from him being forcibly prevented from charging the enemy, to being seized with panic, and everything in between. Indeed, it may well be that amid such carnage he felt all such emotions in turn. Someone finally seized the bridle of his horse and pulled the stunned young man away, tears streaming from his hazel eyes.

The butchery carried out by Cumberland's execution squads on the Highland wounded as they lay helpless on and around the field of battle was disgusting. It had nothing in common with the *coup de grâce*. Likewise the unspeakable punishment meted out to the Jacobite prisoners, the indiscriminate murder, burnings and even roastings alive, gang rapes, wholesale pillage and wanton destruction that was wreaked upon the length and breadth of the Highlands for long after. This was not standard practice. It was savage and it was bad politics. Cumberland reacted to the ultra-loyal Hanoverian Lord President Duncan Forbes's suggestion of tempering the law with princely mercy by shouting: 'Laws? I'll make a brigade give the laws!' before describing him as 'arrant Highland mad [...] that old woman who spoke to me of humanity'. The whig provost John Hossack urged General Hawley 'to mingle mercy with...', but got no further before being kicked from the room, down the stairs and out into the street.

Just as Charles's chivalry towards his prisoners and the Hanoverian wounded will remain a credit to him, so will the violence after Culloden always stain the reputation of Hanover. And though Charles was the initiator of the 'Forty-Five it seems wrong to hold him personally responsible for the unforeseeable sadism that followed. Cumberland's own words, written to the Duke of Newcastle after Culloden, speak volumes: 'I tremble for fear that this vile spot may still be the ruin of this island and our family'.

The speed of events at Drummossie Moor and Charles's inexperience made him commit the cardinal mistake of failing to appoint a rendezvous for his army. Notwithstanding, a few assembled at Fort Augustus whilst large numbers rallied at Ruthven in Badenoch, surprisingly full of fight. There were no fewer than 2,000 of them under Lord George Murray, Duke William of Atholl, the Duke of Perth, Lord John Drummond, Lord Ogilvy, Lord Nairne, Stewart of Ardshiel and Colonel Roy Stewart. With determined leadership their vengeance might have been terrible. At the time few considered Culloden a decisive battle. However, their prince had escaped along a line parallel with the southern shore of Loch Ness. One who went with him wrote:

> Our troops retired, some by Badenoch, some by Inverness and some by Ranach. The French Ambassador and a great many of our volunteers gave themselves up at Inverness. Barisdale, the MacGregors and others that were towards Dornoch retired by Lord Seaforth's country. His R.H. took the road in the mountains of Ranach, and brought with him Sir Thomas Sheridan, O'Sullivan, John Hay and Sandy MacLeod, one of his Aide de Camps, and FitzJames' horse.

In fact there were also Lord Elcho, O'Neil and a Gaelic speaker from North Uist called Edward Burke. That night Charles instructed his ADC, MacLeod, to write to Macpherson of Cluny:

> We have suffered a good deal; but we hope that we shall soon pay Cumberland in his own coin. We are to review to-morrow at Fort Augustus the Frasers, Camerons, Stewarts, Clanranalds and Keppoch's people. His R.H. expects your people will be with us at furthest Friday morning. Dispatch is the more necessary that His Highness has something in view which will make ample amends for this day's ruffle [...] For God's sake make haste to join us; and bring with you all the people that can possibly be got together.

O'Sullivan, also present that evening, described the moment to King James's agent in Paris in an encoded letter dated July 26th, 1746:

> My associate and I after our unlucky shipwreck of the 15th of April last, retreated into a spot where we hoped to be able to collect a little of the remains of our property and to try and re-establish our business as far as was possible and thus to give time to our correspondent in France to arrange our affairs with our creditors and to extricate us from the awkward situation in which we were. But all the efforts we were able to make proved useless. Our property was too much scattered and in so many different hands that we were never able to gather together so much as half

a farthing and we were so harassed by our creditors that we were obliged for our own safety to retire.

From Ruthven, where the two thousand had rallied, came a letter written by George Murray a few hours after Charles's to Cluny:

As no person in these Kingdoms ventured more frankly in the Cause than myself and as I had more at stake than almost all the others put together, so to be sure I cannot but be very deeply affected with our late loss and present situation [...] I thank God I have the resolution to bear my own and family's ruin without grudge.

Murray went on to issue a barrage of accusations against the prince, especially for coming without French aid and for the defeat at Culloden. Then he turned on O'Sullivan and Hay, blaming them for incompetence, before resigning with the words:

I would of late when I came last from Atholl have resigned my commission, but all my friends told me it might be of prejudice to the Cause at such a critical time. I hope your R.H. will now accept my demission.

In the light of these words from his senior commander written from where the main body of men had assembled there can have seemed little point in any course other than returning to France to try and obtain the aid referred to by Murray. But Charles penned an ill-worded letter to the chiefs that misjudged the patriarchal culture of Gaeldom which ultimately looked to him for leadership. In an aloof style he told the men to fend for themselves whilst he would try and make it back to France to raise support from the country that the Scottish leaders were already coming to feel had betrayed them – but which had always been, and still remained, crucial to success and which Charles consistently did everything in his power to secure.

Lochiel, joined in Lochaber by Murray of Broughton, saw clearly just how destructive to Jacobite unity Charles's proposed course would be and dispatched his brother, Dr Archie, to Arisaig to dissuade him. Lochiel wrote to Charles that his plan was 'dishonourable to himself and so harmful to the whole Scottish nation'. But Dr Archie was too late. Charles had sailed from Loch nan Uamh for the Outer Isles with

O'Sullivan, O'Neil, Father Allan MacDonald, Alexander MacLeod, Edward Burke and seven boatmen on the evening of the 26th, two days earlier. Continuing the fight would prove impossible without the prince at their head. Yet fate now played a cruel trick. Just four days after Charles had stood in that very same place the means to carry on arrived. Two frigates from Nantes dropped anchor in Loch nan Uamh with no less than 36,000 louis d'or and sufficient arms to sustain a campaign right through the summer.

Some chose to escape to France with the returning ships, such as Sir Thomas Sheridan, Lord Elcho, Lord John Drummond and the dying Duke of Perth. But as Murray of Broughton wrote: 'Mr Cameron of Lochiel retired into a little hut with Mr Murray where he expressed unwillingness to desert his Clan' so as to 'raise a body of men sufficient to protect the country and to keep on foot during that summer until they should see whether or not the succours promised from France were really intended'. The plan was to take the newly arrived ships and news of the money and arms across to Charles and persuade him to return. But this was prevented by the sudden appearance of three Hanoverian frigates. The French ran for the Continent.

Yet on the shores of Loch Arkaig the chiefs from Barisdale and Moidart began to rally again. By May 8th a convention had been called by Lochiel and Murray of Broughton. It included Lord Lovat, Clanranald, Lochgarry, Barisdale, Keppoch's nephew, Colonel Roy Stewart and Gordon of Glenbucket. They decided that their clans should gather at Lochiel's Achnacarry in the Braes of Lochaber on May 15th whilst 'the Frasers of Aird and other loyal men north of the Ness shall join the people of Glenmoriston and Glengarry; and that the Frasers of Stratherrick, the Mackintoshes and Macphersons shall assemble and meet at the most convenient place in Badenoch'. The MacGregors, Menzies and Glenlyon people were to march to Rannoch and join the local people and the Atholl men whilst Glenbucket and Roy Stewart were to rally Lord Lewis Gordon, Lord Ogilvy, Lord Pitsligo, the Farquharsons and the other northern Jacobites.

But Charles was no longer present. Nor were all made of the same stuff as Lochiel. At Achnacarry four hundred Camerons, MacLeans and MacDonnells from Barisdale came in with more Camerons to follow from Sunart and Ardnamurchan under Major Alexander Cameron of Dungallon. But before they could move off to join up with the MacDonalds of Keppoch at Braelochaber, Lochiel's force was caught in a pincer movement with six hundred Hanoverians approaching from the South and two thousand from the North. They retreated to the foot of Loch Arkaig where they saw 'the melancholy and dismal prospect of the whole country on fire'. In the face of impossible odds Lochiel ordered his force to melt into the hills and glens whilst he himself went to an islet on Loch Shiel adjacent to Cameron of Dungallon's house at Glenhurich. With that order, the 'Forty Five was over.

Norman Davies writes: 'After each of the Jacobite Risings, the draconian English law of treason was improperly introduced into Scotland, and prisoners illegally removed to England for trial'. Their horrific fate almost defies description. 'In several respects the Act of Union was flagrantly breached'. Michael Lynch writes that what had been extraordinary during the whole period from 1688 until 1746 was 'the incredible and repeated good luck of the London regime' and how 'truly marginal was the narrow gap which separated success from failure, whether in 1708 or 1745'. Two hundred years earlier Sir Walter Scott wrote that: 'If Prince Charles had concluded his life soon after his miraculous escape, his character in history must have stood very high'. He was referring to the five months following Culloden during which Charles was constantly on the run from the huge military and naval search encompassing the entire north-western seaboard. The price on his head was £30,000. Yet though poverty reigned everywhere and 'we hang or shoot everyone that is known to conceal the Pretender', as one English officer wrote, only one attempt to betray him was ever made. On the other hand a string of individuals helped the prince, most of whom were later imprisoned. There was also an extensive underground intelligence system in which parents organised their innocent-looking children to ferry information about Hanoverian troop movements to Charles and the others who were with him.

Charles crossed in early June from South Uist to Skye in a dramatic escape organised by a Hanoverian officer, Hugh MacDonald of Armadale, who told the Prince that 'though an enemy in appearance' he was 'yet a sure friend in his heart'. Charles had dressed up as a maid of Armadale's step-daughter, Flora MacDonald. Under his disguise he wanted to hide a loaded pistol but Flora protested, saying that were he to be searched it would give the game away. Charles answered: 'Indeed, Miss, if we shall happen with any that will go so narrowly to work in searching me as what you mean, they will certainly discover me at any rate'. For her loyalty Flora was later imprisoned in the Tower of

London. Then, upon parting with the prince as he was to leave Skye for Raasay in late June, Donald Roy MacDonald said that 'though Sir Alexander[1] and his following did not join Your Royal Highness, yet you see you have been very safe amongst them; for though they did not repair to your standard, they wish you very well'.

Raasay offered no refuge. But it provided a chilling insight into Cumberland's policy. In the words of his successor: 'Nothing but fire and sword can cure their cursed, vicious ways of thinking [...] For God Almighty's sake don't spare those whom you have in your power'. In May the whole island had been plundered, burnt and pillaged without mercy. The laird's house had been reduced to ashes and every habitation on the island left in ruins except for two tiny villages that the Royal Navy officers had overlooked. The orders were given by Captain Ferguson, a man of evil reputation, whose men marched through the island in three bodies, killing everything alive in their paths and leaving the animals' carcasses to rot so they couldn't be used for food. On the small rocky island of Rona, just north of Raasay, they raped a blind girl and horse-whipped two Highlanders so brutally that one died and the other never recovered. They then returned to steal the clothes of the remaining poor of Raasay, kill what cattle had been missed the first time and rape two more women, one of them crippled. Such cruelty was no exception. As John Prebble's book *Culloden* chillingly records, this was now the rule throughout the Highlands and Isles. Of these horrors Charles enquired in detail, aghast at what he heard, whilst the cousin of the heirs of Raasay, Captain Malcolm MacLeod, told him of the cruelty meted out by Cumberland after Culloden. The stories were so appalling that Charles had difficulty in believing them.

MacLeod had the further task of removing about eighty lice from the prince's body, noting that Charles never once complained at his discomfort and that, despite his awful condition, there was 'something about him that was not ordinary, something of the stately and the grand'. A couple of MacKinnon clansmen who had last seen Charles before Culloden recognised him and 'lifted their hands and wept bitterly'. O'Sullivan said that: 'The Prince was in a terrible condition, his legs and thighs cut all over from the briers; the midges or flies which are terrible in that country, devoured him and made him scratch those scars which made him appear as if he were covered with ulcers'.

By mid-July, having at times almost relished the extraordinary

---

[1] Sir Alexander MacDonald of Sleat, officially a Hanoverian.

physical and mental hardships in which a bed at night was a rare comfort and cooked food a luxury, Charles was back on the mainland, moving from Moidart to Knoydart. There his small band had to break through a military cordon, the tightness of which was remarkable. From the head of Loch Eil to the top of Loch Hourn there were camps at intervals of half a mile, sentries within shouting distance of one another and patrols to maintain strict vigilance everywhere.

By the third week of July, Charles was joined at Corriegoe, north of Loch Cluanie, by a group of destitute men who had all served in his army and who took it upon themselves to become his bodyguard. They are known to history as the Seven Men of Glenmoriston, though in fact there were eight. They swore that their 'backs should be to God and their faces to the Devil; that all the curses the Scriptures did pronounce might come upon them and all their posterity if they did not stand firm to help the Prince in his greatest danger'. They proved not only loyal but also strict disciplinarians. When Charles wanted to move on before they considered it safe, they threatened to tie him up rather than comply. He commented: 'Kings and Princes must be ruled by their privy council, but I believe there is not in all the world a more absolute privy council than what I have at present'.

On August 23rd, a year to the day since Charles had stayed the night at John Cameron's Fassiefern House, Cameron's elder brother, Lochiel, hiding in Mullach Coire an Iubhar, discovered that the men of Glenmoriston with Charles and a couple of others were hiding nearby, to the north of the ruins of Achnacarry which had been burnt on Cumberland's orders. Exactly a week later they were reunited at Ben Alder, east of Fort William, when the still-crippled Lochiel tried to kneel before the prince, who would not allow him to. Two days after, Macpherson of Cluny returned, having been out looking for Charles. He too tried to kneel, but Charles stopped him and 'kissed him, as if he had been an equal'. They then all moved higher up the hill to a hide-out known as 'Cluny's Cage' where they passed a week of relative comfort. Invisible from below, it was a wooden construction on two floors, roofed with turf and screened by a holly grove. Yet its view of the terrain below was excellent. Seeing the mass violence, wholesale destruction and widespread starvation caused by the Hanoverians, Lochiel said that Charles was 'cut to the heart by the evils the country had endured'. Women and children had been found on the hillsides dead from want. Lochiel's sister-in-law, Jean Cameron, recalled that many Highland women were forced to beg the Hanoverian soldiers for the guts and green hides of slaughtered cattle which Cumberland's men had stolen from them in the first place. Then, whilst the women boiled this offal, the soldiers would sometimes amuse themselves by shooting them, 'for diversion and for wagers etc'. Charles and his companions agreed he should leave for France to try and obtain help. Moreover, if he appeared elsewhere, George II would see that Charles was no longer in Scotland and send his troops back to the Continent.

'Cluny's Cage' was to be their winter quarters if a rescue ship from France did not come and a chain of communications had already been set up, from Clanranald's South Uist and Moidart through the Camerons' Lochaber, to the hide-out on Ben Alder. However, two ships from St. Malo made it, the *Heureux* and the *Prince de Conti*. Charles, Lochiel and Dr Archie Cameron, joined by Roy Stewart and Macpherson of Breakachie, travelled under cover of darkness to Loch nan Uamh during the six days from September 13th, passing ruined Achnacarry on the way. There they sailed into exile with about a hundred others. Cluny Macpherson remained behind. In Charles's words he was 'the only person in whom he could repose the greatest confidence'. The job with which he was entrusted was to prepare for the next Jacobite rising which never came. Cluny returned to his 'Cage' where he remained hidden by his clansmen for ten years. Finally Prince Charles thanked the Highlanders who had escorted him by moonlight to the loch's shore and bade them a tearful farewell with the words: 'It'll not be long before I shall be with you'. Not only were the hills disappearing into the night, but so too was the ancient culture of Gaeldom. And he had been the instrument of its terrible destruction.

The very day Charles landed at Morlaix in Brittany he wrote to his brother Henry asking him to immediately arrange a meeting with Louis XV. However, King James was already being informed by Colonel O'Brien, the Stuart representative at the French Court, that they were, 'more of a mind to seek peace than think about a new expedition to Scotland'. Henry had been staying at the Navarre estate of the Duke de Bouillon, but the two brothers were reunited at Fontainebleau. The shortish, ebullient younger prince rushed up and threw his arms around his taller, more serious sibling. Fearing this to be an assault, Lochiel drew his sword but Charles turned quickly in protection, saying, 'He's my brother!' They all appeared at Court on October 20th. The prince was greeted with exceptional warmth by Louis and his queen, Princess Marie Leszczyńska, a cousin of Charles's mother. He was also fêted by the rest of the French royal family,

Madame de Pompadour, Louis' ministers and a string of others. But Louis proved evasive on providing material help. The Stuart brothers had even been obliged to attend incognito, as Baron Renfrew and the Count of Albany.

Despite a reluctant public appearance with Henry and de Bouillon on the 28th at the Opera at which the public exploded in wild applause, Charles was intensely frustrated. He sent Louis a forceful memorandum from his base at Clichy asking for an army of eighteen to twenty thousand, arguing that their cause was one and the same. He also urged the French king to strike now whilst the Highlands were seething, before the far-reaching penal laws rapidly being introduced by Westminster could take full effect. He received no reply and repeated the message. Finally Louis proposed six thousand troops to his ministers. But whereas Charles believed the French would sooner focus on England, Lochiel was for a re-run starting in Western Scotland during early 1747. At that time Hanoverian spies were reporting a readiness to rise again amongst the people of Mull, Morvern, Appin, Sunart, Moidart, Arisaig, Knoydart, Glenmoriston, Glen Spean and Glen Roy, not to mention the Cameron country around Loch Eil itself. Indeed, only the Glencoe MacDonalds 'seemed to be weary of rebellion'. But Charles, more cynical now, rejected Louis' proposal, realising that it lacked critical mass, was only enough to distract the Hanoverians from Flanders, and therefore careless of the Scottish lives which would be sacrificed.

Meanwhile James was writing from Rome to his son, criticising him for pushing the French Court too aggressively. But time was slipping by, and, despite his hero's welcome in France, Charles had nothing to show for his efforts. In mid-October 1746 he wrote: 'How can you imagine that I can enjoy any pleasure or amusement when I have continually before my eyes the cruelty with which my poor friends are treated?'

The Treaty of Fontainebleau was now forgotten by the French Government and the cynical reason for its secrecy revealed. As they retreated ever further from giving support of any kind, so did Charles's frustration begin to boil over into anger directed against an ever larger number of people. His mood blackened into an isolated, explosive depression. For his character was not like that of his father who stoically endured defeat, a fact underlined by James's wise but tedious letters urging his 'dear child' to be patient and prudent with the French Court. However, on his mother's side, Charles came from legendarily dynamic stock. The person Clementina Sobieska had once been when escaping from Innsbrück might well have understood her son now. But she was long since dead, killed by her self-destructive anorexia.

Since birth Charles had been steeped in the myth that the Stuarts' royal birthright had been granted by God and that he had been born to win back their thrones which had been wrongfully taken away. But this childhood fairytale had been smashed by a shocking avalanche of brutal reality. And there was no-one with whom Charles could share the responsibility for the terrible things being done to the land and people which had once had been the beautiful, legendary theme of his youth.

CHAPTER SIX

Expulsion from France

Gae bring to me a pint o'wine
And fill it in a silver tassie
That I may drink before I go
A service to my bonnie lassie.

Robert Burns

Prince Charles's inability to control his anger at his powerlessness was reflected in the hostility of his letter of December 29th, 1746 to Sir James Steuart, his plenipotentiary for negotiations with the Court of France:

> If the ministers pretend that the King has a mind to undertake something in our favour, you are to demand proof of his sincerity. Let that be either his daughter in marriage or a large sum of money, not under a million. If you find them cold and backward, you are to communicate to them my orders to leave the Court until matters are riper [...] You are to concur in no measures which seem only to work the affairs of France by occasioning a diversion on the part of Great Britain, but on the contrary to take all possible measures to prevent and disappoint any such scheme.

Charles's great-grandmother had been a royal French princess. But to expect the hand of one now and to equate her to a sum of cash whilst displaying open contempt for Europe's greatest ruler, was an indication of Charles's mental state. Perhaps it was misguided bargaining, but he then went on to gracelessly refuse a French allowance for himself and Henry, expressing outrage at its modesty, preferring instead to live in penury and debt. He similarly rejected their proposal for a residence which he described as 'scandalous'.

Frustrated by Louis and the cynicism of his ministers, Charles looked about desperately for a way forward. He even came up with the idea of marrying the Tsarina of Russia whose dowry would be twenty thousand soldiers for an immediate invasion of England. Regarding his brother, he had plans for a marriage to one of their Polish cousins and on November 27th, 1746 wrote to his father that Henry 'should not lose a minute's time [...] If Prince Radziwiłł has any daughters of age, I should not think one of them to be an unfit match'.

In Rome James was revisited by the same fear with which he had beheld the apparently unfathomable behaviour associated with his wife's anorexia. His elder son was simultaneously a celibate young man, humbly attending confession and protesting devotional obedience to God, yet a veteran of the most appalling scenes of military horror who was beginning to display a drinking habit which was already generating warnings from his friends by the end of 1746. Moreover, Charles's plans were becoming ever more divorced from reality, whilst his pathologically suspicious mind was severely testing the bond of trust with his father and brother as he moved towards self-imposed isolation. Just as James had once interpreted his wife's illness as dissimulation and hypocrisy, so now he was unable to comprehend his son's uncontrollable emotions. He concluded that the explanation had to lie elsewhere and must be the work of 'wicked advisors'. His view was understandable, for he was still receiving letters such as Balhaldy's, which spoke glowingly of Charles in April 1747, but added: 'when I considered the animals about him, my heart was torn to pieces'.

Few of the good men remained. In November of that year Balhaldy said of Lochiel, to whom Charles had kept his promise of a French regiment:

It becomes cruel in me now to be obliged to begin to inform you of the loss Your Majesty has of the most faithful and zealously devoted subject who ever served any Prince, in the person of Donald Cameron of Lochiel. He died the 26th of last month of an inflamation of the head at Borgues where he had been for some time with his regiment.

Charles might have been helped by the venerable George Keith, Earl Marischal, whom he almost begged to come to Paris and act as his general agent. For James was refusing to correspond via his son's 'wicked' secretary, George Kelly. However, Marischal refused on the grounds of 'broken health'.

Recognising that relations between his two sons were degenerating, James tried to arrange for Henry to visit the Spanish Court. But when Charles found out, he adamantly refused to agree and went himself, unannounced, wildly hoping to gain military assistance and the hand in marriage of one of the king's sisters. But he failed completely and came back with nothing except even greater contempt for that court than for the French one. Upon returning to his underground and incognito life in Paris, Charles yet again fruitlessly pressed Louis and his War Ministry for action. But news of another variety was on its way. In May 1747 Henry secretly left Paris for Rome, informing the enraged Charles only when safely on his way. In that letter he lied several times, doubtless fearing his brother's dominating tendencies, but thereby 'confirming' to Charles that his suspicions concerning his family's 'loyalty' were justified. Henry said that his sole motive was to visit his father, that he would only be staying a fortnight, and referred to his return journey. In fact there never was to be a return journey. James and Henry had been secretly planning the latter's accession to the College of Cardinals. And this was the real reason for Henry's sudden departure. When Charles discovered in June, he knew exactly what the effect on Stuart supporters would be. It was not only a major propaganda gift which Hanover would gloatingly exploit by whipping up anti-Catholic religious phobia, but it ruled out Henry's prospects of providing heirs to the succession and represented his withdrawal. James also took the opportunity to give up. Almost with relief, he effectively retired from all political activity aimed at a restoration. About this time he wrote to his heir: 'My age and infirmities increase [...] I am really unfit to do anything but to pray for you'. Charles's response was brief: 'Had I got a dagger through my heart it would not have been more sensible [...] my love for my brother and the Cause being the occasion of it'. He then proceeded to ignore his brother for twenty years and stopped sharing any private thoughts with his father whom he hereafter placed in the same base category as Louis XV. All had become his enemies, together with Lord George Murray, whom Charles wanted to arrest for treason.

Amongst Stuart supporters the shock of Henry's move was extreme. Even Francis FitzJames, a Catholic bishop, pleaded with James to reverse the catastrophic decision, arguing that it was not only the worst thing possible for the Stuarts, but that its repercussions would be damaging for Catholicism. Similarly, the Catholic priest, Father Myles MacDonell, wrote to James from Paris describing Henry's move as 'a mortal deadly stroke to the Cause'. Back at the Palazzo Muti the new Cardinal was starting a career of party-giving for friends who were described by his father as 'low company'. Before long he scandalized the Romans, and still more so his father, by introducing into his household a suspiciously attractive young priest. Yet when his father insisted on the latter's dismissal, according to Horace Walpole: 'Instead of parting with his favourite, the young Cardinal with his minion left Rome abruptly, and with little regard to the dignity of his purple'. Charles was incredulous and turned to his maternal aunt's family of de Bouillon for support. The duke's son, de Turenne, had married Princess Louise-Henriette of Lorraine, whilst his daughter, Louise, had married Prince Jules-Hercule de Rohan, the heir of Hercule, Duke de Montbazon and Prince de Guéméné. Both marriages between these sovereign princely houses had taken place in 1743. Both men had been Henry Stuart's enthusiastic ADCs at the time of the French invasion preparations. And both were away campaigning in the summer of 1747. It was then, in August, that Charles found support and understanding through his uncle's criticism of Henry, James and even Louis.

Following the Battle of Lawfeld, when the 'Butcher' Cumberland had to flee for his life, Charles's optimistic vitality was briefly rekindled and his bitterness vanished in the joyful letters he dashed off to the French king and his War Minister. He hoped their superb victory might bring about a positive change regarding the Stuart cause. But it didn't. So his mood turned to defiance. Having been given Louis' permission to hunt on the Plain of St. Denis, Charles deliberately offended him by doing so in an area strictly reserved for the sovereign. Then, whilst de Turenne and Jules-Hercule de Rohan were away winning the military honours in which he so badly wanted to share, Charles fell desperately in love for the first time. Towards the end of that summer, at Navarre, the prince and his first cousin, Louise de Rohan, became lovers. Their affair reached almost insane heights of intensity during which Charles astounded his father by writing to him about the way in which the Sobieski inheritance had been divided between his mother and Louise's. The love-stricken Charles said that Louise had been 'extremely wronged' and that, concerning the Sobieski jewels, he was 'entirely resolved to yield my share if your Majesty thinks it reasonable'. But his amazed father did not and openly suggested that he and Henry would be more appropriate recipients.

Charles swept Louise away in an unrestrained flood of the most passionate love, both physical and emotional. And when she became pregnant, his ardour increased to fever pitch. But towards the end of the year, upon Jules-Hercule's return from campaigning with the Marshal de Saxe, Charles became insanely jealous. For Louise now had to share a bed with her husband so that he would think their child his. Careless of any problems he was causing, Charles became more and more demanding of proofs of Louise's adoration. Furthermore, they were nightly making love in the de Rohan Paris mansion, the Hôtel de Guéméné, where Charles once became so enraged that he fired off his pistols in hysterical anger. It was hardly discreet, especially as Louise's far from naive mother-in-law was lady of the house.

In January 1748, when the still unaware Jules-Hercule returned to the front, Louise's father and mother-in-law confronted the devastated girl shortly after she had written to Charles: 'I will never leave you [...] Only death can separate us [...] Be sure that your faithful mistress will never cease to adore you. You will see when I am in your arms if I love you. I love you insanely!' Thereafter her words became filled with panic:

Remember, I am bearing your child and that I am suffering because of you. If you stop loving me, it will be more than I can endure. But if you still love me, we will somehow keep in touch [...] One day, I swear, we will be happy again.

The child, whom Louise called Charles, was born weak and died on January 18th, 1749 aged five months and twenty-one days. He was buried as the son of Jules-Hercule in the crypt of St. Louis in the Convent of the Feuillants which was detroyed in the early nineteenth century.[1]

The exposure of their illicit romance destroyed not only the affair, but more than soured Charles's relationship with the previously supportive de Bouillon who, though himself no angel when young, now stung his nephew to the quick with all too justified accusations of ingratitude and worse. Charles consigned his uncle to the same category as James, Henry, Louis and George Murray. Another set of relationships lay in ruins. Yet more knives of perceived rejection were being sharp-

---

[1] This child's birth was only discovered in 1986 by Prof. L.L. Bongie. Doubtless it had earlier given rise to the legend described by A. Lang in *Redgauntlet* that Clementina Walkinshaw bore Charles 'two children of whom the elder, a boy, died early'.

ened. For France and England were moving towards peace. And with that would come the self-pitying prince's expulsion from France, as once had happened to his stoical father. It was against this background, peppered with Louise's tragic letters begging him to stay in love with her and the alienation of his immensely influential de Bouillon and de Rohan relations, that Charles fell in love again. It was April 1748.

He turned now to an older woman. Once more the object of his passion was a cousin on his Polish mother's side. As Louise de Rohan sat in the Opera on Sunday, April 28th, having begged Charles in a note written the day before to 'look at me with the eyes I adore', she found herself tormented by the appearance beside her former lover of their mutual cousin, Marie-Anne de la Trémouille, Princess de Talmont. At forty-seven, twice the age of Louise, this notorious woman was from the ducal family of Jabłonowski. Her grandfather had been one of King John Sobieski's field marshals at the Battle of Vienna; her mother was Prince James Sobieski's first cousin; and her brother had been the Stuarts' plenipotentiary for the Sobieski inheritance in 1739. Furthermore, Marie-Anne's father was the uncle of ex-King Stanislas Leszczyński, exiled in Lorraine, to whom she and her sister had both been mistresses. Not only was Marie-Anne beautiful, but she was brilliant, quick-witted and held convention in contempt. Charles was powerfully attracted to the fact that she made her own rules. No-one ordered her around. Indeed, people feared her.

At much the same time, the approaching peace between France and England, as well as the need to offset his brother's damaging appointment as a Roman Catholic cardinal, pushed the prince into sending Sir John Graeme to Berlin on a secret mission to ask for the hand of the King of Prussia's sister, or any other Protestant princess of the king's recommendation. He also asked for a suitable residence in view of his inevitable expulsion from France. Frederick the Great was a known admirer of Charles, but his hands were tied by recently established friendly relations with Hanover which he wasn't prepared to endanger. The next Protestant candidate was the daughter of Prince von Darmstadt. This also failed. It seemed that the House of Hanover's tentacles reached everywhere throughout the German principalities.

Yet pressure on Charles was increasing as the peace talks of Aix-la-Chapelle progressed. It was now June 1748 and the French government was pushing for clarification of the prince's future plans. The Hanoverian negotiator, Lord Sandwich, was categoric in his insistence that Charles's expulsion from French territory was a *sine qua non* for peace. Upon the treaty's terms becoming public on October 18th both James and his son formally protested. But Charles printed his with the place of writing ostentatiously given as Paris, where he was officially incognito. Louis could no longer deny knowledge of his whereabouts to the English. And such was the prince's phenomenal popularity in France that his protest became a bestseller. He laid out all that the 'Forty-Five had achieved for France by way of diverting Hanoverian attention from the continental theatre and the appalling cost that his supporters had suffered as a result of French inaction. The defiant but futile note of the people's hero could change nothing. Nor was this an insult to a private family such as with the de Bouillons and de Rohans. It was a public challenge to the King of France himself and it did not matter that men such as Montesquieu admired the manifesto for its 'nobility and eloquence'.

From then on Charles conducted an unwinnable war with the French authorities in which they progressively hardened their methods to enforce his departure. For his part the prince used every technique possible to whip up popular feeling. But whilst he couldn't possibly succeed in overturning an international treaty in an authoritarian state not yet ripe for the Revolution, nevertheless the ground was fertile for mischief. His heroic reputation amongst the citizenry of Paris was of legendary proportions and his appearances at the Comédie, the Opéra, the Tuilleries, and even church generated mass adulation. Moreover, the French people were deeply unhappy about a peace agreement which seemed unnecessarily generous to the despised Hanoverian regime. If it was Charles's intention to capture the public's imagination by presenting himself as the innocent victim of a treacherous state which rewarded those who helped it by brutal eviction, then he certainly succeeded.

Realising that Charles's public threats of armed resistance and suicide were beyond even her extraordinarily elastic interpretations of acceptable behaviour, Marie-Anne distanced herself from events. Yet this only provoked her lover to explode in rage at the very doors of the de Talmont residence. Meanwhile, at Louis' request, James wrote Charles a long letter condemning his refusal to leave France. He told him:

I see you at the very edge of a precipice, ready to fall in, and I would be an abnormal father if I didn't at least do the little I can so as to save you, and that is why I find myself obliged to order you, as your father and your King, to conform without delay to the intentions of His Most Christian Majesty.

Louis then took advantage of the opportunity to 'enforce a son's obedience to his father's wishes'. He not only published James's letter but, fearing public rioting in support of Charles, outraged Paris by sending an armed force of 1,200 troops under the Duke de Biron to arrest him on December 10th as he walked to his nightly adulation at the Opéra with three Highland officers. Biron's men tied Charles hand and foot and threw him into a coach as he mockingly asked: 'Where are we going? Are you taking me to Hanover?' They imprisoned him in the tower of the Château de Vincennes, holding him under permanent armed guard in a cramped cell. His officers were locked up in the infamous Bastille.

The number of men used in the operation exceeded the total Highland army that had rallied at Glenfinnan on August 19th, 1745. It was only three years since Charles had stayed at Exeter House in Derby, expecting to commence the final leg of his victorious campaign as the French were putting the finishing touches to an invasion force of 12,000. He had reached that high point of success against all the odds and with unimaginable speed. Yet now, locked up by his former French ally and cousin who had made peace with their mutual enemy of Hanover, the turn of events seemed no less incredible. Vicious satire circulated in Paris, inspired by Marie-Anne de Talmont and Charles's supporters, accusing Louis of being in the pay of Hanover. Typical was:

> George, you say, forced you to refuse shelter
> To the valiant Edward;
> And if he had demanded of you,
> Faithless King, to exile your whore,
> Tell me, miserable creature, would you have done that too?[2]

Amongst those disgusted at the arrest was Voltaire. The Dauphin publicly wept in shame. The Marquis d'Argenson commented: 'We shall be placed, without doubt, alongside Cromwell, who decapitated his King, and we, we have uselessly strung up the legitimate heir

---

[2] Charles was always called '*le prince Edouard*' by the French, whilst the whore in question was Louis' mistress, Madame de Pompadour.

presumptive of that crown!' Such was the groundswell of sympathy for Charles and universal condemnation of Louis that the Government even made a ludicrous attempt to outlaw public conversation about the prince.

Yet however much of a storm he had provoked, Charles had no choice but to quit France. For good measure Louis exiled Marie-Anne to Lorraine and refused her permission to bid farewell to her lover as he passed through Fontainebleau on his way to the Papal state of Avignon. He arrived there at seven in the morning on December 27th and was announced at James Murray's front door as an Irish officer. His host said: 'I was never more surprised to see him at my bedside'. He had come with Sheridan, one officer and three servants. Soon after, he was joined by the indomitable Marie-Anne and got in touch with John Hay. With them he saw in the New Year of 1749 and celebrated his twenty-ninth birthday, writing to his father in Rome: 'I arrived here on Friday last, and am in perfect good health, notwith-standing the unheard of barbarous and inhuman treatment I met with'. Another person who wrote to King James that New Year was the woman Charles had once adored and who loved him still. The letter was signed 'Louise de la Tour d'Auvergne, Princess de Rohan, Duchess de Montbazon'. When she sent her greetings, her child by Charles was still at her side. Eighteen days into the New Year the baby boy died. It is not known if, when he was at Avignon, the prince was informed. He left the city on February 28th accompanied only by his equerry, Henry Goring, and three servants. His every move was observed, recorded and passed back to Westminster by the Hanoverian spy, Walton.

Derby in 1745 had been the watershed, Culloden in 1746 the mili-tary defeat. But it was Charles's arrest in December 1748 that ended his desperate struggle to rescue something from the 'Forty Five. It was this which destroyed him. Professor L.L. Bongie in *The Love of a Prince* writes: 'Afterwards, moral integrity and tranquillity of mind left him forever [...] During the last forty years of his life, he who was once so ambitious to succeed, and who seemed in the beginning so richly deserving of success, attempted little that was commendable and accomplished even less'. Up until Charles's arrest, Bongie speaks of 'all his early promise, the hopes, prayers, and single minded sacrifices, the high sense of purpose, the courage, the magnanimity and basic fairness of a true hero'. But thereafter all those fine qualities 'rotted away'. It would not be too long before Charles would scribble:

> To speke to ete
> To think to Drink

then cross it out and write instead:

> To ete to think
> To Speke to drink.

Henry referred to it as 'the nasty bottle'.

CHAPTER SEVEN

The Web

But I cannot forget, so I wait and wonder
How long will the thinly dividing window hold?
How long will the dancing drown the terrible anger
Of those, the unwanted, who peddle their grief in the cold
Wrapped in their own despair's thick and unkindly fold?

Maurice Lindsay

From Avignon Charles went to Lunéville in Lorraine where ex-King Stanislas Leszczyński of Poland had become duke of that semi-independent principality and held his enlightened, intellectual, bustling court at the enormous Château de Lunéville near Nancy, designed by Germain Boffrand, which rivalled Versailles in magnificence and splendour. There too Marie-Anne de Talmont had estates. The relationship between the ruling classes of France and Poland had long been a close one but it was particularly so at this period. Bearing in mind the Stuarts' close family relationships with the Bourbons, de Bouillons and de Rohans as well as the Sobieskis and Radziwiłłs, this political centre was of key importance.

The Cousins

Lunéville was not only a focus for members of the French Court but also the rallying point for all Polish aristocrats and political activists disinclined to the Russian hegemony over Poland's eighteenth-century sovereigns. Charles's cousin and lover, Marie-Anne de Talmont, and her sister, Catherine Ossolińska, were both at one time or another mistresses of their relation, Leszczyński, whose daughter was Louis XV's queen. The latter was also a cousin of Charles's mother and de Bouillon aunt whose daughter, Louise, had married Henry Stuart's ex-ADC, Jules-Hercule de Rohan, to whose son Henry was godfather and name-sake. Here could be found nearly everyone who mattered in Polish and French politics. One such example was Voltaire. He was staying at Lunéville when Charles's arrest in December 1748 was announced. At the very time he was reading passages to a group including Leszczyński himself from a manuscript describing the prince's 'noble exploits and heroic sufferings'.[1] Another was Bishop Joseph Załuski. He was a distant cousin of the Sobieskis who had known the Stuart family from his early days in Rome.[2] James even made him his plenipotentiary alongside Marie-Anne de Talmont's brother for matters concerning the Sobieski inheritance.[3] That act was dated May 18th, 1736 and signed by both James and Charles.[4] The exiled Stuart king corre-sponded with Załuski for over three decades. In his letters he spoke of Poland as a nation which 'will always be dear and respected'.[5] He would enquire about Polish politics, such as in his letter of March 24th, 1741 concerning the governor of Sandomierz and Prince Radziwiłł, which he signed 'Your affectionate cousin, James R.'.[6] In a later one dated March 28th, 1760 James referred to 'our old friendship', finishing by offering Załuski all the best wishes 'that you could want for you and all your family'.[7] Indeed it had been at the Stuart king's initiative that Załuski had been nominated a Papal prelate. Later he was given a bish-opric in Burgundy by Louis XV, another in the Lorraine by Leszczyński and was appointed bishop of Kiev by the King of Poland in 1758. He took enormous pride in knowing everyone who was anyone throughout Europe, was extremely snobbish and, like so many Polish aristocrats, banked with Fergusson-Tepper.[8]

The Bankers

It is important to appreciate the role played by the financiers who shad-owed the elite habitués of Lunéville: men such as the Stuart family

[1] L.L. Bongie, *The Love of a Prince*, Vancouver 1986, p.265.
[2] *Encyklopedia powszechna*, vol.28, Warsaw 1868, p.247.
[3] A. Boniecki, *Herbarz polski*, vol.8, Warsaw 1905, p.109.
[4] Biblioteka Narodowa (National Library in Warsaw), sygn.3215, mkrf.12127, pp.3–4.
[5] Biblioteka Narodowa, sygn.3222, mkrf.12239.
[6] *Ibid.*
[7] Biblioteka Narodowa, sygn.3260, mkrf.12221.
[8] *Encyklopedia powszechna*, vol.28, *op. cit.*, pp.244–249.

banker Waters in Paris, the de Rohan bankers Turnbull, Forbes & Co. in London, or Fergusson-Tepper and Prot Potocki in Warsaw. The latter, who collaborated closely with Tepper, was doubly relevant in that he alone amongst the leading Polish bankers was an aristocrat by birth and therefore linked by social and blood ties with his clients. These men executed currency and bill of exchange transactions, payments, held deposits, made investments, arranged loans and acted as merchants for international commissions. They also usually owned large stores trading in expensive imported goods. They were the trusted and discreet advisers, financiers and intimates of the monarchs, statesmen and nobles without whom such men could not function in this relatively cash-starved, credit-based environment.

Besides Załuski, Tepper's clients included the King of Poland, Stanislas August Poniatowski, and even the Russian Tsarina, Catherine the Great. The latter used him to import expensive jewels from Western Europe to St. Petersburg.[9] And in her honour Tepper named a ship he used for his Black Sea trading activities, *La Grande Catherine*.[10] Tepper's background was typical of the banking community whose origins were usually foreign. This was because they nearly all had started off as merchants, only later metamorphosing into bankers because of their importing activities which involved a rich array of international contacts, currency transactions and deposit holding. Just as today, this milieu formed a trans-continental, cosmopolitan network, criss-crossed by overlapping relationships.[11]

When in 1791 Poniatowski sought an enormous loan, it was secured and negotiated on the Polish Crown's behalf by Peter Fergusson-Tepper and Peter Blank (another pre-eminent Warsaw banker and also a Protestant) with the Amsterdam bankers, van Hoorn, Gulcher and Milder who syndicated it elsewhere in Europe.[12] Further international credit lines for the Polish treasury and king were sourced out of other financial centres such as Italy.[13]

The origins of some of Warsaw's foremost bankers were: Fergusson-Tepper – Scottish-German;[14] Pierre Riaucourt – noble French; Anthony Prot Potocki – aristocratic Polish; Mathew Łyszkiewicz –

---

[9] T. Korzon, *Wewnętrzne dzieje Polski za St. Augusta*, Cracow 1882, vol.2, p.159.
[10] W. Kornatowski, *Kryzys bankowy w Polsce 1793r.*, Warsaw 1937, p.IX.
[11] A. Magier, *Estetyka miasta stołecznego Warszawy*, Wrocław 1963, p.136.
[12] T. Korzon, *op. cit.*, pp.72–73.
[13] W. Kornatowski, *op. cit.*, p.16.
[14] *Ibid.*, p.12.

Polish-Armenian;[15] Frederick Kabryt – Prussian.[16] Almost as if to emphasise the borderless nature of this community, both Mrs Fergusson-Tepper and Mrs Kabryt used to send their dirty linen all the way from Warsaw to Paris to be laundered, whilst the Fergusson-Tepper children were tutored at home by Abbé Antoine Juet from Perpignan.[17] These financiers did everything possible to integrate and fraternise with the nobility, using their new wealth to gain grants of nobility for themselves and acquire landed estates. Fergusson-Tepper, for example, befriended Poniatowski, with whose dog young Walter Fergusson-Tepper was portrayed in 1785. And, though protestant, Fergusson-Tepper was appointed treasurer and agent of the elitist Roman Catholic Order of Malta in 1777, was granted nobility in 1790, and acquired several country estates and two palaces in Warsaw, entertaining there on the grandest of scales.[18]

Amongst the rich and aristocratic clients of the Tepper bank was the closest Polish cousin of the Stuarts, a man identified with the pro-French lobby. He was the swashbuckling Prince Charles Radziwiłł,[19] and there survive no fewer than 192 letters from the Teppers in the Radziwiłł Archive in Warsaw.[20] Radziwiłł was governor of Vilnius, Duke of Nieśwież, one of Europe's richest men and son of Prince Michael who, when young, used to hunt with Louis XV and the Duke de Bouillon. It was this Michael who, as the closest Polish-domiciled relation of the Stuarts and de Bouillons, had bought the seven towns and 140 villages comprising the ex-Sobieski Żółkiew estate from Prince Charles's aunt in 1739.[21] And it was these Polish relations whom Charles had in mind when he wrote to his father in 1746 recommending a bride for Henry.[22] Such was Radziwiłł's prominence that in 1787 he became one of the men who it was proposed should join a cross-party ruling committee of four to replace the monarchy in a plan which for a while gained Prussian support.[23]

15 *Ibid.*, p.24.
16 T. Korzon, *op. cit.*, p.158; A. Magier, *op. cit.*, pp.326 & 361.
17 T. Korzon, *op. cit.*, p.163; A. Magier, *op. cit.*, p.161.
18 T. Korzon, *op. cit.*, p.158; A. Magier, *op. cit.*, pp.137 & 192; J.& E.Szulc, *Cmentarz Ewangelicko-Reformowany w Warszawie*, Warsaw 1989, p.244.
19 *Polski słownik biograficzny* (hereafter PSB), vol.30, pp.248–261. Radziwiłł was popularly known as '*My Dear Chap*' ('*Panie Kochanku*') – this being his universal form of address!
20 Archiwum Główne Akt Dawnych (hereafter AGAD), Archiwum Radziwiłłów, dz.5, sygn.16223.
21 PSB, vol.30, pp.240, 299 & 303.
22 L.L. Bongie, *op. cit.*, p.149.
23 A. Zamoyski, *The Last King of Poland*, London 1992, p.301.

If the flow of wealth around the exalted community to which Radziwiłł belonged was usually credit-based, we can imagine the network of bankers who shadowed these potentates. And such was the baroque extravagance of Radziwiłł's career that he succeeded in the almost impossible. So many and so large were the debts with which he encumbered his vast estates that in the last years of his life he was technically bankrupt. In the end Żółkiew and many other properties were split up amongst his creditors, a group which included Fergusson-Tepper and Anthony Prot Potocki.[24] In a country where a 10,000-acre freehold estate of good arable land with a large manor house, palace or castle cost about 200,000 zloties, Radziwiłł's debt was estimated at about 50 million just prior to his death.[25] Such figures give an idea of how busy he kept his bankers during his lifetime.

Active amongst the French high nobility associated with Lunéville was another who, like Radziwiłł, tried to draw Poland away from the Russian sphere of influence. He was the brother-in-law of Charles's first cousin and ex-lover, Louise de Rohan, namely Cardinal Louis de Rohan, co-adjutor of the Strasbourg bishopric of his uncle, Cardinal Louis Constantin de Rohan.[26] This bishopric was the richest in France and a sovereign principality which the de Rohans had made their own for most of the eighteenth century. Louis became a member of the Académie Française in 1761, Ambassador Extraordinary in Vienna in 1772, cardinal in 1778 (mainly thanks to the King of Poland) and Prince-Bishop of Strasbourg in 1779.[27] Unfortunately he became best known for the scandal of the *Affaire du Collier de la Reine* to which he fell victim due to the unscrupulous plotting of the parvenue Madame de la Motte. Cardinal Louis was led to believe that if he arranged the purchase of a diamond necklace of stupendous value for Marie-Antoinette, then she would welcome his attentions. For his credulity he was arrested, incarcerated in the Bastille, acquitted by Parliament and then exiled to Strasbourg. The manner in which Louis XVI treated this grand seigneur so shocked his contemporaries that it was later regarded by Napoleon as one of the catalysts of the French Revolution. After that event, as a prince of the Holy Roman Empire whose sovereign bishopric was strategically placed between France and the

[24] PSB, vol.30, p.259; AGAD, Archiwum Radziwiłłów, dz.5, sygn.10496 (pp.27, 30, 34, 36, & 39) & 7240.
[25] PSB, vol.30, p.259.
[26] E. de Haynin, *Louis de Rohan – le cardinal 'Collier'*, Paris 1997, p.59.
[27] *Ibid.*, pp.94–95.

German principalities where his immediate family took refuge, the Cardinal de Rohan refused to acknowledge the laws of revolutionary France and permitted instead the raising of troops for the counter-revolutionary émigré army of the Bourbon Prince de Condé.[28]

In the Radziwiłł Archive is correspondence with the de Rohans dating from 1723 to 1772. From early 1749 there are letters to Michael Radziwiłł concerning money owed to Louise de Rohan from the purchase of Żółkiew. Louise's mother-in-law writes that she wants to give instructions 'to Monsieur Riaucourt' regarding this payment 'in consequence of which a note has been drawn up by her relations which the Duke de Bouillon has signed as his daughter's guardian and the Prince Constantin de Rohan, my brother-in-law, has signed as guardian of my son.[29] It was from the same Pierre Riaucourt that Tepper bought the *Under the Four Winds* palace on Warsaw's Długa Street in 1765. The Radziwiłł Archive also contains letters from both Cardinals de Rohan and other family members as well as from the de Talmonts and de Bouillons.[30] Some concern financial arrangements, others politics, still more are purely social. Similarly, the links between the Radziwiłł and Załuski family of the Stuarts' plenipotentiary are demonstrated by no fewer than six hundred letters from 1685 to 1763[31]. In the Załuski Archive of the National Library in Warsaw are yet more letters from the de Rohans[32] and Radziwiłłs[33] as well as Marie-Anne de Talmont.[34] Even the most cursory glance at either collection gives a vivid picture of just how close the contacts were which linked the French and Polish élites, all of whom were directly or indirectly connected with Leszczyński's Court.

The 'Secret du Roi'

France had a many decades long interest in Poland, typified by Andrew Mokronowski, another Lunéville regular. He was the lover of Izabela Branicka, the second wife of Radziwiłł's ally, the pro-French Field-

---

[28] *Ibid.*
[29] Namely, Prince Jules-Hercule de Rohan, Duke de Montbazon. AGAD, Archiwum Radziwiłłów, dz.5, sygn.4873.
[30] *Ibid.*, sygn.1301, 13184–13187, 16063.
[31] *Ibid.*, sygn.18403–18421.
[32] Biblioteka Narodowa w Warszawie, Katalog rękopisów, see: de Rohan, de Guéméné, de Montauban, de Soubise & Stuart.
[33] *Ibid.*, sygn.3262/2, 3268.
[34] *Ibid.*, sygn.3269, pp.1–2.

Marshal John Clemence Branicki who failed in his bid to become elected King of Poland in 1764. Yet Izabela Branicka, who bore a child to Mokronowski, also happened to be the sister of the victorious candidate, Poniatowski. Furthermore, Branicki's first wife, Princess Catherine Radziwiłł was yet another Stuart cousin. Mokronowski was also one of the closest friends of the Count de Broglie who succeeded the Bourbon Prince de Conti as the director of the organisation known as the *Secret du Roi*. This was the name of the personal secret service of the French king which for decades was used to infiltrate and influence every meaningful Polish political centre and court, including Radziwiłł's, as well as the banking community. Its aim was to further the Bourbon family's interest in placing a candidate of their choice on the only elective throne in Europe – that of the Polish-Lithuanian Commonwealth. Albeit senior, Mokronowski was just one of de Broglie's extensive organisation of agents and informers.[35] Tepper was another. Nor was such lucrative activity viewed as unpatriotic by Poles opposed to Russian hegemony. One key French member was Cardinal Louis de Rohan.[36]

The Freemasons

Another of Mokronowski's incarnations was that in Paris during the 1730s he had become one of the first Polish freemasons. As opposed to the English version, French freemasonry was knightly in origin and profile and a condition of acceptance, according to a 1742 regulation, was an 'inviolable attachment to religion, the King and morality'.[37] Secrecy was also a key element and for Poles the whole movement acted as a magnet for opposition groupings, especially the pro-French Lunéville-related lobby. Polish freemasonry followed the aristocratic French model, quickly becoming fashionable, surprisingly pluralistic and very patriotic. It was started in Poland in 1721 by, amongst others, Princes Michael and August Czartoryski and became so extensive that by the late 1780s there were over a thousand members including Poniatowski, most of the aristocracy, banking families such as Tepper

---

[35] G. Perrault, *Le Secret du Roi, la passion polonaise*, Paris 1992; idem, *Le Secret du Roi, l'ombre de la Bastille*, Paris 1993.

[36] D. Ozanum & M. Antoine (ed.), *Correspondance Secrète du Comte de Broglie avec Louis XV*, Paris 1961; M.E. Boutaric (ed.), *Correspondance Secrète de Louis XV*, Paris 1866.

[37] L. Hass, *Ze Studiów nad wolnomularstwem polskim ostatniej ćwierci XVIII w.*, Warsaw 1973, pp.588–589.

and Szulc of Warsaw (including even Peter Fergusson-Tepper's French Huguenot wife) and Longchamps de Berier of Lwów, as well as foreign diplomats, officers and wealthy merchants.[38] Furthermore, by the 1770s, there were already a large number of Poles who belonged directly to French lodges at the head of which stood the Bourbon Duke of Orléans at whose inauguration in 1773 place of honour was given to Prince Adam Czartoryski.[39] And though the movement grew significantly larger, nevertheless the second half of the eighteenth century was the 'golden' period for both French and Polish freemasonry. It is widely accepted that ex-King Stanislas Leszczyński was a freemason, but beyond doubt that his nephew, Czapski, was accepted into the 'Ville de Tonnèrre' Parisian lodge in 1737 alongside two Princes de Villeroy, one of whom had been tutor to Louis XV.[40]

One of the most picturesque and active freemasons in France during the second half of the eighteenth century was Charles-François Radet de Beauchaine. His relevance is not only that he was instrumental in recruiting large numbers of French aristocrats, but that he presided over a Parisian lodge which had been reconstituted there in 1762 after having spent the Seven Years' War in Germany alongside the French Army. It was called the 'Ecossaise et Anglaise de la Constance'. Previously based in Germany this lodge was part of the European-wide Jacobite Catholic freemasonry movement which supported the restoration of the Stuarts. Within it there reigned a spirit of profound religiosity and loyalty as well as fidelity to monarchy in general. The documents of the 'Constance' indicate that they were approved by the grand master, none other than Prince Charles himself.[41] Other members of this 'Stuart' lodge included the Poles, Prince Sapieha and Szembek as well as the son of Count Brühl, the penultimate Polish king's all-powerful minister.[42]

It was during the 1750's that Prince Charles seems to have most

---

[38] A. Zamoyski, *op. cit.*, pp.262–263; S. Małachowski-Łempicki, *Wykaz członków polskich lóż wolnomularskich w latach 1738–1821*, Cracow 1930; L. Hass, *Wolnomularstwo w Europie Środkowo-Wschodniej w XVIII i XIX w.*, Wrocław 1982; E. Szulc, *Cmentarz Ewangelicko-Augsburski w Warszawie*, Warsaw 1989, pp.503, 562–565; J.& E. Szulc, *op. cit.*, pp.244–245.

[39] L. Hass, *Ze Studiów nad wolnomularstwem …*, *op. cit.*, p.601.

[40] *Ibid.*, p.590.

[41] L. Hass, *La Franc-maçonnerie et les sciences occultes au XVIII siècle: Jean-Luc Louis de Toux de Salvert*, Warsaw 1986, p.102; G. Bord, *la Franc-maçonnerie en France des origines à 1815*, vol.1, Paris 1908, p.158, 180–181; A. le Bihan, *Franc-maçons et ateliers parisiens de la Grande Loge de France au XVIIIe siècle (1760–1795)*, Paris 1973, pp.101–103.

[42] L. Hass, *Ze studiów nad wolnomularstwem …*, *op. cit.*, p.592.

energetically used freemasonry's secret international network. He was known as the 'Soleil d'Or, Milete de Bretagne' as chief of the Order of the Temple. Frank McLynn describes Charles as being 'always at least one step ahead of those who sought him [...] Techniques of disinformation, the art of disguise, the ability to cover his tracks, all those came as second nature'. Though he had drifted away from such intense activity by the 1760's nevertheless during that period the Count de Clermont maintained an ultra-secret 'Royal Lodge', deeply loyal to Louis XV as well as its Grand Master, Charles. In the succeeding decade Gustav III of Sweden and his brothers took up the initiative by strengthening the Jacobite element in Swedish freemasonry. They corresponded with Charles throughout the years 1776–1784. In 1776 the prince created Gustav's brother, Frederick Adolph, 'Vicar of all the Lodges in the North'; was assured by another brother, Charles, that Sweden recognised Charles' role as 'Unknown Superior' of the Templars; whilst Charles in turn assured Baron von Wächter that grand mastership was hereditary in the House of Stuart. Other Jacobite 'Ecossais' Lodges of note were those in the de Rohans' Strasbourg as well as the 'Parfaite Harmonie' founded in 1749 by Clermont in Liège – a place and period of great significance to both Prince Charles as well as Jules-Hercule de Rohan's youngest brother, Ferdinand. Even Louis XV was almost certainly a freemason and held a secret 'Loge du Roi' at Versailles.[43]

Another lodge of significance was the 'Grand Orient de Bouillon' whose first grand master was Charles's uncle, the Duke de Bouillon. He was succeeded by Henry's former ADC, the Prince de Turenne upon his accession to the dukedom in 1771. It is extremely unlikely that Henry's other ADC, de Bouillon's son-in-law, Jules-Hercule de Rohan, would not have been a member. What is certain, however, is that either Jules-Hercule or one of his brothers belonged in 1775 to the 'Saint Jean de Montmorency-Luxembourg', a component of the Grand Orient of France;[44] Prince Camille de Rohan was a mason associated with the de Bouillon lodge;[45] and Cardinal Louis de Rohan was embroiled with Swedenborg and Cagliostro.[46]

[43] M.K. Schuchard, *The Young Pretender and Jacobite Freemasonry: New Light from Sweden on his role as 'Hidden Grand Master'* (revised), in: the *Consortium on Revolutionary Europe 1750–1850*, Selected Papers, Florida State University, 1994.

[44] P. Chevalier, *Histoire de la franc-maçonnerie*, Paris 1992, vol.1, pp.139 & 154.

[45] G. Bord, *op. cit.*, p.186.

[46] P. Chevalier, *op. cit.*, pp.258–263; S.Beswick, *The Swedenborg Rite and The Great Masonic Leaders*, New York 1870.

1 One of the salons in the Castle of Grzymałów where the Prince de Rohan's letters were kept (c. 1900)

2 The Palazzo Muti in Rome

3 Prince Charles Edward Stuart (c. 1735)

4 Stanislas Leszczyński, exiled King of Poland

5 The Château de Lunéville

Mon Cousin; Votre obligeante lettre du 15
Xbre sur le renouvellement d'année, me fait
un vrai plaisir, mais elle n'ajoute rien à
ma sensibilité, a l'egard de votre zéle et de
votre attachement pour moi J'en conserve
en tout tems un singulier souvenir, accompag-
nés de l'estime la plus distinguée et de
l'amitié la plus sincere. Sur ce je prie
Dieu qu'il vous ait, Mon Cousin, en sa
sainte et digne garde. A Rome le 5. de
l'an 1742.

Votre affectionné Cousin

Jacques R

A Mon Cousin.
L'Evêque de Culm, Grand
Chancelier de Pologne. —

6 *Letter from King James to Bishop Andrew Załuski (1742)*

ac perficiendi, aut agere prosequi et perficere
permittendi ac disponendi, cum clausulâ ad
lites amplissima latissimé extendenda, juxta
stilum Curiæ Loci seu Locorum ubi præsens —
nostrum Diploma exhiberi contigerit. Promittentes
et spondentes Nos ea omnia quæ per prædictum
Plenipotentem ac Generalem Commissarium —
Nostrum tamquam Nos alter ego actum, gestum
et statutum fuerit Nos quoque pro acto gesto
statuto rato et grato habituros. In quorum
omnium majorem Fidem præsens nostrum Diploma
manu propriâ tum et Ser.mi Principis Walliæ Filij
nostri Dilectissimi subscriptum, Sigillo nostro —
Regio muniri fecimus. Datum Romæ in —
Palatio Residentiæ Nostræ in plateâ Sanctorum
XII Apostolorum Decima octava die mensis —
maij Anno Domini millesimo septingentesimo —
trigesimo sexto.

Jacobus R

Carolus P

7 *Power of Attorney signed by King James and Prince Charles for Bishop Joseph Załuski*
with regard to the Sobieski inheritance (1736)

8 Clementina Walkinshaw

9 Prince Charles (c. 1795)

10 *The Palazzo Guadagni in Florence, today known as the Palazzo di San Clemente or the Palazzo del Pretendente, Via Gino Capponi 15 – it is Florence's most haunted building.*

11 The Château de Couzières, Montbazon nr. Tours

12 The Château d'Ussé

13 The baptismal certificate from the parish records of Veigné, Montbazon nr. Tours, signed by the head of the de Rohan family, Prince Jules-Hercule de Rohan, Duke de Montbazon, in which be simultaneously legitimised and granted the title of the demoiselle de Thorigny to Charlotte Stuart's daughter, Marie-Victoire

14 Prince Ferdinand de Rohan, Archbishop of Cambrai (1773)

*15 Prince Louis de Rohan, Cardinal and Prince-Bishop of
Strasbourg (1770)*

Je pense que nos auttres parents seront tranquils à brunswick; hélas quelle dispersion!... —
je compte partir toujours pour rome eu naples le 20 maï, mon voïage sera de peu de durée,
j'ai le tems encore de recevoir icy vottre reponse, eu vos commitions pour rome, si vous le voulez;
en tout cas in addressant toujours icy les lettres elles me seront renvoïées exactement. —
je crois que l'italie sera tranquille, je logerai à rome chez mon cousin le pce. camille. —

Je rouvre ma lettre parceque je recois dans l'instant la reponse de mr. Thomas Coutts;
ce fameux banquier si riche u qui est il avec tout ce qu'il y a de mieux, eu d'aplus considerable
en angleterre; je lui connu a paris, eu a liège; il me mande positivament qu'il y a très peu
d'assurance que les indes occidentales, francaises et particulièrement St. domingue, restent sous la
domination anglaise même pendant la guerre. il ajoute, que les hommes les mieux informés de l'angleterre
regrettent, que le gouvernement au adopté la mésure de les subjuguer dans ce tems, où l'idée de les retenir
sous la protection de la gde. bretagne même quand il y auroit une paix... la lettre est très récente, car
elle est datée du 24 mars; — il trouve aussi que le séjour d'angleterre peut devenir mauvais pour un
étranger surtout, qu'il voudroit lui même que ses affaires lui permissent de venir à Venise qu'il regarde
comme l'endroit le plus sûr. — il me mande du bien de mr. Turnbull qu'il dit être un negotiant, marchand
de bonne réputation; il me semble qu'on nous avoit dit qu'ils etaient banquiers très riches, de la cour?...
je suis, mon cher frere, très faché d'apprendre d'aussi mauvaises nouvelles, mais elles viennent d'un
homme bien instruit; en consequence je ne compte presque plus sur st. domingue, ce ne sera encore
qu'un beau rêve, amoins que l'on ne fasse stipuler à la paix que les francais laisseront jouir paisiblement —

1180

16 Letter from Ferdinand to Louis, dated April 17th, 1795, sent from Venice to Ettenheim

17 Charlotte Stuart's daughter, Young Charlotte (?)

L'an dixhuit Cent et Six, le Vingt huitième
jour Du mois De novembre aux quatre heures
après midi,
Par devant Nous, Charles hautotte, maire adjoint
et officier De l'état Civil De La Ville de huy, chef
Lieu Du troisième arrondissement du département de l'Ourthe
Sont Comparus joseph otis, Ecrivain agé de Vingt huit
ans, Domicilié En La Commune De Tihange et nicolas
joseph Degueldre Employé Dans Les Droits réunis
agé De trente ans Domicilié En Cette Commune
tous Deux amis De Charlotte maximilienne amelie
De Stochenstard, née à paris, Domiciliée En Cette Commune
agé De Vingt Six ans, Epouse à jean Louis Lucien
Lucien Cousin De Lamortier receveur principal Des
Droits reunis, fille De maximilien de Stochenstard
et De Clementine de Wavvelz, Lesquels nous ont
Déclaré que Ladite Charlotte maximilienne amelie
De Stochenstard est Décédée Le Vingt Six du présent
mois a trois heures après midi, En Son Domicile
Section du Nord rue de l'aplé
et ont Les Déclarants Signé avec nous, Le présent
acte des décès après Lecture.

18 *Young Charlotte's death certificate from the Archives de l'État à Huy, Belgium*

19 Walter Otton Fergusson-Tepper, playing with Kiopek, King Stanislas August's dog (1785)

20 The Fergusson-Teppers' palace on Długa Street in Warsaw

21 The 'Black House' in Lwów which belonged to the Nikorowicz family

*22 Lwów. In the centre is the six windowed façade of King John Sobieski's 'Royal House'
(No. 6). One away on either side stand the Nikorowicz brothers' 'Black House' (No. 4) and
'Bernatowicz House' (No. 8)*

Recomendatus obsequijs Sacra Regia Majestatis à Celsissimo Duce Radziwiłł Pro sub tempus Comitiorum, mediante Patrocinio Illustrissima Excellent obtinui literas favorabiles secretariatûs et Commissoriatûs, dabam ope per hoc spatium temporis; ne videar communi plerimis acquiescere desidere ut possim particulare aliquod exequi obsequium, mittebam Famulos Constantinopolim et nihil inde singularis potui conducere, et sic pensatis pensandis assumpsi propositum migrandi in Persiam, ubi speciosissima et singularis res reperiuntur et fabricantur, quoniam vero ad illud Regnum ob magnam stantiam loci difficilis et periculosus est aditus, constitui supplicare Illustrissi Excellentia, quatenus possim ob securitatem tam vitæ, quam subtilis fortundæ in charactere Legati seu Missarij hoc iter conficere, sicuti practicavit piæ defor Jacobus Murkiewicz à Serenissimo Divæ Memoriæ Augusto II ad Regem Persiæ Missarius. Advolutus itaq. plantis Illustrissima Excellentia Domini mei Clementissimi humillime supplico ut similem expeditionem à Serenissimo Rege feliciter nunc regnante, mediante interpositione Illustri sima Excellentia obtinere possim, non quæro inde privatum lucrum, sed alia modo desidero alacris animi mei ad obsequia, exhibere documenta prætereà om possibilitate procurare studebo, ut consideratis maturè Regni Persici Incolarum nego tionibus, correspondentiam constituere, et commercium cum Incolis Poloniæ et hîc quam optimè modò stabilire possim, quoniam vero tam pro famulatu charactr adæquato, quam pro donariis Regi Persarum, et ejus Ministris spectantibus fr um impendam peculium, quod debebit esse notabile, idcirco ut aliquod levam in expensis habeam, humillimè supplico quatenus possim per Imperium Mos vilicum postiles equos sine exactione solutionis ex Recomendatione Sacræ Reg Majestatis pro commoditate mea et famulatûs mei habere, in felici verò in Poloniam ab exactione Teloneorum liber esse, quæ omnia Gratiæ, meq Patr Illustrissima Excellentia inimus.

Illustrissima et Excellentissima Dominationis Vestra Domini, Domini mei Clementissimi

humillimus servus
Gregorius Nikorowicz

S. R. mttis

23 Gregory-Simon de Nikorowicz's letter, mentioning his patronage by Prince Charles Radziwiłł, requesting diplomatic protection from King August III for his mission to Persia

Polish membership of French lodges received a boost after the failure of the anti-Russian Confederation of Bar. Paris filled with refugees. And many who had not been freemasons before, seeing its usefulness now, flocked to join. Meanwhile the Confederation's leadership found itself exiled at Prešov in Slovakia. One of the first things it did was to found the lodge of the 'Virtuous Voyager' in 1770. Amongst its founders was the ubiquitous Stuart cousin, Radziwiłł.[47] Not long after, at the time of the first partition of Poland, he would seek the support of Versailles via the same Duke d'Aiguillon[48] who had just appointed Cardinal Louis de Rohan ambassador in Vienna[49] and become such a close friend of Prince Charles.[50] From Vienna de Rohan corresponded about the troubled politics of Poland in May 1772 with Radziwiłł, now based in Cieszyn,[51] as well as with Załuski.[52] A year later the itinerant, exiled Radziwiłł spent the six summer months of 1773 at de Rohan's Strasbourg prior to going to Paris to try and use his highly placed friends and relations to gain support for a Confederate mission to Turkey.[53] One of them was Marie-Anne de Talmont. She died on December 20th, 1776. To the end of her days she wore a bracelet with a hidden spring which caused a tiny portrait of Christ to appear alongside that of Prince Charles.[54] She kept in close touch with Radziwiłł, and their letters amply demonstrate how family ties fast-tracked political ends:

Fontainebleau, August 12th, 1772.
I am waiting, dear Prince, for your news from Strasbourg [...] Your merit and the injustices of all your misfortunes affect me as much as they do you. Of the ties of blood that unite us, I have spoken often to the late Queen, our Mistress, to whom you have the honour to be related as well as to me [...]
Your loving aunt, Marie-Anne de Talmont

Radziwiłł to the Duke d'Aiguillon;

[47] L. Hass, *Ze studiów nad wolnomularstwem ...*, *op. cit.*, p.593.
[48] PSB, vol.30, p.255.
[49] *Nouvelle biografie générale*, Paris 1863, vol.42, p.529.
[50] L.L. Bongie, *op. cit.*, p.210.
[51] AGAD, Archiwum Radziwiłłów, dz.5, sygn.13186.
[52] Biblioteka Narodowa w Warszawie, Katalog rękopisów, sygn.6942, 6943.
[53] PSB, vol.30, p.256.
[54] L.L. Bongie, *op. cit.*, p.274.

Paris,
Madame the Princess de Talmont, my Aunt, shall be present at
Fontainebleau on Monday, and will present me to you.

De Talmont to the Ambassador of Turkey:

Fontainebleau, October 1st, 1773.
My letter accompanies that of my friend, the Duke d'Aiguillon, in
recommending to you my nephew, the Prince Radziwiłł. I have
the honour to be related to the late Queen, as you without doubt
will know, and furthermore that I am a Pole and consequently
infinitely concerned and occupied by the misfortunes of my
unfortunate homeland.[55]

To sum up: the more senior of the Polish and French nobility, their
bankers and those from amongst them or their entourages involved in
the *Secret du Roi* or freemasonry, all either frequented Leszczyński's
highly politicised court in Lorraine or had direct contacts with those
who did. Taken together Lunéville was a melting pot of contacts facil-
itating all manner of political, personal or financial deals. And it was
precisely here that the Stuart family had so many friends and relations.
Never would this extensive Franco-Polish web of contacts prove more
crucial than in the anguished years of the French Revolution. At that
time Louis XVIII and the French royal family found shelter in Warsaw.
So too did the daughter of Princess Charlotte de Rohan, Louise de
Bourbon-Condé, as well as many other high-born refugees.[56]

* * *

And so it was at Lunéville, in April 1749, that Prince Charles planned
his return to Paris via Dijon and Ligny to see his banker, Waters and
stay a week, hidden by Marie-Anne de Talmont. In so doing Charles
broke his word to Louis XV never to return to France. But of that he
cared little. He was not alone in believing that Louis had been the first
to prove faithless.

The prince's presence in Paris was soon known to the authorities
who put their internal security forces on nationwide alert. They issued

---

[55] AGAD, Archiwum Radziwiłłów, dz.5, sygn.16063.
[56] A. Magier, *op. cit.*, p.374. Charlotte was the daughter of Jules-Hercule's first cousin, Charles de
Rohan, Duke de Rohan-Rohan, Prince de Soubise, Marshal of France and minister of State.

standing orders to arrest Charles on sight, distributed 'wanted' posters bearing his likeness and later carried out regular police searches for him both in Paris and Lunéville. By the end of April he had returned with Marie-Anne de Talmont to Lorraine whence he left via Strasbourg for Venice from which he was promptly expelled after just a week, despite a personal appeal to the Empress Maria-Theresa. By early June he was back again in Paris and on the recommendation of his lover approached her friend, Mademoiselle Ferrand, asking if she would agree to act as recipient for letters to be sent to him by Waters, addressed to Mr John Douglas, Charles's pseudonym.

Yet things developed further than that. For Mademoiselle Ferrand and the Countess de Vassé had rooms in the Convent de Saint Joseph on the rue Sainte Dominique. Such guest houses of convents were recognised dwelling places for ladies and their children. It was there that Charles installed himself, secretly enjoyed the company of these two women as well as his lover and observed their intellectual friends. At night a secret staircase led him directly to Marie-Anne's rooms. But it could not be a permanent arrangement for several reasons. Firstly, Charles was in France illegally and had to keep on the move (by November 1749 he was back again at Lunéville). Secondly, he was still obsessed by the Stuart Cause which he could scarcely advance whilst hiding. Thirdly, his paranoia was deepening and he felt the threat of assassins ever more frequently – though not without reason, for Sir Charles Hanbury Williams in Dresden and Lord Hynford in Moscow had both enthusiastically offered to organise his murder. Fourthly, his passionate affair with Marie-Anne de Talmont was degenerating. Ultimately the lovers came to blows and their violent fights became so noisy that Madame de Vassé had to ask them to leave. However, their stormy relationship had more than a year to run until ended abruptly by Charles.

Up until this time the prince had been being financed by credit from Waters against the money that had arrived at Loch nan Uamh after Charles's escape from Culloden to the Outer Isles. It was known as the Loch Arkaig treasure and was being looked after in the Highlands by Cluny Macpherson. Now, in 1749, Charles received some £6,000 of it via Major Kennedy as well as £15,000 through Henry Goring from English Jacobites who made it conditional upon Charles removing certain undesirable drinking companions from his household. At the same time there were promising signs of renewed Jacobite activity in England, where Dr William King of St. Mary's Hall, Oxford claimed that 275 English supporters were ready to present signed testimonies, and where one or two public pro-Stuart demonstrations had occurred. Thus, in 1750, Charles resolved to go on a reconnaissance mission to London, writing that he 'is determined to go over at any rate' and that he 'will expose nobody but himself, supposing the worst'. He asked Sir Charles Goring to send a ship to Antwerp in mid-August, deposited 186,000 livres with Waters and through a merchant, Mr Dormer, his 'chief medium of intelligence with England', ordered 'twenty thousand guns, bayonets, ammunition proportioned, with four thousand swords and pistols for horses in one ship which is to be the first, and in the second, six thousand guns without bayonets but sufficient ammunition, and six thousand broadswords'. He wrote to his father in July, asking in an encoded message for a renewal of his commission of 1745.

James's weary reply makes a stark contrast to his son's feverish activity. He felt Charles to be 'a continual heartbreak'. Nevertheless he reluctantly agreed:

for I am sensible that should I have refused to send it, it might happen to be of great inconvenience to you. But let me recommend to you not to use other people as you do me, by expecting friendship and favours from them while you do all that is necessary to disgust them, for you must not expect that anybody else will make you the return I do.

The journey to London achieved almost nothing except for the fact that he went to the 'New Church in the Strand' and became a Protestant. Just as Charles had been in 1747 when Henry had become a cardinal, so now were his father and brother 'ill with grief' when they heard of his conversion. His supporters rued the fact that he had not done so in 1745. In London Charles probably stayed at the house of the widow, Lady Primrose. After he appeared there unannounced, his astounded hostess immediately sent for Dr King who wrote:

If I was surprised to find him there, I was still more astonished when he acquainted me with the motives which had induced him to hazard a journey to England at this juncture. The impatience of our friends in exile had formed a scheme which was impracticable [...] No preparations had been made [...] He was soon convinced that he had been deceived.

Apart from this Charles met about fifty English Jacobite leaders including the Duke of Beaufort and the Earl of Westmorland. But nothing concrete came of it and he left on September 2nd, deeply disillusioned, arriving in Paris via Antwerp on the 24th, where he described his existence as 'sad loneliness'.

Staying only a short time, he left once more for Lunéville where he took his frustration out on Marie-Anne de Talmont who wrote: 'I love you too much and you love me too little [...] I see clearly, and with extreme grief, that you want to pick a lover's quarrel and set yourself at variance with me'. Next he hid in a château described as 'a lonely and solitary place', moved on to Boulogne-sur-Mer by January 1751 and then to Germany a month later where he was received by Frederick the Great 'with great civility'. Having greatly admired Charles's bravery in the 'Forty Five, the Prussian king could do little for him now, though he continued to stay in touch through Henry Goring and the Earl Marischal. So the thirty-two-year-old Charles returned to Paris.

Most of that year was spent between Paris and Lunéville. Yet once again his optimistic nature picked up. For at this time a plan which came to be known as the 'Elibank Plot' was being hatched by Alexander Murray and his brother, Lord Elibank. Both were ardent Jacobites though neither had been out in the 'Forty-Five. Murray's plan was to enlist some officers of Lord Ogilvy's regiment, cross over to England and raise a body of several hundred supporters who would then storm St James's Palace and assasinate George II and his family on November 10th, 1752. Murray had promised to find five hundred loyal men in and around Westminster. Charles had become convinced that he was about to form a strong alliance with Frederick the Great, whilst the conspirators hoped that General James Keith, brother of the Earl Marischal (who was now Prussian Ambassador to Versailles) would agree to land in Scotland with some Swedish troops just prior to the outbreak of a rising to be led by the late Lochiel's brothers, John Cameron of Fassiefern and Dr Archie Cameron as well as Cameron of Glen Nevis, Ewen Macpherson of Cluny, MacDonell of Lochgarry, Forbes of Skellater, Robertson of Woodsheal and Blairfelty. Conspicuous amongst the Scottish leaders was Alastair Ruadh MacDonell, Younger of Glengarry, who promised to have 'above four hundred brave Highlanders ready at my call'.

Prince Charles briefed the Cameron brothers as well as Lochgarry and the others at Menin in Flanders and two days later was joined by Young Glengarry. But the man who had promised four hundred men was in fact a Hanoverian spy, code-named 'Pickle', who was relaying all the details of the plot back to Westminster. Perhaps the Jacobites got wind of some betrayal for the plan was postponed and never revived. However, the still deeply unpopular Hanoverian regime, not wanting to publicise the existence of significant Jacobite activity, decided to make an example of one conspirator whom they charged under the seven-year-old Act of Attainder for the 'Forty-Five. In March, following the collapse of the plot, Dr Archie Cameron failed to escape back to the Continent and was hiding at Brenachyle on Loch Katrineside at the home of David Stewart of Glenbuckie. Another Hanoverian spy, Samuel Cameron, brother of Glen Nevis and known as 'Crookshanks', told the commander of the garrison at Inversnaid of Dr Archie's presence. Redcoats surrounded the house and arrested him despite the fact that some children had tried to warn the doomed forty-five-year-old. He was taken to the Tower of London and hanged, drawn and quartered on June 7th, 1753 at Tyburn, without trial.

During his imprisonment Dr Archie had not been allowed pen, ink or paper. But with an overlooked, blunt pencil he wrote a testimony on five scraps. The last one read:

I pray to God to hasten the restoration of the Royal Family, without which these miserably divided nations can never enjoy peace and happiness, and that it may please Him to preserve the King, the Prince of Wales, and the Duke of York from the power and malice of their enemies, to prosper and reward all my friends and benefactors, and to forgive all my enemies, murderers, and false accusers, from the Elector of Hanover and his bloody son down to Samuel Cameron, the basest of their spies, as I freely do from the bottom of my heart.

Archibald Cameron

Elsewhere, on another scrap of paper, Prince Charles wrote: 'De vivre et pas de vivre, c'est beaucoup pis que de mourir'.

What is striking about the Elibank plot is the treachery of a member of a Highland chieftain's family. Similarly, Archie Cameron's death was the result of betrayal by one of his own clansmen. Though France's military and political situation had not been conducive, perhaps Charles had been right when pleading with Louis XV for military intervention in 1746 before, as he had written, the demoralising policies of Westminster could take full effect.

Regular and large amounts of alchohol, as well as his violent and tormented affairs with Louise de Rohan and Marie-Anne de Talmont had momentarily exhausted much of the emotional turmoil that had engulfed Charles since Culloden. Then the Elibank Plot had again raised and dashed his hopes. Another loyal supporter, the brother of his friend Lochiel, had been horribly executed. Another wife was widowed. Another eight children left fatherless. Such see-sawing of intense emotions, suppressed guilt, continual disappointment, fear of the assassin's knife, drink and the life of an outlaw constituted a level of stress that was unsustainable. In response Charles sought refuge in domesticity. Even prior to the Elibank Plot some signs of this had appeared as he had gone through a phase of frenetically collecting books, paintings, marble busts and fine wines despite the fact that he had no home in which to put them. Waters the banker had to house them all. He would receive detailed and meticulous instructions from the prince. Even more telling was Charles's acquisition of a house in mid-1751.

CHAPTER EIGHT

Flight from Carlsbourg

My life is done, yet all remains
The breath has gone, the image not
The furious shapes once forged in heat
Live on, though now no longer hot.

Edwin Muir

Be pleased, dear Sir, to give a distinct address how to find Mrs Clemi in writing to the bearer as he is an absolutely trusty servant. Also a letter to the bearer by which you are to say to the said Mrs Clemi that she may give entire credit to my servant (he will deliver the letter) as to anything whatsoever he may say to her. All this must be an inviolable secret betwixt us and you may be assured of my sincere friendship.

John Douglas

Cambrai, May 29th, 1752.
Sir, Nothing in life could have surprised me more than the sight of Your Royal Highness' letter. I kissed it a hundred times [...] As to the person Your Royal Higness speaks of, I can assure Your Highness, upon my word of honour, I don't know what directions to give the bearer about her [...] Her letter to me was from Dunkirk where she gave me to understand that if she had no account from you, that her intention was to go into a convent, and expressed to me that she wasn't very opulent [...] As soon as I am informed of anything about her, I'll take the liberty to write by the way of Mr Wolf, to inform Your Highness of what comes to my knowledge.

Champville

Cambrai, May 31st, 1752.

Mademoiselle, Since your last letter I have received a reply to yours sent to me without an address. This is entirely to your satisfaction, being that which you desire, and worthy of the person who has sent it. The matter at present is that you should be by this person's side, as the person absolutely desires.

J. O'Sullivan

The first of these letters is from Prince Charles and the last two are from John O'Sullivan who had been so devoted to Charles during the 'Forty-Five, escaped after Culloden with him, shared the first half of those punitive five months skulking in the Outer Isles and finally helped send the ships from France which rescued him. Mrs Clemi is Clementina Maria Sophia Walkinshaw whom Charles had met at the Bannockburn home of her grandfather, Sir Hugh Paterson, when she had nursed him during his illness just after the Jacobite victory at Falkirk. Since that time there exists no evidence to suggest that Clementina and Charles had been in touch. Indeed, Charles had been far too involved with Louise de Rohan and Marie-Anne de Talmont. Yet something now stirred both to seek each other out, and the desire to do so seems to have been spontaneous and mutual judging by all surviving material.

Perhaps Charles's need for tranquillity brought to mind the gentle Jacobite nurse from the land of his beloved Highlanders for whom he was perhaps still a hero. She had tended to his fever during his ten-day convalescence at Bannockburn House when his dreams seemed within grasp. That he might still for her be a knight in shining armour calls to mind the fairytale Italian chivalry that pervaded the atmosphere of his innocent Roman childhood when his mother was still alive. Charles knew that Clementina's father had been out in the 'Fifteen, a Jabobite Ambassador in Vienna and involved in the arrangement of his parents' marriage. Moreover, according to legend, the Scottish lass was his mother's namesake and god-daughter. Had she not been symbolically linked to him since childhood?

Charles's exhaustion and disillusionment, the expectation of some role he expected Clementina to act out is almost palpable. Maybe he hoped she might help him find some way forward. But if such a hope existed, she had no chance to fulfil it. As for her, it would appear that Clementina might have believed that some platonic love or mutual attraction had earlier sprung up between them. Though Lord Elcho claimed the two became lovers in 1746 his views are of little value as he had tried to make his peace with the Hanoverians after Culloden and was a man of cruel and vindictive character who had grown to despise Charles. And whilst it seems even probable that a man suffering from high fever should feel tenderness to his nurse, it seems much less likely that he should attempt his first sexual conquest whilst in such a state. Furthermore, Charles's lack of interest in women was widely commented upon by contemporary observers during the 'Forty-Five. In Balhaldy's words, it was not until his affair with Louise de Rohan that he abandoned 'the resolution he had taken of being singular in that virtue'. His valet also confirmed that he had previously been 'given to no vice'.

Later Clementina spoke of a promise she had made in 1746 'to follow the Prince anywhere in the world' – something, however, that many Jacobite girls must have said, and that between 1744 and 1747 she was 'undone' – which in the language of the time can be made to mean whatever the reader wants. It is also said that about this time she refused the marriage proposals of Archibald Stuart, Provost of Edinburgh, and John Campbell, 5th Duke of Argyll. What is certain is that her uncle arranged a place for her as a canoness of a noble chapter at Douai. Having arrived at Dunkirk, she wrote to O'Sullivan, in what presumably constituted her last chance to avoid that fate and see her prince again. The couple met in Paris in the Summer of 1752 and went to Liège, living together as husband and wife and using the name Count and Countess Johnson. According to Young Glengarry, Prince Charles 'keeps her well and seems to be very fond of her'. This was more than can be said of the ever-cautious English Jacobites who feared she might be a spy because her sister, Catherine, was at that time a lady-in-waiting to the Hanoverian Princess of Wales. Nor was Clementina approved of by James, Henry or many of the more ardent Jacobites, all of whom felt that her presence would stand in the way of some advantageous political marriage for Charles which might further the Stuart Cause. Each, over the next few years, would do everything possible to influence Charles against his *maitresse-en-titre*, either by way of parental pressure, insults against her person, base insinuations that she was a spy or straightforward bribery.

Nevertheless, the couple were very happy at first, and when Clementina appeared in public, Charles was always at her side, appearing courteous, attentive and making no secret of their liaison even when she was pregnant a year later. Clementina's sole motive for being with

Charles seems to have been selfless love. For she made no apparent attempt to persuade him to marry her, even in 1753 when she gave birth to a baby girl who was christened on October 29th in the Church of La Bienheureuse Vierge Marie des Fonts at Liège. Their happiness may even be reflected in the baptismal entry: 'Charlotte, daughter of the noble Seigneur William Johnson and the noble Dame Charlotte Pitt'. It is hard to believe that they were not laughing when they chose as her alias the surname of that contemporary English statesman and enemy.

It was Clementina's unswerving loyalty that seems to have appealed so much to Charles. But as his paranoid suspicion of ever more people grew, so in time she too was fated to become a victim. An indication of the prince's unbalanced state of mind appears in a letter to his father dated November 18th, 1756: 'Allow me to take the liberty to mention some persons you should have guard against and not trust, Tencin, O'Brien and his Lady, Warren, Lord Clare, MacGregor, Sir J.Harrington, Aeneas MacDonald, O'Sullivan, the two Glengarries [...]' The significance of this blacklist lies in the fact that these were the names of most of Charles's remaining friends.

Shortly after the daughter was born whom the prince adored, with whom he loved to play and whom he called 'Pouponne' ('little baby'), his relationship with Clementina began to deteriorate. In the aftermath of Dr Archie's execution and the collapse of the Elibank plot his view of the future was bleak. For the present, no matter where he went, he was followed by Hanoverian and French Government spies. Haunting him also was the ever-present fear of assassination which would cause him to rush off and spend odd weeks hiding in German towns. To make matters worse, his finances were now in a dreadful state and he had to sell his two jade-handled pistols. When he called at the house of the Duke and Duchess d'Aiguillon, he was almost turned away as 'an ill-dressed stranger'.

In these circumstances Charles began to drink even more heavily, suffer black depressions, take offence at the drop of a hat and fly into rages. For Clementina the stress of such an atmosphere and worry about the future of their young child whilst living in ever more strait-ened circumstances was unbearable. Inevitably the couple quarrelled both frequently and publicly. In November 1753 Charles wrote to Henry Goring telling him, with regard to the household he was still maintaining there: 'I have written to Avignon to discard all my Papist servants [...] My Mistress has behaved so unworthily that she has put me out of all patience and as she is a Papist too, I discard her also!'

Clementina was sent away to some friends of hers in Paris but Charles immediately regretted it and the couple were reconciled.

Thereafter they lived for a while in the French capital, but the problem hadn't gone away. O'Sullivan described one quarrel in the Bois de Boulogne as 'a devilish warm dispute'. Charles was also plagued by English Jacobites who came to try and persuade him to get rid of Clementina whom they described as 'a harlot'. But he would not hear of it. He described France as an 'abominable country' and said that he was 'not able to breathe as much as the fresh air without the greatest apprehension'. Communication with James in Rome now ceased completely and his father wrote: 'I should not so much know he were alive did I not hear from second and third hands that those who have the same share in his confidence say he is in good health; for it is now more than two years since he has writ here at all'. The ever-faithful Henry Goring could take no more and resigned, having pleaded: 'For God's sake, Sir, have compassion on yourself'. But the prince flew into a rage and, despite Goring's long years of service and hardship, turned him out with nothing but insults. Charles was foolish enough to complain of the incident to George Keith. But Keith knew better and, taking Goring with him to Berlin in 1754, permanently broke off relations with Charles who consequently fell into despair. He wrote to Keith: 'My heart is broke enough, without that you should finish it'. Even the heroic Ewen Macpherson of Cluny, finally authorised to abandon his extraordinary decade of hiding in the Highlands and come over with the remnants of the Loch Arkaig treasure, tried to get Charles to drink tea instead of beer when thirsty and to raise him from his depression. But he just met with hostility. Cluny must have wondered whether this was the same person as the dynamic, optimistic prince with whom he had once hidden in the 'Cage', who, when he had tried to kneel, had stopped him and kissed him instead.

Towards the end of 1755 until 1756 Charles, Clementina and Charlotte lived in Basle in the guise of Dr and Mrs Thompson. In the words of the Hanoverian Minister in Berne, they lived as 'persons of easy fortune, but without the least affectation of show or magnificence'. Still their life together continued to be dominated by financial difficulties. Charles was even reduced to begging money from Louis XV whose pension he had once refused. Waters the banker, in a letter to King James, told him that: 'as to the supplies from England, they have apparently stopped for good'. The English Jacobites had cut off Charles's funding because of their unjustified suspicion of Clementina and a growing abhorrence of the prince's behaviour. The couple's life was unstable for other reasons. In a letter dated May 28th, 1756 the British Minister in Berne wrote that 'though the young Chevalier was often backward and forward, Basle was still his abode, and . . . his family continued there at this time'. It was this relentless coming and going, sometimes with his family, sometimes alone, usually under a pseudonym, which was so unsettling. No doubt associated with Charles's fear of assassination, it was also prompted by his grand mastership of the pan-European Jacobite masonic lodges and the multiplicity of plots and schemes they were incessantly inventing.[1]

Such was the dismal psychological and financial condition of the *de jure* heir to the Kingdoms of Scotland, England and Ireland when, in 1755, France and Hanoverian England once again found themselves at war. With war came renewed interest in the Stuart Cause. Prospects seemed so good that even Lord George Murray, who had been so bitter in 1746, declared his readiness to fight for the Cause once more. Charles's prospects of a politically advantageous marriage were also in the ascendant for the same reason. This was something about which his father had been becoming progressively more anxious. On March 28th, 1756 he wrote to Charles that with regard to the Courts of Europe: 'I have never been abandoned by them, and they have so much at heart the preservation of our family'. But, concerning the French Court's proposal to arrange a marriage with a lady 'who [said James] it would not have been at all unbecoming to me to accept of it', James pointed out in reproach that it would not be forthcoming because Charles had 'taken care to let it be known that he would not enter into such proposals'. The old king was desperately anxious and wrote to Louis as well as to Cardinal Tencin asking them to help. He also sent Sir John Graeme to his son. But to no avail. Finally, in October, James wrote to Charles, trying to persuade him to come to Rome in the hope that he could somehow bring him to his senses: 'You will not grudge this one journey to see your old father that he may embrace you, bless you, and give you his best advice once more before his death [...] I shall keep you here but a few days and as privately as you please'. At first Charles agreed and, leaving Clementina and Charlotte in Liège, left for Paris. Then he changed his mind.

In 1757 the French asked Charles if he would like to lead their attack on Minorca. But he refused. There then followed meetings with Louis

[1] L. Hass, *La Franc-maçonnerie* . . ., op. cit., p.102; M. K. Schuchard, *The Young Pretender and Jacobite Freemasonry* . . ., *op. cit.*

XV's ministers, the Duke de Richelieu and the Duke de Choiseul.[2] Such was the prince's attitude that they concluded it was impossible to work with him. So long had Charles been consumed by bitter cynicism towards French ministers, so long had that cynicism been magnified by drink, that the thought of gathering his remaining strength and raising his hopes once more was more than he could manage. His father wrote: 'Act at least your part as a true Patriot, a dutiful son and a man of honour and sense; if you are in lethargy rise out of it, if you are not show it by your action'. Charles was too burnt out. Yet there was no other Stuart the French could harness to their plans. Henry, by becoming a cardinal, had disqualified himself; the long suffering James was too old; whilst Charles's daughter, Charlotte, was still a child and in any case a girl.

Later the same year the French began preparations to launch an attack on Ireland. Again Charles was offered a role. Again he refused. Several months later, in February 1759, he was invited to discuss matters with de Choiseul, now Foreign Minister. He turned up drunk. Notwithstanding, such was even an alchoholic Stuart prince's political importance at that time that the French carried on with the talks, mainly through Alexander Murray and Lord Clancarty. But Charles kept upping his demands and conditions – all of which 'Pickle' the spy was relaying back to the Hanoverians in Westminster who must have been rubbing their hands with satisfaction.

Finally, when large-scale naval preparations had been made, the French asked Charles to ready himself and come to Brest. He even went so far as to write a proclamation in which he was to publicly announce his renunciation of Roman Catholicism. But the invasion under the Count de Conflans sailed without him, which was fortunate, because it was destroyed in Quiberon Bay by Admiral Hawke in November 1759. Writing in January 1760, Sir Richard Warren reveals the optimism about a Stuart restoration which had been felt by the Jacobites just prior to embarkation:

> This last sea fight has suspended for some time the execution of a scheme that could not but be advantageous to the Cause. Once landed we were sure to bring our neighbourhood to a better understanding. Never troops could show such impatience to be at the other side of the water nor could anything express the confidence they had in the Duke d'Aiguillon, our General.

[2] Etienne François de Choiseul.

However, with the French fleet destroyed there was now no power in Europe with the naval potential to launch a successful invasion of England. No hope remained. A few months later George III ascended the Stuarts' throne with neither worry nor hindrance.

Charles returned to the Château de Carlsbourg on the Bouillon estate of his uncle with whom he was back on better terms. He had stayed there before and besides Clementina and Charlotte had the company of his uncle's plenipotentiary, Monsieur Thibault. With him he would shoot or fish by day and drink himself into oblivion by night. One day, deep in his cups, Charles wrote:

> Thinking not Drinking
> Drinking not Thinking
> Can not be a Tool
> Or like a fool.

In Rome James was more worried than ever about his son. In March 1760 he begged him to come and see him, pitifully telling him that he could do so in complete secrecy, and sending him money for the trip. Perhaps aware that he was in no fit state to be seen, Charles wrote back claiming to be 'suffering from nerves'. Someone more genuinely in that condition was Clementina with whom Charles argued incessantly, not least about Charlotte whom her mother wanted to send away to be educated in a Parisian convent. But her doting father was categoric that his little 'Pouponne' should always remain beside him. According to Lord Elcho's lurid description Charles would beat Clementina as often as fifty times a day and at night construct a defence system of chairs, tables and bells around their bed, presumably out of fear of assassins. However much truth there may have been in this, it is clear that Charles was violent when drunk and suffering from delusions even when sober.

The prince now compared women with men, writing of them as 'being so much more wicked and impenetrable'. As for Clementina, deeply concerned about the effect on Charlotte, it was more than she could bear. They had lived together as a family for eight years, yet Charles was going from bad to worse. Later, when writing of this period, she would say that she had been pushed 'to the greatest extremity, and even despair, and I was always in perpetual dread of my life from your violent passions'. Consequently, at the end of July 1760, when Charles, Clementina and Charlotte were staying at

Bouillon, she hired a coach and, taking their daughter with her, drove to Paris. She wrote: 'There is not one woman in the world who would have suffered so long as what I have done [...] I quit my dearest Prince with the deepest regret and shall always be miserable if I don't hear of his welfare and happiness'. She showed her toughness in that she had undertaken the whole thing herself so as to prevent any member of their household becoming victim to Charles's inevitable fury: 'You may not put the blame on innocent people, ... there is not one soul either in the house or out of it that knew or has given me the smallest help in this undertaking'.

Grief-stricken over the loss of his beloved daughter, Charles wrote to the Abbé Gordon whom he had sent with his servant, John Stewart, to try and find Clementina and Charlotte: 'I shall be in the greatest affliction until I get back the child which was my only comfort in my misfortunes'. But on July 31st Stewart wrote of his meeting with Clementina: 'I reasoned the matter with her, but all to no purpose. She told me that she would sooner make away with herself than go back, and as for the child, she would be cut to pieces sooner than give her up'. Charles tried frantically to find out where they were living and on September 6th Gordon wrote: 'Of all the places you mentioned there was only Mr Stak and Sir John O'Sullivan of whom as yet I have not got sufficient information. I can assure you she is not at St. Germains, Lord Nairn's, Gasks's, Lady Ramsay's and not at the Convent of Conflans, nor rue Cassette.' Charles was beside himself and even threatened to set fire to the nunneries of Paris until he found his daughter. Thanks to the Hanoverian spies who relentlessly continued reporting back to London, we know that the search for Charlotte lasted a full month.

Prior to her flight from Bouillon, Clementina had been in correspondence with James who helped organise her escape and granted her an annual allowance of 6,000 livres. Louis XV also took her under his protection and she and Charlotte were placed in the care of the Archbishop of Paris at the Convent of the Nuns of the Visitation. To Charles, still at Bouillon, she wrote: 'Nothing can be more sensible to me than this fatal separation. I can't express to you, my dearest Prince, how much my heart suffers on this account'. She went on to explain that her 'one principal object was the child's education' and that Charlotte 'has a vast desire to see her dear Papa'. Louis replied to Charles's letter of protest bluntly: 'I cannot force the inclination of anybody in that situation'. By his own father Charles was told:

It was many months before I had undoubted information of her desire to leave you, to satify her own concience in the first place, and to stop the mouths of those to whom she knew herself to be obnoxious and suspected, and lastly to be able to give her daughter in a convent a Christian and good education [...] You cannot but be sensible that I could not do otherways than grant her request not only on her own account, but even on yours, that her child might have a decent education, which you could not give her in the situation you are; and in reality it would be ruining that poor child if you were to keep her with you in the uncertain and ambulatory life you lead, and if you have a true love and tenderness for her, you should prefer her good education to all other considerations [...] Oh my dear child, could I but once have the satisfaction of seeing you before I die, I flatter myself that I might soon be able to convince you that you never could have had a truer friend.

Of Charlotte, Clementina wrote to Charles:

I will make it the study of my life to neglect nothing to have her well and virtuously brought up and to make her worthy of you and of the Blood she has the honour to come of. I never intend to break the tie that unites her to you. She will always be yours, but my ambition is that she should do you honour.

Charles's recourse was to the bottle. Alexander Murray wrote: 'Your Royal Highness is resolved to destroy yourself to all intents and purposes. Everyone here talks of your conduct with horror, and, from once being the admiration of Europe, you are become the reverse'. A report from the British Embassy in mid-1761 reports that Charles 'is drunk as soon as he rises, and is always senselessly so at night, when his servants carry him to bed'. He hadn't seen his father since 1743 when he had ridden off into the night to stand at the head of what was to have been the 1744 French-led restoration of the Stuart birthright. He had gone bursting with faith and energy. To return now to his father's dark eyes which had known him since birth would have been to see reflected in them the true extent of his failure and degenerate state. With Clementina, Charlotte and all hope of military help from France gone, Charles shut himself away from the world at the Château de Carlsbourg. He refused all contact, with the exception of one or two of his closest friends, and replied to no-one, neither the French court, nor his Jacobite supporters, nor his father. In early 1762 James wrote: 'If you make no reply to this letter, I shall take it for granted that in your present situation you are not only buried alive, as you really are, but in effect you are dead and insensible for everything'. Clementina also continued to write. So did Charlotte. She addressed her letters to 'Mon Auguste Papa'. They were signed: 'Pouponne'.

CHAPTER NINE

Lochaber No More

Now the New Year reviving old desires
The thoughtful Soul to Solitude retires
Where the white hand of Moses on the Bough
Puts out, and Jesus from the ground suspires.

Edward FitzGerald

In 1760 old King James had fallen seriously ill and, though it did not kill him, he never fully recovered. In 1764 illness struck again, this time heralding the end. In February, James's secretary, Andrew Lumisden, wrote to Prince Charles spelling out the seriousness of his father's condition. The months passed by and the old king clung on. But no word came from his elder son.

Henry wrote to his brother asking for an end to nearly two decades of silence. The reply came through a secretary telling him that His Royal Highness neither wished to see nor write to anyone. In February 1765 Henry wrote once more, encouraging Charles by telling him that Marie-Anne de Talmont was in Rome and 'really seems sincerely attached to you. She complains she never can hear of you, and thinks she deserves a share in your remembrance'. The cardinal, who in the intervening years had built up a position of considerable wealth and influence, also described the terms of James's will and volunteered to pass on to his brother any bequests granted him by their father. He added: 'Among the misfortunes of our family I cannot but consider as the greatest of them all the fatal at least apparent disunion of two Brothers'. But he got no reply. So he wrote again, receiving a curt note in October telling him that he should ensure the Pope recognise Charles as the king's heir when the time came. And though at least it had been written by Charles himself, still it was out of touch with reality. Not only was Charles formally a Protestant but Westminster had been putting pressure on the courts of Europe not to recognise the Stuart succession. And the Vatican was indicating it would not risk Hanoverian wrath.

Henry carefully explained to his elder brother that though their family would always be extremely well regarded in Rome, it was nonetheless imperative to come in person, find a way to become quietly accepted back into the religion of his birth and re-establish relations with the Pope. Otherwise there was no chance of being formally acknowledged as the *de jure* King Charles III. And if there was a sense of urgency about Henry's advice, it was because if his elder brother was not recognised, then it might rule out his own succession at some later date. For Henry keenly felt his family's moral right to their royal titles and support from the Vatican. Had it not been for the sake of Catholicism that those thrones had been sacrificed in the first place?

The dying king, despite his illness, had been writing pleading letters to Charles: 'Is it possible that you would rather be a vagabond on the face of the earth than return to a father who is all love and tenderness for you?' Finally, Charles forced himself away from the bottle and isolation at the Château de Carlsbourg and on December 30th, 1765 set out for Rome. He left it too late. A life begun on June 10th, 1688 in St. James's Palace in London, which had been lived under a perpetually evil star, yet weathered with grace, ended on the night of New Year's Day 1766. And though neither of his sons was by his side, as Lumisden wrote, James died 'without the least convulsion or agony, but with his usual mild serenity in his countenance'. He had outlived all the usurpers – William of Orange (d. 1702), Queen Anne (d. 1714), George I (d. 1727), George II (d. 1760) and even the 'Butcher' Cumberland (d. 1765).

The next day Lumisden wrote to Charles: 'I most humbly beg to condole with you on the death of your Royal Father of blessed memory, and at the same time to congratulate you on your accession to the throne'. The Hanoverian spy, Sir Horace Mann, commented that: 'The Romans were vastly impatient to bury him, that their theatres might be opened'. Yet James's body lay in state on a cloth of gold for a full five days, after which it was carried to St. Peter's in a procession led by twenty cardinals along a route illuminated by a thousand candles and thronged with large crowds. In the great basilica the sermon was preached by Clement XIII himself.

Not long after, the Pope, who had continued the Vatican's lease of the Palazzo Muti for the benefit of the Stuarts, ordered that the royal arms of Great Britain be taken down from the building's façade. It was an act done with indecent haste and behind Charles's back, at a time when he was away at Albano. Just beforehand, Clement had shied away from recognising Charles as heir to his father's rights by passing the decision over to the College of Cardinals. In fact the matter had already been decided. Mann wrote back to London in triumph.

No-one except his younger brother came to greet Charles when he arrived in Rome on January 23rd. Once there, he spoke of his unhappy feelings and memories from childhood. Almost at once he wrote to his drinking companion at Carlsbourg, that he wished he had his 'dear Thibault to amuse and comfort' him. The only moral support he received was from Henry, who seated him on his right when driving in his Cardinal's carriage* and from the Scots, English and Irish Colleges in Rome who defied the Pope by receiving the prince with royal honours and singing a *Te Deum* for his restoration as King Charles III. Henry also helped his brother financially, passing over to him his £250,000 inheritance from their father and his annual Papal pension of 20,000 crowns.

The first year back at the Palazzo Muti was doubly hard because Charles was shunned by Roman society which took its lead from its Papal arbiter. Unable even to go out and enjoy the music which had been the principal childhood happiness he shared with his mother, the prince passed his time hunting in the *Campagna* and drinking. It shocked Henry now that he witnessed it at first hand. Occasionally Charles received visits from Jacobite supporters and sympathisers. One Englishwoman wrote:

> His person it is rather handsome, his face ruddy and full of pimples. He looks good-natured and was overjoyed to see me; nothing could be more affectionately gracious. I cannot answer for his cleverness, for he appeared to be absorbed in melancholy thoughts, a good deal of distraction in his conversation, and frequent brown studies. I had time to examine him for he kept me hours. He has all the reason in the world to be melancholy, for there is not a soul that goes near him, not knowing what to call him. He told me time lay heavy upon him. I said I supposed he read a great deal. He made no answer.

* A mark of respect extended to reigning monarchs.

A little later another described the prince as:

> above middle size, but stoops excessively; he appears bloated and red in the face; his countenance heavy and sleepy, which is attributed to his having been given in to an excess of drinking; but when a young man he must have been esteemed handsome [...] He is by no means thin, has a noble person and a graceful manner [...] On the whole he has a melancholy, mortified appearance.

However, Prince Charles began to slowly lift himself out of this trough. Henry pressurised the Pope into receiving him, though this was made conditional upon being in private audience and Charles being announced anonymously as 'the brother of the Cardinal York'. Primed by Hanoverian propaganda to expect some drunken brawler, the Pope was delighted to find that Charles knelt before him, kissed his ring and spoke with friendship and respect for about a quarter of an hour. Afterwards the clerics informed Horace Mann of the meeting, stressing its insignificance. Yet whatever the dubious loyalty of Clement XIII to the Stuarts, the visit opened the doors of Roman society and Prince Charles was able to breathe more freely. Furthermore the fresh air when hunting in the Italian countryside had improved his health, and a period of sobriety began which restored his natural kindness. An English traveller noted:

> His person is tall and rather lusty. His complexion has a redness in it, not unlike the effects of drinking [...] He talked very rationally, reads much and is fond of music. The Romans had conceived him to be a debauchee, but his behaviour in Rome has been perfectly sober and affable.

Charles even sent letters to his former friends, such as Marie-Anne de Talmont, to whom he wrote of feelings which 'will always be engraved on my heart'. But Clementina Walkinshaw in Paris was not included. As Lumisden wrote: 'His passion must still greatly cool'. It was typical of Charles that he could only cope with the loss of his daughter by shutting out all thought of her.

But the improvement evaporated when, as a contemporary witness put it: 'he was met with things that vexed him'. In 1767 Charles wrote to Henry: 'What is in my breast cannot be divulged until I have occasion. God alone is Judge'. Henry could only:

deplore the continuance of the bottle [...] It is impossible for my brother to live if he continues in this strain [...] I am severely afflicted on his account when I reflect on the dismal situation he puts himself under, which is a thousand times worse that the situation his enemies have endeavoured to place him in, but there is no remedy except for a miracle.

Until 1771, the prince's existence continued to be characterised by dips into and out of intoxication, typical of an alchoholic. They were punctuated only by trips to the spa at Pisa during which he tried in vain to buy a home in Florence so as to escape from the Palazzo Muti in Rome. But the Grand Duke gave in to Hanoverian pressure and issued orders to ignore the unrecognised Stuart King. Henry succeeded in persuading his brother to rent a villa in Pisa for the winter months instead.

Then came a major surprise initiated by Charles's cousins, the Duke of FitzJames and Louis XV, as well as his old friend, the Duke d'Aiguillon. Such was the state of France's international position in the aftermath of the Seven Years' War that it was time for one last play of the Stuart card. A bride would be found to keep alive the prospect of a male heir to the Stuarts' rights. Westminster now became seriously alarmed (the surviving exchanges are panic stricken) when they heard of the prince's arrival in Paris in late August 1771. The British Ambassador demanded an explanation from d'Aiguillon who fobbed him off with calculated vagueness. Charles's cousins, the Dukes of FitzJames and Berwick, were both illegitimately descended from James VII and II by Arabella Churchill, and Berwick's heir was engaged to be married to the impoverished but well-born Princess Caroline von Stolberg-Gedern. Given the hostility of the Hanoverians as well as the disastrous state of the Jacobite Cause, it was no small success to gain the hand of Caroline's teenaged younger sister, Princess Louise Maximiliana – a girl who proclaimed herself 'very impatient to assume her position'. The delighted French government provided the penniless bride-to-be with a substantial dowry, and Louise and Charles were formally married by proxy on March 28th, 1772.

Louise was an attractive, spirited girl, one of four sisters whose father had been killed at the Battle of Leuthen as a colonel in the Imperial Army. She had been placed from the age of six in a convent at Mons in Belgium from which, having enjoyed little maternal love, she had been anxious to escape. She was an intelligent though manipulative person who, whilst aware of Charles's exiled status, only partly realised the extent of his alchoholism. However, it was not initially evident, for his regenerated optimism had made him considerably fitter by the time he travelled to meet his young bride at Macerata where they were married in a small ceremony conducted by the local bishop. The marriage was even consummated the same day in satisfaction of a condition laid down by Louise's mother. Charles mischievously reported to his younger brother that 'the marriage was made in all the forms'.

Receptions followed, money for the poor was distributed and on April 19th the nineteen-year-old bride and fifty-two-year-old groom left for Rome in high spirits. For once Charles was anxious to arrive, in the hope that France's open support for his match would bring Papal recognition of the Stuart rights. Their arrival was commented upon by an eye-witness:

> First four couriers, the Chevalier's post-chaise, then the Princess's coach-and-six, followed by two other post-chaises, the Chevalier and the Princess in their coach, followed by the coaches-and-six with his attendants. The confluence of people at the cavalcade was surprising [...] She is pretty and young, he strong and vigorous. They may produce a race of pretenders that will never finish, which the French will be always playing upon every quarrel. May they increase fruitfully!

But the new Pope, Clement XIV, continued to refuse recognition of the Stuarts' legal rights despite French, Spanish and Maltese support. Nevertheless, the newly married couple were invited everywhere. They attended the opera and concerts, receptions at the residences of foreign ambassadors, held open house at the Palazzo Muti and went out for long drives in the *Campagna*. The prince drank less and his natural warmth remained in the ascendant. He wrote to his old loves, Marie-Anne de Talmont and Louise de Rohan as well as to his new mother-in-law. He told them all how happy he was. It was a happiness, however, inextricably linked to his hope of a male heir. The months went by, and though there were rumours which spread excitement throughout the Highlands, still no pregnancy materialised. Louise, it transpired, was barren. When that realisation set in, Charles returned to the bottle. On December 11th, 1773 Sir Horace Mann informed London that: 'He is seldom quite sober, and frequently causes the greatest disorders in his family'.

Bitterly hurt by the Vatican's refusal to acknowledge his family's rights, Charles and Louise left Rome in August 1774 and took a villa between Parma and Pisa, moving in the Autumn of that year to Florence where they lived in a palace offered them by Prince Corsini – a family long friendly to the Stuarts. The Corsinis' generosity was all the greater as it was in opposition to the Grand Duke Leopold who again gave in to Hanoverian pressure by ordering that no official recognition be given to Charles and Louise. The rest of the Florentine nobility sheepishly followed the shabby example of their duke. It was not only wounding but made life dull. This, the continued lack of an heir, financial problems and the pointlessness of his existence pushed Charles deep into the pit of drunkenness. 'Poor man, behaves well when he is not drunk', observed Horace Mann. Most evenings, with no-one for company, Charles would sit in his box at the theatre and drink himself unconcious, the unpleasant details of which filled the reports which Mann sent back to Westminster.

Inevitably Charles and Louise's relationship deteriorated. In 1775 she wrote:

> If Your Majesty goes on sulking, I shall be obliged to justify myself before the world and make it clear why the Royal Countenance is not quite so dazzlingly glorious as usual and its beautiful eyes not quite so radiant. I shall send all my friends a copy of the enclosed memorandum I have already sent to Your Majesty in which I set out the facts as best I can in the belief that I am in the right and that people will realize this.

In some letters Louise openly expressed her hope that her husband would die and she might 'become mistress of my own destiny'. In 1775, she described how she and Charles 'go out walking and get bored, and that is no relief'.

The prince bought the Palazzo Guadagni for himself in 1777 in the quiet, north-eastern outskirts of Florence. Though little more than a large villa it had beautiful views over the surrounding countryside. To Charles it was more than a mere building. It was the only home that ever belonged to his family during their century of exile. He displayed an immense pride in it, devoting all his energy to overseeing every detail of the building and garden's decoration. It is said that there was one small room with tartan frescoed on its walls. There was also a weather vane decorated with a royal crown, cipher and date, '*C.R.1777*'

(Carolus Rex 1777), whilst over the portal of the main doors in the entrance hall was painted the Stuart version of the British Royal Arms together with a small thistle, white rose and the inscription '*CAROLUS III M.BRIT.ET HIBERNIAE REX*'. In public, however, Charles used the title 'the Count of Albany'.

It was at this time that Louise acquired a lover. He was the twenty-eight-year-old Italian playboy, Count Vittorio Alfieri, a talented poet with whom Louise shared an interest in literature and the arts. At first Alfieri's animated conversation also won Charles's friendship – until Charles realised what was going on. In 1779 jealousy and alchohol combined to drag him down to hitherto unplumbed depths. As he had done twenty years before to Clementina Walkinshaw, so now the seriously ill prince began to physically abuse Louise when drunk and construct a mad system of alarm bells around her bed at night. Horace Mann wrote that:

> he has a declared fistula, great sores in his legs and is insupportable in stench and temper, neither of which he takes the least pains to disguise to his wife.

Returning home drunk from a St Andrew's Day celebration on November 30th, 1780, Charles burst into Louise's room, accused her of being unfaithful and assaulted her. She calmly made it the pretext she had been waiting for to terminate the relationship. For she had ensured that those who mattered remained unaware of her affair with Alfieri. Mann described the sixty-year-old prince as having performed, almost acrobatically, 'the most nauseous and filthy indecencies from above and below upon her'.

Presented with her chance, Louise immediately contacted the grand duke and solicited his protection. She and Alfieri then devised a scheme with their friends, a young Irishman called Gehegan and his mistress, Signora Orlandini – the ex-mistress of the French Minister in Florence. Whilst out driving with Charles, Louise and Signora Orlandini disappeared into a convent and the protection of the grand duke. Charles was outraged and realised at once what was going on. But his all too accurate accusations were met with Gehegan and Alfieri's theatrical poses of moral indignation. No-one of any consequence was prepared to accept the word of an ageing alchoholic against an intelligent, attractive young woman skilled in deception. So successfully did Louise plead the virtuous innocent to Henry that she forgot he was a cardinal who could, and did, immediately arrange for her removal from Florence to a Roman convent. With horror she realised this would be a far greater obstacle than Charles had ever been to the sort of life she envisaged leading with her playboy lover.

The prince frantically tried to get his wife back, but to no avail. She departed in secret for Rome in late December with Alfieri, in disguise, travelling on the box of her carriage. Mann reported that:

> The mould for any more casts of the Royal Stuarts has been broken, or, what is equivalent to it, is now shut up under the double lock and key of the Pope and Cardinal York, out of reach of any dabbler who might foister in any spurious copy.

The Pope received Louise in private audience and promptly cut Charles's pension by half. Protesting illness, she persuaded Henry to lend her his seldom-used official residence, the Cancelleria. Alfieri then moved into the nearby Villa Strozzi and the two lovers took promiscuous advantage of the Vatican residence and Papal protection. The news drove Charles wild. But even Prince Corsini failed to open the eyes of the Pope and Henry. So badly did Charles want Louise back that those close to him became convinced he would die from apoplexy. Even Mann observed: 'He has totally altered his way of living and behaves in every respect with proper decency'.

Louise continued to push her luck. Having asked Henry to write to Charles for some books which he was refusing to release, she completely forgot herself: 'Your letter to the King is admirable, and if you will excuse the expression, it is full of malice; I think on reading it he will be at his wits end'. Even now Henry did not see through her. Of him she wrote: 'He belongs to a race of amphibious creatures who are intended to be seen from a distance but whom an evil chance has brought close to our eyes'. On one occasion she created a sensation by turning up at a peformance at the Spanish Embassy adorned with the magnificent Sobieski and Stuart jewels. The playwright and her partner for the evening was, of course, Alfieri. Rumours began in earnest.

In late March 1783 Mann informed London that Charles was extremely ill and had received the Last Sacrament. So Henry hurried to spend most of each day by his brother's side. Once there the truth about Louise and Alfieri was finally brought home to him. Mortified, he immediately informed the Pope and the poet was expelled

forthwith from Papal territories, ridiculously protesting his innocence and confessing himself 'stupefied'. Louise, however, kept her
nerve and behaved with humility and dignity to avoid disgrace and
ruin. The point was not lost on her mother who arrived to try and
convince her daughter that she should return to her husband. Mann
commented: 'The cat, at last, is out of the bag. The Cardinal of York's
visit to his brother gave the latter an opportunity to undeceive him,
proving to him that the complaints laid to his charge of ill-using her
were invented to cover a plot formed by Count Alfieri'. Of Charles
Louise wrote to a friend: 'Reassure me, that he cannot last long [...]
Of course, he may at any moment succumb to the gout in his chest.
What a brutal thing it is to expect one's happiness through another's
death! [...] His legs are become useless, yet he survives despite this
malady'. The Hanoverians also wanted him dead. But just as they had
been unable to finish him off after Culloden, so now he proved unac-
comodating. Though the sixty-three-year-old had suffered a punish-
ing illness, nevertheless he more or less recovered, and detoxified
himself sufficiently for his old self to resurface. So much so that he
spent much of the summer of 1783 convalescing, attending race
meetings, fêtes, festivals and travelling around Tuscany. But Charles
was no longer a twenty-six-year-old. He collapsed in complete
exhaustion and was described as 'decrepit and bent; he walks with
great difficulty, and is so impaired in his memory that he repeats
himself every quarter of an hour'.

Later that year King Gustav III of Sweden arrived in Italy and spent
the winter there. He and Charles had become linked by freemasonry
and corresponded since 1776. Now they became personal friends and
nothing could have been more welcome, for Gustav had great diplomatic skills and undertook to arrange a settlement between the royal
couple. Gustav travelled to Rome, conferred with Henry and finally
agreed between the parties that they would sign a formal document of
separation and that Louise would return the Sobieski and Stuart jewels
as well as her share of Charles's Papal pension. He even arranged new
pensions from the French and Spanish. Charles's declaration was
signed on April 3rd, 1784:

> Our common misfortunes have rendered this event useful and
> necessary for us both, and in consideration of all the arguments
> she has adduced to us, we declare by these presents that we freely
> and voluntarily give our consent to this separation.

Both Louise and Charles wrote letters of gratitude to Gustav. The prince told him: 'I cannot sufficiently express my thanks [...] It would be impossible to find anyone to whom I could better confide my honour and interests'. Charles' thanks took another form as well. He pledged to Gustav the hereditary right of succession as Grand Master of the Masonic Order of the Temple.[1] Part of the separation agreement was that Louise would reside within the Papal states under the formal care of the Pope. Nevertheless this was to prove a flexible enough arrangement. Having learned her lesson once, Louise was careful not to throw caution to the wind when reunited with Alfieri at the 'Inn of the Two Keys' at Colmar in Alsace on August 17th. For as long as Charles was still alive she remained his legal wife. Her delicate but precious freedom was only the product of a formal separation overseen by a Pope whom she was not willing to anger again for mere weakness of the heart. Of Louise one epitaph comes from the usually sympathetic pen of Sir Compton Mackenzie:

> She was entirely without religion. She had no faith in humanity. She was mercenary. She was a liar. She was cold to the very core of her being. She was pretentious. She was self-complacent. Such humour as she had was of the privy. She began life as a chatterbox with good teeth and a pretty complexion. She ended as a dowdy, interminable old bore in a red shawl.

It seems a harsh judgement but whatever she was like the twelve years of the French Court's scheme to produce a male Stuart heir had come to an end, its sole aim unrealised.

Charles now lived alone in Florence amongst his servants and the portraits of his ancestors. Mann observed that he lived decently, with his drinking more or less under control. To pass the time he played music most evenings with the well-known Italian musician he befriended, Domenico Corri. According to Corri, the prince and he would sit in a room hung with crimson damask dimly lit with candles. On the table lay an ever-present pair of silver pistols in case of some assassination attempt. Sometimes Charles would rise, silently check they were loaded and primed, then resume the duets, with Corri accompanying on the harpsichord. On other occasions the prince, unaccompanied, would play old Scottish and Gaelic melodies on the

---

[1] M.K. Schuchard, *The Young Pretender and Jacobite Freemasonry ...*, op. cit.

French horn, violoncello, flageolet or Highland pipes. Almost always the evening would finish with the air, *Lochaber No More*, for which Allan Ramsay had written words some fifty years earlier including lines from before 1704 by Drummond of Balhaldy for Jean Cameron of Lochiel. It was a song which had often been sung by Jacobite prisoners awaiting execution. According to Corri the old man's hazel-brown eyes would run blind with tears by the time he reached its final verse:

> I gae then, my lass, to win honour and fame
> And if I should chance to come gloriously home
> I'll bring a heart to thee with love running o'er
> And then I'll leave thee and Lochaber no more.

The candlelit room hung with crimson damask which witnessed those sad evenings was in Charles's palace on the Via Gino Capponi. Today it is called the Palazzo di San Clemente and sometimes the Palazzo del Pretendente. It is Florence's most haunted building.

CHAPTER TEN

The Duchess of Albany

This lovely maid's of Royal blood
That ruled Albion's kingdoms three
But oh, Alas, for her bonnie face
They've wranged the Lass of Albany.
We'll daily pray, we'll nightly pray
On bended knee most fervently
The time will come, with pipe and drum
We'll welcome hame fair Albany.

Robert Burns

In 1760 Clementina Walkinshaw was created Countess of Albestroff, reputedly by Emperor Francis I, Duke of Lorraine and husband of Maria Theresa of Austria. But it did nothing to improve her modest circumstances. For the first six years after Clementina's flight with Charlotte from the Château de Carlsbourg at Bouillon, they lived in the Convent of the Visitation in Paris, paid for out of the pension granted by King James. But its value had declined significantly because of the inflation affecting what had become the world's most expensive city.

After James's death in January 1766, Charles angrily refused to support Clementina. He passed the responsibility on to Henry who, though he had always strongly disapproved of his brother's relationship, carried on paying the allowance. However, the Cardinal did two things. Firstly he reduced the pension from 6,000 to 5,000 livres. Secondly, having heard a rumour in 1767 that Charles had secretly married Clementina, and fearing that this might dissuade any prospective bride who might yet produce a Stuart male heir, Henry threatened

to stop Clementina's allowance altogether unless she sign a formal declaration that she had never been married to his brother. This she did
and, no longer able to afford to live in Paris, left for cheaper lodgings
at the Convent of Notre Dame de la Miséricorde in Meaux-en-Brie.
From there she wrote to Charles:

> Although I have been continually told that my letters weary you
> and it would be wisdom on my part to discontinue them, I should
> think myself guilty of ingratitude to Your Royal Highness if I did
> not express to you at the beginning of the New Year all the affec-
> tion I have for you.
>
> Meaux, December 16th, 1768.

Half a year later, Charlotte's letter to her father from the same place
mentions that her previous three had gone unanswered:

> Oh my King, it is from you that I derive life, you fondled me at
> my birth, the tenderest and most worthy of Mothers thought it
> her duty to remove me from your love to give me the best masters
> to direct my education and make me worthy of your Majesty. [...
> That] I may have the consolation of weeping one day, one day
> only, on the breast of my august Papa [...] this affectionate
> Pouponne, who was once so dear to you, see her fly, or rather
> throw herself into your arms.

By the same post Clementina added:

> This charming creature whom you brought into the world and
> who surely has never done anything to deserve to be abandoned
> by Your Majesty, because she is, I venture to say, worthy of you,
> of all you could do for her, this unfortunate child only claims the
> rights of her blood from you who are her King and father. And
> what will become of her if you refuse her this justice? [...] She is
> now at an age when thought begins to become serious and she
> already feels only too keenly and with the greatest grief Your
> Majesty's neglect and indifference. The unhappy child repeatedly
> says to me: 'What will become of me if my Papa abandons me?'
> [...] These sayings pierce me to the heart, and she also very often
> says to me: 'I am fit, Mama, to share the misfortunes of my King
> and father, but at least let him recognise me as his daughter' [...]

Can it be possible that you resolve to abandon a child who belongs to you and who has loved you? [...] She is charming as regards all the qualities of heart and mind [...] If we had been a little more affluent, her education would have been finished and completed, but we have retrenched in everything for that since the death of the King, who spared nothing to render this child worthy of Your Majesty [...] She is a very good musician. She has a very beautiful voice, she has begun the harpsichord [...] I could not give you, Sire, a greater proof of my attachment and respect than that of forming a creature worthy of you. I hope one day you will do me justice and I will die content [...] These are the wishes which the unhappy mother of your child will always make, who will be faithfully and inviolably attached to you until her last sigh.

Yet such was Charles's fury at Clementina that Waters the banker was told by Henry to mention her existence only when absolutely necessary, and only in letters marked with an 'X': 'for she must never be mentioned to His Majesty'. Then, upon hearing the unexpected news of her father's marriage to Louise von Stolberg-Gedern and horrified by the implications for her own situation, the eighteen-year-old Charlotte wrote to her father from Meaux on April 27th, 1772:

Having exhausted all the sentiments of my heart in the infinite number of letters that I have had the honour to write to you, none of which have made any impression upon you, my august Papa, which is a very clear proof to me of your total abandonment which I have never merited [...] I can only share in the honour of being your daughter, as one without hope, because I am without future and portion and consequently condemned to lead the most wretched and miserable life in the world.

She even came with her mother to Rome to appeal for recognition, refusing to see her father without her mother. However, their visit infuriated Charles who let it be known through a third party that his daughter could stay – but Clementina, never. The teenager refused the offer and returned with her mother to their simple existence at Meaux after Henry let them know that he would cut off their income if they did not do so immediately. The Cardinal added harshly that he would also do likewise if Charlotte lived anywhere but in a convent. During their stay in Rome her mediator had been Monsignor Lascaris, Henry's acting treasurer. To him Charlotte directed her thanks and hoped 'that His Eminence will not refuse my demand for exchanging my convent in Meaux for one in Paris'. Nevertheless, despite Charles's anger, it was after this episode that the prince's affection for Charlotte was reawoken. This is hinted at in the 'Memorial' which Charlotte sent to the French Court appealing for material assistance:

> The Lady Charlotte, daughter of Prince Charles Edward [...] baptized under the name he was then bearing, brought up as his daughter in his household until seven years old, and presented in that quality to all [...] Her mother, of one of the first Scottish families, allied to the House of Stuart, for which many of her relatives have shed their blood and lost their lives, and at that time treated by the Prince as his wife, and known on his different journeys by the same name as himself [...] The news of the marriage of the Prince has altered the condition of both [mother and daughter] [...] The Lady Charlotte, his daughter, is fully persuaded of his [Charles's] tenderness for her; she has received recent proofs of his attachment [...] She reminds the King that she is the last scion of a sovereign house, allied to the House of France, celebrated for its misfortunes and which has sacrificed its dominions for the sake of religion [...] The services rendered to his father [Louis XV] by the Scottish gentlemen have gained for them an annual subsistence. She dares to hope that the same assistance will not be refused to the daughter of him who fought at their head.

But despite Charlotte's kinship with Louis by shared descent from the great King Henry IV of France, Horace Walpole observed that: 'The House of FitzJames, fearing their becoming a burden to themselves, prevented the acknowledgement of the daughter'. Despite being shunned by him, Charlotte continued to write to her father who, when she was at her most eligible age, made her promise never to marry or take the veil. These orders were communicated to her by Abbé Gordon, Principal of the Scots College in Paris, who wrote back to Charles on February 27th, 1775:

> I communicated to the young lady in question the contents of your letter of the 10th, it touched her to such a degree that I was sorry that I had spoken to her so freely [...] The Doctor says that

her grief has given her an obstruction of the liver [...] She was only six years old when she was carried off, so that she ought not to be entirely ruined for a fault of which her age hindered her to be anybody's partner. I am heartily sorry for her misfortunate situation and think she deserves better, being esteemed by all who know her as one of the most accomplished women in this town ...

Charlotte was twenty-two, outgoing, full of common sense, very patient and, though she had inherited Charles's stubbornness, had a charm which would win her some extraordinary diplomatic victories. She had dark blond hair and bright blue eyes. Horace Mann described her as having 'a good figure, tall and well made, but the features of her face resemble too much those of her father to be handsome'. Another Englishman commented: 'She was a tall, robust woman of a very dark complexion and a coarse grained skin with more of a masculine boldness than feminine modesty or grace, but easy and unassuming in her manners'. Placed in the most impossible of financial, political and social situations, she decided, in early 1776, to apply to become an honorary canoness of the Noble Chapter of Migette, a convent near Besançon in Franche-Comté. On her way there she was invited to a reception and dinner given by Lord Elcho. Another guest that day was the young Archbishop of Bordeaux with whom Charlotte had more than a little in common.

Of all the people with whom she should form a relationship it is interesting that Charlotte should choose the thirty-seven-year-old blonde-haired, blue-eyed Prince Ferdinand Maximilian Mériadec de Rohan.[1] For whilst the Stuarts' protoplast was Flaald, the 11th century hereditary High Steward of Dol in Brittany, Ferdinand was the scion of another great Celtic Breton family whose name came from Rohan, no more than fifty miles south-west of Dol. The de Rohans descended from Guethenoc, Viscount de Porhoët, who built the massive Castle of Josselin in 1008 and were recognised as direct descendants of the

---

[1] In his book, *Roehenstart – A Late Stuart Pretender*, Edinburgh & London 1960, p.13, George Sherburn quotes Henry Sage's description (see Bibliography below) of a pastel portrait of Ferdinand de Rohan at Cambrai. This author is grateful to the diocesan archivist, Abbé Machelart, for confirming that this portrait is in fact of Archbishop Henri Marie Bernardin de Rosset de Reconzel de Fleury (+1781), painted by Louis François Durrans. Apart from the white marble bust illustrated in the present work, at the Duke de Rohan's Château de Josselin in Brittany, there also exists a rather weak portrait of Ferdinand by either Antoine or Joseph Hickel, dated 1773, which was sold at auction on December 11th, 1996 by Mes.Etienne et Damien Libert & Alain Castor, 3, rue Rossini, Paris.

ancient Celtic Kings of Brittany and sovereign princes in their own right by the Dukes of Brittany and Kings of France, Louis XIV declared: 'The House of Rohan should be treated in all matters equally with the Houses of Savoy and Lorraine'. Likewise they were formally acknowledged by the Kings of Sweden and Spain as well as the Vatican and the ruling Houses of Saxony, Hesse and Württemberg. Furthermore, the Stuarts and de Rohans had become linked by blood after King James I's daughter, Princess Isabella, married François I, Duke of Brittany. Both families were also many times related through the French royal family as well as that of Lorraine. Indeed, it had been Ferdinand's ancestor, the French Huguenot leader, Duke Henri de Rohan, who had carried the future King Charles I to his christening at Holyrood Palace in Edinburgh in late December 1600 and become his godfather. Duke Henri, who married Marguèrite de Béthune, the daughter of the great Duke de Sully, had even been the heir presumptive of his cousin, King Henri IV of France, to the kingdom of Navarre until the birth of the future Louis XIII of France. One of the very few families with the status of 'sovereign prince resident in France', the de Rohans had two family mottoes. The first, from the Dukes of Britanny, was: 'Sooner Death than Disgrace'. But the second better articulates their intense family pride: *'Roi ne puis, Duc ne daigne, Rohan suis'*.[2]

Ferdinand was born in 1738, the son of Prince Hercule-Mériadec de Rohan, Duke de Montbazon and Prince de Guémené by Princess Louise-Gabrielle de Rohan-Soubise, the daughter of Prince Hercule-Mériadec de Rohan-Soubise, Prince de Rohan-Rochefort, Prince de Soubise, Duke de Rohan-Rohan and Duke de Frontenay, by Anne-Geneviève de Lévis, the daughter of the Duke de Ventadour. His pedigree was hard to better. He was the youngest of four brothers of whom the third was Prince Louis, Cardinal-Bishop of Strasbourg; the second was Admiral Prince Louis-Armand, Prince de Montbazon, who was guillotined in 1794 and died childless; and the eldest was Henry Stuart's old ADC from the 'Forty-Five, Lt.General Jules-Hercule, Duke de Montbazon and Prince de Guémené. It was he who was the cuckolded husband of Prince Charles's lover and first cousin, Princess Louise de la Tour, the demoiselle d'Auvergne, daughter of Prince Charles-Godefroy, Duke de Bouillon, by Princess Charlotte Sobieska.

For generations the fate of the de Rohan family had been intertwined with that of the Stuarts. And they were nothing if not integral

---

[2] 'King I cannot be, nor condescend to be a duke, I am Rohan'.

to that transcontinental network of Franco-Polish, Stuart-related aristocrats and politicians centred upon ex-King Stanislas Leszczyński's Court at Lunéville. Indeed, was it not from the de Bouillons' Château de Carlsbourg that Charlotte had been separated from her father as a little girl? After that the de Rohans proved themselves the most loyal of friends to Clementina and Charlotte, inviting them to Paris even when they were forced to move to Meaux. In particular Jules-Hercule's wife, Louise, must have felt sympathy for Charles's daughter to whom she was linked by close ties of blood and a shared rejection by the man they both loved. Yet whether or not Charlotte had met Ferdinand before that dinner at Lord Elcho's, the two soon discovered how much they had in common. All would have been perfect had it not been for the fact that Ferdinand had been pushed into the traditional church career of a youngest son, about which he would write later with bitter regret. An intelligent man, he had won a doctorate of theology at the Sorbonne, become Grand Prior of the chapter of Strasbourg at the age of twenty-one, Abbé of Mouzon in 1759 and a Canon of Liège. Then, in 1769, Louis XV nominated him Archbishop of Bordeaux at the age of thirty-one. However, this was pre-revolutionary France where many great aristocratic families pushed younger sons into becoming clerics for the considerable income it could bring.

Charlotte's situation when she met Ferdinand was acutely difficult. For years she had been ignored by her father and still remained unrecognised by him. She had seen her mother's modest pension cut by Henry as well as her own appeal for a pension from the French Court blocked by her FitzJames cousins. And she was completely without a dowry. Yet she was the last of the ancient Royal Stuart dynasty and at twenty-two was in her prime. But, held in reserve by Charles in case of political need, he had forbidden her either to marry or become a nun. A more contradictory and impossible social position in the eighteenth century is hard to imagine. That was the context in which she fell in love with Ferdinand for whom marriage had also been ruled out. Needless to say, Charlotte changed her plan to become a canoness and returned to Paris where she and her mother were 'lady pensioners' at the Convent of the Visitation on the rue St. Jacques. Ferdinand took a lease on a house in the same street, belonging to the Abbé de laVillette and acquired a country home for them all at Anthony, a few miles south of Paris in the direction of Fontainebleau.

During the remaining years of the 1770s Ferdinand completed a magnificent palace in Bordeaux (today it is the Mairie) whereupon, in

1781, he was elevated to the more lucrative Archbishopric of Cambrai. There he instructed Bishop d'Amycles to act as his deputy so as to be free to live in Paris, not only with Charlotte and her mother, but also with the two daughters and son by Charlotte whom he fathered between 1778 and 1784. However, though Charlotte began to move in the court circle of Versailles and her friendship with the de Rohan family became public knowledge, the existence of her children was such a well-guarded secret that not even Sir Horace Mann found out.

In March 1783 fate played the cruellest of tricks on Charlotte. She was almost thirty years old and since 1775 had given up hope of being recognised by her father. Consequently she had started her secret family. At that time Charles was so ill that he had been given the Last Rites and was convinced he was dying. Finally realising how disgracefully he had treated his once adored 'Pouponne', he suddenly decided to make his only child the sole heir of his last will and testament dated March 23rd with a codicil of March 25th. In addition he created her Duchess of Albany, a dukedom traditionally reserved for the heirs of Kings of the Scots. Then, by an act dated March 30th, Charles raised Charlotte to the status of legitimate child with the additional title of 'Her Royal Highness'. Never a man to do things by halves he even ensured that all of this was recognised by the Vatican as well as by the King and parliament of France. Ten months later, between January 24th and February 14th, 1784, Charles was again struck down, this time with a suspected stroke. For two days he lay unconscious and once more received Extreme Unction. But his extraordinary constitution rallied. When he recovered, he sent word to his daughter in Paris telling her of his decisions and asking if she would come to Florence and live with him. Nothing could have been more unexpected, especially as at the time she was pregnant with her third child.

On July 10th, 1784 Mann wrote from Florence to London that Charles:

> acknowledges his natural daughter who with her mother resides in a convent at Paris in the quality of pensioners by the name of Lady Charlotte Stuart. She is about thirty years of age and as she is not obliged to conform to any of the rules of the convent she is often absent from it and frequents the Prince of Rohan, Archbishop of Bordeaux. Count Albany says that he will send for her to live with him here.

A week later Mann's next report to London reads:

> He often talked of sending for his natural daughter from Paris, to
> live with him here, though nobody then believed he would so
> soon put it into execution, but two days ago only, he took the res-
> olution to send his old servant Stuart who has attended him in all
> his excursions for that purpose to Paris [...] He has wrote to his
> daughter [...] to inform her that he had acknowledged her by a
> public deed, and by his will had appointed her his sole heiress [...]
> He has wrote likewise to the Count de Vergennes[3] to desire that
> he will get the deed of acknowledgement of his daughter regis-
> tered in the Parliament of Paris.

That Act of Parliament was signed by Louis XVI on September 7th
and Charlotte's rights, titles and royal status were not only recognised
but she was additionally granted the 'right of tabouret'.[4] Mann wrote
again on September 18th:

> Count Albany has received notice from Paris that his natural
> daughter whom he calls Lady Charlotte Stuart, to which name in
> the Act to acknowledge her he added the title of Duchess of
> Albany, was on the point of setting out on her journey hither [...]
> He is very busily employed in making preparations and furnish-
> ing his house [...] He received a large quantity of plate and his
> share of the jewels which belonged to his mother, except the two
> large rubies which were pawned by the Republic of Poland to his
> grandfather, Sobieski [...] Count Albany's health continues daily
> to decline, of which he is very sensible, and it makes him the more
> impatient for his daughter's arrival.

On October 9th, he continued:

> On the 5th instant Count Albany's daughter arrived here [...] She
> has appeared every evening since with her father at the theatre
> very richly adorned with the jewels that the Pretender had lately
> received from Rome [...] All the ladies and gentlemen of the
> country leave tickets of visits at her door [...] The Pretender has

---

3 Louis XVI's foreign minister
4 The privilege of remaining seated in the presence of the queen – a right reserved exclusively
  for French princesses and duchesses of the blood royal.

wrote letters to the Pope, to the Cardinal his brother, to the Courts of France and Spain and probably to many others, to announce the arrival of his daughter here.

Then, on December 7th:

> Though Count Albany is extremely infirm nevertheless [...] he has private balls three times a week at his own house [...] On the 30th of last month being St Andrew's Day [...] he performed the mock ceremony of investing his daughter with the order of St Andrew [...] Your Lordship will perceive [...] how weak the understanding of the Pretender is grown.

This last was a curious conclusion. Because the Order of the Thistle had been revived by Charles' grandfather in 1687, from whom the Hanoverians were not descended.

The prince began to enjoy life once more and, with his daughter, became so regular an attendant at the theatre and Opera that the Grand Duke of Tuscany had the Stuarts' boxes redecorated, the former in yellow and the latter in crimson damask. However, Charles's health continued to plague him. Horace Mann wrote that at their soirées 'he drowses most part of the time', had high blood pressure, breathing difficulties and suffered badly from gout, his legs being so badly swollen that he had to be carried everywhere in his chair. As for his drinking, Charlotte kept this under reasonable control, dissuading her father with her *'ton de fermeté'*. In April 1785, when Charles had a terrible attack of gout, Charlotte told her mother: 'My father has been in continual rages [...] Wine is not the cause, he drinks almost none'. Senility was also now beginning to set in. Mann noticed that 'he is quite incapable of transacting his own business, and his mind seems to approach that of imbecility'. Charlotte wrote to her mother that 'Lord Nairn and my father dispute and quarrel all day long. He's quite gone in the mind'. Even Charles admitted to his brother: 'I am so bothered in the head'.

Also troubling Charles were financial problems from which he and his daughter sought relief by trying to obtain the £50,000 capital and even greater amount of accrued interest for the jointure of his grandmother, Mary of Modena. But though the money had been outstanding since 1685, voted through by Act of Parliament, confirmed by William of Orange at the time of the Treaty of Ryswick and by Queen

Anne in the Treaty of Utrecht, nevertheless the London government had never honoured the debt, even in part. Charlotte likewise had problems. She had become the mother of three children. Yet she could not reveal their existence to anyone, for the scandal would be seized upon by the Hanoverians to destroy what little was left of the Stuart Cause. Worse, Charlotte's own position as the Stuart heiress would also be ruined and, by extension, that of her children and mother. She herself had had to wait more than two decades before coming into her own. Hopefully it would not be that long before she would inherit, her father and uncle would be no more, and then she would be able to help them. In the interim all she could do was write letters to her mother and Ferdinand in Paris, rather naively encoded in the hope that the Hanoverian spies would not understand them. Ferdinand, whom she initially forbade to write back because of this danger, was described as 'my friend' who was 'jealous as a tiger'. And the children were 'my little flowers' which 'need to be watered and tended every day', which she and Ferdinand had 'planted together in the garden'. In twice-weekly letters to her mother, Charlotte constantly wrote of hoping to see her flowers 'before they grow much higher', and of them 'not forgetting her'. In January 1785 she wrote to Clementina: 'What I give you will serve for your comfort and for the upkeep of my garden. My worthy friend has so fair a soul that I don't doubt that he will attend to everything, but for myself I wish to have my little part, otherwise I should be jealous'. One letter, dated March 25th, 1785, written several months after the birth of her youngest, contained instructions which presumably referred to his wet-nursing: 'He who is in the country will no doubt soon be returning to the city, and it is quite time that he did so. I count on you, dear Mama, to watch over his health and see that he wants for nothing'. Also from this period comes Charlotte's comment to her mother that she hopes 'my friend' will be pleased with his new child and love and cherish him tenderly. In a later letter she writes to Clementina asking for the latest news on the developing scandal of the '*Collier de la Reine*' owing to which Ferdinand's brother, Cardinal Louis, had been arrested in the Galerie des Glaces at Versailles and then imprisoned in the Bastille where he was visited by a stream of his famously loyal de Rohan relations who were lobbying vigorously for his release and exoneration.

Another problem was Henry's attitude. On November 2nd, 1784 Charles wrote to his brother:

I am very glad to tell you myself that my very dear daughter, having been recognised by me, by France, by the Pope, is Royal Highness for all, and everywhere. I do not dispute your rights. They are established, because you are my brother; but I beg of you also, not to dispute those of my very dear daughter.

But dispute he did, for Henry, who was still supportive of, and still being manipulated by, Louise von Stolberg, was more than a little offended by his brother's recognition of Charlotte and her honours. So he issued a formal declaration, publicly protesting that his permission had not been asked, that what Charlotte had received constituted a slight to himself and his sister-in-law, and objecting to the elevation of the new duchess to the right of Royal Succession which not even the FitzJames's had received. Undaunted, armed with her father's stubbornness and grandfather's patience, Charlotte began to correspond with her uncle in Rome, writing him warm, courteous letters. At first they went unanswered, yet little by little her star began to wax in Henry's eyes just as surely as her stepmother's began to wane.

In addition to being Charles's permanent nurse, Charlotte also began to bring order to the household's finances, finding in this another pretext to communicate with her uncle on matters of family 'business'. Her letters were largely concerned with her father's health but they also became increasingly condemnatory of Louise and Alfieri's conduct. At length she began to be answered. Meanwhile, Charles' health remained dire. On May 9th Charlotte told Henry: 'The leg is very bad; the swelling enormous'. And in July: 'He complains much of his stomach and is obliged to remain in bed a great part of the day'. Nevertheless, Charles pushed his daughter's cause as hard as possible, writing to Henry on April 9th, 1785: 'My daughter is doubly dear to me when I see her occupied in recalling to me a way of thinking which I hope will not change again, and which I love to assure you of the endurance of'. Later, on July 9th, he added: 'I cannot describe to you, my very dear brother, the happiness I feel in expecting that some day you will play the part of a father to a daughter I have every reason to love tenderly'.

At first Henry's rapprochement with his niece came on paper, accompanied by expressions of disgust at Louise's relationship with Alfieri which he described as 'a union so offensive to our family. It makes me furious [...] She has deliberately broken her word to me'. But, regarding Charlotte: 'I am greatly obliged to your daughter for interesting herself so with you on my behalf. It proves the kindness of her heart, to which everyone bears witness'. Shortly after, even Pope Pius VI congratulated Henry on the improved spiritual condition of his brother, openly attributing it to Charlotte. That summer's correspondence began to discuss when she and Henry might finally meet. The opportunity presented itself when Charlotte discovered her uncle would be visiting Perugia. So she obtained her father's permission to travel to Monte Freddo to see him. Their meeting proved such a success that it removed any residual reluctance Henry had in recognising her and cemented his reconciliation with his brother which remained unbroken till the end.

Charles, ignorant of his daughter's relationship with Ferdinand de Rohan, had ambitions to marry Charlotte into a reigning family. The Baroness de Castille commented: 'Many Italian princes have offered to her, and one of the brothers of the King of Sweden. Her father who wished to see her on a throne, presses hard for the latter'. A description of the duchess in 1785 comes from Abbé Dupaty:

> If benevolence alone were necessary to entitle her to the throne of her ancestors she would soon ascend it [...] Her attention to her father is extremely affecting. When this old man calls to mind that his family has reigned, his tears flow not alone.

With extraordinary energy Charlotte now succeeded in persuading Charles to leave Florence for Rome, ostensibly only for the winter, believing this to be the best thing for his health and the Stuart Cause. On December 1st, 1785 they started off on the eight-day journey to the detested city of Charles's birth, bidding farewell to the Florentine nobility with a huge party. Henry came to meet them at Viterbo and saw to his considerable surprise with what firmness, yet tact, his niece managed his notoriously difficult brother – that she was succeeding where all before had failed. He had given her his complete trust. For Henry too she became unique as the only woman who entered his intimate life and retained his love. Not long after he gave Charlotte the ultimate symbolic proof of this:

> Cardinal York has given up to his niece all his own jewels [...] including the Great Ruby, which was mortgaged by the Republic of Poland to the King Sobieski, which is supposed to be of very extraordinary value.
> Florence, January 28th, 1786, Sir Horace Mann

On December 31st, 1785 Mann had noted that Henry presented Charles 'to the Pope to whom likewise he had presented his niece some days before; and as she does not assume or pretend to any distinction, she has been received by the Roman Ladies with great civility'. Furthermore, the Pope at last agreed to treat Charles with some of the dignity reserved for reigning monarchs. For although the Vatican still would not formally recognise him as a sovereign, nevertheless he was granted the right to use the Royal Tribune at St Peter's, as previously granted to King James. The Pope also paid for the refurbishment of the Palazzo Muti. Charles and Charlotte went out to parties, concerts, the theatre and opera and lived for the moment, furiously making up for the lost years. It exhausted Charles. Local wags said that Charlotte was trying to kill him off. But living life to the hilt was what she understood her father wanted. When she gave musical parties for Rome's dignitaries and nobility Charles sat quietly, radiant with happiness. In April 1787 the Tuscan Envoy reported: 'The Count of Albany was openly insulted by the Marchese Vivaldi, owing to which the Marchese was arrested by the troops in the Theatre of the Valle, and by order of the Pontiff was imprisoned in Castel Sant'Angelo; he was liberated through the request of the Count of Albany'. Ill, old and badly stooped, the man who once kissed Cluny Macpherson 'as an equal' was back; who, after Prestonpans, when his prisoners broke parole, granted it to them a second time; who, after Falkirk, refused to let his officers cut the musket thumb off the right hands of the captured enemy; and who, in September 1745, wrote to his father about 'the errors and excesses of my grandfather's unhappy reign'.

Having won over Henry, Charlotte not only brought the two brothers together again, but also returned Charles into the bosom of the Church. Then she managed the unthinkable. Since 1785 Charlotte had been relaying back to her mother words of tenderness from Charles. And on January 3rd, 1787 Charles wrote to Clementina:

Although I have charged my dear daughter, the Duchess of Albany, to tell you how much I was moved by your letter of the 18th of the past month, I cannot refrain from indicating also my sincere gratitude. The prayers that you address to Heaven, the wishes that you make for my happiness and felicity I believe most sincere, and it seems that they may be realized since I enjoy perfect health, and hope in return that you may always be in the same state. My dear daughter, the Duchess of Albany, is also at this moment in the best of health. The sweetness of her nature, her good qualities, and her amiable companionship diminish greatly the pains and inconveniences that are indispensably joined to my aged condition. Rest assured that I love her, and that I shall love her with all my heart, and that I am and shall be your good friend,

Charles R.

With Rome's black associations forgotten, and no return to Florence planned, Charles and Charlotte spent the summer months at the Palazzo Savelli at Albano where a small theatre was opened for them. Visitors came in droves. Not all were tactful. The ironically named dramatist, Robert Greatheed, pushed his reluctant host to tell him about the Rising:

> For a brief moment the Prince was no longer the ruin of himself, but again the hero of the 'Forty-Five. His eyes brightened, he half rose from his chair, his face became lit up with unwonted anima-tion, and he began the narrative of his campaign. He spoke with fiery energy of his marches, his victories, the loyalty of his Highland followers, his retreat from Derby, the defeat at Culloden, his escape, and then passionately entered upon the awful penalties so many had been called upon to pay for their devotion to his Cause. But the recollection of so much bitter suf-fering – the butchery around Inverness, the executions at Carlisle and London, the scenes on Kennington Common and Tower Hill – was stronger than his strength could bear. His voice died in his throat, his eyes became fixed, and he sank upon the floor in con-vulsions. Alarmed at the noise, his daughter rushed into the room, 'Oh Sir! What is this? You must have been speaking to my father about Scotland and the Highlanders! No-one dares to mention those subjects in his presence'.

At last Charles's strength began to ebb away. But at least he had the grim consolation of outliving the British Minister who for decades had relentlessly monitored his every move. For Sir Horace Mann died in Florence in November 1786. As James Lees-Milne put it: 'more than a year before the wretched victim of his acidulated pen'. Having been suffering from recurrent dropsy, Charles returned with Charlotte from Albano in the Autumn of 1787 by which time Charles was lapsing into

115

unconciousness and would pass the time lying on a couch with his favourite dog. On January 7th, 1788 he suffered a major stroke which paralysed him down one side. It was the first of a series which attacked him as he lay in semi-conciousness for the next three weeks. Finally he could take no more. The Irish Franciscans of Saint Isidore gave him the Last Rites and on the 30th of that month he joined his comrades with whom the romantics regretted he had not fallen on Drummossie Moor in 1746. In the Highlands the Gaelic poet, William Ross, wrote the last genuine Jacobite song. It was called *An Suathneas Ban* after the Stuarts' White Rose:

> *Soraidh bhuan do'n t-Suaithneas Bhan*
> *Gu latha luain cha ghluais o'n bhas*
> *Ghlac an uaigh an Suaithneas Ban*
> *Is leacan fuaraidh tuaim a thamh.*[5]

Six altars were erected in the antechamber and two hundred Masses were said, a cast was made of Charles's face and his body was embalmed and placed in a coffin of cypress wood with the Orders of St. Andrew and St. George on his breast. Throughout the thirty hours before Charles's body was removed, the Irish Franciscans chanted the office of the dead. The Pope, however, despite Henry's efforts, refused to bury him in the same style as his father. So Henry had his brother's body carried on a litter to Frascati where it lay in royal robes, sword by his side, crown on head, sceptre in hand and the great seal on his finger. On his coffin was the inscription: 'Carolus III Magnae Britanniae Rex'. In tears, Henry celebrated High Mass before 'a very great crowd of people, largely foreigners and the Nobility, who when the service was over were in the Sacristy to cordially compliment the Duchess who was found there with the Cardinal Carandini'. The entombment followed the next day. On the third a requiem. Some time later the coffin was removed and placed in the crypt of St. Peter's with the coffins of his mother and father.

In February Gustav III of Sweden learnt of Charles's death. Straight away he sent a masonic emissary to Rome who obtained from Charlotte the latin document drawn up five years earlier in which Charles promised Gustav the formal transfer of the grand mastership

---

[5] A long farewell to the white rose, Till the day of doom it'll not move from the state of death, The grave has taken the White Cockade, And cold ashes form the tomb in which he rests.

of the masonic Knights Templar. To this day it remains the prized possession of the Swedish Grand Lodge.[6]

Charlotte's father was dead, but in his last three and half years he had enjoyed greater peace, contentment and fulfilment than at any time since Derby in December 1745. His thirty-four-year-old daughter, who had been the authoress of this happy twilight, who had suffered so much beforehand, surely deserved some measure of relief from the ill star that had hung over her family for so long. Yet during Charles's last months of life her letters to Paris had steadily grown more anxious and she longed to be reunited with her mother. Would her children recognise her? Did Ferdinand still love her? Had he found another? Would she see any of them again? Her alarm was caused by malignant cancer of the liver. Barely a soul knew of it. For, apart from her mother, she never complained until she could conceal it no longer.

In Florence Charles had revealed his belief that the only hope for the Stuart Cause lay with his daughter to whom he had granted the Right of Succession. He had designed four versions of a medal of honour, one side of which depicted Charlotte herself, whilst for the other there were four alternate versions. One portrayed the Figure of Hope pointing to a crown with the legend: *Spem juvat amplecti, quae non juvat irrita semper.* The second was of Charlotte with one arm pointing towards the Stuart arms and her eyes gazing at an empty throne alongside the inscription: *Spem etsi infinitam persequar.* The remaining two were along the same lines. Notwithstanding, Henry at once transformed his ducal coronet into a royal crown, struck a commemorative medal as Henry IX, instructed his household to address him henceforth as 'Your Majesty' and signed his letters with the prefix *denominato*, signifying that he continued to call himself the Cardinal of York only for the sake of convenience. He even published a proclamation to underline that it was he who had inherited his brother's rights. Charlotte showed no sign of protest. But at least the Pope granted her the right to use the Royal Tribune at St. Peter's. In any case she had far more serious problems. For her cancer was incurable and its pain was growing worse each day. She also had to deal with the legal consequences of her father's death. And though she had inherited her father's estate, nevertheless it was not enormous. Furthermore, the French and Papal annuities had ceased with his death and the jointure under Charles's separation settlement with his estranged wife, Louise, had to be paid. What

---

[6] M.K. Schuchard, *The Young Pretender and Jacobite Freemasonry ...*, op. cit.

remained was an annual pension of 20,000 livres which the French court granted Charlotte, as well as the palace in Florence with all its contents. This she sold with all its furniture to the Duke di San Clemente, clearing all financial obligations to her stepmother by passing over to her the proceeds. All the family portraits, plate and jewels, valued at £26,740 were sent to Rome. Most had come from the Sobieskis and were described as: 'Many precious ornaments that belonged to King John of Poland, especially those acquired by him at the deliverance of Vienna from the Turks and the Grand Vizier who commanded them, being arms and armaments from his tent'.

With the Florentine palace gone and the tenure of the Palazzo Muti terminated, Henry now made available to Charlotte a fine suite of rooms in the Cancellaria. To this he added three rents from French properties amounting to 8,750 livres per annum from which Charles had previously benefited, as well as his £2,200 cardinal's allowance. In return she made over to him the Crown Jewels (now at Edinburgh Castle). With this much-needed income Charlotte was able to continue supporting her mother and secret family in Paris as well as settle the various legacies her father had made which in total exceeded the potential of the assets she had inherited. Thereafter, Charlotte spent much of her time in Henry's company, as his diaries record, sometimes singing to him after dinner. She also stood Godmother at Countess Mary Norton's confirmation at Frascati, the latter being a member of Charlotte's modest court which also included Monsignor Stonor, the young and bright Duke of Berwick and the distinguished and intellectual Cardinal Consalvi.

In March 1789 she sent a new portrait of herself to Ferdinand de Rohan. But her feelings at the time must have been deeply influenced by her health which was continuing to deteriorate. As early as June 1786 she had written to her mother: 'I have a swelling on my side which pains me when I breathe'. On January 11th, 1788, during her father's last days, she was 'unable to leave her bed owing to her wretched state of health [...] For the lady this was a cause of great affliction, the more so that until this morning her father's illness had been concealed from her'. A day later she 'was in bed afflicted with the constant torment of hernicrania, the sharp pain being much worse at night than by day. Distress at her father's illness and being unable to help him sensibly increased her trouble'. On November 29th 'the Duchess of Albany was suffering from fever and a cold, and pains about the waist and chest for which she had been bled, and again this morning. Doctor Mora feared it was the beginning of a serious illness'. Finally, in the Summer of

1789, her doctors ordered her to take the waters at Nocera in Umbria. It did her little good. In early October she moved to Bologna, considered the best centre of medicine and surgery in Italy. On the 10th of that month she wrote to Clementina: 'Don't worry. I am well; I love you and will send you news as soon as possible'. She also asked her mother to 'kiss my dear friends for me'.

In Bologna she stayed at the Palazzo Vizani which belonged to her friend, the Marchesa Giulia Lambertini-Bovio, who wrote to Henry:

> She has had a very serious relapse with terrible chills and a high fever. The doctors in treating the wound have drawn off a great quantity of matter of very bad colour and odour, whilst her pulse is very far above normal. I cannot sufficiently express my anxiety.

On November 13th she wrote again:

> I must tell you the fever increases every moment, so that we fear to lose her very shortly. My Lord, the Cardinal Archbishop[7] remains constantly with her, nor does he mean to leave her bedside so long as she is alive.

A day later:

> The doctors are confirmed in their opinion that this is a fever of re-absorption, and therefore of a fatal type. Her resignation continues unaltered in the face of imminent danger, and she has already put her Will into the hands of the Cardinal Archbishop.

Three days later, on November 17th, the Marchesa informed Henry that Charlotte had:

> passed to the Other Life this evening at nine o'clock. So blessed was her death, that the tears I pour out from grief are tears of tenderness.

Charlotte had made her will that same day. She asked to be buried in the Church of San Biagio as simply as possible. She was thirty six. Her friends called her 'the angel of peace' and 'her father's guardian angel'. Her detractors accused her of shallowness, resentful that she

---

[7] Cardinal Andrea Giovanetti, Archbishop of Bologna.

wrote to her mother of girlish things such as the latest fashions in Paris. How quickly were forgotten her long years of denial. But, though neither political nor military, none can deny her extraordinary achievements at the human level. Henry held a grand memorial service at Frascati and a few months later, in August 1790, came and prayed at her graveside. Seven years later the Church was closed by the French and pulled down. In 1801 the bodies from San Biagio were reinterred in the Certosa. But the Duchess's name was not amongst them. Where her remains lie nobody knows. Her memorial stone was reset into the pavement of the adjoining Trinità. Some time later it was removed and has since disappeared. In her will Charlotte remembered everyone, including her negro page. But she could not write openly of her three secret children. To her mother she left 50,000 francs and, meaningfully, 'any of her necessitous relatives'. The rest of her property went to Henry on condition that he continued paying her mother's allowance. Amongst the objects he inherited were the Garter jewel worn by Charles I at his execution.

At the time of Charlotte's death the *de jure* King Henry IX was in his mid-sixties. And whilst his hereditary right to the triple throne of Great Britain was now indisputable, he nevertheless became the first Stuart prince to make no attempt to regain it. A childless Roman Catholic cardinal was not acceptable to Protestant England. Henry lived between Rome and the Villa Muti in Frascati[8] until his declining years were interrupted by the French Revolution which lost him his income from that country. Then the Spanish Court stopped their pension to him. Next, in 1796, the Pope squandered the Stuart jewels in a forlorn bribe aimed at keeping Napoleon out of the Papal States. For this purpose Henry sold the great Sobieski ruby for an astonishing £60,000. And in 1798 the invading French Army chased the elderly cardinal out of his rural home and forced him to leave behind everything he cherished, which they then plundered.

In September 1799 Cardinal Borgia sent a letter to Sir John Cox Hippisley in which he said: 'It is very afflicting to me to see so great a personage, the last descendant of a Royal House, reduced to such circumstances'. On February 28th, 1800 the Times newspaper wrote: 'The malign influence of the star which had so strongly marked the fate of so many of his illustrious ancestors was not exhausted and it was

---

[8] Henry had been appointed Bishop of Frascati in 1761 and the Villa Muti there was his favourite country residence.

peculiarly reserved for the Cardinal of York to be exposed to the shafts of adversity at a period of life when least able to struggle with misfortune. At the advanced age of seventy-five he is driven from his episcopal residence, his house sacked, his property confiscated, and constrained to seek his personal safety in flight, upon the seas, under every aggravated circumstance that could affect his health and fortune'. George III responded by granting Henry an allowance of £4,000 a year to be paid through Coutts the banker. Henry replied through Lord Minto: 'I am, in reality, at a loss to express in writing all the sentiments of my heart; and for that reason leave it entirely to the interest you take in all that regards my person to make known in an energetic and convenient manner all I fain would say to express my thankfulness'.

France concluded a concordat with the Vatican in 1801 which permitted the titular King Henry, soon to become Dean of the College of Cardinals, to return to his home for which he commissioned frescoes by the Polish artist, Thadée Kuntze. And with just a little of his elder brother's panache, he used to enjoy himself by galloping at full tilt in his coach and six across the Roman *Campagna*. But whereas Charles had cut off his means of escape in 1745 by sending Antoine Walsh's *du Teillay* back to France, Henry made sure he was always followed by a second, empty coach in case of disaster.

PART TWO

 The Secret

Over the two hundred years since the death of Prince Charles in 1788 and Charlotte, Duchess of Albany in 1789 there has been no shortage of would-be descendants of the last Stuarts. Some have been absurd but colourful, others disturbed fantasies. None have ever produced evidence acceptable to historians. There has only been one exception – Charles, the youngest of Charlotte Stuart's three children by Prince Ferdinand de Rohan. His biography was published in 1960 by Professor George Sherburn who discovered his letters and personal documents and purchased them on April 8th, 1935 in a sale at Sotheby's. Sherburn left them to the Bodleian Library in Oxford where they remain.

From 1784 on, when Charlotte was living with her father in Florence and then in Rome, she wrote to her mother in Paris twice weekly. This correspondence, also in the Bodleian, reveals the existence of Charlotte's two daughters and son. However, 'nothing is known about the two daughters', as the late James Lees-Milne writes in his book *The Last Stuarts*. Which is why others, such as John MacLeod, in *Highlanders*, have assumed that Charlotte's son was 'the last of the line by blood'.[1]

Most of the material which follows is either almost unknown or has never been published before.

---

[1] J. Lees-Milne, *The Last Stuarts*, London 1983; J. MacLeod, *Highlanders*, London 1996.

CHAPTER ELEVEN

From Out of the Mist

*Finally the Stuart Papers found their way to the Royal Archives
at Windsor, where they remain to this day, and are guarded
with astonishing exagerration, as if the dynasty of Windsor
is still somehow threatened by the Stuarts.*

Maria Niemojowska[2]

W hen she went to live with Charles, Charlotte Stuart left her three
'flowers in the garden' to be looked after by their grandmother,
Clementina and her 'worthy friend', Ferdinand de Rohan. It was the
year 1784 and the children barely knew their mother. The eldest was
five and the youngest had been born just a few weeks before. Their
material situation was better than Charlotte's had been, for she regularly sent money from Italy and Ferdinand also supported them.
Nevertheless, practically speaking, they were orphans, hidden from
public view as some unfathomable, political secret. Their single fixed
point was their devoted grandmother, Clementina Walkinshaw, the
much maligned, unsung hero of their mother's upbringing.

Charlotte Stuart's two daughters – Legend and Myth

Until now only the youngest child's story has been known. Concerning
that boy's two elder sisters, there have been just scraps of legend and
hearsay, distorted over the passage of time. The two daughters' dates
of birth have been variously given as between 1778 and 1783. One
claim is that the eldest was called Aglaë and born in 1778 whilst the

---

[2] M. Niemojowska, *Ostatni Stuartowie*, Warsaw 1992, p.293.

second was called Marie and born in 1780.[3] Others state that Aglaë was born in 1780 or 1781 and Marie a couple of years later;[4] or that the daughters were born in 1780 and 1782.[5] In each case the assertion is unsubstatiated.

Aglaë is the only name given in Charlotte's letters and, according to one biographer: 'She seems to have been prone to illness and may not have survived the French Revolution'.[6] However, by the time Charlotte was corresponding from Italy with her mother in Paris she had become intimate with most of the de Rohan family. On May 29th, 1781 Ferdinand's great nephew, Prince Charles de Rohan, married Louise-Aglaë, the daughter of the Marquis Gabriel de Conflans d'Armentières. There is no doubt that Charlotte knew Charles de Rohan's bride. Was this the origin of one of the girls' aliases? For it scarcely seems credible that in deliberately obscuring all the other names connected with Ferdinand and her 'garden', Charlotte should reveal the real name of one of them. The conclusion would be that if the name Aglaë was used openly in Charlotte's letters, then it is the one name that daughter was definitely not called.

Concerning the other daughter, whilst most legends speak of her as Marie,[7] some biographers have claimed she was called Zemire. This is a misunderstanding. In one of Charlotte's letters to Clementina she continues a section devoted to her three 'friends' with the question: 'And how is Zemire'?[8] Elsewhere in her letters Charlotte refers to her three dogs. Their names were Jacquot, Moustache and Zemire.[9] That is not all. In March 1788 Charlotte wrote to her mother: 'You tell me nothing of V. I know that she has been very ill and this news has cruelly worried me'. Then on April 5th: 'You assure me that my dear V. is better. I assure you that this news causes me nothing but joy'.[10] Disguised as a mere initial there seems no reason to doubt that one daughter's name began with V. Yet it is curious how persistent is the name Marie in legend.

In 1977 C.L. Berry wrote: 'Romantic tales have been invented. One relates that Aglaë became Duchess de Bouillon and her sister a teacher

---

[3] E. Cassavetti, *The Lion and the Lilies*, London 1977, p.289.
[4] J. Lees-Milne, *The Last Stuarts*, *op. cit.*, p.229.
[5] M. Forster, *The Rash Adventurer*, London 1973, p.285.
[6] C.L. Berry, *The Young Pretender's Mistress*, London 1977, p.157.
[7] E. Cassavetti, *op. cit.*, p.289; J.Lees-Milne, *op. cit.*, p.229; G. Sherburn, *op. cit.*, p.4.
[8] G. Sherburn, *op. cit.*, p.4.
[9] C.L. Berry, *op. cit.*, p.159.
[10] *Ibid.*, p.156.

in Paris […] It is not difficult to disprove the first, but the same cannot be said for the second'.[11] The genealogy of the Dukes de Bouillon disproves the first claim, not only with regard to the dukes themselves but all other males of that family, both legitimate and legitimised – the latter having also been published.[12] However, it will become apparent that the extraordinary first claim was not invention, but a distortion of the truth.

One confident-sounding but unsubstantiated assertion is that: 'Nothing more was heard about the two Stuart girls beyond the fact that they both died unmarried at the Château de Beaumanoir near Tours. Aglaë died in 1823 and Marie in 1825, and they were buried at St Cyr-sur-Loire'.[13] It is interesting that this claim should pick out Tours, because the Duchy of Montbazon belonging to Ferdinand's eldest brother, Jules-Hercule, lay just south of that town. St. Cyr-sur-Loire is today the north-west suburb of Tours and Beaumanoir is in the nearby Commune de Fondettes, whilst there is another in the more distant Commune de Crotelles. All registers of deaths for these areas are complete, but there is no evidence in them to support this claim. It should therefore be dismissed.[14]

Why hide the children's true identity?

With regard to Charlotte Stuart's three children the whole point was to prevent anyone from ever discovering their true parentage. Such a revelation would have been seized upon by the Hanoverians to whip up a scandal designed to finally kill off the last vestiges of the Stuart Cause. That would have destroyed Charlotte's position as Stuart heiress and ruined her mother and children's prospects as well as Ferdinand de Rohan's. Just as Prince Charles and Clementina Walkinshaw disguised their true identities when they baptised Charlotte, using the aliases Seigneur William Johnson and Dame Charlotte Pitt, so now, with the stakes far higher, will there never be a document explicitly naming Charlotte and Ferdinand as their children's parents.

[11] *Ibid.*, p.207.
[12] *Livre d'Or des Souverains*, Tours 1907, pp.550–552 & 787.
[13] E. Cassavetti, *op. cit.*, p.300.
[14] Archives Départementales d'Indre-et-Loire, Chambray-les-Tours, Commune de St. Cyr-sur-Loire, N.M.D. & Table Décennales; Commune de Fondettes, N.M.D. 1820–1832; Commune de Crotelles, N.M.D. 1793–1836.

Why were the de Rohans predisposed to help?

In unravelling the story of Prince Charles's three grandchildren, several points about the de Rohan family are relevant. As will become clear, Ferdinand's immediate relations knew all about Charlotte and his secret family. In particular, Ferdinand's sister-in-law, Louise (Jules-Hercule's wife), was Charlotte's first cousin once removed and her father's ex-lover. Charlotte and Louise were not only close blood relations but both had been rejected by Charles. It seems probable Louise felt sympathetic towards the traumatic situation of Charlotte's blameless children. Furthermore, during the decades after the exposure of her affair with Charles by Jules-Hercule's mother and her own father, Louise led a quiet life of domestic tranquillity, remaining on the best of terms with her husband, mother-in-law and father till the end. She appears to have been a kind and understanding person.[15] In any case, Louise herself had given birth to an illegitimate boy by Prince Charles. Her own brother, Godefroy-Charles[16] had fathered and recognised three natural children between 1762 and 1767 by Marie Blondin; whilst her nephew, Jacques-Léopold[17] had fathered and recognised a natural son by Marthe Serson in 1775.[18] Illegitimacy, therefore, was not alien to Louise. Nor did it seem to disturb Jules-Hercule who, until the end of his life, remained close to Louise's brother with whom he had been Henry Stuart's ADC in 1745.[19]

After Louise's death in 1781 and their only son Henri's massive 34 million livres bankruptcy a year later,[20] Jules-Hercule became more or less penniless, was hounded by creditors and fell into a depression. It was Louise's brother who provided for him, lending him the Château de Carlsbourg where Jules-Hercule died in December 1788.[21] Jules-Hercule was also considered pliable, so much so that his brothers considered him 'in the pocket'.[22] And in the words of L.L. Bongie: 'Though a military leader of unquestioned bravery he, like Louise, is revealed as dutiful and tender; indeed, his style almost drips with family

---

[15] L.L. Bongie, *op. cit.*, p.282.
[16] Duke de Bouillon from 1771.
[17] Duke de Bouillon from 1792.
[18] *Livre d'Or des Souverains, op. cit.*, p.787.
[19] Louise's brother was still the Prince de Turenne at the time of the 'Forty Five.
[20] Announced of September 30th, 1782.
[21] L.L. Bongie, *op. cit.*, p.285.
[22] E. de Haynin, *op. cit.*, p.137.

sentimentality'.[23] This is evident in a letter to the Duke de Bouillon dated June 17th, 1760, written just six weeks before Clementina's dramatic flight with Charlotte from the Château de Carlsbourg: 'Adieu Cher Papa! Please receive with kindness my most sincere assurances of attachment for our most tender friendship that will not cease except with my death. For a dear father-in-law whom I love in the extreme, The Prince de Rohan'.[24] Finally, the de Rohans were not only related to the Stuarts, but were both anglophile[25] and of legendary clan solidarity.[26]

The First Evidence – Charlotte Stuart's Daughter 'Marie' or 'V'

Jules-Hercule's Duchy of Montbazon was centred upon the Parish of Veigné just south of Tours. His three times great-grandfather, Hercule de Rohan, became Duke de Montbazon, married Madeleine de Lenoncourt, then Marie of Brittany and built the Château de Couzières which still overlooks Montbazon from the north-east. There, in 1619, Hercule had orchestrated the reconciliation of the Stuarts' ancestress, Marie de Medici, with her son, Louis XIII. Then, in November 1645, as governor of Paris, Hercule had bidden farewell to the future Queen Marie-Casimire Sobieska when she left Paris as a young girl in the retinue of King Ladislas of Poland's bride, Marie de Gonzague. And it was at the Château de Couzières that Hercule died in 1654. A century later, on March 2nd, 1781, the property was sold as part of a string of Loire Valley sales by Jules-Hercule and his son. Until then it had been the summer residence of the Dukes de Montbazon together with the Château de Sainte-Maure some ten miles further south.[27] A more modest but much older property than Couzières, the Château de Thorigny which lies on Montbazon's north-west flank, was bought on February 20th, 1757 by Jules-Hercule from François Ferrand de la Bastèrie and sold on July 13th, 1781.[28] On the other

---

[23] L.L. Bongie, *op. cit.*, p.283.

[24] *Ibid.*, p.284.

[25] E. de Haynin, *op. cit.*, p.51.

[26] *Ibid.*, p.43 & 138.

[27] J.X. Carré de Busserolle, *Dictionnaire Géographique d'Indre-et-Loire*, 1883, Couzières; *Nouvelle Biographie Générale, op. cit.*, vol.42, p.523. For the rest of the year Jules-Hercule's residences were either the Château de Saint-Ouen, now in the suburbs of Paris; a part of the Tuilleries overlooking the rue de Rivoli which is still called the *Pavillon de Rohan*; or his principal mansion, the Hôtel de Rohan-Montbazon at 29, rue du Faubourg St. Honoré near the Elysée Palace.

[28] J.X. Carré de Busserolle, *op. cit.*, Thorigny; L.Vieira, *Le Château de Thorigny*, Tours 1997.

hand, Jules-Hercule and his son acquired the vast Château d'Ussé on February 19th, 1780 – though it too was sold in the aftermath of Henri's bankruptcy, on July 5th, 1785.[29]

Charlotte Stuart's two daughters are generally accepted as having been born around the year 1780 and one of them had the name 'Marie', 'V.' or 'Marie-V.' At that time Charlotte's uncle Jules-Hercule was fifty-six years old and his only child Henri had been born no less than thirty-four years earlier. On June 19th, 1779, in the chapel of the Château de Couzières, Jules-Hercule signed the following document:

> On the nineteenth of June in the year Seventeen Hundred and Seventy Nine was baptised, with the sub-condition by us the under-signed, Marie, born yesterday, the natural daughter of the very high and powerful and very excellent Prince Jules-Hercule, Prince de Rohan-Guéméné, Duke de Montbazon, Peer of France, Lieutenant-General of the King's Armies, who has come in person to recognise her by the present act which he has signed with us, and by which he has named her the demoiselle de Thorigny; and of Mademoiselle Marie Grosset; the Godfather was the lord Simon Pierre Cevest de la Clémencerie; and the Godmother Mademoiselle Victoire Jeanne Wallin, the wife of the said lord Cevest, the steward of my said lord, who has signed with us.
>
> Jules-Hercule, Prince de Rohan   Cevest de la Clémencerie[30]

By this act Ferdinand's eldest brother, the head of the de Rohans, baptised and legitimised as his own a baby girl called Marie. And her godmother's name began with V. It was common practice at the time for a child to be given its godparent's name – Marie being so universal in Roman Catholic France that it was often dropped for the more individual second name. This infant would therefore have been formally called Marie, though more familiarly, Victoire. In this book she is described as Marie-Victoire[31]. As a consequence of her baptismal act

---

[29] J.X. Carré de Busserolle, *op. cit.*, Ussé. The Ussé estate and château was sold for 902,000 livres.

[30] Archives Départementales d'Indres-et-Loire, Chambray-les-Tours, Commune de Veigné, N.M.D., Table pour l'an 1779, naissances, nr 35, Marie THORIGNY naturel.

[31] To give another example: when Jules-Hercule's wife was a girl she had the title, la demoiselle d'Auvergne and the first names Marie-Louise. She was known, however, as Louise. After her marriage she usually signed herself 'Louise de la Tour d'Auvergne, Princesse de Rohan, Duchesse de Montbazon'; Livre d'Or des Souverains, *op. cit.*, p.551; L.L. Bongie, *op. cit.*, pp.186 & 269. The title 'la demoiselle de …' was a title given to chosen daughters of such pre-eminent

the legitimised girl enjoyed exactly the same legal rights of inheritance from Jules-Hercule as his only child, Henri. Having been legitimised by a sovereign prince her correct style was 'Princess Marie de Rohan-Guémené, the demoiselle de Thorigny'. In the custom of the day this would have been abbreviated to de Rohan-Thorigny or de Thorigny.[32]

It is also worth noting the other actors in this vignette: the 'mother' was Mademoiselle Grosset, the daughter of Jules-Hercule's castellan at Couzières; Monsieur Cevest de la Clémencerie was Jules-Hercule's steward or personal secretary; and the godmother was Monsieur Cevest's wife.[33] More subservient people would have been hard to find.

Equally, it was a rarity for the Dukes de Montbazon to legitimise natural children. The previous case was in 1691 when Jules-Hercule's grandfather, Duke Charles III, baptized a natural son with the title 'le Sieur de Narbonne' after a manor belonging to him at Joué-les-Tours. Earlier, a natural son called François had been given the title 'le Sieur de Boistoneau' on September 7th, 1634. And on April 3rd, 1619 a boy was legitimised by Duke Louis VIII who granted him the title of 'le Sieur du Verger' after a de Rohan castle in the Commune de Seiches-en-Anjou.[34] In each of these three cases the legitimised child was a boy and the father a young man. Moreover, all are recorded in genealogical almanacs.[35]

footnote 31 (*cont.*)

    families. Of those born during the 18th century only three other de Rohan princesses were thus distinguished: Louise, la demoiselle de Rohan (1765–1839), Marie-Louise, la demoiselle de Guémené (1728–1737) and Charlotte-Louise, la demoiselle de Rohan (1722–1786); G. Martin, *Histoire et Généalogie de la Maison de Rohan*, Lyon 1998, pp.63–78.

[32] Had the de Rohans been granted their princely title by a sovereign then Marie-Victoire would only have had the right to that title with the formal consent of that ruling house. However, the de Rohans had been recognised as direct descendants of the ancient Kings of Brittany in 1080 by the Duke of Brittany, in 1420 by Duke Jean V of Brittany, in 1457 by Duke Artus III of Brittany and in 1748 by the Estates General of Brittany. Likewise were they acknowledged by the Kings of France – in 1549 by Charles IX, then Henri III, Louis XIII in 1626 and then in 1667 and 1692 by Louis XIV who declared that the House of Rohan was to be treated equally with the Houses of Savoy and Lorraine, whilst Louis XV described the de Rohans as: 'Princes of a Sovereign House'. In 1501 they were recognised by the Vatican, in 1602 by the King of Sweden, in 1629 by the King of Spain and later by the ruling Houses of Saxony, Hesse and Württemberg. They held the status of 'Sovereign Princes resident in France' thereby distinguishing them from mere French dukes and non-royal princes. The de Rohan princely title was 'granted by the grace of God' and Jules-Hercule's sovereign status meant that he needed no-one else's consent for Marie-Victoire to automatically enjoy the title of princess upon legitimisation. Whether or not she was aware of her legitimised status is unclear. It appears she was not, for later she assumed the title '*la Comtesse de Thorigny*'. My thanks to Monsieur Georges Martin, author of *Histoire et Généalogie de la Maison de Rohan*, for his opinion on the above.

[33] L. Vieira, *op. cit.*

[34] *Ibid.*; G. Martin, *op. cit.*, p.51.

[35] *Livre d'Or des Souverains, op. cit.*, p.787.

Significantly, no Duke de Montbazon nor head of the de Rohans had ever legitimised a natural daughter before Marie-Victoire. If she was so important as to warrant such a thing, why is there no later trace of her as Jules-Hercule's daughter in any almanac, memoir or archive? And as her 'mother' was only a member of Jules-Hercule's household at Couzières, what was so special about this 'daughter' anyway? Money was the usual pay-off for an accidental pregnancy, not legitimisation, for that raised the child to the same legal status, with the same rights of inheritance, as legitimate offspring. Its consequences were significant in the extreme. Why also, in the extensive correspondence between Jules-Hercule and his son during the decade following her birth, is there not a single mention of Marie-Victoire? This is extraordinary because almost every letter is partly devoted to the financial implications of Henri and Jules-Hercule's bankruptcy. If Marie-Victoire really was the Jules-Hercule's daughter, and so important as to have been uniquely legitimised, why did neither 'father' nor 'brother' ever write about her either in general or in particular when considering their complex financial problems, which would have directly affected her had she really been Jules-Hercule's daughter[36]? And why was Jules-Hercule never even once described as Marie-Victoire's father in any of her later correspondence nor in any memoir, but a different paternity is given?

Another exceptional factor is that previous de Rohan legitimisations had always been confirmed by the King of France, just as Charles did when he legitimised Charlotte Stuart in 1783. Such was the de Rohans' position at the French court in 1779 that the matter would have been a mere formality. Yet Marie-Victoire's legitimisation by Jules-Hercule was not confirmed by Louis XVI. No legitimisation at all would have suggested that Mademoiselle de Grosset really was the natural mother – for there would have been no reason to bother; whilst for Jules-Hercule to have openly requested Louis' confirmation would have suggested that he was indeed the natural father – for there would have been no reason not to. Why then was everything avoided which might have drawn attention to Marie-Victoire? What was her mysterious importance that warranted all the legal consequences of legitimisation yet demanded such complete discretion?[37]

---

[36] Státni Oblastní Archiv Litoméřice, Pobočka Děčin, Rodinny Archiv Rohanové (hereafter: Archiv Rohanové), Inventař Děčin, 1973, Inv.č.429, k.č.170.

[37] L. Vieira, *op. cit.*; G. Martin, *op. cit.*

Nor does the story end there. Just before mid-day on September 2nd, 1782 another document was signed by Jules-Hercule, this time at the Château d'Ussé:

> Signed before us, the under-signed royal notaries resident at Bourgeuil, is a settlement of the very high and powerful lord, his Highness Jules-Hercule, Prince de Rohan and de Guéméné, Duke de Montbazon, Peer of France, Lieutenant-General of the King's Armies, living at his Château of Ussé, by which, wanting to recognise the services that Mademoiselle Marie Grosset de Villeneuve, living at the said Ussé, has rendered him and for his sincere attachment for her over several years and to ensure a commodious and honest life, gives her and constitutes by way of an irrevocable donation, in the best form that he can, the sum of three thousand livres as a life annuity [...] The first payment will fall due here between three and six months and the second six months after and as such will continue from term to term until the death of the said Mademoiselle de Grosset at which point the annuity will be extinct and amortised, which the said Mademoiselle Grosset, here present, has accepted, thanking very humbly his Highness for his benevolence and reward.

Jules-Hercule, Prince de Rohan   Marie Grosset de Villeneuve
Beauvallet, royal notary   Ruelle, royal notary[38]

Striking is the fact that there is no provision for, nor any mention of, a child. Yet this 'reward' for 'services rendered' is a life annuity which explicitly ceases with Miss Grosset's death. If Marie-Victoire was really her child, to be brought up by her, why would Jules-Hercule leave the self-evidently important Marie-Victoire destitute in the event of the premature death of her 'mother'? The eighteenth century was hardly safe and disease-free. If, however, Marie-Victoire was to be brought up by her 'father' why is there no trace of her being with Jules-Hercule at any later date? After all, Marie-Victoire was now a recognised member of the de Rohan family. It makes no sense. Unless, of course, Jules-Hercule and the daughter of his castellan were only standing in for the real parents. And Charlotte Stuart's natural daughter, 'Marie', 'V.' or

---

[38] Archives Départementales d'Indre-et-Loire, Centre des Archives Historiques, Tours, Insinuations des Donations, Généralité de Tours, C855, 1782, p.13/14, (original dated September 2nd, 1782, minuted November 16th, 1782); L. Vieira, *op. cit.*

'Marie-V.' by Ferdinand de Rohan, born circa 1780, was one and the same as Marie, god-daughter of Victoire, who was so discreetly baptised on June 19th, 1779 in the remote Parish of Veigné in the exclusive company of her uncle's employees. Does Charlotte's letter, apparently referring to her third child's wet-nursing 'in the country', not echo the events at the rural Château de Couzières? Indeed, would it not have been eminently wise of Charlotte to have spent her confinement there, rather than in central Paris where she was well known and her pregnancy might have been discovered? And in legitimising Marie-Victoire, did Jules-Hercule not formally bring her into the same family to which she would have in any case belonged if not for the extraordinary political circumstances of which Charlotte Stuart was victim?

First homes

After completing the magnificent bishops' palace at Bordeaux, the forty-two-year-old Ferdinand was elevated to the richer Archbishopric of Cambrai in February 1781. Though he delegated its administration to his auxiliary, Bishop d'Amycles, nevertheless he had to spend some time there, not least because of the superb gardens he was having laid out. Instead Ferdinand was mainly based in Paris where he had a house on the rue du Regard and another in Auteuil, or in the Hôtel de Rohan on the rue Vieille du Temple. For Charlotte, her children and mother, Ferdinand provided a house on the rue St. Jacques adjacent to her convent, as well as a country house at Anthony. It was in these homes that Charlotte's three children were brought up until the outbreak of the French Revolution. One wonders what Ferdinand had in mind in 1790 when despairing of his Church career: 'With my brother-in-law much regarded by the King of Spain, I should have probably entered that service: I should have had real advantages and honours – not to mention an advantageous marriage such as perhaps I might have made'.[39]

Further Evidence – Charlotte Stuart's Other Daughter and Son

One document suggests that Charlotte's other daughter was born in Paris during or after the Summer of 1780 but before November 28th.

---

[39] H. Sage, *Une République de Trois Mois: le Prince de Rohan-Guéméné*, Verviers 1909, p.251.

24 King Charles I with the future King James VII & II as Duke of York

25 King John III Sobieski with Queen Marie-Casimire and their children (l. to r.), Princes Constantine, Alexander and James with his wife, Princess Hedwig Elisabeth of Bavaria-Neuburg holding their daughter Marie-Léopoldine, and Princess Thérèse Sobieska

26 *James VIII and III*

27 *Princess Clementina Sobieska. This portrait of 1740 by Louis Stern served as the model for the mosaic on Clementina's tomb in St. Peter's.*

28 Prince Charles (mid-1748). This portrait, for which Charles paid 1,200 livres, he gave to Marie-Anne Jabłonowska, Princess de Talmont.

29 *Charlotte Stuart, Duchess of Albany*

30 *Marie-Victoire, the demoiselle de Thorigny (c. 1800)*

31 Antime, Chevalier de Nikorowicz (c. 1825)

32 Countess Julia Thérèse Pinińska née de Nikorowicz, 1864. (She is in mourning after the failure of the 1863 uprising.)

33 Professor, Count Leon Piniński (c. 1905)

34 Count Mieczyslas Piniński (1925)

However, no second baptism took place in the Parish of Veigné during this period.[40] In March 1783 came Prince Charles's major health scare when he took the decision to make Charlotte his sole heir, legitimise her and create her 'HRH the Duchess of Albany'. But he neither informed her of this nor sent for her until after he recovered from his second crisis. It wasn't until July 17th, 1784 that he sent his 'Master of the Household' John Stewart to Paris. Yet Charlotte did not leave straightaway for Florence. She arrived there only on October 5th, almost three months later. The reason for her delay was because she had recently given birth to a son. In 1816, that boy wrote that he had been born in Italy on June 11th, 1784.[41] But at that time he had every reason to conceal his true place and date of birth, for his baptismal entry inevitably contained false identities for his mother and father. That document, described in detail in the next chapter, states that Charlotte's son was born and baptised in Paris on May 13th, 1784. Such a date ties in with Charlotte's letter to Clementina dated March 25th, 1785 suggesting his wet-nursing should come to an end.[42] Moreover, that his wet-nursing took place 'in the country' also ties in with an astonishing extract from the memoirs of the great-nephew of Abbé Barnabé, the parish priest of the same Veigné where Marie-Victoire had been baptised. It relates to an incident in which Jules-Hercule again plays the central role, which occurred about the time of the birth of Charlotte's son:

> The Prince de Rohan arrived therefore at the Church in Veigné and presented the newly born boy as his natural son [...] My great-uncle agreed to baptise the child, but absolutely refused to register him under the name of the Prince. He, however, being used to wielding power, and because of the violence of his character, threatened the priest, imagining he could intimidate him; but the latter resisted firmly. He declared that there is no power in the world that can make him act against his conscience, and that he will never dirty one of the best and most ancient names of France, by a written proof of a relationship disapproved of by the Church [...] The Prince, astonished and furious at this sign of

---

[40] Archives de l'Etat à Huy, Archives Générales du Royaume et Archives de l'Etat dans les Provinces, death cert. for Charlotte Cousin de la Morlière née Roehenstart, deceased at Huy on November 26th, 1806, registered at Huy on November 28th, 1806.

[41] G. Sherburn, *op. cit.*, p.16.

[42] *Ibid.*, p.9; E. Cassavetti, *op. cit.*, p.293; see also ch.10.

resistance, so forgot himself as to threaten to have his men seize the old priest and take him to the dungeons of his castle. The curate replied with still greater force that he is master in his place of worship, just as the Prince is in his gilded salons; then, with the greatest dignity, added: 'Go! Go! I fear neither your men nor your threats! As a priest, I must give the water of baptism to this child, but as a man of honour, I will never dirty such a great name with the fruit of debauchery – and perhaps intrigue!' These last words, said with such vehemence, produced an effect on the Prince such as would lightning. He withdrew immediately with all his following, ordering that the newly-born child be baptised as the son of an unknown father. This matter reverberated around the entire province, and the honourable family of de Bouillon addressed their sincerest congratulations to my great-uncle [...] Some time later, the Prince himself visited the priest and, without betraying the slightest resentment for what had happened, was happy enough to tell him, as he shook his hand: 'You are a minister worthy of the Lord'.[43]

This description is a transparent glorification of Abbé Barnabé by his great-nephew. Hence the vilification of the near sixty-year-old Jules-Hercule. The content, however, is striking. And, though there is no record in the perfectly preserved parish registers of any natural child having been baptised during this period, it is inconceivable that the story was pure invention. Several aspects are worthy of note. Jules-Hercule had earlier organised Marie-Victoire's baptismal legitimisation at Veigné with, apparently, no questions asked. Yet though he no longer owned the Château de Couzières nor any other in the parish, it was to Veigné he returned to try and do the same for her brother. It is also explicit that Jules-Hercule wanted not merely to baptise, but to formally recognise and therefore legitimise the child, exactly as in the case of Marie-Victoire. Yet that was not the cause of Abbé Barnabé's protest. Nor was the fact of the child's illegitimacy. Those were not grounds for refusal – as was evident from Marie-Victoire's baptism. What caused this lowly parish priest to challenge one of the most powerful men in France was Abbé Barnabé's conviction that Jules-Hercule was lying about the child's real identity – his key accusation being: 'intrigue!'. That speaks volumes about what he must have heard from

---

[43] C.-L. Bouilly, *Les Récapitulations*, Paris 1840, vol.1, pp.91–95.

local gossip subsequent to Marie-Victoire's baptism in 1779 and Mademoiselle de Grosset's 'pay-off' in 1782. It is also noticeable that Jules-Hercule not only conspicuously failed to push his case, but beat a suspiciously hasty retreat for a general, and then later tried to humour his opponent.

It is possible that Charlotte's son was whisked off to Paris to be baptised under an invented surname as the son of fictitious parents as a consequence of the event at Veigné. But it is probable that prior to his wet-nursing 'in the country' he had indeed been born in Paris and, as his baptismal entry states, baptised on that same day of May 13th, 1784, for if a child appeared weak at birth it was customary for baptism to take place immediately. As both his name and those of his parents as well as their address were all false, the existence of that almost worthless baptismal entry did not stand in the way of an attempt by Jules-Hercule to baptismally legitimise Charlotte's son at Veigné, thereby giving him the legal status and enormous prestige of a de Rohan as well as formally making him a member of the family of his natural father. If this had been worth doing for a daughter, Marie-Victoire, how much more important it must have seemed for a son. That Charlotte was in direct contact with Jules-Hercule is demonstrated by the fact that even as late as February 26th, 1788 he was told by his son, Henri: 'I shall send you the letter of Madame la Duchesse d'Albanie whose address is at Rouen'.[44]

The 1780s – On the Eve of Revolution

In the autumn of 1784 Charlotte left her three children in Paris with their grandmother, Clementina, and went to live with Charles in Florence. Time moved inexorably towards the two momentous events of their mother's premature death and the French Revolution. In April 1785 Clementina took her grandchildren to the country house at Anthony for the summer. It was there that Charlotte addressed her letters. They usually spent the remainder of each year at the house on the rue St. Jacques where the children lived innocent but parentless lives in the shadow of the events of the 1780's which affected their relatives.

Fate was no shorter on drama for the de Rohans than it was for the Stuarts during that decade. In 1781 Jules-Hercule's wife Louise died.

---

[44] Archiv Rohanové, Inv.č.418–429, k.č.170. By 'address' Henri was referring to Charlotte's forwarding address.

On May 4th, 1782 Berthe de Rohan was born. She was the daughter of Charles, grand-daughter of Henri, and great-grand-daughter of Jules-Hercule and Louise.[45] On September 30th that year Henri's massive 34 million livres bankruptcy was announced making European-wide news. However, Henri's children were saved by the vast fortune of their mother, Princess Victoire de Rohan-Soubise who was the last of her line.[46] In March 1784, Ferdinand's second eldest brother, Armand, Prince de Montbazon, was promoted to the rank of Vice-Admiral after his return from the American War of Independence. Then on August 15th, 1785 the third of the four de Rohan brothers, Cardinal Louis, was arrested at Versailles by Louis XVI for the *Affaire du Collier de la Reine* and imprisoned in the Bastille. As the shock waves reverberated around Europe the de Rohan clan flocked to support their relation. At the same time the population of Paris began to sympathise with the cardinal, believing the king to be arrogantly disregarding the law and the queen to be in any case evil. Electing to be tried by Parliament, the cardinal was wise enough to conduct himself with uncharacteristic modesty, found innocent and released. Nevertheless Louis XVI exiled him to Strasbourg where he remained until the outbreak of the Revolution.

1788 saw mutual distrust creep into Charlotte and Ferdinand's twelve-year-old relationship. He had become jealous of Charles's ambitious matches for Charlotte and she reacted in the same way when he tried to provoke her with courtesans.[47] Unaware of the legal problems after Charles's death, as well as Charlotte's declining health, Ferdinand tried to pressurise her into an early return to Paris, talking of their children's future and telling her 'to remember her obligations'.[48] Writing to her mother, Charlotte said firmly: 'I have replied to him that I know the full extent of them, and that I will gladly, in that matter, walk in his footsteps'.[49] Friction spilled over into the area of money. By Spring 1788 Charlotte was warning her mother not to let Ferdinand know how much she had been receiving in Paris since 1786 via the Stuarts' bankers, M.M.Busoni & Co.[50] This occurred in the context of an argument as to who would pay for the renewal of the lease

---

[45] Berthe and Marie-Victoire were almost exactly the same age. Yet, if Marie-Victoire had really been Berthe's great grandfather's daughter, then she would have been her great aunt!

[46] Together with her sister, Princess Charlotte, the wife of Louis de Bourbon, Prince de Condé.

[47] G. Sherburn, *op. cit.*, p.8; E. Cassavetti, *op. cit.*, p.297.

[48] E. Cassavetti, *op. cit.*, p.298.

[49] G. Sherburn, *op. cit.*, p.8.

[50] E. Cassavetti, *op. cit.*, p.297; F. Skeet, *H.R.H. Charlotte Stuart, Duchess of Albany*, London 1932, pp.96–97 & 148–149.

on the rue St. Jacques house. Charlotte finally wrote to Clementina: 'I am renewing the lease for only three years because I hope very much that before then we shall be reunited, and then the prolongation would be embarrassing [...] My friend has notified me that he has paid the rent. I replied that I hoped he would pay it as a good father. I don't know how pleasing that proposition may be'.[51] Ferdinand couldn't understand why, with his relatively limited resources, he had to pay for everything. He also presumed Charlotte to have inherited a much larger fortune than was the case and wrote openly suggesting that she pay for 'our friends'. But Charlotte refused.[52] Despite such misunderstandings she sent Ferdinand a new portrait of herself in March 1789[53] and then helped him become Prince-Coadjutor of Liège[54] by obtaining a recommendation for him from the King of Prussia whose army had just driven the Austrians out of that principality.[55]

One small incident from this period was Charlotte's request to her mother that she introduce a young English traveller to her friend 'the Princess de Rohan' in Paris. Clementina Walkinshaw was evidently intimate not only with Ferdinand but also the rest of his family.[56] Charlotte was almost certainly referring to Louise-Aglaë, the wife of Jules-Hercule's grandson, Charles.[57]

One other relationship was formed during the 1780s which would prove crucial to Clementina and her grandchildren. The London-based court banker of Scottish origin, Thomas Coutts, was a distant relative of the Walkinshaws and was invited with his family to come and stay at Ferdinand's houses in Paris and Liège.[58] In 1788 his daughters were placed in a Parisian convent to improve their French and Clementina was asked to act as chaperon.[59] Coutts also put Clementina in touch with a number of his international financial contacts who could assist her in his absence.[60] In 1789 help was desperately needed, for in July the Bastille was stormed by the Paris mob. It was the beginning of the French Revolution in which parliament was hijacked, the king was caught trying

[51] G. Sherburn, *op. cit.*, p.9.
[52] *Ibid.*
[53] E. Cassavetti, *op. cit.*, p.299.
[54] A ruling position analogous to his brother Louis' sovereign bishopric of Strasbourg.
[55] G. Sherburn, *op. cit.*, p.8.
[56] E. Cassavetti, *op. cit.*, p.299.
[57] *Livre d'Or des Souverains, op. cit.*, p.623.
[58] G. Sherburn, *op. cit.*, p.9.
[59] C.L. Berry, *op. cit.*, pp.165–166.
[60] *Ibid.*, p.176.

to escape in 1791 and then guillotined in 1793, followed by the Great Terror. Amongst those executed was Ferdinand's second eldest brother, Admiral Armand, who didn't escape when he could, was tried before the Revolutionary Tribunal on July 23rd, 1794 and guillotined the next day.

Charlotte's last weeks of life were agonising. Not only was she dying from cancer but she was beginning to realise she would never see Ferdinand, her mother or children again. From the time her doctors ordered her to take the waters in the Summer of 1789 until her death in late November she must have been enormously worried by the dramatic events unfolding in Paris. She wrote to her mother: 'Our friend must think up a refuge for our friends!' She urged her mother to take her children to Switzerland or even bring them to Rome. But her strength was fading fast.[61] Most nobles were trying to flee France; and not only the French. Princess Elizabeth Lubomirska fled Paris with Count Adalbert Mier on August 12th, making for Lyon. In September she wrote: 'We're all in a state of uncertainty as to what to do. My banker tells me there's no apartment to be had in Nice, everything there is overflowing already. Perhaps I'll go to Marseilles. To spend the Winter in Béziers would be risky. Because if this blaze consumes everything, how would we get out of there? On the other hand, here I can't find teachers for the children [...] In the end, I don't know where I'll go. Perhaps there'll be such a mess in France that one won't know where to turn one's head. In the longer term it's my intention to return to Poland'. Then, writing to Mier on November 17th to recommend the safety of Sardinian Nice, Lubomirska conveyed the panic of these refugee grandees: 'Madame de Talmont is collapsing in the arms of everyone [...] Madame de la Trémouille, her mother-in-law, who was so superior in Paris, now shows a civility that is almost charming [...] Another meeting-place is the salon of Madame de Rohan, to which I often go'.[62]

On the same day, Marchesa Giulia Lambertini-Bovio wrote from Bologna to Henry Stuart in Rome, informing him that his niece had 'passed to the Other Life'. Only a month earlier Charlotte had written to Clementina: 'Don't worry, [...] I love you [...] Kiss my dear friends for me'. But they never saw their mother again.

---

[61] G. Sherburn, *op. cit.*, p.9; E. Cassavetti, *op. cit.*, p.299.
[62] E. Rabowicz, *Poezje zebrane Wojciecha Miera*, Wrocław 1992, pp.40–41. Those mentioned are: Marie, Duchess de la Trémouille (1744–1790), daughter of the Prince von Salm-Kyrbourg; Henriette, Princess de Talmont (+1831), daughter of Count d'Argouges; the identity of the de Rohan princess is unsure; Princess Elizabeth Lubomirska (1736–1816), daughter of Prince August Czartoryski by Marie-Sophie Sieniawska; and Count Adalbert Mier (1759–1831).

CHAPTER TWELVE

The Dying Years

Maman told me to love You and I do it very much.
I shall be happy if I can obtain your protection,
for I am a good boy,

Your respectful nephew, Charles
Munich, January 1st 1799.

By the end of the Great Terror, those of Ferdinand's immediate family who survived, apart from himself and Charlotte's three children, were his brother, Cardinal Louis, and their nephew, Henri, who had succeeded Jules-Hercule as Duke de Montbazon and Prince de Guéméné. Henri had four children of whom the eldest was Charles (1764–1836), the father of Berthe (1782–1841). The second was Marie-Louise (1765–1839) who married her cousin, Charles de Rohan-Rochefort and Montauban (1765–1843). The third was Victor (1766–1846), who married Berthe but had no offspring. And the fourth was Jules-Armand-Louis (1768–1836). He was known as 'Prince Louis' and married Catherine de Biron, Duchess de Sagan, daughter of the Duke of Courland. They divorced less than five years later, in 1805, with no children. There being no male heir, the senior Guéméné line of the de Rohans died out and its titles passed to the younger branch descended from Marie-Louise's husband by whom she had two sons and three daughters.

In the Revolution's Wake – Ferdinand and Charlotte's Mother

After the storming of the Bastille in 1789 Ferdinand left his Archbishopric of Cambrai and was named Regent of the Principality of Liège in 1790 where he had brief ambitions to set himself up as a reigning prince. Ferdinand was initially seen as representing the liberal wing of the clergy and even swore an oath to 'the Nation of Liège to maintain the principles of the Revolution'. However, a few months later, an army of the Holy Roman Empire under the Archbishop-Elector of Cologne restored order. So in January 1791 Ferdinand fled back to Cambrai only to discover that things there were even worse than in Liège. He then withdrew to the Abbey of Saint-Ghislain in the Austrian part of his diocese and refused to swear the revolutionary oath to the civil constitution for the clergy. When the revolutionary French army advanced he was forced to flee again, this time to Munster in Westphalia.[1]

In mid-1789 Charlotte had implored Ferdinand to 'think up a refuge' for their children. It seems he must have done so by 1791 as Clementina's letters no longer mention them after that date.[2] It also appears that Ferdinand had ensured Clementina's own safety. Abbé Count Henri-Gabriel de Montrichard was a man who had been close to Ferdinand for many years. From 1777 he was vicar general at Bordeaux, then in 1781 at Cambrai, whilst in 1784 he was appointed canon co-adjutor in Liège. When the Revolution broke out de Montrichard took refuge in his family's Château de St. Martin near Voiteur whence he left for Switzerland, arriving at Fribourg in September 1792. He lived there until January 1798 and organised a scheme to help refugee nobles and clergy settle in the town and support those in need.[3] There can be little doubt that Clementina's escape to Fribourg, where she lived from 1792 until her death ten years later, was organised by Ferdinand through his former right-hand-man, de Montrichard.

Ferdinand and Louis – Charlotte's Children Hidden Away

After the scandal of Marie-Antoinette's necklace, Cardinal Louis led a quiet life in his principality of Strasbourg, concentrating for once on his pastoral duties. But after the Revolution erupted he was elected a

[1] H. Sage, op. cit.; Nouvelle Biographie Générale, op. cit., vol.42, p.536; G. Martin, Histoire et Généalogie des Maisons de Chabot, de Rohan-Chabot et de Rohan, Lyon 1977, p.117.

[2] C.L. Berry, op. cit., p.199.

[3] T. de Raemy, L'Emigration Française dans le Canton de Fribourg (1789–1798), Fribourg 1935, pp.263–264, Archives de la Société d'Histoire du Canton de Fribourg, vol.14. Abbé Henri-Gabriel de Montrichard (1748–1816).

deputy of the clergy to the Estates General where he was initially viewed with sympathy as a victim of regal despotism. However, his situation was untenable as he was far from being a supporter of the Revolution. So in mid-1790 he left Paris for his diocese on the Rhine and, like Ferdinand, refused to sign the oath of the civil constitution for the clergy. Yet Louis' position was unique. For when it became impossible for him to remain on the French side of the Rhine and he crossed over to Ettenheim, he was not in exile, like the Bourbons, but still a sovereign ruler in the eastern half of his principality which was formally a part of the Holy Roman Empire. Consequently Louis was able to provide a recruitment and organisational centre there for the counter-revolutionary army of the Bourbon Prince Louis de Condé who had married his cousin, Charlotte de Rohan-Soubise. Louis de Condé's army, whose high command was at Worms, was not the only royalist force being assembled. The king's brothers were also putting together the 'Army of the Princes' at Coblenz. But de Condé's was far more professional and disciplined. Nor was Ettenheim a centre only for exiled politicians and the military. Many other refugees found shelter there, such as Charlotte de Rohan-Rochefort who became engaged to de Condé's grandson, the Duke d'Enghien.

Concerning the circumstances of Charlotte Stuart's children during the 1790s, there are only hints in Ferdinand's correspondence. It is evident he took a great interest in a certain boy's education but mysteriously witheld the boy's name.[4] There are also clues in Ferdinand's surviving letters to his brother:

Mulheim near Cologne on the Rhine, September 3rd, 1794.
My dear brother, I received this morning your letter dated August 29th from Baden-Baden [...] I see that you haven't received mine. I have nevertheless put the address just as Madame de Marsan[5] told me. Please pass a million compliments to my cousin, the Prince de Rochefort[6] and Mademoiselle de Rohan[7] and tell them of my feelings and sadness concerning the tragic end suffered at the hands of the monstrous regicides [...] Mr Rocheplatte is going to embark in Holland and from there go to London, whence he will leave for San Domingo after having conferred with the

---

[4] E. Cassavetti, *op. cit.*, p.301.
[5] Marie-Louise de Rohan-Soubise, the widow of Gaston de Lorraine, Count de Marsan.
[6] Charles Armand de Rohan-Rochefort.
[7] Charles' daughter, the finacée of the Duke d'Enghien.

negotiators[8] [...] I am no wiser than you as to where our poor brother is situated[9] [...] Farewell, my dear brother; [...] a thousand tendernesses for our relations.[10]

Louis replied on September 16th, devoting most of his letter to the legal and financial arrangements concerning the attempted sale of their San Domingo property, but adding: 'All my relations here thank you for remembering them'.[11]

On December 17th Ferdinand was in Venice and wrote to Louis again, deeply concerned about their financial problems and banking relationship with Turnbull, Forbes & Co. of London.[12] Still in Venice he wrote on April 17th, 1795 to Louis in Ettenheim in similar terms, adding:

> The Jacobins carry themselves with an air of triumph. Oh my God, without luck we are lost! [...] Just to have something certain in order to survive [...] I am so pleased that all our relations and you, my dear brother, are well. Assure them, I beg you, of my tender attachment [...] I think that our other relations will be tranquil at Brunswick; Ah, what dispersion! [...] I am counting on leaving for Rome and Naples on May 20th [...] I will stay in Rome with my cousin, the Prince Camille[13] [...] I have just received from London the reply of Mr Thomas Coutts, the famous banker [...] I knew him in Paris and Liège [...] He thinks that the best informed people in England fear the government has adopted a policy of subjugating (*San Domingo*) [...] He tells me that Mr Turnbull is said to be a negotiator and merchant of good reputation.[14]

Then once more from Venice, on April 29th: 'My cousin and our relations are at Wolfenbüttel and not at Brunswick [...] A thousand and a thousand more tendernesses for my relations who have the good luck to be with you'.[15] By June 9th Ferdinand was in Rome and in his letter

---

[8] Louis and Ferdinand were urgently trying to raise money from the sale of an estate there.

[9] Their brother, Admiral Armand, had in fact been guillotined on July 24th.

[10] Archiv Rohanové, Inv.č.418–429, k.č.170.

[11] *Ibid.*

[12] Archives Nationales, Paris, Archives Privées, Archive de Rohan, Letter F.M. de Rohan to L.de Rohan, December 17th, 1794, AP 388.

[13] Camille de Rohan-Rochefort, born 1737.

[14] Archiv Rohanové, Inv.č.418–429, k.č.170.

[15] *Ibid.*

to Louis added: 'I would ask you to give a thousand compliments for me to all our relations'. Then on August 20th, from Venice to Ettenheim: 'Is Madame de Marsan still in Wolfenbüttel? [...] I have heard all the details concerning the death of the young King [...] I hope that God will one day punish these monsters [...] A thousand tendernesses to all my relations'.[16]

It is noticeable that there are two groups of relations – one with Louis at Ettenheim and the other with Marie-Louise de Marsan at Wolfenbüttel.[17] Ferdinand also seems considerably warmer to the group staying with his brother, twice referring to them as 'my' rather than 'our' relations, once when expressing significant concern for their well-being. There also exists a curious unsigned letter from Rome to Clementina dated April 18th, 1794. Its content is inconclusive but form of address extraordinary: 'Chez la Veuve Friend' (sic).[18]

Ferdinand – Return from Exile

As for Ferdinand's circumstances, though he had little money, he had enough to survive on: 'Venice, November 22nd, 1794. I live as cheaply as possible; for this business may last long, even if all is not lost'. In July 1795, he felt he could 'still live a long time without importuning anyone'.[19] It seems he then spent some time in Bologna before moving to Waldeck near Kassel and, at least once, was in Warsaw – on May 11th, 1799 – where there were many other French emigrés.[20] Not least of them was the future King Louis XVIII as well as Ferdinand's cousin, Princess Louise-Adèlaide de Bourbon who was de Condé's daughter by Charlotte de Rohan-Soubise.[21]

Five months later Cardinal Louis died at the age of sixty-eight at Ettenheim with Charlotte de Rohan-Rochefort and the Duke

---

16 *Ibid.*

17 E. de Haynin, *op. cit.*, p.322. Marie-Louise had moved to Brussels almost immediately the Revolution began and provided accomodation there for Henri de Rohan's sons. Later she moved to Linz where she died in 1802.

18 Bodleian Library in Oxford, Documents and Letters of C.E. Roehenstart (hereafter Documents of C.E. Roehenstart), Ms Fr b7 13.

19 A. Theiner, *Documents inédits relatifs aux affaires religieuses de la France, 1790–1800,* 1857–1858, vol.1, p.435; vol.2, p.65.

20 H. Sage, *op. cit.*

21 A. Magier, *op. cit.*, p.374. When, on September 20th, 1802 Louise-Adèlaide finished her two years as a novitiate at the Warsaw convent of the Holy Sacrament, she took her Holy Vows there in the presence of the assembled members of the French royal family. The Stuarts' aunt, Princess Charlotte Sobieska is buried in the same church.

d'Enghien at his side.[22] Just over a year later d'Enghien was abducted by Napoleon and executed by firing squad at the Château de Vincennes near Paris where Prince Charles had been imprisoned after his arrest in 1748. Despite everything Ferdinand made his peace with Napoleon after the Concordat with the Vatican was signed in 1801. He returned to France but failed to get back his Archbishopric of Cambrai. Nevertheless Napoleon liked to have some of the great names of the *ancien régime* amongst his courtiers. Consequently, in 1804, Ferdinand was appointed grand almoner to the Empress Josephine, then to the Empress Marie-Louise, was granted a pension of 12,000 francs and given the title of Count of the Empire by letters patent dated July 2nd, 1808. Five years later, on October 30th, 1813 he died in Paris at the age of seventy-four. He was the last of the Princes de Rohan-Guéméné still domiciled in France. His nephew, Henri, had died in 1809 and his wife in 1807. The old Breton-French chapter of de Rohan history had closed, but a new Austro-Hungarian one had begun. Of Henri's three sons, Charles and Victor both became Austrian field-marshals and Louis a general. None left a male heir, so Marie-Louise and her husband from the younger branch of de Rohan-Rochefort and Montauban became the ancestors of those de Rohans whose new home from 1820 until 1945 was the beautiful estate of Sychrov, north of Prague. To them passed too the de Rohan-Guéméné Dukedom de Montbazon.

In Close Touch – Henry Stuart and Ferdinand's Great-Nephew, Victor de Rohan

By the 1790s both Prince Charles and Charlotte Stuart were dead. Their immediate relations who were still alive were Henry Stuart, Clementina Walkinshaw and Charlotte's three children. Having been forced by Napoleon's troops to flee Frascati in 1798 the seventy-six year-old Henry returned there after the Concordat between France and the Vatican. Correspondence from the period shows how close the youngest generation of de Rohans was to him. There are seven surviving letters to Victor de Rohan from Henry's two most trusted men, Cardinal Albani and Angelo Cesarini, Bishop of Milevi. Indeed, the latter became Henry's heir and inherited all that was left of the Stuart fortune. Most of these letters are concerned with the rights of succes-

---

[22] E. de Haynin, *op. cit.*, p.329.

sion to the former Sobieski property of Oława which had been seized by the Prussians years before – yet certain passages are curious:

Frascati, November 19th, 1803.
His Eminence will shortly be leaving and shall not fail to give your Highness[23] his explanations and suggestions which will bring things to a happy conclusion. And you will be abreast of these operations which he will undertake. Your brother, the Prince, has been informed of everything – a person very favourably perceived by His Royal Highness,[24] and for whom he has great respect – and he will be able to come to a full understanding after his[25] return to Vienna.

Cesarini

Rome, July 17th, 1805.
I received your Highness' letter together with the letter to His Royal Highness who is very pleased and sends his best wishes for the forthcoming marriage. He also expresses his happiness that you have not resigned from our business, so advantageous to both sides.

Cesarini

Vienna, February 15th, 1804.
I have received from the person that you earlier indicated the packet which contains copies of new information about which we didn't know here in Rome, and I undertake to give them to the Bishop of Milevi [...] I beg you to do nothing without the agreement of the Cardinal Duke of York, and to agree all with the Bishop of Milevi and myself when I am in Rome.

Albani[26]

Clementina Walkinshaw – Her Final Years

As for Charlotte Stuart's mother, her removal from Paris to Fribourg in 1792 was probably simultaneous with her separation from

---

[23] Victor de Rohan.
[24] Henry Stuart.
[25] Cardinal Albani.
[26] Archiv Rohanové, Inv.č.418–429, k.č.187, *Victor Louis Mériadec de Rohan – Kardinal Albani (1803–1804) & Cesarini Angelo (1803–1805)*

Charlotte's three children. In Switzerland Clementina survived on the irregular income from the pension granted under her daughter's will which was sent by Henry. But it was heavily devalued by high exchange rate costs as well as financial turmoil caused by the Revolution and Henry was not always co-operative. On August 8th, 1793 Hyacinte Bruni wrote to Clementina from Florence saying that her pension had not been sent and advised her to put pressure on Henry.[27] But when Henry had to flee Frascati in 1798 these funds dried up altogether. Thomas Coutts interceded on Clementina's behalf with the British Government in January 1800, however, they refused help. Nevertheless, the banker proved a loyal friend. As Clementina's servant, Couppey, wrote: 'In all her distresses the Countess of Albestroff at times received some help from Mr Thomas Coutts, Esquire, banker in London who, having learned of her misery, had pity on it. He was indignant at the conduct of the Cardinal. Madame knew him very well in Paris with his wife and three daughters'.[28] In her now shaky hand Clementina wrote to Coutts in gratitude, describing him as a man of 'unending kindness'.[29] Her pension was restarted in mid-1802 at which point Coutts corresponded on Clementina's behalf with Abbé Waters, Charlotte's old *major domo* and executor. The latter spoke of Clementina's 'very difficult life' which had been the case 'for some time'.[30]

Clementina died on November 27th, 1802 and was buried two days later in the cemetery of the Parish and Collegiate Church of St. Nicholas in Fribourg, close to her last home. It seems she remained in love with Charles until the end and always spoke of her daughter's father with great respect and affection.[31] In her will she made special mention of 'a gold box surmounted with a medallion showing a woman crying next to an urn'.[32] She also referred to a 'Genealogical act made in Edinburgh and dated October 4th, 1769, signed by Douglas and Stuart, which is in a tin box and locked in the secretaire'. Clementina added that these and other papers and letters in her desk should be sent to Mr Coutts and given to her family together with a copy of her will.[33]

[27] Documents of C.E. Roehenstart, Ms Fr b7 11.
[28] M. Forster, *op. cit.*, p.304; G. Sherburn, *op. cit.*, p.40; Documents of C.E. Roehenstart, Ms Fr b7 37.
[29] Documents of C.E. Roehenstart, Ms Fr b7 38.
[30] *Ibid.*, Ms Fr b7 27 & 30.
[31] M. Forster, *op. cit.*, p.304.
[32] Documents of C.E. Roehenstart, Ms Fr b7 39.
[33] *Ibid.*

As Ferdinand had made separate provision for Charlotte's children, what little Clementina had was left to Couppey who had been with her since 1784 and must have known her grandchildren.[34] Clementina's reference to her family is enigmatic, because her own siblings had predeceased her and where their wills exist make no mention of her.[35] Therefore, when Clementina died, she had no close family except for Charlotte's three children. Couppey writes: 'When the tribunal of the District of Fribourg lifted the seals from the effects of Madame d'Albestroff, there was found a tin box which contained a genealogy on parchment and some other papers which a clause in her will charged her executor, Mr Weck [...] to have sent to Mr Coutts in London'. Weck sent six parcels of Clementina's papers to Coutts in 1804. But when he had earlier tried to send them to him they had been returned and Weck kept them because: 'I opened one, and seeing that different persons could be compromised if they became public, I thought it proper to retain them [...] But the relatives of the Countess of Albestroff being very desirous of having them, to whom they are destined by the will of the deceased, and I relying greatly on the intelligence and discretion of those relatives, I now decide to send them on in the manner indicated to me. I beg you then, Monsieur, to send them to Mr Coutts'.[36] There also exists an unsigned letter dated September 5th, 1806. It complains of delays by Thomas Coutts in returning Charlotte's letters. The author says: 'He knows that various persons may be compromised if the letters become public [...] but the relations of the Countess of Albestroff very much want to have them'.[37]

Charlotte's Children – Parentless in Exile

The formative years of Charlotte's children, lived just before and during the French Revolution as parentless homeless exiles, must have been bewildering. Compounding this was the fact that they never knew which of the four de Rohan brothers was their real father. And though proof exists of Marie-Victoire's legitimisation, it appears she never knew of it. As for the de Rohans, they kept the children's existence firmly in the shadows, whereas Charlotte Stuart had left them when Marie-Victoire was five and none of them ever saw her again. They

[34] G. Sherburn, *op. cit.*, p.40.
[35] F. Skeet, *op. cit.*, p.6.
[36] G. Sherburn, *op. cit.*, pp.40–41.
[37] Documents of C.E. Roehenstart, Ms Fr b7 43.

were brought up by Clementina, but separated from her when the eldest had only just reached her teens and the youngest was nine. Ferdinand's letters to Cardinal Louis hint at the daughters, or perhaps all three children, being at Ettenheim during the years 1792–95. Amongst Charlotte's son's letters are four which convey the atmosphere of his early years. One is written to his 'Bonne Maman' whilst two are adressed to his 'Papa', and mention his 'protector and uncle' as well as 'grandmother'. One letter is dated January 1st, 1799 and is addressed to Cardinal Henry from Munich, though it is unclear if it was ever sent:

> My Lord, I avail myself of this New Year to present to Your Royal Highness the wishes which I form for You. Maman told me to love You and I do it very much. I shall be much happy if I can obtain Your Protection, for I am a good boy.
>
> Your respectful nephew, Charles
PS. Je prie toujours le Bon Dieu pour Your Royal Highness. C.[38]

In a letter from Munich to his 'Bonne Maman' dated January 4th, 1799 Charlotte's son writes with extraordinary tenderness and affection, telling her how she 'made up for my unhappy childhood' and concludes by enclosing a copy of the letter to Henry, commenting that it is 'to my Great-Uncle whom I don't love as much as you, because I believe him to be very bad'.[39] On June 6th, 1800 he writes again from Munich, mentioning his 'grandmother' and 'uncle and protector'. The boy is reduced to asking his 'Papa' to write him a letter, urging him to do so by telling him how happy he is 'each time we are reunited after so long a separation [...] during this unhappy time'.[40] But his 'Tendre Papa' did not reply. So the boy wrote once more, asking: 'What am I to think of this silence?' before going on to plead for 'your letter which will give us so much pleasure and a joy, which, however, will not be perfect until we are all re-united', emphasizing that 'Your kindness will be forever engraved upon our hearts'. His closing words, perhaps more question than statement, were: 'You cannot doubt our sentiments for you'.[41]

[38] *Ibid.*, Ms Fr b7 18. The date on the letter is unclear and may be 1793.
[39] *Ibid.*, Ms Fr b7 17.
[40] *Ibid.*, Ms Fr b7 19.
[41] *Ibid.*, Ms Fr b7 20. See page 211, note 43. Charles's 'uncle and protector' and 'Papa' may have been one and the same. Compare with Marie-Victoire's letters.

Charlotte's daughter – Charlotte Maximilienne

There is contradictory evidence as to which of Charlotte Stuart's two daughters was born first. All legends state that they were born close together and that Marie-Victoire was the younger. Charlotte's letters to Clementina suggest the same. So too does the choice of their respective Christian names as well as the fact that Marie-Victoire appears to have been the second to marry and that it was she and the youngest sibling who were found homes through the same intermediary. On the other hand her death certificate suggests that she was younger than Marie-Victoire by a year.

Five pieces of evidence identify Charlotte Stuart's daughter. One is an old, unidentified family portrait of a young woman still in the possession of the descendants of her sister, Marie-Victoire. The girl portrayed is strikingly similar to the de Rohans.[42] Moreover her style of dress and age indicate she was born at the right date and there is no other appropriate candidate from amongst the ancestors of Marie-Victoire's descendants. There is also a note on the reverse of the canvas saying that the 'painting comes from Frankenberg'.[43] There are only two places with that name in Europe and both are in Germany. One is extremely close to Waldeck where, or near where, Ferdinand was staying at about the time this portrait must have been painted. Furthermore, in a letter written after her sister's death, Marie-Victoire asks if her 'family pictures which were always in the Gros Caillou might momentarily be placed in your mansion? [...] There are only two big pictures, the others are busts of an ordinary dimension'.[44]

The second piece of evidence was recorded about 1900 by Alfred Testot-Ferry, a naval officer decorated with the Legion of Honour and a descendant of the uncle of the husband of Marie-Victoire's sister. His notes were made from a marriage contract, the original of which no longer exists because the Paris registers were destroyed during the

---

[42] Compare hers with the portrait of Cardinal Louis de Rohan illustrated in the present work.

[43] The portrait is in the possession of the author's family in Poland.

[44] Archiv Rohanové, Inv.č.562, k.č.193 II. The *Gros Caillou* refers to the *quartier* in which stands the Church of St. Pierre de Gros Caillou on the rue St. Dominique parallel to the rue de Grenelle. It is a small area bordered by the Quai d'Orsay, the Hôtel and Esplanades des Invalides, the avenue de Tourville and Parc du Champs de Mars. Marie-Victoire rented an apartment there on the rue de Grenelle near General Prince Louis de Rohan's mansion.

Paris Commune in 1871 and only a small percentage later reconstituted. They read[45]

> Jean Louis Lugle Luglien Cousin de la Morlière, born at Montdidier September 13th, 1763, baptised the next day at St Pierre [...] Died in Paris on December 20th, 1846, Receveur Principal des Contributions Indirectes. He married in Paris, to the great dissatisfaction of his brother with whom he was never reconciled, on the 21st of Thermidor in the Year XII (*August 9th, 1804*), Mademoiselle Charlotte Maximilienne Amèlie Roehenstart, said to be the daughter of the late Maximilien Roehenstart and of Clementina Ruthven; but in reality the natural daughter of Cardinal (sic) Ferdinand Maximilian Mériadec de Rohan, Archbishop of Cambrai [...] and Charlotte Stuart, grand-daughter of the Pretender. The name Roehenstart was but a rebus more or less discreetly recalling the two names de Rohan and Stuart. The contract of marriage states that it was made in the presence of their relations and friends, hereafter named:

> On the side of the Groom:
> Madame Anaclète-Julie Deleinte, widow of Monsieur Cousin de Méricourt, first cousin.
> Hubert-Aubin Cousin, Ancien Maître Particulier des Eaux & Fôrets at Dijon, first cousin.
> Claude-Marie Besson, first cousin.

> And on the side of the Bride:
> Monsieur Auguste Maximilien Roehenstart, brother.
> Mademoiselle Victoire Adèlaide Roehenstart, sister.
> The Cardinal (sic) de Rohan, friend, who by this contract grants the bride a debt of 20,000 francs.
> Madame Henriette Jeanne Gauné de Cazau, wife of Monsieur Louis Raymond Sarra de la Bérarde.[46]

---

[45] The records for the period were searched by the author using every variation for the names of both bride and groom. Nothing was found. Confirmation of the destruction of the original records and the extent of their reconstitution for the period 1800–1810 may be obtained from les Archives de Paris, 18 Boulevard Sérurier, 75019 Paris.

[46] The notes were made by Alfred Testot-Ferry (1854–1932), the grandfather of Robert Testot-Ferry of Marseilles. They were descended from General Baron Claude Testot-Ferry

De la Morlière's father was Jacques-Luglien Cousin de Beaumesnil, a noble from Montdidier who was a *conseiller du roy* as well as Mayor of Montdidier from 1765–1768. And the groom's grandfather was Jean Cousin, Seigneur de la Vose and a *conseiller du roy* in Montdidier where his family had lived since the 15th century.[47] Various things about this document are striking.[48] The author of the notes, who obviously had a copy of the marriage contract in front of him at the time of writing, was only a distaff descendant of the groom's uncle. He was therefore not making any claim of Stuart ancestry for himself. The groom's brother's disapproval of the marriage has the ring of authenticity. The author could hardly have known that 'the late Maximilien Roehenstart' did in fact match the alias for his father that Charlotte's son was using elsewhere (as will become evident). The choice of the mother's alias of 'Clementina Ruthven' is impressive as it links the bride's grandmother's Christian name to a surname with strong Jacobite associations. Neither would Testot-Ferry have known that 'Auguste Maximilien Roehenstart' was indeed a name the bride's brother was using at the time.[49] Nor would he have known that the names on the bride's sister's previously unknown baptismal certificate included Victoire. Nor even that the initial 'V.' for one of her daughters was used in Charlotte's letters to her mother, attention to which has been drawn only recently. Also, the choice of the name 'Charlotte' is in keeping with Stuart tradition whereas Aglaë is not. The settlement of 20,000 francs by the 'friend' Ferdinand is in line with the financial settlement granted to Young Charlotte's brother (as will also be seen), whilst the term 'friend' alongside Ferdinand is exactly the formulation by which Charlotte Stuart referred to her children's father. Lastly, if the marriage contract

footnote 46 (*cont.*)

(1773–1856) by Josephine Fabry (1786–1836), the latter being the daughter of Bernard Fabry (1755–1826) by Adèlaide-Henriette Cousin de Méricourt (1759–1785), the latter being the daughter of Jean-Edouard Cousin de Brière et de Méricourt (1725–1797) *conseiller du roy* in Montdidier and uncle of Young Charlotte's husband. A copy of these notes, obtained from Monsieur Testot-Ferry, together with other material concerning the Cousin family is in the Piniński Archive in Warsaw, Gabinet Genealogiczny, Royal Castle (hereafter the Piniński Archive in Warsaw). Note also the name of Young Charlotte's witness on the de Rohan side: Henriette de Cazau. The original was a hand-written document and spelling variations were common at the time. Compare the phonetically identical name of Cazeaux in Marie-Victoire's letter 7 (see appendix). The Pierre Cazeaux mentioned was obviously a de Rohan employee of high standing because he was known to Marie-Victoire. It seems possible that Henriette and Pierre were related.

[47] *Ibid.*

[48] Testot-Ferry's information has been published previously: *Héraldique et Généalogie*, 1981, July-August 1981, vol.XIII, D.4927. Stuart., but was unsupported by any other evidence.

[49] Documents of C.E. Roehenstart, Ms Fr b7 65 for example, and others.

was spurious, why would its author disguise the very families with which he was presumably trying to claim some indirect relationship?

Three further pieces of evidence confirm the authenticity of the above. The Parisian family of Berryer became famous in France during the two generations of Pierre-Nicolas and his son, Antoine-Pierre. Both of these talented lawyers acted for the successful defence of Marshal Ney during his trial before the Court of Peers. In 1816, Berryer senior also defended the former Bourbon agent, Fauche-Borel, by which time he had a reputation as one of the best lawyers in the field of high commerce. Berryer junior was deeply religious, an ardent French royalist and not only a brilliant barrister but a pre-eminent political orator as well as a member of the Académie Française.[50] In the Berryer Archive in Paris are four letters addressed to father and son. Each suggests an intimate long-term relationship with them: 'Have you thought of me today, Monsieur, being here in Paris, relying on your goodwill towards me? I am going to quite probably bore you, but my curiosity is greater than my discretion'. This undated letter is addressed to Berryer senior and signed: 'Countess de la Morlière'.[51] The three remaining ones are addressed to both 'Monsieur Berryer' and 'Monsieur Berryer – fils'. All are undated but one bears a post-mark in the style of 1830–35.[52] They refer to 'whist evenings', 'our friends' and even 'an intimate little soirée'. Two are signed: 'Countess de Thorigny'; the other: 'V.de Thorigny'.[53]

Marie-Victoire's contacts with the Paris legal circles in which the Berryers moved are revealed in two of her other letters. In the first, post-marked 1820, she asks to be told 'about the case successfully won, relating to the Duchy of Bouillon' mentioning 'the documents that one had often asked to put before the eyes of one's friends, so that they could, in case of need, support your legitimate rights with the benefit of full knowledge of the matter'. Then again, circa 1824: 'If you don't know anyone from the Paris bar, I could ask a lawyer for a model of the declaration'.[54]

That both sisters should assume the title of countess is not untypi-

---

[50] *Dictionnaire de Biografie Française*, pp.162–166. Pierre-Nicholas (1757–1841) & Antoine-Pierre (1790–1868).
[51] Archives Nationales, Paris, Archives Privées, Berryer Papers, 223 AP 34.
[52] *Ibid.*, 223 AP 40.
[53] *Ibid.*
[54] Archiv Rohanové, Inv.č.562, k.č.193 II.

cal for the France of that period. Nevertheless it hints at a shared complex. And though Marie-Victoire was married at the time it is not surprising she referred to herself by her title of de Thorigny. Such was the custom of the day that one could either call oneself by way of a title, surname or both, whether by birth or by marriage. Even after her first marriage, in the company of her siblings or relations, Marie-Victoire used the 'maiden' name de Roehenstart; although her monogram was 'M.R.' – for Marie.[55]

The next piece of evidence is the baptismal certificate for Young Charlotte's brother. That document reads:

> Thursday May 13th, 1784 was baptised Auguste Maximilien, born the same day, the son of the noble Maximilien Roehenstart and the noble Clementine Ruthven, his wife, of this parish, the Cul de Sac des Anglois. The godfather Thibault Etienne Lauverjat, master in surgery, of the same house, the godmother Anne Victoire Lauverjat, under-age daughter of the godfather, of the same abode, the father absent on business.[56]

All details on this document, which was unknown to Testot-Ferry, agree entirely with his extracts from Young Charlotte's wedding certificate which it pre-dates by twenty years. However, it warrants comment. Neither mother nor father were present at the baptism, for the act almost stresses that the child was born the same day and no mother in the late eighteenth century would have jumped out of bed immediately after childbirth and gone off to church. It is also clearly stated that the father was not undiplomatically 'absent on business'. So the only people

---

[55] *Ibid.* For example, Marie-Victoire's uncle, Jules-Hercule de Rohan who held the titles 'Duke de Montbazon' and 'Prince de Guémené' called himself by any, or a combination of: 'de Rohan', 'de Montbazon' or 'de Rohan-Guémené'. His wife, born Louise de la Tour, la demoiselle d'Auvergne, referred to herself after marriage as 'de la Tour d'Auvergne de Montbazon' or 'de Rohan de Montbazon' as well as other permutations.

[56] Archives de Paris, Baptismal acts, 5 mi.2/1018, 5 mi.1/66, Roehenstart, May 13th, 1784. This act, described as a birth certificate, is in fact a baptismal certificate. Because it is a copy of the original made after the destruction caused by the Paris Commune in 1871 – and the original was a baptismal certificate. Therefore we cannot be sure the child really was born that day, only that a baptism took place that day. The original belonged to a Maître de la Guerre who presented it for copying on May 29th, 1879. That title usually, though not exclusively, referred to a public notary. Unfortunately de la Guerre was not a notary, otherwise it might have been possible to find his archive in which there might have been further information. That he was not a notary is clear from the absence of his name in: *Notaires Parisiens des Origines à Nos Jours*, MC/3 (a), (b) & (c), Archives Nationales in Paris, as well as *Almanach National* for 1879 which covers all of France.

present were the godfather and his young daughter. Nor did the house in the Cul de Sac des Anglois belong to the 'noble' Roehenstarts but to the surgeon Lauverjat who had qualified in 1774 and appears thereafter in the *Almanach Royal* with this as his address.[57] Unfortunately it is impossible to discover whether Lauverjat acted as surgeon to the de Rohans. However it is striking that his house was just 350 yards from the Hôtel de Rohan.[58] Nor is there any other trace whatsoever in the Paris Archives of the name of Roehenstart or Ruthven or anything like either. Moreover, Young Charlotte's brother was baptised in the Parish Church of St. Merry on the rue St. Martin. And that just happened to be the church where Pierre-Nicolas Berryer married in 1789 and his son was baptised in 1795.[59] Was this the origin of the Berryers' intimate friendship with Young Charlotte and Marie-Victoire?

It now transpires there was some substance to C.L. Berry's claim that the first of Prince Charles's grandchildren 'seems to have been prone to illness and may not have survived the French Revolution'.[60] The letters of Marie-Victoire's brother suggesting the survival of only one sister by the year 1813[61] are explained by the fact that at five o'clock on the morning of November 26th, 1806 Young Charlotte gave birth to a still-born boy at her home on the rue l'Apleit at Huy.[62] Later that day, at three o'clock in the afternoon, she too died. Her husband of just two years, Jean de la Morlière, never remarried and died childless in Paris forty years later.[63] All the details of Young Charlotte's death certificate match not only Testot-Ferry's extracts from her marriage contract but also her brother's baptismal certificate:

Charlotte Maximilienne Amélie de Roehenstart, born in Paris, domiciled in this Commune, aged about twenty six, the wife of

[57] *Almanach Royal 1784*, ed. L. d'Houry, Paris 1784, p.616.

[58] *Nomenclature des Voies Publiques et Privées*, 7th ed., Paris 1951, p.48. The Cul de Sac des Anglois, or Anglais, is today called the Impasse Beaubourg and entry to it is at 37, rue Beaubourg, 3rd arr.

[59] C. Baloche, *Eglise Saint Merry de Paris*, vol.2, 1912, p.748: 'January 4th, 1795: birth and baptism: Hippolyte-Nicolas Berryer, son of Pierre-Nicolas Berryer and Anne-Marie Gorneau, married at Saint Merry in 1789'.

[60] C.L. Berry, *op. cit.*, p.157.

[61] G. Sherburn, *op. cit.*, p.37; Documents of C.E. Roehenstart, Ms Fr b7 158.

[62] Formerly called the rue de l'Aplé.

[63] See notes 46–48 above. Jean de la Morlière's brother who so disapproved his marriage was Pierre de Luxembourg Elizabeth Luglien Cousin de Beaumesnil, born in Montdidier on January 8th, 1761, died there on July 21st, 1839, president of the Tribunal of the First Instance in Montdidier 1818–1838, mayor of Montdidier 1791, member of the Legion of Honour.

Jean Louis Lugle Luglien Cousin de la Morlière, receveur principal des droits réunis,[64] the daughter of Maximilien de Roehenstart and Clementina de Ruthven [...] died on the 26th of the present month.[65]

The first of the Duchess of Albany's 'three flowers' had been cut down.

---

[64] Principal Collector of Indirect Taxes.
[65] Archives de l'Etat à Huy, Archives Générales du Royaume et Archives de l'Etat dans les Provinces, Death Certificate for Charlotte Cousin de la Morlière née Roehenstart, deceased at Huy on November 26th, 1806, registered at Huy on November 28th, 1806.

CHAPTER THIRTEEN

The Road to Poland

As they gazed at the high walls and noble towers
that ringed it around,
and the splendid palaces and towering churches,
they were amazed by it,
and especially by the height and breadth of the city,
which was sovereign above all other cities.

Geoffrey de Villehardouin

The 'Oban Times' Letters

A strange series of articles appeared in the *Oban Times* between April and July 1939. The first, by Iain Gordon, recounted the history of Prince Charles, Clementina Walkinshaw and Charlotte Stuart but went on to add:

> The Duchess of Albany [...] married the Swedish Baron Roehenstart by whom she had two children, John and Marie Stuart Roehenstart. These children were secretly adopted by a family in Poland, friends of the House of Stuart [...] The granddaughter, Marie Stuart Roehenstart, married James Sobieski, a cadet of the House of Sobieski[1] who died early in life. Her brother went to Scotland where he remained for some time.

Gordon also said that Charlotte's son wrote to his sister in Warsaw asking her to send him their grandmother's genealogical papers which

---

[1] The Sobieski family became extinct in 1740 upon the death of Princess Charlotte Sobieska, Duchess de Bouillon.

she had received after Clementina's death and that his sister brought them to Scotland herself. She then accepted the offer of a cheap return passage to the Baltic in a ship belonging to a Dundee whaler who abducted her, stole the gold box with the family documents and left her to die on Campbell Island off New Zealand. Gordon's article generated a reply from Professor George Sherburn:

In 1935, almost by accident, I purchased in Sotheby's auction rooms the personal papers of this 'baron' who for years quietly insisted he was the grandson of Bonnie Prince Charlie. According to documents in my possession Roehenstart in 1816 asked the support of the Prince Regent in establishing claims to the supposed property of Charlotte Stuart, Duchess of Albany [...] Naturally, Roehenstart was asked to produce documents in support of his claims, and since he was illegitimate he could not. It is possible that at this time he invented the story Mr Gordon tells about the remote Campbell Island grave. For many reasons the grave had to be remote!

A man signing himself 'Morvern' then wrote:

Coleridge's *Life of Coutts* states that a certain 'R' wishes to repay a loan of two hundred and sixty two guineas lent by the banker to Countess d'Albestroff. The same 'R' states at the time: 'I have every reason to believe that more money has been paid to my grandmother'. Baron Roehenstart's sister, Marie Stuart Roehenstart, was born in 1778. Both children were adopted by a family in Warsaw named Fergusson-Tepper. Marie Stuart Roehenstart married James Sobieski and was early left a widow with one daughter, Carolina Sobieska.[2]

Professor Sherburn was undoubtedly right to point out that Charlotte's son needed to invent the abduction story to explain away the lack of documentary evidence for his claim of legitimacy. Hence, as Sherburn points out in his biography, he kept his sister's existence deliberately obscure, mentioning her only once in his correspondence. He was concerned that in presenting himself as legitimate, his older sister might

---

[2] *The Heather Grave on Campbell Island*, The Oban Times, 15 IV 1939; *A Jacobite Echo*, ibid., 24 VI 1939; *Baron Roehenstart*, ibid., 5 VIII 1939.

reveal the truth if someone contacted her. The legend described in these articles almost certainly originated from Charlotte's son when he was in Scotland a century earlier. And though it contains distortions, exagerrations and comical embroidery it also provides clues. Reduced to its bare essentials the following remains: by the time they were young adults only two of Charlotte's three children were still alive, a boy and a girl. Coutts the banker was in contact with the former. The latter's name was Marie. She had received Clementina Walkinshaw's genealogical papers and married a Pole but been widowed young and left with one child.

There were indeed only two children left, a boy and a girl – Young Charlotte having died in 1806. Marie really was the surviving sister's first name, Victoire being her familiar one. And as described in the previous chapter, Marie-Victoire and her sister 'very much wanted to have' their grandmother's genealogical papers. The legend also states that a Warsaw family called Fergusson-Tepper played some key role in the early lives of two of Charlotte Stuart's three children.

Poland's Bankers – who were the Fergusson-Teppers?

Only specialists in the history of eighteenth-century protestantism in Warsaw or early banking in Poland might recognise the name today. Even at the time of the Oban Times articles the Polish scholar, Dr Victor Kornatowski, wrote in 1937: 'Peter Tepper, Charles Szulc, Frederick Kabryt, Prot Potocki, Mathew Łyszkiewicz and John David Heyzler – these names are today practically forgotten' though they were 'the great and famous Polish merchants and bankers at the end of the eighteenth century, concentrating in their hands enormous amounts of capital' and the owners of companies 'known throughout the contemporary world of commerce'.[3] They have been forgotten because the Tepper bank, along with all the other major Polish banks except one, crashed in 1793 when it became obvious that the credit-worthiness of the Polish king and state was fast disappearing in the troubled last months prior to the final partition of Poland in 1795. That prospect provoked a sudden run on each bank's funds causing a domino effect. The winding-up of the Tepper bank took ten years until 1803,[4] after which it and the once fabulously rich Fergusson-Tepper family disappeared from the Polish scene for ever.

---

[3] W. Kornatowski, *Kryzys bankowy w Polsce 1793r. – upadłość Teppera, Szulca, Kabryta, Prota Potockiego, Łyszkiewicza i Heyzlera*, Warsaw 1937, p.1.
[4] *Ibid.*, p.2.

Peter Tepper was from Poznań but moved to Warsaw. He started his career as a merchant supplying the Polish nobility and rich bourgeoisie with every conceivable luxury which he imported from abroad and sold from a shop on Warsaw's old market square. By 1774 he had become so successful that he could afford to build the 'Tepper Palace' on Miodowa Street, the first such building by a member of Warsaw's merchant class. In parallel he began his banking activities, exchanging currencies, organising domestic and international payments, lending cash secured on real estate, extending credits to the king, cities and even the Polish treasury. Likewise he became a shareholder in several government-supported companies, especially in the textile industry, and acquired the right to run the National Lottery with fellow-banker, Peter Blank.[5] In 1765 Tepper bought the 'Under the Four Winds' Palace on Długa Street from the de Rohans' French Warsaw-based banker, Pierre Riaucourt.[6] Yet for all his wealth, Tepper was described by E.A. Lehndorff as: 'a millionaire to whom, so to speak, all Poland belongs. All the more, therefore, does his simplicity and humility astonish me [...] He is without pretension in his behaviour and sparing in his domestic life'. He also played a leading role in the protestant movement in Poland, occupying some of the highest positions in the Evangelical-Augsburg Church where he was a generous benefactor as well as an organiser and financier of their new church in Warsaw. In 1766 his wife died and he was left heirless. So in 1768 he adopted his nephew, also called Peter, whom he made his heir.

Peter was the son of Catherine Tepper and the Poznań-based, Edinburgh-born engineer, William Fergusson. In 1762 he married a Gdańsk-born woman of French huguenot descent, Marie Philipina Valentin Hauterive and after his adoption used the name Fergusson-Tepper, gradually taking over the management of the Tepper empire which he brought to the summit of its success just prior to the crash of 1793. However, Peter was quite unlike his uncle when it came to social ambition. In 1776 he succeeded in gaining parliamentary permission to acquire land (the preserve of the nobility) for himself and his sons-in-law. Then in 1779 he gained a grant of arms as well as an official but substanceless genealogy in 1786 from the Elders of the City Council

---

[5] E. Szulc, *op. cit.*, p.562. Piotr Tepper (1702–1790).
[6] AGAD, Archiwum Radziwiłłów, dz.5, sygn.4873; (see also ch.7).

of Edinburgh,[7] thanks to which he managed to obtain Polish nobility in 1790 for himself and his sons-in-law.[8] Fergusson-Tepper not only inherited his uncle's Warsaw palaces on Miodowa and Długa streets but acquired other properties in the capital and extensive landed estates nearby as well as in Volhynia. Furthermore, together with the banker-aristocrat, Anthony Prot Potocki, he took an active role in the French-inspired development of the Black Sea trade, centred on bi-lateral commerce with Constantinople and Turkey and the movement of goods along the established route from Poland through Lwów and the Ukraine down to the Black Sea, then by ship through to the Mediterranean and back.[9] At his peak, Fergusson-Tepper's gross assets were valued at about 60–65 million Polish zloties, equivalent to about 3.25 million acres of good arable land, whilst the king alone owed him 11 million. Fergusson-Tepper became an intimate of the monarch and the aristocracy into whose class he did everything to establish himself, entertaining on the most lavish scale at his various residences. He was also an active and generous member of the Reformed-Evangelical Church, yet managed to become the treasurer of the elite catholic Knights of Malta. Together with his wife and family he was a member of the Warsaw masonic lodge, the 'Göttin von Eleusis', whilst his son-in-law, the banker Charles Szulc, belonged to the 'Parfait Silence'.[10] Fergusson-Tepper was undoubtedly involved in the *Secret du Roi* in his earlier career whilst later he acted as banker to the Russian Embassy in Warsaw which was even located on his premises. Amongst his many aristocratic clients were not only the Stuarts' plenipotentiary, Załuski, but also the Stuarts' closest Polish-domiciled cousin, Prince Charles Radziwiłł. It was he who had inherited the vast ex-Sobieski property of Żółkiew which his father bought from King James's sister-in-law in 1739. However, by the end of Radziwiłł's extravagant life in 1790, the Żółkiew estates found themselves in Austrian Galicia after the first partition of Poland, bankrupted by a massive burden of debt. It was Peter Fergusson-Tepper who helped try and sort out Radziwiłł's financial

---

[7] AGAD, Dokumenty pergaminowe 2145 i 3323, genealogical descent of Piotr Tepper. The grant of arms is signed by Thomas Browne, Garter Principal King of Arms and Ralph Bigland, Clarenceaux King of Arms. Peter Fergusson-Tepper (1714–1794) & Marie Philipina Fergusson-Tepper (1739–1792).

[8] AGAD, Księgi kanclerskie 100, Indygenat dla Piotra Fergussona-Teppera, 1790r.

[9] M. Mądzik, *Powstanie i pierwsze lata działalności Kompanii Czarnomorskiej 1782–1785*, Rocznik Lubelski, vol.21, 1979.

[10] E. Szulc, *op. cit.*, pp.503, 562–565; J.& E. Szulc, *op. cit.*, pp.244–245; S. Małachowski-Łempicki, *Wykaz polskich lóż wolnomularskich w latach 1738–1821*, Cracow 1930.

mess.[11] Indeed, the Radziwiłł relationship was one reason why it took so long to wind up the Tepper bank after its own bankruptcy.

To an extraordinary extent, therefore, the Fergusson-Tepper family sat at the very centre of the web of contacts born out of Leszczyński's Court at Lunéville. And the socially ambitious, incredibly well-connected, so-called 'Greatest Banker of the North' would have loved nothing better than to help an illustrious Prince de Rohan find an appropriate refuge for the children of a royal Stuart duchess. The more so as Peter Fergusson-Tepper also had children the same age as Charlotte's[12] whilst the eldest child of Peter Charles, his son, partner and heir, was also near in age, having been born in 1792.[13] This, then, was the family which was mentioned in the 1939 Oban Times articles.

Why were the Fergusson-Teppers predisposed to help?

Considering that Clementina Walkinshaw's letters no longer mention her grandchildren after 1791, that the Tepper Bank crashed in 1793 and Fergusson-Tepper senior died in 1794, it seems reasonable that Charlotte's son and daughter were found homes before the latter date. It is also possible that they were with Cardinal Louis de Rohan at Ettenheim until about 1795 and were 'placed' sometime later, perhaps through Peter Charles Fergusson-Tepper. After all, the bank was not wound up until late 1803. Yet, though the precise timing and nature of the Fergusson-Tepper involvement is not known, nevertheless the context of the event is revealed by examining certain key relationships.

Fergusson-Tepper, like Radziwiłł, was a freemason. In 1810 the following speech on the guiding principles of freemasonry was made at a meeting of the 'Grand Orient of Poland':

> To be a good husband, a good father and a good citizen [...] Leniency is one of the first virtues of a freemason, and is a foundation of our institution and of our secret friendship [...] A second virtue, which without doubt you possess, is charity [...] I should speak to you also of discretion [...] Discretion, Charity and

[11] PSB, vol.30, 1987, pp.248–260.
[12] Library of the University of Warsaw, Katalog Rękopisów Synodu Ewangelicko-Reformowanych, vol.3, cz.III, k.1074. The youngest of the ten children were: Peter (b.1777), Izabella (b.1778) and Otton Walter (b.1779).
[13] W. Kornatowski, op. cit., p.18.

Leniency, there you are – that is what should guide your conduct.[14]

They were the very qualities Ferdinand de Rohan was looking for in the person who would find a refuge for Charlotte Stuart's children. Furthermore freemasonry provided an extensive, reliable and discreet set of contacts for Ferdinand as either he or one of his brothers belonged to the 'Saint-Jean de Montmorency-Luxembourg' whilst Louis was engaged with the movement and Jules-Hercule almost certainly belonged to the 'Grand Orient de Bouillon' with which Prince Charles himself was closely associated, being the nephew and first cousin of successive grand masters and himself grand master of the pan-European Jacobite 'Ecossais' lodges as the 'Soleil d'Or, Milete de Bretagne'.

Fergusson-Tepper was also treasurer of the Order of Malta, another high-level contact-providing organisation.The following letter of thanks was written in 1791:

For your sincere attachment to my order [...] I am therefore once again thanking you [...] One cannot be more sensitive to the esteem and the confidence that you have accorded this Minister Plenipotentiary of Religion.[15] I am persuaded he deserves all considerations and that you will not cease to continue them for him, and I would like, in turn, that you should never doubt the distinguished sentiments that you have inspired in me and with which I am,

de Rohan
Grand Master[16]

It was written by François-Emmanuel de Rohan. He was not only grand master of the Order of Malta but since youth an active freemason, initiated into the Maltese lodge founded at Floriana in 1785. Though from the junior de Rohan branch of the Counts de Poulduc, Emmanuel had been for years close to Ferdinand's paternal uncle, Cardinal Louis Constantin – a knight of Malta. Emmanuel was also an intimate of Ferdinand's maternal aunt, Marie-Louise de Marsan, née

14 AGAD, Archiwum Masońskie, MF 25304.
15 'Of Religion' was a term for the Order of Malta itself.
16 AGAD, Archiwum Masońskie, 341 MF 25303. François-Emmanuel de Rohan (1725–1797).

de Rohan-Soubise. He had furthermore been having a passionate affair throughout the late 1780s with Ferdinand's niece. And since his election as grand master in 1775 he had been in close contact with Poland over a legal wrangle concerning the Order of Malta's claim to estates there, bequeathed by Prince Ostrogski in the seventeenth century. He was also responsible for ratifying the institution of a Grand Priory of Poland with six family commanderies created out of that bequest.[17]

Emmanuel de Rohan's letter was addressed to Count Stanislas Kostka Potocki, one of Poland's foremost freemasons. It was Potocki who had gone to France in 1787 to sign an agreement between the two countries' senior lodges designed to bind them together as closely as possible.[18] Potocki was not only Fergusson-Tepper's fellow freemason but also the cousin of Anthony Prot Potocki, Fergusson-Tepper's banking partner. All three were founding partners in the 'Black Sea Company' together with King Stanislas August Poniatowski, Prince Anthony Jabłonowski (Marie-Anne de Talmont's nephew) and his son-in-law, Prince Joseph Czartoryski.[19]

The Fergusson-Tepper and Württemberg Connection

Another series of relationships is eye-catching. Not only was Ferdinand himself in Warsaw in 1799 but his nephew, Henri, was intimate enough to enter into interest-free loans with Prince Adam Czartoryski.[20] The latter was another pre-eminent Polish freemason closely associated with Potocki and Fergusson-Tepper as well as the Polish king with whom the Czartoryski family could not have been more closely related.[21] In 1784 Czartoryski's daughter married the younger brother of the future King of Württemberg, Prince Louis – a general in the Russian Army.[22] At the same time Henri de Rohan's son, Charles, was on friendly terms with Louis of Württemberg's brother,

---

[17] H. Sire, *The Knights of Malta*, New Haven-London, pp.188–189 & 223–230.

[18] L. Hass, *Ze studiów nad wolnomularstwem polskim …, op. cit.*, p.602. Stanislas Kostka Potocki (1757–1821) & Anthony Prot Potocki (1761–1801).

[19] No less than ten members of the Potocki family were active freemasons prior to the year 1800; see S. Małachowski-Łempicki, *op. cit.*, & M. Mądzik, *op. cit.*, pp.83 & 86.

[20] Archiv Rohanové, Inv.č.430–438, k.č.172, Letters 1806. Adam Czartoryski (1734–1823).

[21] L. Hass, *Ze studiów nad wolnomularstwem polskim …, op. cit.*, p.601.

[22] *Livre d'or des Souverains, op. cit.*, pp.396 & 470. Sophia Maria (1759–1828), the sister of Louis (1756–1817) and his brothers had married the Russian Tsar Paul I (1754–1801) the son of Catherine the Great. Louis was also brother-in-law of Princess Louise von Stolberg-Gedern (1764–1834) – a cousin of Prince Charles's wife Louise (1752–1824), King George III's daughter Charlotte as well as Emperor Francis I of Austria.

Prince Ferdinand. Both were the same age and both became Austrian field-marshals.[23] It is very striking that Louis of Würrtemberg was the only non-Polish prince of a reigning family to have been a client of Fergusson-Tepper. He was even a client of Fergusson-Tepper's son-in-law, Szulc.[24]

There was another Württemberg brother, Prince Alexander. He too was a general in the Russian service with whom Fergusson-Tepper's contacts were intimate, being not only Catherine the Great's banker but also banker to the Russian Embassy in Warsaw. It was here in the household of Prince Alexander that Charlotte Stuart's son first reappeared as a young adult. Significantly, the Württembergs treated him as a privileged member of their closest family circle. Alexander of Württemberg's wife was Antoinette of Saxe-Coburg-Saalfeld. Amongst Charlotte's son's papers is a description of the Battle of Saalfeld written in 1806 as an eye-witness.[25] And the earliest recorded Christian name, patronymic and surname by which he was known was 'August Maximovitch Roehenstart' – in 1810 – precisely the formula used on Young Charlotte's 1804 marriage contract with de la Morlière.[26]

The Oban Times Letters and Marie-Victoire

But what of Charlotte's daughter, Marie-Victoire, legitimised at baptism in 1779 by Ferdinand's brother as the demoiselle de Thorigny? Were the articles in the *Oban Times* right to suggest that the ubiquitous Polonised Scot, Fergusson-Tepper, had helped find her a start in life too? The final partition of Poland had taken place in 1795. At the beginning of his career with the Württembergs, Marie-Victoire's brother was based in the former Polish city of Vitebsk, then under Russian control. To the south lay the former Polish city of Lwów which had become the capital of the newly created Austrian province of

---

[23] Archiv Rohanové, Inv.č.498–499, k.č.181, Letters 1801–1802. Prince Ferdinand of Württemberg (1763–1834).

[24] AGAD, Archiwum Królestwa Polskiego, pudło 88/11–12, *Etats des Débiteurs et Créanciers, Fergusson-Tepper & Charles Szultz*. There was one other prince, namely Potemkin, but he was not from a reigning family and his involvement was not as a private client but a consequence of Fergusson-Tepper being banker to the Russian Embassy and Catherine the Great.

[25] Documents of C.E. Roehenstart, Ms Fr b7 47. It is curious that this account, written in Roehenstart's hand, is signed 'Amèlie' – one of his sister Charlotte's names. Prince Alexander of Württemberg (1771–1833).

[26] Documents of C.E. Roehenstart, Ms Fr b7 65 onwards; G. Sherburn, *op. cit.*, p.18 onwards.

Galicia, Lodomeria and the Grand Duchy of Cracow. Lwów was a rich, cosmopolitan city, strategically placed on one of Europe's great trade routes. Apart from its protestant and orthodox churches as well as synagogues, it boasted no less than three archbishoprics – roman catholic, greek catholic and armenian catholic. The latter community was Lwów's richest.

Armenia's Ancient Nobility

In the year 314 Armenia became the world's first Christian state. For centuries she struggled to maintain her independence against constant invasion until the middle of the eleventh century when the Seljuk Turks swept out of Central Asia, conquered Persia and in 1064 sacked and occupied Christian Armenia. Huge numbers went into exile. Many crossed Asia Minor and travelled to what was then the world's most magnificent city, Constantinople. The thirteenth century chronicler, Geoffrey de Villehardouin, commented that people 'never imagined that so rich a city could exist in the world'. There, for centuries, the highly cultured descendants of the Christian Armenian exiles held key positions at the heart of the Byzantine Empire. Others went further and settled in the Ukraine, Transylvania, Wallachia, Moldavia and the Polish-Lithuanian Commonwealth where some became wealthy merchants. One can see memorials and grave-stones engraved in their script in the Armenian Cathedral of Lwów. They date from the seventeenth and eighteenth centuries by which time the Armenians had come to dominate the trade routes from Central Europe down to the Black Sea and beyond, monopolising the silk trade with Persia. So keen was the East India Company to establish trade with these merchants that the company granted them free passage on all their ships and even offered to build churches for them wherever forty or more settled.

But most of the exiled Armenian nobility went towards Cyprus. There, to the south of the Taurus Mountains, north of Antioch, they established a new Kingdom of Lesser Armenia in Cilicia. It was composed of a multiplicity of principalities engaged in near-constant war with the Turks. From their new homeland these devout Christians and ferocious warriors played an outstanding role in the Crusades, fighting alongside the eleventh century first crusader, Godfrey de Bouillon, the 'Advocate of the Holy Sepulchre', and his brothers, Baldwin and Eustace – all descended through their mother from Charlemagne. Baldwin became King of Jerusalem and married an Armenian princess.

The Armenian knighthood even found themselves fighting alongside Scots, described by Guibert de Nogent as 'wearing short tunics of bristling fur which left their knees bare and with their baggage slung over their shoulders'. Lesser Armenia became a vassal state of the Mongol Empire which had become well established in Persia. And by the second half of the thirteenth century King Hettum and then King Leo formed a Christian-Mongol alliance which included the Knights Templar. Its purpose was to counter the Mameluke invasion of Cilicia, whose main aim was to drive the crusaders out of the Holy Land. In 1281 the two sides fought one of the bloodiest battles in history, the Battle of Hims. Two hundred and fifty thousand men took part. Ten years later the final outpost of the crusaders' kingdom of Jerusalem fell and the Muslims set about erasing every trace of Christian civilisation. Palestine became a desert. For a brief moment, however, the Armenian-Mongol alliance freed the Holy Land once more and the Armenians retook their ancient homeland for which they had been fighting for over two hundred years. But no help came from the West. In 1303, when their combined army was defeated, the Holy Land was lost again and the King of Armenia withdrew to Poitiers where he became a monk. Lesser Armenia was forgotten. Her ancient dynasty died out and her nobility elected a new ruler from the famous Frankish family of Lusignan, kings of Cyprus. It was to this last crusader stronghold that the remnants of the Armenian nobility escaped when the Mamelukes finally conquered Cilicia in 1375 and deported its last king, Leo V Lusignan, to Egypt. He died in Paris in 1393. Then the Turks invaded Cyprus and the island capitulated. Again the Armenians were forced into exile, but they never founded another Lesser Armenia. Some found their way to south-east Poland where many of their compatriots had established themselves. Early fourteenth century sources record the existence of thriving Armenian communities in Lwów, Kamieniec Podolski, Łuck and Kiev. They were proverbially intelligent and those in Lwów became wealthy and trusted enough to lend money to the Polish king and conduct diplomatic missions to countries like Turkey and Persia whose languages, culture and ruling classes they knew from their merchant activites. Like the 'Brotherhoods of Scots' in the Polish-Lithuanian Commonwealth, the Armenians governed themselves directly with their own sovereign judiciary answering only to the Polish Crown. The Armenians' catholicism facilitated assimilation with the Polish population until that process was more or less complete by the end of the nineteenth century. Their foremost families gradually gained Polish nobility and used their merchant wealth to acquire landed estates, becoming ardent patriots and intermarrying with the Polish nobility. It was a process which began in the seventeenth century when many played important roles in the defence of the Polish south-eastern marchlands during the Cossack and Turkish wars of Field-Marshal Żółkiewski and his grandson, King John Sobieski.

Poland's Armenians – who were the Nikorowicz's?

One of the leading families which Armenian tradition acknowledged as being of ancient aristocratic origin was originally called Arvabec'i. Their coat of arms displayed a vertical anchor with an arm in armour brandishing a sabre as its crest. An example is still visible on the right of the entrance to Lwów's Armenian cathedral.[27] The final form of their surname developed as follows – Nikohor Arvabec'i had been living in Jazłowiec, south-east of Lwów. For centuries Jazłowiec had been the second most important Armenian bishopric behind Lwów and its Armenian community one of the oldest, most numerous and richest in the Polish-Lithuanian Commonwealth. But in 1672 it was overrun by the Turks and devastated during an occupation which lasted until 1684. In 1672 Nikohor moved to Lwów, was accepted into the Polish nobility and his descendants became known as 'Nikorowicz', meaning 'son of Nikohor'.[28] Nikohor's father-in-law was Theodore Seferowicz-Spendowski, an Armenian-born noble who had moved to Poland. Having become the *wójt* of Jazłowiec, in other words the superior of its Armenian community, he was ennobled by Sobieski in 1676 for military leadership and bravery in defending the town against the Cossacks in 1648 and against the Turks throughout the succeeding period until 1672.[29]

Nikohor had three sons. Nicholas was a member of the Polish Embassy to Constantinople in 1710, a chamberlain of King August III

---

[27] It is the memorial stone of 'The noble Catherine Nikorowicz, died in 1755, aged thirty six, wife of Piramowicz, Secretary to His Royal Highness', (secretaryship being usually an honorific rank). It displays the escutcheon with an anchor quartered with the Piramowicz's arms of *Odrowąż*,

[28] K. Krzeczunowicz, *Historia jednego rodu*, London 1973, p.52. Krzeczunowicz was a careful researcher but the author has no other evidence for this ennoblement. What is beyond doubt is that the Nikorowicz family was accepted by their fellow Armenians as noble and armigerous.

[29] AGAD, Metryki Koronne, ks.nr 213, p.235; S. Barącz, *Żywoty sławnych Ormian w Polsce*, Lwów 1856, pp.244–254 & 303–310; J. Ostrowski, *Kresy bliskie i dalekie*, Cracow 1998, pp.50–53.

and an expert linguist in Latin, Persian and Turkish to the extent that he could write poetry in the latter. His brothers were Gregory and Simon. They travelled regularly to Constantinople on both trade and diplomatic missions, sometimes accompanying Poland's ambassadors to the Ottoman Porte. Simon married Rozalia Bernatowicz from one of Lwów's richest and oldest Armenian families, records of which go back to about the year 1400 when the family founded the chapel of St. James there.

Simon and Rozalia had four sons and a daughter, Ursula. Of their sons, Theodore became a priest. He rose to the top of the Lwów church hierarchy and was so wealthy that he personally bought a new residence for the Armenian archbishop in 1750. Two of his brothers, Gregory-Simon and Dominic, were both owners of magnificent renaissance houses with arcaded courtyards on Lwów's principal square. Dominic's was the famous 'Black House' (no. 4), whilst his elder brother Gregory-Simon inherited the 'Bernatowicz House' (no. 8). Since the early seventeenth century the latter had provided a home for the king's retinue whilst in Lwów. This tradition, which brought with it royal privileges, began when King Ladislas IV urgently needed a large loan of 100,000 ducats. Irritated when Christopher Bernatowicz asked whether that amount should be in gold, silver or coin the king thought he would teach his subject a lesson by asking for a third in each. Bernatowicz then coolly sent the full amount in each currency. Almost symbolically the 'Black' and 'Bernatowicz' houses stood on either side of King John Sobieski's 'Royal House' (no. 6).[30]

Dominic Nikorowicz became an honorific secretary of King August III in 1758 and a director of the independent Armenian judiciary until the first partition of Poland in 1772 whereupon the independent judiciaries were disbanded. In 1782 he became senior assessor of the Galician Bill of Exchange Court and in the same year Emperor Joseph II ennobled him as a hereditary chevalier of Galicia (baronet or *ritter*).

However, the scale and range of his elder brother Gregory-Simon's interests were astonishing. In 1744 he became an honorific secretary of King August III. He also stood at the apex of the independent Armenian judicicial system, being its elder and president of its court. Consequently, in 1760, King August III granted him the

---

[30] The Nikorowicz's were also the owners of other houses on the square – nos. 41 & 42. Theodore (+1757), Gregory-Simon (1713–1789) & Dominic (1729–1800).

privilege of being removed from the jurisdiction of the city of Lwów and subject only to the court of the Crown Marshal himself. Gregory-Simon was also appointed director of the Lwów Trade Court, president of the Galician Bill of Exchange Court in 1775 and president of the Bill of Exchange Tribunal in 1781. In other words he wielded decisive influence in this central pillar of the banking system as well as in trade disputes. This was especially significant as Gregory-Simon acted as merchant banker to some of the Polish-Lithuanian Commonwealth's richest aristocrats as well as the king himself. In connection with this he was the owner of retail houses in Warsaw, Lwów and Constantinople specialising in artistic fabrics and rugs of the highest quality from Turkey and Persia. Throughout the eighteenth century Gregory-Simon's business was one of the biggest importers of the exquisitely ornamented sashes universally worn by the nobility. Likewise he was the leading specialist in the equally beautiful sabres assembled in Lwów from parts imported from the Orient. Polish Armenians with such extensive international contacts as his had long been used by Poland's rulers for espionage. That would certainly have been one of the purposes of Gregory-Simon's 1746 mission on behalf of King August III to travel the collosal distance to Esfahan in Persia to purchase for him and other aristocrats 'the most beautiful and singular things'. One can imagine the size of the armed escort he needed to ensure the safety of that treasure-laden expedition as it travelled through the vast expanses upon which roamed Cossacks and Turks. An insight comes from Gregory-Simon's letter to the king asking for diplomatic status 'for myself and for my servants and that I might have post horses through the Muscovite Empire free from the burden of expense, and with my safe return to Poland that I might be relieved of the obligation of paying taxes' owing to the need to personally fund 'appropriate gifts for the King of Persia and his ministers'.[31] Active also in the field of charity, he paid for the refurbishment of the Armenian school in Lwów in 1772 and purchased for it a library. He even became a member of the Galician Parliament in 1781 and that same year was ennobled by Emperor Joseph II as a hereditary chevalier of the Holy Roman Empire. A landowner too, by 1773 he owned Cypurów near Lwów and, having leased Lipniki and Skwarzawa Nowa near Żółkiew since

[31] Biblioteka Narodowa, Biblioteka Czartoryskich, Akta dotyczące stosunków z Turcją 1699–1756, sygn.617.

before 1745,[32] he acquired their freehold in 1784 describing the latter as 'his favourite country residence'.[33]

A resumé of the next generation completes the picture of the family's position in Polish and post-partition Austrian society. Gregory-Simon had four daughters and four sons.[34] The oldest, John, was the owner of three country estates near Lwów, a diplomat and linguist in both Turkish and Persian as well as a member of the Polish Embassy in Constantinople from 1763 to 1772 whence he departed to tour England. He was a member of the Galician Parliament from 1786 until 1830, a judge of the Armenian judiciary and in 1790 became a chamberlain of King Stanislas August Poniatowski. Furthermore he founded a greek-catholic church on his property of Zboiska and in 1813 became the first person to create charitable foundations on his estates to support the needy. He was also instrumental in establishing the 'Institute for the Poor' in Lwów in 1811 as well as the 'Fund for Deserving Soldiers' and co-founded the 'Emperor Francis' own Cavalry Regiment'. He was decorated with the Austrian Order of Leopold and the Cross of Jerusalem in 1816 and, like one of his sisters, married a descendant of the Armenian Princes Attabek, Sophie Augustynowicz.[35]

The second son, Mark, became a priest in 1772, gained a doctorate of theology in Rome in 1775 and rose to the rank of vicar-general of Lwów in 1807. The fourth son was Joseph who, in 1786, became a councillor of the Supreme Tribunal of Justice in Vienna; then, in 1799, an imperial privy councillor to Emperor Francis with the title of 'Excellency' as well as president of the Court of Nobility in Cracow.

---

[32] AGAD, Archiwum Radziwiłłów, dz.5, sygn.10496, (6).

[33] *Ibid.*, 10496, (30). Gregory-Simon's wife was born Anna Zachariasiewicz Kopczyk, from a noble family of Armenian origin which, like Gregory's, conducted merchant activities in both Warsaw and Lwów. The family of his mother-in-law, Susannah née Muratowicz, had become Polish nobles in 1600 and in the early seventeenth century had been responsible for re-establishing diplomatic relations between King Sigismund III and the Shah of Persia.

[34] Of the daughters Marie-Anne (1739–1797) married the descendant of an Armenian crusader family which had settled in the Ukraine in the eleventh century. He was Bernard Rosco-Bogdanowicz, co-owner of the estates of Przymiwółki near Żółkiew and nine others in the district of Brzeżany, Kołomyj and Stanisławów. Another was Elizabeth (1756–c.1820) who married into the noble family of Piramowicz. Then came Margaret (+ c.1820) who married Judge Florian Augustynowicz (1748–1832), an assessor of the Galician Bill of Exchange Court. According to Armenian tradition his family was descended from the Kings of Armenia through the Princes Attabek. From his family came John, Armenian archbishop of Lwów in 1751 and a house prelate to Pope Clement XI. The family was intermarried with magnatial families such as the Princes Poniński, Counts Łoś and nobles Olizar.

[35] Their only son, Ignatius, died in his teens. John (1746–1830), Mark (1749–1820) & Joseph (b.1757).

From 1813–1816 he was president of the Appeal Court there and later president of the Senate of the Grand Duchy of Cracow. He translated the works of Wilhelm de Reibnitz into Polish, was an honorary member of the Cracow Society of Learning and a knight of the Order of St. Stanislas. But he left no children by his wife of French origin, Baroness Marie-Anne de Bourguignon who died in Vienna in 1817 and was buried at the Maria Hietzing Cemetery on July 20th.

Who was Paul, Chevalier de Nikorowicz?

There was also the third son, Paul Anthony Louis Bertrand, Chevalier de Nikorowicz. His life is shrouded in mystery. For although his father was a wealthy man, nevertheless Paul was only one of eight children and each inherited an equal part of their parents' wealth.[36] Paul died intestate – suddenly, one presumes – so the Imperial Court of Nobility in Lwów had to decide upon his children's inheritance. Those papers are all intact and from them it is clear he was extremely rich. Much more so than his father.[37] Yet there is a striking absence of any biographical information for him. What was the nature of that career or activity which must have existed to generate such wealth? For Paul owned eighteen country estates including his main residence of Krzywczyce just outside Lwów. Seven were in the district of Stanisławów and five in the district of Sanok. Significantly, the other five were all properties which had previously belonged to Prince Charles' grandfather, Prince James Sobieski, as part of the Żółkiew complex which Prince Michael Radziwiłł had bought in 1739 from the Stuart's aunt.[38] Paul also owned

---

[36] Paul (1751–1810) fathered the following offspring: by Catherine Tamburini he had three children – Josephine (1779–1844) who married Joseph Bołoz-Antoniewicz, a noble Armenian landowner and doctor of civil and canon law; Roman (1780–c.1828) and Ignatius (b.1783). The latter became a member of the Galician Parliament (1820–1852) and his son, Joseph (1827–1890) wrote the music for the poet Kornel Ujejski's 'Chorał', later adopted as an informal national anthem of mourning after the failure of the 1863 Uprising. By his second wife, Marie-Anne Skrochowska (married Lwów 1785, the widow of Bleydzmier), Paul had a daughter, Rengarda (b.1790), who married a landowner of Armenian origin, David Jędrzejowicz. Paul's third wife, Joanna Bohdanowicz de Oroszeny, was from a noble Armenian family which made a fortune supplying the Austrian army with provisions, for which Joanna's father was ennobled in 1781 by Emperor Joseph II. By her Paul had Spirydion (b.1795) and Martha who died young.

[37] The Lwów W. Stefanyk Scientific Library of the Ukrainian Academy of Science, The Piniński Archive (hereafter the Piniński Archive in Lwów), fond 79, nr 1–2.

[38] They were Lipniki, Skwarzawa Nowa, Skwarzawa Stara, Lubella and Glińsko. The latter was particularly valuable because of its porcelain factory, managed later by the leading Warsaw porcelain expert, Frederick Wolff. The Glińsko works included the Habsburgs amongst its clients.

the *Jurydyka* of Łyczaków. This was the term for a country estate formerly outside a city but which had become absorbed as the city boundaries expanded. In other words Paul owned a large piece of land within the city of Lwów itself lying between the eastern section of the old city walls and running right out to the boundary of his main country estate of Krzywczyce. Its value was truly exceptional.[39] However, Paul was four times married and after his death his various estates and other wealth were divided between his six surviving children.

Nine years earlier, on April 10th, 1801, Paul's third wife had died at Krzywczyce, six weeks after the birth of a daughter who died in infancy. For the next five years nothing is known of his whereabouts or activities. Yet during that time he remarried. For at the age of fifty-five he became a father for the last time. His youngest child's baptismal entry at the Armenian-Catholic Cathedral of Lwów reads:

April 20th, 1806, Antime (given in baptism) Mark (given in confirmation), baptised and confirmed by Father Mark de Nikorowicz, Vicar General, the son of Paul de Nikorowicz and Victoire de Thorigny Nikorowicz.[40]

Charlotte Stuart's daughter had reappeared. However her marriage did not last long. Paul died in early 1810 aged almost sixty. Marie-Victoire was barely thirty. Their son was three. Just as the core of the *Oban Times* legend said: Charlotte's daughter, Marie, married a Pole, was widowed young and left with one child.

Because Paul died intestate the court had to decide not only what each child would inherit but who would become the under-age children's guardian. Paul's eldest two under-age children were placed under the sole guardianship of their eldest brother. Yet though Antime inherited the estate of Krzywczyce his mother, curiously, was not granted sole guardianship of her son. The decree of May 2nd, 1810 reads: '[...] but for the under-age Antime, his mother, Marie de Thorigny Nikorowicz, shall be guardian together with John Nikorowicz' – Paul's eldest brother. It is also significant that the formal

---

[39] Piniński Archive in Lwów, fond 79, nr 1–2.

[40] Central State Historical Archive of the Ukraine in Lwów, Archive of the former Court of Nobility, Baptismal Register for the Cathedral of the Armenian Rite for the year 1806, p.29/17: '20 April.1806, Antimus in baptis., Marcus in confirm., Catholica, puer, legitimi. Parentes: Paulus de Nikorowicz et Victoria de Thorigny Nikorowicz, bapt.et confirm. Marco de Nikorowicz, Vicario. Patrini: Josephus de Bołoz Antoniewicz, advocat., et Rengardis de Nikorowicz, virgo.'

court documents use Marie-Victoire's strict baptismal name of 'Marie' whilst nearly all others refer to her as 'Victoire'.[41] But how had Marie-Victoire come to marry the Chevalier de Nikorowicz? Had the Fergusson-Teppers really been somehow involved?

The Nikorowicz and Fergusson-Tepper Connection

No fewer than six areas of contact existed between Paul's family and the Fergusson-Teppers. Regarding freemasonry, Paul's sister-in-law and brother-in-law's family, the Augustynowicz's, had been active in the movement since 1785.[42] Secondly, like the Teppers, the Nikorowicz family had also had a merchanting business in Warsaw. Moreover the Teppers' shop had been located on Warsaw's Old Market Square where many neighbouring ones were owned by families of Armenian origin related by blood and marriage to the Nikorowicz's.[43]

Thirdly, as Anthony Magier, commented: 'The bankers [...] Tepper, Blank, Kabryt, Heyzler, Szulc, Rafałowicz, Prot Potocki etc, would make out in each other's favour Wechsels or Bills of Exchange'.[44] Bills of Exchange were central to the eighteenth century banking system and disputes concerning them legion. Consequently it was in the interest of every banker to have the best possible relationship with the Bill of Exchange Court. Paul's father was president of the Galician Bill of Exchange Court from 1775 and president of its Tribunal from 1781. In other words he held the highest positions relating to this central aspect of banking in former South Poland. Nor was banking or commerce inhibited by redrawn political boundaries. Moreover Paul's uncle and brother-in-law were both senior assessors of the Bill of Exchange Court. It is not only probable that Fergusson-Tepper knew Marie-Victoire's in-laws, in fact there was no way he could have avoided them.[45]

Fourthly, the Fergusson-Teppers and the Nikorowicz family had in common another family of significance, that of the Silesian-born lawyer Ernst von Kortum. From 1773 he was associated with Warsaw

---

[41] Piniński Archive in Lwów, fond 79, nr 1–2.

[42] S. Małachowski-Łempicki, *op. cit.*

[43] T. Korzon, *op. cit.*, vol.2, p.153. According to Korzon: 'In Warsaw the shops facing onto the square of the Old Town were in large measure stocked with Turkish goods being sold by Armenian traders.'; W. Smoleński, *Mieszczaństwo warszawskie w końcu wieku XVIII*, Warsaw 1976, pp.1 & 61.

[44] A. Magier, *Estetyka miasta stołecznego Warszawy, op. cit.*, p.136.

[45] S. Barącz, *op. cit.*, see 'Nikorowicz'; S.Górzyński, *Nobilitacje w Galicji w latach 1772–1918*, Warsaw 1997, pp.60 & 200–201.

where, like Fergusson-Tepper, he was ennobled in 1775 by the Polish parliament and became an active freemason. Whereas Paul's brother was a chamberlain, von Kortum was a privy councillor of King Stanislas August. Moreover, von Kortum belonged to the same tightly-knit group of Warsaw protestants as the Fergusson-Teppers. In 1783 von Kortum settled permanently in Lwów having been appointed an advisor to Emperor Joseph II's governor and himself the administrator of the State's landed properties and forests. Not only did this new and prominent citizen of Lwów undoubtedly know Paul's family but, like him, became the owner of land bordering the city. His property was in Kleparów on Lwów's north side. Later it became known as Kortumówka, or Kortum's Hill.[46] Ernst's younger brother was Charles Louis. Though educated in Cracow he lived in Warsaw from 1768 where he too, alongside the Fergusson-Teppers, was a leader of the protestant community. Moreover he was a banker and in 1793 became a member of the winding-up commission for the bank of Fergusson-Tepper's son-in-law.[47]

Fifthly, Fergusson-Tepper and Anthony Prot Potocki were pioneers in trying to open up the Black Sea Trade and founding partners of the 'Black Sea Company' along with Emmanuel de Rohan's correspondent, Stanislas Kostka Potocki. This activity greatly interested the French government who instructed their ambassador in Constantinople to support the Polish initiative.[48] No group was better informed, more experienced nor linguistically qualified to assist this enterprise than the Lwów-based Polish Armenians of whom few were as able as the Nikorowicz family which had for generations been trading with the Black Sea. From at least the beginning of the eighteenth century they had owned a merchanting business in Constantinople and had belonged to the Polish Embassy there. Evidence of their pre-eminence was Paul's father's mission to Persia on behalf of King August III. Furthermore, Paul's brother was based in Constantinople during the years 1763–1772 from where he corresponded directly with King Stanislas August who had a personal interest in Fergusson-Tepper and Potocki's Black Sea initiative. Then in 1770 Paul's father wrote to the king asking him to recall his son from Constantinople as he wished him 'to complete his education in

[46] W. Smoleński, *op. cit.*, p.95; PSB, vol.14, pp.120–121. Ernst von Kortum (1742–1811).

[47] *Ibid.*, pp.121–122. Charles von Kortum (1749–1808).

[48] M. Mądzik, *op. cit.*, pp.77–91; PSB, vol.28, pp.133–137.

Vienna or Turin or some other European city', requesting 'a passport and letters of recommendation'.[49]

Paul's father gives a further idea of his family's connections in Persia and the Ottoman Empire in three letters from 1767–68. In the first he writes that he has organised for a 'splendid fellow' to go to Constantinople and bring back the wife and family of the Persian staying at the Castle of Nieśwież. In the next he explains that 'Madame the Princess Field-Marshal' asked him a year earlier in Warsaw to obtain oriental fabrics woven with gold and that he had written to his son in Constantinople to get an oriental merchant to send the material by way of Chocim. Then, a few months later, his son 'who knows quite a few of the Turkish lords' was commissioned to buy some 'beautiful specimens of Arab horses' to which end Paul's father sent an expert to Constantinople with sufficient money for their purchase.[50]

The Nikorowicz and Radziwiłł Connection

The identity of the person to whom Paul's father sent those letters reveals perhaps the most important of all the relationships which shed light on how Paul came to marry Charlotte Stuart's daughter. For those letters are part of his family's surviving correspondence with the Stuarts' closest Polish cousin, Prince Charles Radziwiłł. It was from amongst Radziwiłł's sisters that Charles had suggested finding a wife for Henry after returning from the 'Forty-Five. It was from the Stuart brothers' aunt that Radziwiłł's father had bought the Żółkiew estate, part of which had now passed into Paul's ownership. It was Charles and Henry's first cousin, Louise de Rohan, who had asked Radziwiłł's father to repay the Żółkiew-related debt via Tepper's colleague, Riaucourt.[51] Then it was Radziwiłł who had corresponded with Charles' other ex-lover, Marie-Anne de Talmont. And Radziwiłł who had stayed at the de Rohans' Strasbourg residence and corresponded with Marie-Victoire's uncle, Cardinal Louis. Moreover, it was Peter Fergusson-Tepper, Radziwiłł's fellow freemason, who had been a merchant banker to him in his earlier years and who later tried to sort out his huge debts

---

[49] Biblioteka Narodowa, Biblioteka Czartoryskich, sygn.628 & 677.

[50] AGAD, Archiwum Radziwiłłów, dz.5, sygn.10496, (15), (18) & (22); T. Mańkowski, *Pasy Polskie*, Cracow 1938, p. 33 – the Persian was Jan Madżarski, the Constantinople-domiciled Armenian whom Prince Michael Radziwiłł had employed in 1758 as director of the famous manufactory of sashes and 'oriental' fabrics initially based at Nieśwież, then at Sluck.

[51] *Ibid.*, sygn.10496, 10497 & 10498.

and bankrupt Żółkiew estate.[52] The ostentatious, Warsaw-based Fergusson-Tepper was therefore not alone in being close to Prince Radziwiłł. So too was Paul's Lwów-based father, Gregory-Simon, who had been discreetly acting for him as merchant, banker, lease-holder and financier. Put simply, the Stuarts' closest Polish cousin was a joint client of both Paul's father and Fergusson-Tepper, both of whom were linked by mutual interests and contacts. Even Radziwiłł's most trusted secretary was Paul's immediate cousin.[53] And when Paul's father had asked King August III for diplomatic immunity for his mission to Persia his letter began: 'Recommended to His Royal Highness by the Prince Radziwiłł in Grodno during the meeting of Parliament there, and through the good offices of Your Excellency, I received the privilege of being appointed a Royal Secretary'.[54] Other letters from Paul's father paint a vivid picture of his relationship with the Radziwiłł family: 'Lwów, July 27th, 1755 [...] organised payment for the chest marked no.55 from Biała' which had been taken into safe-keeping, whilst returning 'the iron chest in a wooden container'. Then: 'Lwów, July 20th, 1758 [...] According to your order the Chinese sash has been given to Monsieur Kamiński', whilst Paul's father sent Radziwiłł 'a gold sabre and a few other items that might please you' in thanks for 'your ceaseless protection of me throughout my life'. 'Lwów, January 22nd, 1769' concerning Radziwiłł's order from four years earlier to acquire 'gold vessels from Hungary' the price of which had been agreed with another of Radziwiłł's right hand men, General Fryczyński who had already taken them. But as payment was long overdue Paul's father asked 'that at the earliest convenient moment, and without much delay, the outstanding amount of 500 ducats be paid'.[55] And when Fryczyński died and was buried in Lwów, it was Paul's father who, on June 6th,

---

[52] *Ibid.*, sygn.16223, Letters from P.Tepper, 192 from 1738–1778; W. Kornatowski, *op. cit.*, pp.18, 73, 122, 188, 193–197; PSB, vol.30, p.258.

[53] PSB, vol.30, p.258. These cousins of Paul were Lawrence and James Bernatowicz. The latter was firstly secretary to Prince Michael Radziwiłł and then to his son, Prince Charles. A measure of the Bernatowicz-Radziwiłł relationship can be guaged from the fact that Prince Charles Radziwiłł bestowed upon the Bernatowicz brothers a version of the Radziwiłł arms *Trąby* with a crest of ostrich feathers of which the two central ones are sharpened to form quills. These arms were then called *Wierność* (Fidelity) – *Materiały do biografii, genealogii i heraldyki polskiej*, vol.IX, Buenos Aires-Stockholm 1987, p.119.

[54] Biblioteka Narodowa, Biblioteka Czartoryskich, Akta dotyczące stosunków z Turcją 1699–1756, sygn.617.

[55] AGAD, Archiwum Radziwiłłów, dz.5, sygn.10496, (11), (12) & (24); PSB, vol.30, p.254. General James Fryczyński was the commanding officer of Prince Charles Radziwiłł's private militia whilst Adalbert Fryczyński was marshal of his court – together with the Bernatowicz brothers they were Radziwiłł's most trusted employees.

1776, broke the news to Radziwiłł. It is even just possible that Paul's father might have come into contact with the Stuart prince himself. On May 24th, 1752, long after Nikorowicz had become a trusted adviser of the Radziwiłłs, Pope Benedict XIV referred to a report that the Prince Charles was in Poland staying with his Radziwiłł cousins on their Lithuanian estates. Nor did the Pope doubt it, whilst the Tsarina of Russia was so angry upon hearing the news that she wrote to August III of Poland and George II of Great Britain urging them forcefully to make sure he was thrown out of the country.[56]

Then, on February 2nd, 1778 Paul's father effusively thanked Radziwiłł for giving him 'and in such a way as this' his 'favourite country residence' of Skwarzawa Nowa in return for having personally settled Radziwiłł's debt of 45,000 złoties with Judge Leszczyński. Full freehold rights to the ex-Żółkiew manor were passed over to Paul's father in late 1784 when he settled the last outstanding mortgage on the property. The Skwarzawa Nowa and Lipniki estates were then made over to Paul himself on January 23rd, 1785 though how Paul came to own the remaining three ex-Żółkiew estates is unclear.[57]

By 1781 the financial difficulties in which Radziwiłł found himself entangled were already evident when Paul's father apologised that he couldn't help Radziwiłł by releasing the large sum of money pledged to the governor of Bełżec and held on deposit with him despite 'half a century of my life during which I have had the honour of being graced by your Serene Highness'. But he added: 'I know, and know it well, that the Governor will not, however, need this sum for at least the next several contracts'. He then advised Radziwiłł how best to proceed before telling him that the Prince von Thurn and Taxis was due in Vienna.[58]

The Radziwiłł and Württemberg Connection

The casually mentioned name of von Thurn und Taxis was that of the father-in-law of Radziwiłł's brother, Jerome. And Jerome's wife just happened to be the first cousin of the three princes of Württemberg of whom one was so friendly with Charles de Rohan, the second was a client of Fergusson-Tepper and the third had provided such a privileged start in life for Charlotte Stuart's son ... at the same time as Marie-Victoire had been found a husband in the rich Chevalier de

---

[56] E. Heekeren (ed.), *Correspondence de Benoît XIV*, Paris 1912, vol.2, p.189.
[57] AGAD, Archiwum Radziwiłłów, dz.5, sygn.10496, (27–33) & (36–40); Piniński Archive in Lwów, fond 79, nr 1–2, Nikorowicz 1, 'Libro Contractum', vol.14, p.316.
[58] AGAD, Archiwum Radziwiłłów, dz.5, sygn.10496, (34) & (35).

Nikorowicz, the new owner of the five ex-Żółkiew estates and porcelain factory acquired from his father and Fergusson-Tepper's mutual client, and simultaneously the Stuarts' and Württembergs' cousins, Charles and Jerome Radziwiłł.

Nor was it just Paul's father who corresponded with Radziwiłł. His brothers were also in close contact. From 'Rome, April 26th, 1775' Mark wrote of 'the grace and protection Your Highness has always extended to my whole family', grieving that 'in Venice I could not be by your side, for only I know how much I have benefited thanks to you, and how many times I have had the honour of treating with you'.[59] Then the Viennese career of Joseph got off to a flying start in imperial court circles thanks to Radziwiłł's protection. Joseph was clearly trusted by his patron. For he was not only involved in managing Radziwiłł's divorce proceedings but also provided him with legal advice, news on trade matters, political developments and the latest gossip from court.[60]

Vienna and The French Connection

It is also worth considering the family background of Paul's sister-in-law (Joseph's wife), Marie-Anne, who was married in Vienna in 1783. Her father was of noble French origin and had become established in Austria well before the French Revolution at a time when ties between the Bourbon and Habsburg courts had drawn even closer after the marriage of Louis XVI to Marie-Antoinette. Joseph's father-in-law, Jean François de Bourguignon was already a councillor to the imperial court as well as a professor of law at Prague University by 1757 at which time he was created a hereditary chevalier of Bohemia. Then in 1775 the Habsburgs granted him another hereditary title, that of Baron von Baumberg.[61] The Bourguignon's French origin, high social, court and academic connections based on the same Prague-Vienna axis that the de Rohans occupied after the French Revolution, placed Marie-Victoire's brother-in-law, Joseph Nikorowicz, in the heart of the exiled royalist French community which established itself in Austria. And it was precisely then, in 1799, that Joseph himself was given the title of 'Excellency' and created an imperial privy councillor.

---

[59] *Ibid.*, sygn.10498.

[60] *Ibid.*, sygn.10497, (1), (3) & (5).

[61] Biblioteka Narodowa, Zbiór Aleksandra Czołowskiego, Notatki do genealogii różnych rodzin XVIII w., sygn.5569, mkrf.63461–63464, p.122; K.von Frank, *Standeserhebungen und Gnadenakte für das Deutsche Reich und die österreichischen Erblande bis 1806 sowie kaiserlich österreichische bis 1823 mit eningen Nachträgen zum 'Alt Österreichischen Adels-Lexikon 1823–1918'*, Bd.1, Senftenegg 1974, p.117.

There was something else. In a letter written by Marie-Victoire about 1818 she says that her son's 'father died in the service of the King' – namely Louis XVIII.[62] Her own father, Ferdinand de Rohan, had been in Warsaw at about the same time as Louis and various other members of the French royal family to whom he was closely related by blood and status. And Marie-Victoire's uncle, Cardinal Louis, had provided a base in Strasbourg for the Prince de Condé's counter-revolutionary army. Indeed all the de Rohans were pre-eminent courtiers and royalists. But how had Marie-Victoire's husband managed to become so much richer than his father and brothers? His brothers-in-law, through his third wife, had made a large fortune as agricultural suppliers to the Austrian army, alongside which de Condé's royalist French army fought. Did Paul's services for the Bourbons have their origin here? Or had Paul's family once been part of the *Secret du Roi*? For the Bourbons had their well-paid agents at all the main Polish magnatial courts – and none was more important than the Radziwiłł's. Or perhaps Paul had been one of those who lent Louis XVIII large amounts to finance his familt's Polish-based exile?

The 'Oban Times' letters – Conclusion

It is not possible to identify precisely how Charlotte Stuart's daughter and son were found a home with the Nikorowicz and Württemberg families. But it wasn't by chance. These choices were carefully selected by Ferdinand de Rohan through that tightly-knit web of contacts whose genesis was at the Lunéville court of the exiled Polish King Stanislas Leszczyński where the Stuarts and de Rohans had so many French and Polish friends and relations. Evident in this is the hand of that arch deal-maker of Scottish origin, the phenomenally well-connected, Warsaw-based, international banker, freemason and trea-surer to the Knights of Malta, Peter Fergusson-Tepper. Was he one of the international banking contacts whom that other great financier Thomas Coutts had given Clementina Walkinshaw in Paris just prior to the Revolution? Whatever the case, one thing is clear: the letters which appeared in the *Oban Times* in 1939 were not wrong to mention the once great name of Fergusson-Tepper – in fact, they hadn't even begun to appreciate its significance.[63]

---

[62] Archiv Rohanové, Inv.č.562, č.193 II.

[63] Apart from the *Oban Times* articles, there is one other suggestion of a Polish connection for two of Charlotte Stuart's children. In Georges Martin's book *Histoire et Généalogie de la Maison de Rohan*, Lyon 1998, the author states on page 17: 'One of the prelates of the House of Rohan,

footnote 63 (*cont.*)

the archbishop of Cambrai or his brother, the cardinal of Strasbourg, had two children by the last of the Stuarts (one with the names Charles Edward), from whom a posterity which today would be Polish'. The author betrays unfamiliarity with the subject by being unaware that the father of Charlotte's children was Ferdinand. But he makes three remarkably accurate statements: (a) that the number of children associated with a Polish connection is two, not three; (b) that the son's names were Charles Edward; (c) and that there was a posterity (Marie-Victoire's son, Antime) whose descendants would today be Polish. Monsieur Martin had been informed of the above in 1997 by a Frenchman who explained that these facts were based on original documents in his possession which he would photocopy and send to him. Unfortunately he left neither name, address nor telephone number nor sent the photocopies. As Monsieur Martin published his work by prior subscription his informant presumably knew he was preparing a work on the de Rohan family but had no idea of his documents' significance in the context of Charlotte Stuart's children. This author has advertised in various media for Mr Martin's informant to come forward, as yet with no result.

CHAPTER FOURTEEN

Sport of a Sad Destiny

My whole history has been kept
so strictly secret both by my father and grandmother,
that it appears indeed difficult to explain this enigma.

Charles Edward August Maximilian, 1816

Nothing better conveys the confusion of identity suffered by Charlotte Stuart's son than the names and titles he used. Nor was it snobbery. The wide range of acquaintances he acquired in life indicates an enquiring and unprejudiced mind. Indeed, his grandfather always seemed to have a better contact with highland clansman than fellow royals or aristocrats.

The earliest letters of Charlotte's son, from the 1790's, are signed plain 'Charles'.[1] But in 1810 he was known as 'August Maximilian Roehenstart'.[2] A year or two later he is addressed as 'Baron de Roehenstart'[3] and the 'Chevalier de Roehenstart'.[4] Within another couple of years he was not only 'Korff-Roehenstart esquire'[5] but also 'Monsieur de Stuart'.[6] Yet in the same period he also signed himself 'August Maximilian Korff esq.'[7] as well as 'Korff-Roehenstart'.[8] By 1814 he became 'Charles Edward Roehenstart',[9] sometimes with the

[1] Documents of C.E. Roehenstart, Ms Fr b7 17.
[2] *Ibid.*, Ms Fr b7 65, 72 etc.
[3] *Ibid.*, Ms Fr b7 88.
[4] *Ibid.*, Ms Fr b7 98.
[5] *Ibid.*, Ms Fr b7 153.
[6] *Ibid.*, Ms Fr b7 168.
[7] *Ibid.*, Ms Fr b7 158.
[8] *Ibid.*, Ms Fr b7 165.
[9] *Ibid.*, Ms Fr b7 173.

title of 'baron',[10] yet also 'August Maximilian Korff de Roehenstart'.[11] Simultaneously he used the names 'Charles Edward Stuart esq.'[12] and even 'Lord Roehenstart'.[13] By the next year he became 'Count Stuart de Roehenstart'[14] and 'Baron Korff Roehenstart'.[15] In a notarial deed of 1815 he described himself as 'Charles Edward August Maximilian Korff, Baron de Roehenstart'.[16] In 1816 he appeared as 'Charles Edward August Maximilian Roehenstart'[17] as well as 'Charles Edward August Maximilian, Baron de Roehenstart, Count de Korff'.[18] Finally, the Stuart incarnation got the upper hand. By 1824 he was signing himself 'Charles Edward Stuart Roehenstart'[19] and 'Charles Edward Stuart, Count de Roehenstart',[20] sometimes adding the title 'Baron de Korff'.[21] However he often simplified this to either 'Monsieur Stuart' or 'Count Stuart'.[22] His 1826 marriage certificate describes him as 'Charles Edward Stuart, Count Roehenstart – otherwise Charles Edward Roehenstart Stuart'.[23] Nevertheless he also signed himself that year 'Korff'.[24] By the 1830's his surname became more or less permanently 'Stuart' or occasionally 'Lord Stuart'[25] and he wrote to his second wife as 'Madame Stuart'.[26] When the name Roehenstart appeared it was only on formal occasions as the title 'Count of Roehenstart'.[27]

The early use of the name 'Charles' and his return to it later suggests that this was how he was known familiarly in childhood. 'August Maximilian' seems to have been foremost during the early adult period and although 'Maximilian' was his father's second name, nevertheless they feel contrived, as if it was his father's intention to send him into

---

[10] *Ibid.*, Ms Fr b7 178.
[11] *Ibid.*, Ms Fr b7 182.
[12] *Ibid.*, Ms Fr b7 189.
[13] *Ibid.*, Ms Fr b7 186.
[14] *Ibid.*, Ms Fr b7 193.
[15] *Ibid.*, Ms Fr b7 204.
[16] *Ibid.*, Ms Fr b7 208.
[17] *Ibid.*, Ms Fr 44 14.
[18] *Ibid.*, Ms Fr 44 48.
[19] *Ibid.*, Ms Fr 44 113.
[20] *Ibid.*, Ms Fr 44 119.
[21] *Ibid.*, Ms Fr 44 146.
[22] *Ibid.*, Ms Fr 44 133 & 136.
[23] *Ibid.*, Ms Fr 44 191.
[24] *Ibid.*, Ms Fr 44 189.
[25] *Ibid.*, Ms Fr b9 46.
[26] *Ibid.*, Ms Fr 44 263.
[27] *Ibid.*, Ms Fr 44 287.

the world with an identity removed from the Stuart tradition. Likewise the name 'Korff' is alien and probably indicates an important early role played by someone of that name, pre-dating 1804. 'Roehenstart' was a combination of de Rohan and Stuart. But why was it invented? Marie-Victoire had been legitimised in 1779 and had the right to the de Rohan name. Was it that after Jules-Hercule's failed attempt at Veigné to legitimise her brother he never tried again? Or was it that all three children were legitimised but that Ferdinand then had second thoughts and preferred obscurity for Charlotte's children?

The name Korff seems associated with separation from Charles' sisters. On the other hand Roehenstart tends to appear in contexts where other parties present belong to his family circle. The final ascendancy of Stuart probably reflects the fact that it was his mother's family who provided him with his only clear-cut 'parent', Clementina Walkinshaw. For he was kept in the dark as to which of the de Rohan brothers was his real father.[28] His assumption of titles indicates a need to compensate for his natural birth.

After Charles' early childhood he seems to have been found a home among protestants in or near Munich, probably about 1795. But it is unclear if he was already separated from his sisters. In his letters dated 1800 from Munich to his '*tendre Papa*' he wrote of 'so long a separation; [...] this unhappy time'; and 'until we are all reunited'. On the other hand he pleads for a 'letter which will give us a lot of pleasure and will give us joy'; assuring him that 'you cannot doubt our sentiments for you. Your kindness will be forever engraved upon our hearts'.[29]

The family or guardian who looked after him was almost certainly called Korff. That family's background presents a strangely familiar pattern. The Korffs were of Westphalian origin and in the middle ages moved to the Baltic regions of Courland and Livonia which were then under the Polish Crown.[30] In 1692 they acquired the title of baron[31] and during the seventeenth century became strong supporters of the Princes Radziwiłł. At that point Nicholas Korff achieved senatorial rank in Poland.[32] Dating from 1597 to 1809 are some one hundred letters from the Korffs to the Radziwiłłs. A number are from a

---

[28] See appendix – Letters of Marie-Victoire ..., nr 10.
[29] Documents of C.E. Roehenstart, Ms Fr b7 19 & 20.
[30] PSB, vol.14, p.70; A. Boniecki, *Herbarz polski*, vol.11, Warsaw 1907, p.151.
[31] *Gothaisches Genealogisches Taschenbuch der Gräflichen Häuser*, Gotha 1890, p.521–524; S. Konarski, *Szlachta kalwińska w Polsce*, Warsaw 1936, p.141.
[32] PSB, vol.14, pp.70–71. Nicholas Korff (+1659).

Königsburg-based 'de Korff' who in 1782 was acting as a banker or financial adviser to Fergusson-Tepper and Nikorowicz's client, Charles Radziwiłł.[33] Also striking is the fact that Fergusson-Tepper's friend, co-shareholder in the Black Sea Company and fellow banker, Anthony Prot Potocki, also had Korff connections. His tutor had been Captain Charles Korff.[34] Furthermore, during the second half of the eighteenth century the Korffs established strong connections with the Russian Court. They were even related by marriage to the Russian ambassador to Poland, Baron Otto von Stackelberg, whose banking arrangements were managed by Fergusson-Tepper.[35] That the Korffs were mostly protestant explains Charles' upbringing in that religion. But the fact that Young Charlotte and Marie-Victoire were catholic does not preclude them from having lived with their brother during the period after 1795. For in this milieu boys were usually educated as protestants but, where mixed marriages or adoption occured, girls were often brought up as catholics.

Charles' first appearance as a young adult was on August 9th, 1804 with Marie-Victoire and Ferdinand de Rohan when all were witnesses at the marriage of Young Charlotte to de la Morlière in Paris. On that occasion Charles appeared as August Maximilian and the marriage contract recorded their father as the late Maximilian Roehenstart. Charles later claimed that in 1800 he had been an officer of the artillery and by 1803 had won promotion.[36] Whatever the case, by 1806 he was no longer in the army but had joined the household of Prince Alexander of Württemberg. Charles' special relationship with Alexander, who was governor of White Ruthenia, was referred to in a letter of 1807 written to him from Paris by a certain de la Croix who was a friend of both Württemberg and Prince Hohenlohe: 'I received your letter from Coburg [...] I am convinced you will not fail to have a career in a land in which justice rewards ability and in which you will also have the protection of Monsieur the Duke and his wife'.[37]

Charles' career began auspiciously. In St. Petersburg Württemberg recommended him freely, signed letters wishing him 'a thousand com-

[33] AGAD, Archiwum Radziwiłłów, dz.5, sygn.7228–7241.

[34] PSB, vol.28, p.133; N. Ikonnikov, *La Noblesse de la Russie*, vol.46, Library of the University of Warsaw, pp.530 & 554 as well as S. Konarski, *op. cit.*, p.141, suggest that this was Captain Charles (+1787) who married the calvinist Daria von Meyer, or possibly Charles (1746–1814) who emigrated to Germany with two younger brothers.

[35] N. Ikonnikov, *op. cit.*, p.530; A. Zamoyski, *The Last King of Poland*, London 1992.

[36] G. Sherburn, *op. cit.*, p.21.

[37] *Ibid.*, p.22; Documents of C.E. Roehenstart, Ms Fr b7 72.

pliments' and took him into the bosom of his family. Charles' role embraced everything from managing the household expenses to choosing ribbons for the ladies and acting as a trusted and valued tutor. When plays were performed by the family Charles always had a role. When Alexander was invited for dinner Charles received an invitation. Count Golovkin invited Alexander to present Charles to the tsarina. To quote his biographer, he was 'socially desirable in any gathering'.[38] Furthermore his relationship with Alexander's wife, Antoinette, was nothing if not close. She treated him with the interest of a loving sister. And whilst Charles was in St. Petersburg he became initiated as a freemason into the 'Les Amis Réunis' lodge.[39]

In late 1810 Charles organised the removal of the Württembergs' court to Vitebsk where they spent 1811, just one year before Napoleon passed through with his *Grande Armée*. It was then, on October 28th, that the chief of police Krassovsky addressed him as 'August Maksimovitch', just as Charles had appeared on Young Charlotte's marriage contract. And there, mid-way between Moscow and Vilnius, within the borders of the old Polish-Lithuanian Commonwealth, rich prospects awaited him. For the Württembergs had become friends with an old Lithuanian family which had owned the nearby estate of Krynki since 1540. Like Alexander its owner was a general in the Russian service. His name was Vladimir Romejko-Hurko.[40]

Hurko had two daughters, Evelina and Marianna. The Russian tsarina had organised that the former be married to another of her generals whilst Charles' financial agent, Kramer, told him that the owner of Krynki 'desired nothing so sincerely as to see you his son-in-law'. Kramer, Antoinette and Hurko were convinced that the world lay at Charles' feet. However, three events ruined this vision. The vast majority of the fortune that had been made over to Charles had been placed with two companies. The greater part was with his father and uncle Louis de Rohan's company of London bankers, Turnbull, Forbes and Co. Thomas Coutts had recommended the company, which was why they had been entrusted with the management and sale of the de Rohans' San Domingo estate in 1794. But in 1803 the partnership went bankrupt and John Forbes departed for America with the

[38] *Ibid.*, Ms Fr b7 70; G. Sherburn, *op. cit.*, pp.22–29.

[39] Documents of C.E. Roehenstart, Ms Fr b9 4. Antoinette of Württemberg , née Saxe-Coburg-Saalfeld (1779–1824).

[40] *Słownik geograficzny Królestwa Polskiego i innych krajów słowiańskich*, vol.4, Warsaw 1883, pp.758–759; R. Gawroński, *Rodzina Hurków*, Cracow 1895, pp.9–10.

remnants of Charles' inheritance. Another part of his wealth was placed with the Russian banker, Sofniev. In 1811 he too went bankrupt and Kramer advised Charles that he could only expect to recover five per cent of his capital – 5,000 roubles out of an original 100,000. To compound these disasters Charles and Evelina Hurko fell in love. But this wasn't what the tsarina had arranged. It was Marianna who had been ear-marked for Charles. Perhaps he and Evelina had been indiscreet. Or perhaps Charles couldn't bear to marry the sister of the woman he loved. But the main reason was that with most of his fortune gone he felt inadequate. Charles suddenly left Vitebsk for England via St. Petersburg. Alexander couldn't understand it. Antoinette was bitterly upset. 'She is much annoyed with you for leaving', wrote one friend, whilst Kramer told him: 'You have acted wrongly in leaving here without conferring with Her Royal Highness. She would have fixed everything for you; you know very well what she would have done with pleasure; and if she knew the motive for which you have left her, she would not forgive you'. Charles received four heart-broken letters from Evelina. As he set sail from Kronstadt in the Autumn of 1811, with little besides two letters of recommendation from Alexander and Antoinette, he wrote: 'Father of Heaven! What have I done to deserve this misery? Why have I been, at one stroke, deprived of all that rendered existence estimable? Now I am bereft of all; I have neither father, mother, nor country'.[41]

By November Charles was in London. From there he sent a hostile article to *The Sunday Review* in May 1812. In it he accused the Hanoverian prince regent of authoritarianism and reminded him that thrones can be taken away by man, just as happened to 'that race which by birth had a stronger claim to the British sceptre than any of your own family'. With that salvo he left for America in pursuit of John Forbes. He was probably also interested in the San Domingo estate which had been worth one and a half million livres before the Revolution and been owned by his father and uncles. In their correspondence of 1794–95 Louis and Ferdinand doubted whether the bankrupt Henri could inherit.[42] Then in 1803 Louis' share passed to Charlotte de Rohan-Rochefort. So, of the original owners, only Charles' father was still alive at the time of his departure for America in 1812. As San Domingo had been the subject of contested political

[41] G. Sherburn, *op. cit.*, pp.22–29; Documents of C.E. Roehenstart, *op. cit.*, Ms Fr b7 47–100.
[42] Archiv Rohanové, Inv.č.418–429, k.č.170.

control, a simulated sale of the estate had been arranged with Turnbull, Forbes & Co. For a while they passed on the revenues to the de Rohans but stopped when the plantation was expropriated. Nothing could be done without someone being on the spot. Charles might have gone in his father's name but, like Marie-Victoire, he must have been told that their natural father was Ferdinand's conveniently guillotined, childless brother, Admiral Armand.[43] Hence, presumably, Charles' despairing note from 1811 when Ferdinand was still alive: 'I have neither father, mother nor country'. He therefore probably believed himself to have a claim on his late uncle's share.

Charles did go to Haiti. But he got nowhere with the sale of the estate which was still unsold in 1841, according to Charlotte de Rohan's will. From there he arrived in New York in May 1813 whereupon he not only undertook a highly risky venture but evidently had enough capital left or recovered with which to finance it. To judge by his later statement that he 'never knew before coming to this country how painful it is to have debts' it was apparently his last throw of the dice. Having been encouraged by the Russian minister in Washington, Dashkov, to sail under the neutral and then prestigious Russian colours, Charles decided to buy a ship and do some provisions running from the American ports which were being blockaded by the British. In August he bought the *Betsy* in New Haven, which he renamed the *Alexander*, and filled her with a cargo of corn, flour and other items which he declared were bound for Havana. Disaster struck. In September the *Alexander* was intercepted by an American ship, the export of provisions having been declared illegal by President Madison. Such seized cargoes were often ransomed and after a couple of months Charles was trying to negotiate the sale of part of his failed enterprise. However the ship seems to have been forfeited. According to Charles' estimate of November 25th, 1813 his total loss was $17,900. Even allowing for his tendency to exaggerate he had quite obviously suffered a third, major financial loss. He was twenty-nine.

Problems now began in earnest. Earlier that year Charles had borrowed a few hundred dollars from his friend, Count Gabriel Sampigny d'Yssoncourt. At that time such sums had seemed small change. But now he couldn't repay and Sampigny began to threaten lawsuits. The two men knew a French widow in New York called Madame Chapus whom Charles described as his 'good friend'. He wrote to her in late

---

[43] See appendix, Letters of Marie-Victoire ..., nr 10.

December 1813 telling her that 'Sampigny is a monster. I now have only $200 [...] I can give only the half. If you are willing to lend me $200, remit to him the enclosed note [...] I don't wish to tie myself by an uncertain promise; sooner than four months I shall not succeed in repaying, but I will, just in case, give you against all risks a Letter of Exchange on my sister in case I am not in a position to pay sooner'.[44]

This last statement is revealing. For it was Charles' only explicit mention of his sister in his surviving papers. He must have overlooked it, given his policy of erasing all trace of the one person who could reveal his natural birth. In his final will of December 29th, 1853 he gave instructions that those documents not already destroyed 'are to be burnt, particularly the sealed parcels marked: 'To be burnt at my death'.[45] Yet he could hardly have used Marie-Victoire as his financier of last resort had their contact not been close.

Charles returned to Europe on May 3rd, 1814 – seven months after Ferdinand had died in Paris. His return could scarcely have been less triumphant. The bitterness of his feelings was reflected in a startlingly accurate self-analysis:

> It is strange, but it is true, that those who have been thrust by mis-fortune to a state beneath their birth and expectations, consider themselves the object of universal hostility. They see contempt in every eye. They suppose insult in every word. The slightest neglect is sufficient to set the sensitive pride of the unfortunate in a blaze; [...] fancied ills which, however unfounded, keep the mind in a constant fever with itself, and warfare with the sur-rounding world.[46]

Despite his losses Charles still had modest funds from somewhere or someone upon which to live. For he did not work and travelled freely, though living modestly and spending carefully. His debts were never big and he always settled them sooner or later. Nonetheless his return to Europe heralded a fundamental change. He set aside his solemn vow never to publicly mention his parentage and began to pursue the chimera of establishing his legitimacy so as to recover something of the Stuart fortune which he wrongly presumed his mother to have left. He started to write of his 'reclamations' – the word by which he always

[44] Documents of C.E. Roehenstart, *op. cit.*, Ms Fr b7 158.
[45] *Ibid.*, Ms Fr 44 287.
[46] G. Sherburn, *op. cit.*, pp.36–37.

referred to his claims. In his search for funds the Stuart route was the only one open. For by 1814 Marie-Victoire and he were the only living Stuart offspring. The same was not true of his paternal side. He had already received an inheritance from the de Rohans and could scarcely feel cheated. And there were his powerful cousins who wanted him and his sister kept hidden in obscurity.[47] But to successfully press a Stuart claim Charles was convinced he had to present himself as legitimate. Yet he must have believed the same as Marie-Victoire who admitted that 'The brave Admiral, the Prince de M. never married the Duchess'.[48] So Charles dusted down the fictitous identity of his father from Young Charlotte's 1804 marriage contract and upgraded him to 'the late Count August Maximilian Roehenstart'.

Not once did Charles show the slightest pretension to the Stuarts' thrones. He was solely concerned with trying to recover something of his late mother's wealth or obtaining a government pension from the British or French. But it was a road which led nowhere and was littered with forced lies and half-truths which would generate bitter frustration, disappointment and emotional isolation. Only alchohol would have been required for his life to degenerate into a re-run of his grandfather's.

Charles turned first to his grandfather's estranged wife, Louise von Stolberg-Gedern, in Florence whom he all too accurately recognised as 'a woman of great intelligence but she is malicious and vindictive to a superlative degree'. From his step-grandmother he obtained nothing except the address of his mother's former lady-in-waiting, Countess Mary Norton. To her Charles wrote: 'I had taken the engagement never to break the silence which I have so strictly observed, but having been told that the Cardinal Duke of York repeatedly asked for me before his death, this reason alone could induce me to recover a part of my mother's fortune of which I have been so unjustly deprived'.[49] Apart from the ridiculous embroidery concerning Henry, he added: 'An unfortunate circumstance compelled me to go to America, whence I am returned since a few months [...] I flatter myself that the remembrance of my poor mother will act upon your mind in favour of her unfortunate son who has constantly been the sport of Fortune. Fate has

---

[47] See appendix – Letters of Marie-Victoire ...; it is evident from this correspondence that most of their surviving de Rohan cousins knew that Marie-Victoire and Charles were the children of Charlotte Stuart and Ferdinand de Rohan.

[48] *Ibid.*, nr 10. The title 'Prince de Montbazon' was the correct form for the second of the four de Rohan brothers, namely the guillotined Admiral Armand – prince ranking lower than duke.

[49] Documents of C.E. Roehenstart, Ms Fr b7 182.

indeed contrived to pour on my head such a torrent of combined evils that my fortitude has scarcely been proof against them'. But the old lady died before he could meet her.

Another avenue was Fribourg. Charles had learnt of the tin box containing the genealogical act of 1769 signed by 'Douglas and Stuart' as well as other documents mentioned in his grandmother's will. He was given these details by Pierre Couppey, the faithful valet whom Clementina had made heir to her negligible estate. So in late July 1815 Charles went to Fribourg to see his grandmother's executor, Councillor Weck. From him he heard about the six parcels of his mother's letters which had been sent to the Coutts family along with the tin box. Thirty-one documents still in Weck's possession were handed over to Charles. During his time in Switzerland he stayed in Berne. There too was his grandmother's former charge, Coutts' daughter, the dowager Marchioness of Bute. He visited her on August 4th and commented that the three sisters: 'Ladies Bute, Guilford and Burdett were practically brought up by the Countess of Albestroff' and that Lady Bute spoke very warmly of Clementina. She invited him to dine with her. Afterwards he noted that amongst the guests was the wife of the famous Polish General Henry Dąbrowski.[50] Charles and Lady Bute subsequently met several times and she gave him letters of introduction to her father and sister. In the former she wrote:

> This letter will be delivered to you by the Baron Roehenstart, the son of the unfortunate Duchess of Albany, daughter of our old acquaintance, Madame d'Albestroff, whom we all remember at Paris. He is the last of the Stuarts and his history is a very sad one [...] He is a very well bred, agreeable man and should he put his present intention into execution of going to England I hope you will see him and I need not say I am sure you will do him any kindness in your power.[51]

In recording one of his other visits it is curious to see what caught Charles' eye. He noted down old signatures from the guest book of a local auberge. They included: 'General Thadée Kościuszko, Princess Jabłonowska and Princess Lubomirska'.[52]

Next he was in Strasbourg in November where he received a very

[50] *Ibid.*, Ms Fr b7 199.
[51] *Ibid.*, Ms Fr b7 204.
[52] *Ibid.*, Ms Fr b7 229.

friendly letter from Prince Hohenlohe whom he had known in Russia. Hohenlohe wrote: 'I suppose you must await with much impatience the letter that will determine the direction you are to take [...] for this wandering life cannot be agreeable [...] I beg you not to forget that I take a considerable interest in anything that concerns you'.[53] Unsure what course to follow in his uncomfortable situation Charles had asked if he could return to the Württembergs. But though he would appeal to Princess Antoinette more than once over the next year to accept him back her offended door remained firmly closed.[54]

The early months of 1816 were spent in Florence, Ascoli and Venice. Afterwards Charles spent quite a long time in Vienna where he seems to have had a source of income. There he befriended Baron di Carnea who was a chamberlain at the Habsburg court where Marie-Victoire's brother-in-law Joseph was an imperial privy councillor and his wife the daughter of another. Joseph's wife died in Vienna a year later and when Charles' sister died she was buried alongside her.[55]

Finally, Charles arrived in London from Hamburg in September 1816 where he intended implementing two plans simultaneously. One was to use Lady Bute's letters of introduction to the Coutts family to try and get back his grandmother's tin box, its contents and the correspondence between her and his mother. However, the Coutts family had long been bankers to the Hanoverian court and could harm their position if they returned documents which might be used to raise the ghost of Stuart claims. Though the ladies of the family claimed they searched high and low, only a few uninteresting documents were ever handed over. This effectively ruined the second plan. For Charles had anticipated finding documentary proof that he was his mother's son. Enraged by the Coutts' behaviour he considered prosecuting them. For he had already appealed to the prince regent for help in establishing himself as the grandson of Prince Charles Edward Stuart and now found himself unable to substantiate his claim. His 'Memorial' was comparable to his mother's to the Court of France in 1772. Unfortunately Charles was naive enough to believe that the prince

[53] *Ibid.*, Ms Fr b7 205.
[54] G. Sherburn, *op. cit.*, pp.39–50.
[55] *Ibid.*, p.52. The records of the Friedhof Hietzing cemetary in Vienna for: Marie-Anne de Nikorowicz née Baroness Bourguignon de Baumberg, buried July 27th, 1817, grave nr 56 group 4; Anne von Leiner, buried July 26th, 1816, grave nr 57, group 4; and Marie-Victoire de Pauw née de Thorigny, buried April 29th, 1836, grave nr 55, group 4; S. Barącz, *op. cit.*, p.251; AGAD, Archiwum Radziwiłłów, dz.5, sygn.10497; Biblioteka Narodowa, Zbiór Aleksandra Czołowskiego, *op. cit.*; K.von Frank, *op. cit.*, p.117.

regent would receive him privately and chivalrously settle the matter as one royal to another. Instead Charles encountered the deliberate obfuscation of official bureaucracy. Nor did his foolishness stop there, for his prose was exaggerated and he invented a 'great-grandfather' in the Swedish 'Baron Roehenstart, Count of Korff who came over to England in the year 1715 and served in the English Army; he afterwards [...] married Miss Sophia Howard, by whom he had two daughters and a son'. Without doubt this claim was exposed, destroying the credibility of the rest. Yet his childish innocence is scarcely how a shrewd Stuart imposter would have behaved. Certain phrases also cast light on his past. He wrote that his grandmother:

'[...] insisted on my being brought up in the Roman Catholic Church, and my father would never consent to it: she was for this reason much irritated against him [...] I was on the point to make [...] a marriage which answered all that I could wish. But adverse fortune seems to have brought me to a state of prosperity, merely to throw me into an abyss [...] I received the news that a merchant, Mr Forbes, in whose hands was placed the greatest part of my fortune, had become bankrupt, and was gone to the United States of America. This was to me a thunderbolt. If I had not been so foolishly scrupulous, my marriage might still have taken place [...] A short time after my arrival in Philadelphia, I had the satisfaction to recover a part of my money [...] My earnest wish is not to give publicity to this very unfortunate business, out of respect for my grandfather's name. But by merely proving that the Cardinal had no right to enjoy my mother's fortune, to show that I am the first creditor of his succession'.[56]

In an accompanying letter Charles added: 'My whole history has been kept so strictly secret both by my father and grand-mother, that it appears indeed difficult to explain this enigma'.[57] In a private letter to a friend dated November 8th, 1816 Charles commented:

Not having any more money I could not muster courage enough to wait upon the Duke of Gloucester, to whom I have been strongly recommended five years ago by his particular friend, the

[56] Documents of C.E. Roehenstart, *op. cit.*, Ms Fr 44 39; G. Sherburn, *op. cit.*, p.61.
[57] Documents of C.E. Roehenstart, *op. cit.*, Ms Fr 44 16; G. Sherburn, *op. cit.*, p.63.

Duke of Württemberg. One feels indeed very stupid *'sans argent'* [...] Having been several times to Carlton House my papers were sent by Mr Watson to Lord Sidmouth: this distresses me very much, as they were intended for the Prince alone, and the idea of any publicity of my sad story makes me shudder [...] I awake now after a long dream, and I must absolutely forget all my pompous claims; [...] pray mind that I allude only to Frascati and the pension of Government [...] All what I look for at this moment of wretchedness is not to get a Crown, but to get my bread in Scotland. Water and a crust of bread in that country, so endeared to me by so many sad and tender recollections, the theme of my infancy [...] Had I not lost my brig and all I possessed I should have religiously kept my word and never said a thing about my claims.[58]

Charles then travelled to Edinburgh. But his stay there only lasted a couple of months before he returned via London to Paris. He had intended to travel to Russia in the hope of picking up again with the Württembergs and perhaps recovering some of the second fortune he had lost there. But during his six months in Paris an unbelievable event occurred. The British Government instructed their Paris-based agent, John Schrader, to spy on Charles and try to compromise him. An opportunity presented itself when, at Charles' instigation, a young Prussian officer called Augustus von Assig was arrested for theft. Schrader then persuaded von Assig to accuse Charles of trying to organise an army with which to invade England! Today this seems incredible. But in 1817 not that much time had passed since the last period of Jacobite discontent. Furthermore, the Hanoverians had proved themselves capable of relentless, petty persecution of the Stuarts. And Lord Sidmouth, to whom Charles' papers had been passed, had recently been responsible for brutally suppressing civil disturbances in Derby and elsewhere. Moreover Sidmouth was head of the British secret service. In addition, the Hanoverian succession was in serious doubt, for out of the seven surviving sons of George III none, in 1817, had any legitimate offspring and the future Queen Victoria had not yet been born. Notwithstanding, Westminster's initiative was preposterous. On July 3rd, 1817 Charles was summoned by the *Ministère de Police Générale* on the basis of an unspecified charge against

---

[58] Documents of C.E. Roehenstart, *op. cit.*, Ms Fr 44 18.

him. Appalled to discover that he was being accused of high treason he appealed to the British Ambassador, Sir Charles Stuart, saying: 'I am being made an instrument to destroy the peace of the country. To lay any weight upon this charge would be proof of insanity'.[59] A fortnight later, in the presence of several French police officers, a friend of Charles, Edward Storr Haswell, managed to get von Assig to confess that he had acted under pressure from the British spy, Schrader. His statement was immediately sent to the British Embassy. A further exoneration was sent by the French police to their ambassador in London in which the British agent's charges were described as a 'ridiculous exaggeration and culpable bad faith'. They described Charles' situation as 'cramped by financial losses. His behaviour, reserved and discreet, suits his condition. He sees few people and receives few letters'.[60]

The fact that the British Government contrived this bizarre episode clearly implies that they knew precisely who Charles' mother was. They would scarcely have gone to all that trouble if they had believed him to be a mere impostor. Indeed, the background of the British Ambassador, Sir Charles Stuart, reveals that Westminster had in him a truly remark-able source of information about the Duchess of Albany's children. Sir Charles Stuart (created Lord Stuart de Rothesay in 1828) had been sec-retary of the British Legation in Vienna from 1801–04 and in charge of it from 1803–04. One of his main areas of interest would have been the activities of the emigré French royalist forces allied to Austria, for whom that city was a key political centre. Then, though Sir Charles remained chargé d'affaires in Austria until 1806, he became secretary of the British Embassy in Russia from 1804–08, acting as minister *ad interim* from 1806–07. This was exactly the period during which Charles was based there with Prince Alexander of Württemberg and was 'socially desirable in any gathering'. Sir Charles could hardly have avoided him. Then fol-lowed the two periods of Sir Charles' ambassadorship to France: 1815–24 and 1828–31. But that was far from all, for Sir Charles also hap-pened to be the grandson of the 3rd Earl and nephew of the 1st Marquess of Bute. In other words his aunt was none other than Frances Coutts, that same dowager Marchioness of Bute who had been chaperoned in Paris by Clementina Walkinshaw just prior to the French Revolution and had met Charles in Berne in 1815. Her father, of course, was

[59] *Ibid.*, Ms Fr 44 58.
[60] Royal Archives at Windsor, Georgian Papers, 22, 063–5.

Thomas Coutts, who had been responsible for arranging Cardinal Henry Stuart's pension from George III and had been a friend of both Ferdinand de Rohan and Clementina Walkinshaw. Evidently the British Ambassador was nothing if not amply qualified to confirm the identity of Charlotte Stuart's son.[61]

In July 1817 Charles had believed that 'no man could be more firmly attached or more sincerely devoted to England'.[62] Not that he viewed himself as English. That same month he asked a friend: 'Why are all the English so partial to Geneva?'[63] Bitterly disillusioned by the humiliating dismissal of his 'Memorial' and the extraordinary attempt to frame him, his attitude towards England became cynical. He also wrote that, by the Act of Union, Scotland had been 'cheated of her independence' and that 'the wrongs of my country shall be a sharp sword that will at once defend me against all opponents; [...] that at this moment I could communicate to the heart of every Scot an equal ardour to that which burns in mine. Then should our haughty English foes flee as heretofore they died at Bannockburn'.[64]

In the end Charles didn't go to Russia whence he received 'unsatisfactory news'. Instead he spent the winter in Italy which for over a decade became something of an annual migration. The next major event of Charles' wandering existence was mentioned in a letter written to his step-grandmother, Louise von Stolberg-Gedern, in early 1820 after having come back from tutoring two young men around the Middle East. He informed her 'of my marriage with an Italian lady, brought up in Paris, of the Barbieri family. This house, though not rich, is distinguished and of rather ancient nobility'. The union did not last long. His wife died childless in July 1821 and was buried on the 20th of that month aged thirty-one in the Parish of St. Marylebone, Middlesex as Maria Antoinetta Sophia, Countess of Roehenstart.[65]

---

[61] Private Papers of British Diplomats 1782–1900, The Royal Commission on Historical Manuscripts, HMSO London, p.65; National Register of Archives, Chancery Lane, London, Charles Stuart, Baron Stuart de Rothesay (1779–1845), diplomat, http://www.hmc.gov.uk/nra/PIdocs.asp/P-2759.

[62] Documents of C.E. Roehenstart, *op. cit.*, Ms Fr 44 58.

[63] *Ibid.*, Ms Fr 44 57.

[64] *Ibid.*, Ms Fr 44 18.

[65] G. Sherburn, *op. cit.*, p.76. Sherburn gives the name as 'Barbuonei' adding that it is illegible. From the original it resembles either 'Barbuoni' or 'Barbieri'. There was no such noble European family as Barbuoni, only Barbieri. Likewise is there no trace of a Barbuoni family in the Births/Baptisms, Marriages and Deaths records of the Archives de Paris, whereas there are several entries for Barbieri between 1830–1860: J.Rietstap, *Armorial Général*, vol.1, Lyon, pp.112–113; Archives de Paris, 5 mi.2/708 & 5 mi.2/11.

On September 15th, 1823 Charles received a letter from Sampigny d'Yssencourt in which he wrote: 'Mrs Bouchier Smith is the lady to whom you had the kindness to bring a letter for me last year, she has become a widow and thinks to settle in France'. This contact led to Charles' second marriage – to Louisa Constance, the moderately wealthy daughter of Joseph Bouchier Smith who had died earlier that year. Constance's family had belonged to the Oxfordshire landed gentry and had old university connections until her father sold his manor of Kidlington together with Garsington to the Earl of Peterborough. Thereafter he lived in London as well as Godstone in Surrey.[66] Constance and Charles' wedding at St. Pancras on December 13th, 1826 was a far cry from the imperial court at St. Petersburg, Prince Alexander of Württemberg, the estate of Krynki and the prospect of the generously-endowed hand of Marianna Romejko-Hurko. But a lot had changed since then and none of it for the better.

After their marriage Constance suffered the consequences of Charles' inability to form a trusting and balanced relationship. Even Marie-Victoire was not informed of her brother's whereabouts. So Constance was left on her own for long periods while Charles meandered all over Europe and Asia Minor on one pretext or another. She lived for periods in France, where she struggled to learn the language, and also in London. But she hardly features in her husband's surviving papers. Travel seemed the only thing which brought Charles peace. His observations reveal an intelligent, well-informed mind and natural kindness. He wrote with tenderness even about the stray dogs of Constantinople. And his sense of relief is palpable when 'vaulting on my noble arabian I bounded over the desert'.[67] His writings betray a special interest in Turkey though it wasn't the only place free from the suffocating rules of Europe. One wonders if his choice wasn't triggered by the connection with Constantinople and the family origin of his sister's first husband. For in writing about Turkey Charles also referred to Armenia.[68]

Another aspect of his personality is his pretension to grandeur visible

[66] College of Heralds, London, W.L. Chester MSS, Parish Registers, Oxford, St. Giles; ibid., *Bigland's Pedigrees*, vol.2, p.153; ibid., *Victoria County History of Oxfordshire*, Bullingdon Hundred – Garsington 3014/231; Alumni of Oxford and Westminster; Family Records Centre, Clerkenwell, Prerogative Court of Canterbury Wills, Indexes to Estate Duty Wills and the Death Duties Registers, 1823, IR27/187 & IR26/975 f.46, Probate 11/1665/41, Will dated October 9th, 1814, Probate dated January 10th, 1824.
[67] G. Sherburn, *op. cit.*, pp.87–108.
[68] *Ibid.*

35 General, Prince Louis de Rohan (1830)

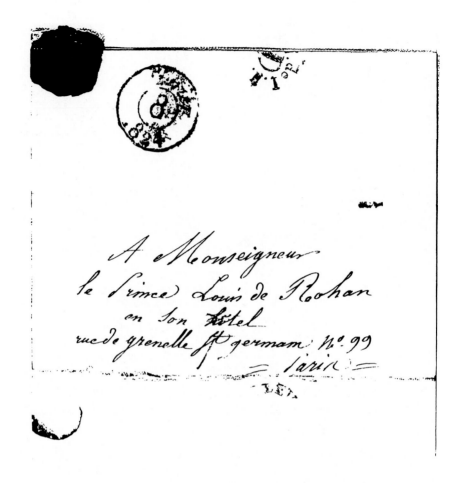

36 The envelope of one of Marie-Victoire's letters to Louis de Rohan

mon courage dans mes malheurs, j'en
gardois la copie soigneusement, et la lecture
de ses grands souvenirs historiques
étoit un talisman pour élever mon ame.
— Je vais envoyer un petit mémoire
pour le ministre avant que le Prince
ait eu la bonté de me dire s'il vouloit
bien s'en charger, je ne sortirai point
de toute la journée ainsi que demain
pour attendre la réponse du Prince,
jeudi je vais à Versailles pour voir
mon fils dont je suis inquiète; sa
santé va bien, mais c'est sa sagesse
qui va mal —.

J'ai l'honneur d'être avec respect,
Mon Prince,
Votre reconnaissante
Roehenstart

37 One of Marie-Victoire's letters to Louis; (note the use of the 'maiden' name Roehenstart whilst simultaneously refering to her son)

Mon premier bonjour est — pour celui
à qui je le dois , c'est un bien heureux
accord que celui du plaisir et du devoir ; j'ai
donc l'honneur de saluer mon Seigneur et
frère et de lui offrir l'expression de ma reconnais-
=sance .   — Je sais qu'il n'est pas
besoin de stimuler l'obligeance du Prince pour
rendre justice à une orpheline du pur Sang
des M. et des S. , mais je prie instamment
Monseigneur de ne point encore s'ennuyer, de
ne pas perdre courage ...... ce serait s'arrêter
en trop beau chemin , la charité chrétienne
soutiendra votre bienveillance au moins jusqu'à
l'époque du mariage !! — Il est des services
qui valent cent fois plus que de l'or." J'ai
réfléchi qu'hier, en vous témoignant mon inquiétude
(qu'une certaine épithète lancée méchamment — ne vînt
affecter la sensibilité du respectable) vous avez
pu croire que je ne lui avais pas très franchement
parlé de Ma naissance toute naturelle , il en sait
là-dessus autant que nous, il n'ignore pas que—

38 & 39 (2 illustrations) *Part of a letter from Marie-Victoire to Louis*

le brave Amiral Prince de M. n'a jamais été
marié avec la D.... J'ai cru nécessaire même, d'avertir
M. d'A. qu'il pourroit peut être entendre dans le
monde répéter une calomnie affreuse qui a plané sur
la tête de mon respectable oncle et tuteur le P.ce J.
aussitôt que M. d'A. m'a parlé de ses espérances
d'union, je l'ai prévenu de tout franchement :
il sait que le P.ce J. nommé tuteur après la mort
du P.ce de M. a seul veillé à mon éducation
et que par ce moyen ayant seul paru s'intéresser
à moi, la calomnie peut s'être exercée sur lui.
— J'ai toujours l'honneur de prier de nouveau le
Prince d'être mon généreux Chevalier dans le monde, s'il
en est besoin, je lui promets de ne jamais déshonorer
l'illustre famille d'où je sors. M. d'A. m'a
dit souvent qu'il aimoit la noblesse de mes sentimens
(je ne suis pas trop modeste de répéter ce compliment)
qu'il savoit bien qu'il me manquoit quelques
parchemins pour prouver d'autres titres de
noblesse, mais que cela lui étoit égal, que
j'étois toujours à ses yeux une M. et une S.
— Dans ce moment je regrette doublement que
Madame la Princesse Charles ne soit pas à Paris,
elle pourroit dire à qui de droit... que si je n'ai pas
de fortune, je possède au moins une réputation intacte

Je suis bien reconnaissante que votre
Altesse ait la bonté de vouloir bien
intéresser en faveur de votre malheureuse
fille, j'espère tout de votre éloquence
persuasive et je compte sur vos
Sentimens paternels.

Vous m'avez unie à la bonté
personnifiée, mon attachement pour
le Prince avait encore augmenté à la vue
des souffrances qu'il supportait avec
un grand courage, depuis un an ; je
vous l'avoue, c'était plus que de
l'affection que j'avais pour le Prince,
j'éprouvais une sorte de vénération
pour le chef de cette noble famille
qui accueillit si généreusement nos
frères dans l'exil, je ne croyais jamais
pouvoir assez montrer de dévouement
à mon malheureux ami, il disait
qu'il ne désirait recouvrer la santé
que pour s'occuper du bonheur de

40 & 41 (2 illustrations) Part of a letter from Marie-Victoire to Louis written on black edged mourning paper

la Victory ..... excusez, monseigneur, je m'oublie, en parlant de celui qui mérite tous mes regrets !

J'ai l'honneur de prier votre Altesse de recevoir l'expression de la reconnaissance et du respect affectueux de votre fille.

Victory d'Auvergne.

ce dimanche 27.

P.S. Veuillez m'excuser si je n'ai personne dans ce moment pour faire déposer cette lettre directement à votre hôtel.
Si je pourrais prévoir le jour où l'état des services aurait reçu votre révision je le ferais prendre pour le recopier, j'espère que vous aurez la bonté de m'instruire des démarches que je devrai faire.

42 Lwów (1825)

Jch, Don _Raul Heinrich Langläß_ **aus der Versammlung der regulirten Prie‑
ster des heiligen Apostel Paulus (insgemein' Barnabiten genannt) der Zeit**
Propst und Pfarrer an **der kaiserl. königl. Hof‑Pfarrkirche zum heiligen Michael in Wien, bezeuge hiermit,
daß laut des pfarrlichen** _Sterb_ = **Protokolles** _die Hochwohlgebornen Frau Maria de Pauw gebornen_

hier Skorigny, von Tours gebürtig, ehemahligen des compromirten K.K. bibliothecaris Gatten,

der Pauw hochwohlgeborn; Ludzigischer Religion, 56 Jahr alt, am Sieben und zwanzigsten

April Eintausend Achthundert Dreyßig und Sechs /. am 27. April 1836 / um 5 Uhr

Abends im Hause Nr. 1732 in der Alservor Vorstadt, sanft an Lungstall gestorben,

und von demselben am Samstag, das ist der 29. April 836 nach ihre Katholischen Ge‑

bräuchen eingesegnet und nach Maria Hitzing bey Wien zur Beerdigung überbracht

worden ist.

Urkund dessen meine ämtliche Fertigung. Wien im Collegium zum heiligen Michael am _14. Juny_
im Jahre 18 _36_

Don _Raul Heinrich Langläß_
ut supra.

43 Marie‑Victoire's death certificate (1836)

44 *The Castle of Grzymałów (c. 1900)*

178	Nr. Do-mus	NOMEN	Religio		Sexus		Thori		PARENTES		PATRINI	
			Catholica	Accatholica	Puer	Puella	Legitimi	Illegitimi	PARENS	MATER	NOMEN	CONDITIO
											PATRINI	
	1806 Menfis											
	26-as = april. 1806.	Antimus in baptis. Manuel in confirm.	1.		1.	—	1.		Paulus de Nike.	Vitoria de Thon	Josephus de Botoz Antonieur	Advocat.
		Baptisaute ab... confirm... clarco de Nitano Pli.								gry — Nitorow Nitorowicz	Rengazos Ct. Nitorowic	Virgo.

45 *Antime de Nikorowicz's baptismal entry in the register of the Armenian–Catholic Cathedral of Lwów (1806). (Note the use of the name Victoire.)*

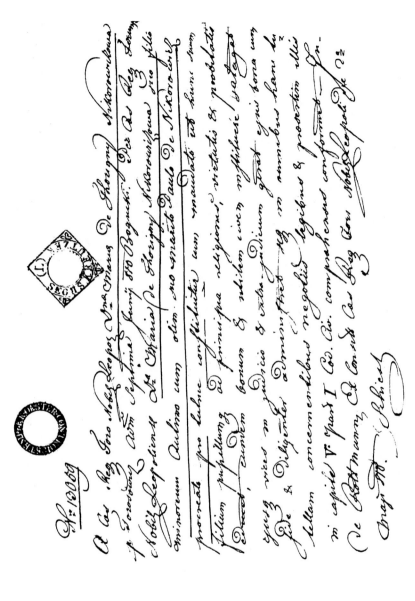

46 One of the documents from the Galician Court of Nobility in Lwów concerned with Marie-Victoire's guardianship of her son after her first husband's death intestate in 1810. (Note the use of the name Marie.)

Nixorowicz Antym

47 *Antime's confirmation of nobility, in the records of Galician Court of Nobility (1829)*

48 Count Leonard Piniński

49 The Castle of Krasiczyn (1835)

50 Elizabeth Robertson-Butler (née Fraser) with Count Leon Piniński in Copenhagen (1925)

51 Count Alexander August Piniński (c. 1900)

52 The manor house at Suszczyn

53 The Castle of Świrz

54 Count Stanislas Piniński, 1944 (right)

55 Stanislas and Jean Graham, May 12th, 1951

in his active membership of various orders of chivalry. From 1825 he had been given permission by the King of France 'to wear the decoration of the Grand Cross of the Chapitral Order of Ancient Nobility and of the Four Emperors and that of the Grand Cross of the Order of the Lion of Holstein'.[69] He could also be terribly hurt and become enraged by the smallest insult. In 1833, having been badly treated by customs officials, he complained to the Prince of Monaco. But the latter's response seemed arrogant and he demanded satisfaction, contemptuously informing him that he was the 'heir of a House far superior to that of Monaco'. He signed himself: 'Stuart'.[70] Then in 1838 he was turned away from the Paris home of Alexander of Württemberg's son. Charles sent him a bitter letter in which he said: 'I used to know several members of your family' and then called Württemberg 'the littlest Kingdom in Europe, the dignity of which was only granted by the grace of Napoleon'.[71]

The final humiliation came with the appearance of the Manning-Allen brothers who posed as the 'Sobieski-Stuarts'. Though now debunked they sought and gained tremendous notoriety during their lifetimes and in the gullible era of romanticism convinced a lot of people that they were Prince Charles' grandsons. Disgusted by their lies and publicity-mongering, Charles wrote to his wife in August 1836:

My dear Constance,
I saw in Galignani's a paragraph copied from a Scotch paper, giving an account of a visit paid to Scotland by two young men, brothers, one Charles Edward, the other John Sobieski, represented in glowing colours etc etc. I felt certainly ruffled, having made up my mind not to stir anymore in this melancholy business'.[72]

He wrote to Mrs Hamilton of Kames Castle, Edinburgh from Wiesbaden: 'As heir to my unfortunate race, isolated, with nothing left but my name, it is not a little vexatious and annoying to see it so conspicuously and falsely assumed by these men'. He told her that he deeply regretted having put forward his 'Memorial', but was

[69] *Ibid.*, p.51; Documents of C.E. Roehenstart, *op. cit.*, Ms Fr 44 165.
[70] *Ibid.*, Ms Fr 44 226.
[71] *Ibid.*, Ms Fr 44 272.
[72] *Ibid.*, Ms Fr 44 261.

'reconciled to my fate', having been 'the sport of a sad destiny and placed in a false position in the world'. He was characterised by a defenceless innocence and people were often drawn to him. As Lady Bute said: 'He is very well-bred' and 'gentlemanlike'. He could also be disarmingly sincere, such as in his observation to Mrs Hamilton that, despite everything, he had 'known moments of happiness'.[73]

According to her death certificate Charles' second wife, Constance, had been born in London and was sixty when she died in central Paris on October 20th, 1853 at their modern, comfortable but not grand, third floor apartment at 9, rue de Notre Dame de Lorette – a house built in 1845.[74] Charles survived her by just one year. He was killed in a coaching accident near Dunkeld in Perthshire. A wheel broke off, the coach overturned and he was thrown. Badly injured in the fall he held on for a couple of days but died on October 28th, 1854. He was seventy. Though twice married he left no children. Nor is there a portrait of him. It is known only that he was not tall and, like his mother and two sisters, had blue eyes. Charles also shared the fair, ruddy complexion and oval face of his grandfather.[75] At least he was buried in Scottish soil. On his tombstone, in the nave of Dunkeld's ruined cathedral, friends added the words: '*Sic Transit Gloria Mundi*'. The epitaph scarcely suited his life. Perhaps it referred to the long and blighted chain of events which had preceded his birth. Over it the unforgiving Stuart star had hung for generations – the sole inheritance Charlotte passed on to her children.[76] Two of Prince Charles' three grandchildren had died childless. Only Marie-Victoire was left.

---

[73] *Ibid.*, Ms Fr 44 276.

[74] Family Records Centre, Clerkenwell, Misc.Marriages & Burials in Consular Records, MS 43/4 1830–81, Stuart, Louisa Constance, 1853, ref.10 631–2, p.316. In this document Charles is described as the owner of the house at 9, rue de Notre Dame de Lorette. In fact it was owned by Martin Gaillard from 1844–54 and then by Paul Galoppe. Charles was the first leaseholder of the 3rd floor apartment, no 13, with four windows onto the street, three onto the courtyard and one other small one. Apart from the drawing-room, dining-room and kitchen there were five other rooms: Archives de Paris, Property Records: 9, rue de Notre Dame de Lorette.

[75] G. Sherburn, *op. cit.*, p.81 – passport description for April 4th, 1835.

[76] *Ibid.*, pp.114–115. (The author is particularly grateful to Roger Powell, researcher to two successive Garter Kings of Arms, *Debrett's Peerage*, *Burke's Peerage and Baronetage* as well as *Burke's Landed Gentry of Scotland*, for his help and research on Sir Charles Stuart, the Bouchier Smith family, the death certificate of Charles' second wife as well as the second marriage of Marie-Victoire and that husband's will.)

CHAPTER FIFTEEN

The Demoiselle
de Thorigny

*'Un Clou de Charette' – I will never forget this last phrase
which was given me by a very kind 'Grand Seigneur'.
I did not see why I should explain my complete indifference
to Society by telling him my Secret.*

Marie-Victoire, 1820

Marie-Victoire is the only one of the Duchess of Albany's three grandchildren for whom there is proof that she was legitimised. And just as her brother struggled with a confusion of names, so did she. As a consequence of her baptismal legitimisation by the head of the de Rohan family she formally became: 'Princess Marie de Rohan, the demoiselle de Thorigny'. However she never called herself this as she appears not to have been told about her legitimisation. In her mother Charlotte's correspondence of 1788 she is referred to as 'V.' for Victoire – her familiar name taken from her godmother. Then, leaving aside her married names, in 1804 she appears on her sister's marriage contract as 'Victoire Roehenstart' and in 1806 as 'Victoire de Thorigny'.[1] But in court documents of 1810 she is described as 'Marie de Thorigny'.[2] From circa 1816 to 1825 she used the surnames 'Roehenstart', 'de Roehenstart' and 'Rohan Stuard', with the Christian names 'Victoire' and 'Virginie'. Nonetheless she simultaneously used the monogram 'M.R.' for Marie.[3] In court documents of 1828 to 1829 she appears as

---

[1] Central State Historical Archive of the Ukraine in Lwów, Archive of the former Court of Nobility, Baptismal Register for the Cathedral of the Armenian Rite for the year 1806, p.29/17.
[2] Piniński Archive in Lwów, fond 79, nr 1–2, Nikorowicz.
[3] Archiv Rohanové, Inv.č., 562, k.č. 193 11. See also appendix, Letters of Marie-Victoire …

both 'Marie' and 'Victoire de Thorigny'.[4] Then in the early 1830's she signed herself: 'the Countess de Thorigny' and 'V.de Thorigny'.[5] Finally, on her death certificate, she is referred to as 'Marie de Thorigny'.[6]

An exaggerated desire to belong is evident in both Marie-Victoire and her brother Charles. The latter first emphasized his loyalty to England and later professed ardent Scottish patriotism.[7] Similarly, Marie-Victoire constantly described an older de Rohan relation as her 'father' and herself as his 'daughter', only occasionally revealing that by this she meant her 'second father' and 'father of the family'.[8] Another element common to both are Marie-Victoire and Charles' peregrinations. Marie-Victoire was born in France, exiled in Germany, married in Polish Lwów, spent ten years 'running around the world',[9] then became based in Paris, returned to Lwów and died in Vienna.[10] Lastly, both chose to live at a distance from Society. Charles was described in 1817 as 'reserved and discreet [...] He receives few people and receives few letters'.[11] Marie-Victoire wrote of her 'anti-social attitude and estrangement from Society'.[12] The children simply didn't fit into any neat, social, legal or psychological category; for the complex political events and social circumstances into which they were born call to mind no obvious historical parallel. And their natural birth could scarcely be dismissed as some typical royal illegitimacy.

To continue Marie-Victoire's story – despite her first husband being

---

[4] Central State Historical Archive of the Ukraine in Lwów, Archive of the former Court of Nobility, *Ustawa Rady Wydziału Stanów Królestw Galicyi i Lodomeryi* nr 448 confirming the inclusion of Antime, Chevalier de Nikorowicz in the Register of the Country's Nobility, vol.22, p.120, dated July 5th, 1829.

[5] Archives Nationales, Paris, Archives Privées, Berryer Papers, 223 AP 34 & 40.

[6] Piniński Archive in Lwów, fond 79, nr 1–2, Nikorowicz; see also appendix, Letters of Marie-Victoire ..., footnote 11; Not included are 'Wiktoria' and 'Victory' as they were only translations into Polish and English; see also part 2, ch.1 for a full explanation of the permutations that could be used according to late 18thc./early 19thc. French custom for someone whose full name and title was: 'Princess Marie Victoire Adèlaide de Rohan, the demoiselle de Thorigny' without confusing matters further by taking into consideration her married names. It should be noted that whilst French custom allowed almost every conceivable combination of maiden and married name and title, the Austrian court system of Polish Galicia was unusually strict. There was no Austrian equivalent of the French title 'the demoiselle'. As far as the Austrians were concerned the final part of the full name was the surname for registration purposes.

[7] See previous chapter.

[8] See appendix, Letters of Marie-Victoire ...

[9] *Ibid.*, letter 5.

[10] This peregrination is described in the present chapter.

[11] See previous chapter.

[12] See appendix, Letters of Marie-Victoire ..., letters 5 & 10.

almost thirty years her senior, nevertheless a son was born. His baptismal entry in the register of the Armenian-Catholic Cathedral of Lwów appears innocuous. Yet it reveals the extraordinary information that a great-grandchild of Prince Charles Edward Stuart had been born. His name was Antime de Nikorowicz, Hereditary Chevalier of the Holy Roman Empire. Nor would his existence be of any interest were it not for one curious thing – he was the sole descendant of James VIII & III, *de jure* King of Scotland, England and Ireland by Princess Clementina Sobieska, grand-daughter of King John III of Poland. However, no-one ever found out. Marie-Victoire and her brother took their 'Secret' with them to the grave.

According to family legend Marie-Victoire refused to agree to the name 'Nicodème' proposed by her husband Paul and hastily found an obscure Saint Antime upon whose holiday his descendants presumed him to have been born.[13] However there must be some confusion because of the four Saints Antime none of their feast days tally.[14] For a while Marie-Victoire also called her son: 'Theodore'. Though a Nikorowicz family name strongly associated with Eastern European and Armenian culture, one can easily imagine why its etymology must have seemed more than appropriate to Marie-Victoire. It means: 'God's gift'.

It is not absolutely certain when and where Antime was born. Perhaps in Paris, but Lwów is more likely. And whilst he may have been baptised on the day of his birth the fact that the feast of St. Theodore fell five days prior suggests that as his birthday – saints' days having a special significance according to Polish custom.[15]

Less than four years later Antime's father died, in early 1810, leaving Marie-Victoire a widow of thirty with one child. But Paul hadn't made a will. Consequently the Court of Nobility in Lwów had to decide how to divide his wealth which included the five estates and porcelain factory which had previously belonged to the Radziwiłłs and Sobieskis. Yet there were certain strange aspects of the court proceedings. The

---

[13] Fundacja-Zakład Narodowy im.Ossolińskich, Wrocław, rkp.sygn.nr 15.971.

[14] Antime, bishop of Nicodemia, martyred 303, feast day April 27th; Antime, martyred Roman priest, feast day May 11th; Antime, 8thc. abbé of Brantôme in Périgord, feast day June 28th; Antime, a doctor who worked charitably in Egée in Cilicia, martyred 287, feast day September 27th. This last mentioned is provocative (see Appendix, Letters of Marie-Victoire ..., footnotes 6 & 7) because he is associated with Cilicia where the Armenian nobility settled and because after his death his colleagues were then interred in Théodoret, Syria. It is surprisingly coincidental that there appears to be a triple link between Antime, Armenia and Theodore.

[15] See appendix, Letters of Marie-Victoire ..., letter 1, footnotes 6 & 7.

first was that Marie-Victoire was absent from the list of beneficiaries, which comprised only her husband's six surviving children, despite being the deceased's wife of at least five years. Whatever else it might imply, clearly Paul's total estate must have been established prior to their marriage. Perhaps Marie-Victoire received some out-of-court settlement from the family. But she cannot have voluntarily resigned. For by law her share would have passed to her son. Yet his portion was no bigger than any other. That Paul's great fortune was split up is no surprise – that was the normal Polish custom. Perhaps it is significant that the four-year-old Antime received the palace and estate of Krzywczyce near Lwów which had been his father's main residence – though the youngest of his father's children. Yet the oddest was that the eldest sibling, Roman, was appointed sole guardian for the other two under-age children whereas Marie-Victoire was not appointed sole guardian of her own son. She was only Antime's co-guardian along with her sixty-four-year-old brother-in-law, John. The income from Krzywczyce was reserved exclusively for its heir's benefit and could not be accessed by Marie-Victoire without the co-operation of her brother-in-law. Furthermore, whilst a guardian's allowance (payable out of Krzywczyce's income) was granted to Marie-Victoire, its amount was set by the joint beneficiaries of her husband's will in agreement with the court. It would not have been more than a figure they considered reasonable for expenses based on Lwów's relatively modest cost of living. Marie-Victoire's late arrival on the scene and mysterious origin would hardly have encouraged over-generosity on their part.[16] Thus it was Antime's uncle John, as co-guardian, who effectively held the purse strings. But whereas he had plenty of income as the owner of three estates near Lwów, Marie-Victoire was apparently totally reliant for income upon her allowance as joint-guardian. John's career suggests an abstemious approach to life. He had pioneered two charitable founda-tions – one to give financial assistance to poor peasants on his estates, another to help small-holders in difficulty pay their agricultural taxes. Furthermore, he had helped set up the 'Institute for the Poor' in Lwów and the city's 'Fund for Deserving Soldiers'. He also lost his only son whilst the latter was still in his teens. He hardly seemed a man likely to look with indulgence upon extravagant expenditure.[17]

The only clue as to what happened to Marie-Victoire after Paul's

---

[16] Piniński Archive in Lwów, fond 79, nr 1–2, Nikorowicz.
[17] S. Barącz, *op. cit.*, pp.251–253.

death in 1810 is contained in a letter post-marked 1820 which she wrote to the youngest of the exiled grandsons of Jules-Hercule. He was Prince Louis de Rohan, a general in the Austrian Army. She described herself as having been 'running around the world throughout the ten years during which I have conserved my liberty'.[18] Even if she had received some dowry from Ferdinand or a cash settlement from her in-laws in 1810, ten years of running around the world was a very effective way of spending both it and her joint guardian's allowance. Travelling was relatively much more expensive than it is today. Marie-Victoire remained in Lwów until at least 1811, looking after her infant son and dealing with the legal consequences of her husband's death. During the same two years her brother Charles was based in Vitebsk with the Württembergs. She must have been in contact with him otherwise he could scarcely have written in 1813: 'I will, just in case, give you against all risks a Letter of Exchange on my sister'. Not long after the absurd attempt by Westminster to accuse her brother of trying to invade Britain, Marie-Victoire wrote from Paris to Prince Louis: 'In prolonging the discussion by my disinterest in better serving my brother, I forgot to ask you [...] to obtain an audience for me with the British Ambassador,[19] [...] during your absence I could ask him to keep me informed as to where my brother is, and who could better know his residence than Lord Stuart?'[20]

These and other letters form one half of the correspondence between Marie-Victoire and Louis de Rohan. They come from the archive of the neo-gothic palace of Sychrov, north of Prague, an estate bought in 1820 by Prince Louis' eldest brother, Charles, who had succeeded as Duke de Montbazon. Louis' replies to Marie-Victoire were kept with the most valuable family documents of her descendants at the castle on their estate of Grzymałów, east of Lwów. Both Sychrov and Grzymałów were in the Austro-Hungarian Empire. However, during the First World War the sixteenth century palace-fortress of Grzymałów was devastated by the Russians who occupied it for several months when the front was nearby. Hardly anything survived. Even the roofs had to be replaced. Only the castle's massive walls remained to await post-war restoration. Consequently the Sychrov half of their correspondence is all that exists today and constitutes an appendix to the

---

18 See appendix, letters of Marie-Victoire ..., letter 5. Louis de Rohan (1768–1836).
19 Sir Charles Stuart, later Baron Stuart de Rothesay; see previous chapter.
20 See appendix, Letters of Marie-Victoire ..., letter 4.

present work. Louis' descendants probably had no idea who Marie-Victoire was, assuming they even realised her letters were in their archive. And though Marie-Victoire's descendants knew of Louis' replies, they assumed the relatively unknown general to be his internationally famous namesake, Cardinal Louis of the *Affaire du Collier de la Reine*.[21] This was because Marie-Victoire repeatedly called Louis her 'father', herself his 'daughter' and only occasionally 'second father' and 'father of the family'.[22] Doubtless echoed in Louis' replies at Grzymałów, this appeared to confirm that her father was 'the' Louis de Rohan. And with that, for over a century and a half, the matter rested, a family secret seldom spoken of even privately, though known to each generation of Marie-Victoire's descendants down to the present day.

All Marie-Victoire's undated letters to Louis were written from Paris. And her admission of having been 'running around the world' between 1810 and 1820 implies that she was based there only latterly. Her letter concerning her brother's whereabouts continues revealingly, for she tells Louis that her 'health which suffers by all these worries needs a rest. I have neglected the business of my lessons with my English ladies ever since your kind attempts on my behalf'. C.L. Berry's legend that one of Charlotte Stuart's two daughters became a teacher in Paris was not without foundation after all.[23] Marie-Victoire must have spoken at least a little English, though obviously teaching French. Yet these lessons cannot have been her only source of income if she was able to neglect them. They were probably a distraction as well as supplement to her joint-guardian's allowance which would not have gone very far in Paris, particularly as she was living on the fashionable rue de Grenelle just down the road from Louis' mansion at no 99.[24] Initially Antime was also in France, for Marie-Victoire wrote to Louis:

> Fearing to be too indiscreet in asking you to help both Mother and Son, I have already told you of the wish I have of trying to enter my son into one of the Paris Colleges [...] He has been educated at the Royal College of Versailles [...] I am unhappy with him since I myself left Versailles [...] I would be very happy if through your protection my son could be brought back to Paris

---

[21] *Ibid.*, introductory text; see also footnote 71 of the present chapter.
[22] *Ibid.*, compare letters nr 3, 5, 8 with 9, 10, 22 and 19, 20, 21, 23.
[23] See part 2, ch.11.
[24] See appendix, Letters of Marie-Victoire ..., letter 2.

[...] and I doubt not but that [...] you might not prior to your departure leave a small portion of happiness for this poor widow.[25]

However, Antime does not seem to have been granted a place in Paris as he was not living there with his mother later on. He must have either remained at Versailles or been sent to Vienna to continue his education, paid for by the income from Krzywczyce.[26] In this same letter there is an echo of Marie-Victoire's childhood:

I am sending you a book which was written in 1785 during the author's trip to Florence [...] The letter which you see and which I beg you to read, has often served to keep up my courage during my misfortunes, and I have kept this copy very carefully, and the reading of these great historical memoirs was like a talisman uplifting my soul.[27]

A little later she asked Louis for 'the pleasure of hearing about the Princesses whom I have always loved' after he had returned from the exiled de Rohans' new home in Bohemia, telling him she has 'prayed for your happy return' after his 'long journeys which always worry me [...] I will send someone before eight o'clock to get your news and find out when you might receive me – that is, if you would not prefer to come and visit me'.[28]

Though there are signs of close contact with the de Rohans from a much earlier period, clearly Marie-Victoire had not been in contact with Louis for at least the decade 1803–1813.[29] Nevertheless, by 1820, she was advising him on affairs of the heart, telling him not to have anything to do with a certain lady who, if she 'presents herself to you during your voyage, tell her pitilessly that you want nothing to do with her'.[30] Marie-Victoire further demonstrated her intimacy with Louis by intervening on behalf of 'Pierre Cazeaux who has lost his place through a great injustice as the guard of the Forest of Saumur', asking that he be reinstated as he is 'worthy of your confidence and has a

---

[25] *Ibid*, letter 1.
[26] *Ibid*., footnote 10.
[27] *Ibid*., letter 1.
[28] *Ibid*., letters 2 & 3.
[29] For example, the fact that she tells Louis in letter 1 where Antime was born implies that he probably didn't know, yet surely would have done had their contact been close.
[30] See appendix, Letters of Marie-Victoire ..., letter 5.

perfect acquaintance of your properties in the Midi'. And again: 'I would be very interested to know if the pregnancy of Princess Gasparine is not causing any worry [...] Please pass on my respects to the Princess Charles and Princess Berthe. I sincerely hope to hear their health is good and likewise that of the Princes'.[31]

Yet her complex of birth generated an exaggerated attitude: 'I am utterly devoted to the interests of your illustrious house'[32] and 'I feel a sort of veneration for the head of this noble family which so generously gave shelter to our brothers in exile'.[33] But she was confused as to whether the de Rohans were only Louis' family or hers too for she wrote elsewhere: 'If it is necessary then I shall promise never to dishonour the illustrious family from which I come'.[34]

Repeatedly she displays her association with the Paris legal world, which was also visible in her own and her sister's letters to the Berryer family. To Louis she writes: 'Please can you tell me all you can about the success of the case relating to the Duchy of Bouillon' the papers of which she wanted 'to put under the eyes of my friends so that they might, in case of need, defend your legitimate rights [...] Send me prior to your departure the précis of the case and the defence of the judgement. All the material will be read with the greatest interest'.[35] And again: 'If the Prince Louis didn't know anyone from the Paris Bar, I would ask a lawyer for a model of the declaration'.[36] Then she 'wishes very much to learn if the case of Liège has been won'[37] and later asks that 'the testimony of Princess Charles (of which I am sending you a word for word copy) will be done as legally as possible'.[38]

One of her most revealing letters to Louis was post-marked 1820:

I must thank you for your visit [...] I completely forgot to tell you something very important [...] It will perhaps be given to me to choose a Chevalier from amongst the Veterans of the Army of de Condé, waiting for the end of five years of the strictest mourning. I shall continue to keep myself far from Society so as to avoid

[31] *Ibid.*, letter 7; see also part 2, ch.12, P.Cazeaux & H.Cazau.
[32] *Ibid.*, letter 7.
[33] *Ibid.*, letter 21.
[34] *Ibid.*, letter 10.
[35] *Ibid.*, letter 5.
[36] *Ibid.*, letter 14.
[37] *Ibid.*, letter 17.
[38] *Ibid.*, letter 18.

hearing those insults which have been numerous, of being 'stand-offish', '*un Clou de Charette*'. I will never forget this last phrase which was given me by a very kind 'Grand Seigneur'. I did not see why I should explain my complete indifference to Society by telling him my Secret [...] How many volumes are full of the romances of the Stuarts and Rohans? This Breton blood which runs in my veins has not been very comforting. It was necessary, therefore, to take an extreme course so as to moderate one's conduct. And that was in running around the world during this ten years during which I have conserved my liberty. Let others judge if there wasn't more merit in resisting so as to triumph [...] There is nothing left, therefore, other than the reasonable choice of becoming united with an old Veteran of the Glory.[39]

Her resigned tone implies that at the age of forty-one she foresaw nothing more for herself than the companionship of a retired cavalry officer from de Condé's royalist army which had fought against Napoleon during the Revolution alongside the Austrians. Indeed it must have felt almost a family regiment given de Condé's relationship with the de Rohans and the political help provided by Cardinal Louis from his safe haven of Ettenheim. But Marie-Victoire had to wait for the end of the veteran's unusually long period of mourning.

In 1821 Marie-Victoire acted as chaperon to Louis' twenty-two-year-old niece, Princess Gasparine, prior to her marriage to Henry XIX, the reigning Prince of Reuss-Greiz. During this period Marie-Victoire complained that 'I have used a large amount to settle old debtors' and over-spent on 'a marriage trousseau worthy of the august person whom I had the honour of accompanying'. But her time spent with Gasparine ended with the latter's marriage in January 1822.[40] Then followed an unexpected change of plan. For Marie-Victoire did not marry the 'reasonable choice' of the noble French veteran of de Condé. Instead she asked Louis to 'honour the promise that you made to come and take tea this evening – I have already invited the respected foreigner.[41] [...] Please choose between Thursday, Friday and Saturday for giving me the honour of taking tea with the noble and honest

---

[39] *Ibid.*, letter 5. To be 'un clou de charette' was an insult. La charette was a contemporary expression referring to the Paris mob during the Revolution. To be a 'nail in the cart' was to criticise Marie-Victoire for associating with the bourgeoisie and disdaining the nobility.

[40] *Ibid.*, letter 6.

[41] *Ibid.*, letter 8.

Englishman'.[42] Clearly the newcomer had charm if he had successfully eclipsed Marie-Victoire's chevalier-in-mourning. Her excitement when writing to Louis is palpable:

> I know there is no need to stimulate your kindness in doing justice to a poor orphan of the pure blood of the R's and the S's, but I beg you not to lose courage; […] that would be to give up when everything is going well. Christian charity will maintain your benevolence, at least up until the time of the marriage!! These services are worth more than gold!! […] You were able to see that I had not spoken very frankly of the natural birth. He is as aware of the above as much as we are. Nor has he overlooked the fact that the brave Admiral Prince de M. (*Armand, Prince de Montbazon*) never married the Duchess (*of Albany*). I believed it necessary, all the same, to warn Monsieur d'A. that he could perhaps hear repeated in Society the terrible lie that hangs over the head of my respected uncle and guardian, the Prince F. (*Ferdinand*). As soon as Monsieur d'A. spoke to me of his hopes for a union I told him about everything quite frankly. He knows that the Prince F., nominated guardian after the death of the Prince de M., only supervised my education and that by having appeared to be interested in me, has fallen victim to this lie […] If it is necessary then I shall promise never to dishonour the illustrious family from which I come. Monsieur d'A. has often said to me that he loves the nobility of our feelings (I am not modest enough not to repeat this compliment!) and that he fully knows I lack certain documents to prove other titles of nobility, but that it is all the same to him, and that I was always in his eyes an R. and an S. Right now I doubly regret that the Princess Charles is not in Paris, who could have told me who has the right and that if I don't have any fortune, at least I possess a spotless reputation. I defy my greatest enemy to say that I have had even a single lover. You will laugh at me for such bourgeois morality, and I believe I can see my friendly and gallant Prince smile at my lack of sociability. But for myself I don't regret it, for it has made me worthy of a gentleman who is giving me his name […] In the midst of my anti-social attitude and estrangement from Society I have kept up relations with a few people of note (once or twice

---

[42] *Ibid.*, letter 9.

a year). For example I know the person […] to whom you are going on Sunday. If by design or by chance he should speak to you of me, I would invoke your deepest paternal feelings not to deny me.[43]

Though her fiancé had evidently heard malicious gossip, Marie-Victoire's marriage went ahead – helped by Prince Louis' reassurances. However she had evidently been convinced, presumably by Ferdinand, that her father was her childless, guillotined uncle, Armand. But who was this mysterious Englishman, Monsieur d'A. who had arrived out of nowhere and was so keen to win the hand of a middle-aged widow of natural birth? Before exploring the man's background it is necessary to remember who Louis de Rohan's grandmother was. She was Louise de la Tour d'Auvergne who had married Marie-Victoire's other uncle, Jules-Hercule de Rohan. Louise's nephew was the last Duke de Bouillon who died without heir in 1802. Shortly after the Bourbon restoration in 1814 the Bouillon rights of succession were awarded to Louis' eldest brother, Charles. However, they were contested.

Some generations earlier a certain Edward d'Auvergne had been born in Jersey. He was the son of Philip d'Auvergne who claimed descent from the last reigning Duke de Bouillon. Edward was a chaplain to the Scots Guards, then to William III and later made a small name for himself as a military historian. His son was called Philip after his grandfather and had a large family including two sons, James and Charles. The former became a major-general and mayor of Southampton in 1795. The latter left the army early and married twice. By his first wife Charles d'Auvergne had four sons of whom the youngest was Philip who became an admiral. By Charles' second marriage there were two further sons, Edward and Corbet James. It is Admiral Philip and his half-brother, Captain Corbet James, Royal Navy, who are relevant. For the former used the title 'Prince of Bouillon' and was the man who in 1816 unsuccessfully contested the de Rohan succession to the duchy of Bouillon. But the legal costs ruined him financially and as a consequence he committed suicide, though not before adopting Corbet James as his heir and successor to his 'title'. It was the latter who was the mysterious Captain d'Auvergne who appeared out of nowhere to oust the 'Veteran of the

[43] *Ibid.*, letter 10. Compare the references to Ferdinand as 'uncle and guardian' with the references to 'uncle and protector' on page 150.

Army of de Condé'. Now it is clear why C.L. Berry's legend also spoke of Charlotte Stuart's daughter becoming the 'Duchess of Bouillon'.[44]

It is not easy to believe that the retired, ageing bachelor d'Auvergne's sudden romantic interest in Marie-Victoire was unconnected with his pretensions to the duchy which had been awarded to her cousin. But Marie-Victoire was vulnerable and passionately believed in her English naval captain.[45] Interestingly, their marriage took place at the British Embassy in Paris whilst Sir Charles Stuart was ambassador.[46] The consular records give the date as November 29th, 1823 and call Marie-Victoire: 'Dame Victorie Adèlaide Roehen Stuart' (though she signs herself 'Roehenstart') and describe her as a 'widow' and d'Auvergne as a 'bachelor'.[47]

Marie-Victoire's description as 'Victorie Adèlaide' provides further confirmation of the authenticity of Testot-Ferry's extracts from Young Charlotte's marriage contract[48] where Marie-Victoire appeared as a 'witness' and 'sister' under the name 'Victoire Adèlaide'. Furthermore, her status as a 'widow' matches her letter to Louis de Rohan in which she describes herself as a 'poor widow', which was indeed her legal status after the death in 1810 of her first husband, the Chevalier de Nikorowicz. There is also another interesting fact recorded on those consular records. Marie-Victoire gave her parish as that of St. Benoît. But St. Benoît had been closed as a church since 1813 and not existed as a parish since 1808. Nor had Marie-Victoire lived in France between 1791 and 1808. However, the former parish church of St. Benoît stood at 96, rue St. Jacques. And the rue St. Jacques was precisely where Ferdinand de Rohan had rented a house from the Abbé de la Villette for Charlotte Stuart, her mother and children. In referring to St. Benoît, Marie-Victoire was accurately giving the parish church of her

---

[44] See part 2, ch.11: C.L. Berry's legend claims it was 'Agläe' who became the Duchess de Bouillon and her sister a teacher in Paris. In fact it was one and the same sister – Marie-Victoire. Legend also spoke of 'Agläe' being the first born. Perhaps the implication is that in Charlotte's letters to her mother, 'Agläe' was her code for Marie-Victoire along with 'V' and that Marie-Victoire was the first-born – see part 2, ch.12 for arguments for and against the above; G. Martin, *Histoire et Généalogie de la Maison de Rohan, op. cit.*, pp.76–77; see appendix, Letters of Marie-Victoire…, footnote 35, for the genealogy of d'Auvergne.

[45] See appendix, Letters of Marie-Victoire …, letters 10–23.

[46] See above as well as part 2, ch.14.

[47] Family Records Centre, Clerkenwell, Misc.Marriages and Burials in Consular Records, RG 33/63, Marriages, Paris, p. 102. Nr 62, Nr 305, d'Auvergne.

[48] See part 2, ch.12.

childhood home.[49] Yet once Marie-Victoire and d'Auvergne became married problems began. To Louis she wrote:

> My good and honest friend, for whom I would like to avoid even the smallest sorrow, had this morning a very unpleasant visit from a creditor set upon tormenting Monsieur d'Auvergne because of his former business people. Since Monsieur d'Auvergne withdrew his proxy they are so enraged that they try to do him all the harm possible. You know, my Prince, that to satisfy my heart, and to give proof of the devotion and respect towards the august family which I cherish, that I have always preached peace (before and after my marriage). To be perfectly sure that no court case would be begun I have had nothing to do with business people. I am thus the cause of new sorrows for Monsieur d'Auvergne [who] gave me his word that he arrived here, happy, in good health with four thousand louis d'or in order to await the justice that is owing him![50]

Time and again d'Auvergne allowed his wife to act as the interface between his claims and her relations. On his behalf Marie-Victoire asked Louis to:

> ... prepare a legal declaration which affirms that the Duke de Montbazon acknowledges that he saw in favour of the late Admiral d'Auvergne the sum of 3,000 pounds sterling which was made out to him as a receipt, that this same receipt has been presented to you intact and without any other signature other than that of the Prince de Rohan, that by this reason the recognition of three thousand pounds was perhaps lost. The Admiral, not having passed the succession to anyone else, his sole heir, the Captain d'Auvergne, has a right to be reimbursed which the Duke de Montbazon cannot refuse [...] It is said to Monsieur d'Auvergne, 'These are the Princes de Rohan who have the estate of your brother, the Admiral, far from persecuting you they should agree to your just complaint.[51]

---

[49] J. de la Tynna, *Dictionnaire Topographique, Historique et Etymologique des Rues de Paris*, Paris 1817, p.53; E.Raunié, *Epitaphier de Vieux Paris*, Paris 1890, vol.1, see Eglise Collégiale et Paroissiale de St. Benoît.

[50] See appendix, Letters of Marie-Victoire ..., letter 13.

[51] *Ibid.*, letter 14.

Marie-Victoire then went on to describe her husband as 'the best of men, and so I feel for him the most sincere affection. I beseech you not to persecute my good and fair benefactor who deserves all the tenderness of his 'Victory' ' and who 'said that he never knew misfortune (to have debts) other than since he has been involved in a just claim with Prince Louis [...] You know how disinterested I am and without ambition. Likewise is Monsieur d'Auvergne. But I cannot resist sorrow when I see my fair friend deceived in all his just hopes'. Shortly after, a new element began to appear in Marie-Victoire's letters: 'Monsieur d'Auvergne returned yesterday quite ill'.[52]

On the one hand Louis did not cave in to d'Auvergne's attempts at extortion. On the other, Marie-Victoire naively wrote about her husband: 'It is awful that a man of honour is tormented for 200 louis when he possesses more than 2,000 francs in England'.[53] To Louis she caustically added:

> Do not fear that I dare to be so indiscreet as to insist on the object of Thursday's request. Your point blank refusal is engraved upon my memory [...] The point of this note is to discover if I could on Tuesday morning send for the declaration that you have promised me? I doubt not that your intention is anything other than to entirely conform to the justice due to the Admiral [...]
>
> Victoire d'Auvergne.[54]

The letter was post marked July 7th, 1824.

Then, ominously: 'As Monsieur d'Auvergne is ill it is better not to speak of business in front of him'.[55] And as d'Auvergne's condition deteriorated so did Marie-Victoire's tone towards Louis soften:

> I was hoping to wish you a happy voyage yesterday, but my duty as an affectionate wife kept me at the side of Monsieur d'Auvergne [...] Since your last visit the oppression on the chest of my dear patient became extreme and it is for this reason that the doctor judged that he should be bled [...] Please be sure of my desire that all your legal cases turn out in the happiest way for you. I hope with all my heart that all the claims of Monsieur d'Auvergne end

---

[52] *Ibid.*, letter 14.
[53] *Ibid.*, letter 15.
[54] *Ibid.*, letter 16.
[55] *Ibid.*, letter 17.

amiably with all the parties concerned [...] I sincerely wish not to find myself at war with the family that I respect. Monsieur d'Auvergne [...] is suffering too much to go out.[56]

Marie-Victoire's second marriage lasted only fourteen months. For in early February 1825 her husband died and was buried in Paris on the 5th of that month as 'Prince Corbet James d'Auvergne, abode Paris, aged 60'.[57] Marie-Victoire's subsequent letters to Louis are on black-edged paper: 'It was not a pension of pure favour that was asked for. You know in part how much the venerable friend for whom I mourn had the right to a benefaction from the Bourbons. I admit to you, at the risk of displeasing you, that I believe in your intention of honouring the memory of the English Prince who was so unhappy in France'. Apart from the ducal coronet on their seal, this was the only time she openly indulged her late husband's pretensions to the title of 'Prince of Bouillon'.[58] She signed herself: 'Your very distressed daughter, Victory d'Auvergne'.[59]

[56] *Ibid.*, letter 18.
[57] *Ibid.*, letter 14; Family Records Centre, Clerkenwell, Misc.Marriages and Burials in Consular Records, RG 33/60, Burials, Paris, p.32, Nr 253, d'Auvergne.
[58] See appendix, Letters of Marie-Victoire ..., letter 19; It might be argued that Marie-Victoire acknowledged her husband's pretensions by occasionally using on her letters to Louis the armorial of the Counts d'Auvergne, namely: a field azure semé of fleur de lis or, with a tower argent masonned sable, surrounded by a belt with the motto 'Nous de changerons ...' (the last few letters are illegible), surmounted by a ducal coronet – Archiv Rohanové, Inv.č.562, k.č.193 II. There was also another armorial apparently used by Marie-Victoire, visible in the quarterings prepared during the 1890's for the Austro-Hungarian authorities for Counts Stanislas and Leon Piniński (Fundacja-Zakład Narodowy im.Ossolińskich ‚Wrocław, see: Piniński; another copy is in the Piniński Archive in Warsaw). Such proofs of nobility were required by the Habsburgs for senior officers of state. On their distaff side the Piniński brothers had to give their great grandparents with respective armorials. But by the 1890's Marie-Victoire's descendants were aware only that she appeared in family documents as 'de Thorigny'. Whilst they knew she was the natural daughter of a Prince de Rohan, apparently Louis, nothing further was known. They probably believed de Thorigny to be her mother's maiden name, such as later generations did. She appears on the quarterings as 'Maria de Thorigny' and armigerous. The probable origin of the heraldic device shown, which in English heraldry would be called a 'Fess Rayonné', was a seal or wax impression on some document which her descendants took to be the arms of de Thorigny. The device shown had nothing in common with either Polish heraldry or armorials associated with the name Thorigny. However it is curious that a Fess is shown, because the Stuarts' heraldic device was also a Fess – a 'Fess Chequy'. The difference may be due to damage or illegibility of the original seal or wax impression. Alternatively the rayonné element might have been used to suggest illegitimacy, doubt or a junior branch. One can only speculate. Because unlike Scottish and English heraldry neither Polish nor Austrian heraldry attributes any specific meaning to this modification. The author is grateful to David Howard and Count Moritz Strachwitz for their help with this analysis.
[59] *Ibid.*, letter 20.

Marie-Victoire's two final, surviving letters convey her deflation after the stormy emotions raised by the litigious d'Auvergne. Louis' patience and loyalty to her is clear as she asked him to:

> ... re-read the list of services and to tell me what would be more useful to mention [...] It is very tiresome at present to be forced to work on matters of business, but the idea of doing all I can to honour the memory of the best of men excites my courage [...] My attachment for you has increased still more in view of the suffering which you have borne with great courage for a year; I confess that it is more than affection I have for you. I feel a sort of veneration for the head of this noble family which so generously gave shelter to our brothers in exile [...] I never seemed able to sufficiently show my devotion for my unhappy friend – he used to say that he didn't want to regain his health other than to bring happiness to his 'Victory' [...] Forgive me, Prince, I am forgetting myself in speaking of him who merits my regret![60]

Her tired words seem to acknowledge d'Auvergne's instrumental treatment of her, especially her final phrase. She then packed up the apartment in which she had spent her brief second married life and asked Louis for:

> ... permission that the family pictures which were always in the *Gros Caillou*[61] might momentarily be placed in your mansion. I have been told that the new tenants of the apartment I was occupying on the rue de Grenelle cannot keep them as they themselves have a lot of engravings to hang [...] Not knowing what apartment I will be occupying when I leave Tivoli I would ask you not to refuse my request. There are only two big paintings, the others are busts of an ordinary dimension. The little *genre* pictures were never taken to the *Gros Caillou*, there are only those of the family [...] The bearer of this letter is the daughter of de Carré (an old servant of the Princes de Rohan) [...] This is a real service that you do for me in my sad situation; [...] you know, my Prince, that I don't have my own place.
>
> Your Respectful Daughter, Victory.[62]

[60] *Ibid.*, letter 21.
[61] The *quartier* in which Marie-Victoire was living prior to her marriage to d'Auvergne.
[62] See appendix, Letter of Marie-Victoire ..., letter 23.

Those family paintings must have included her own portrait as well as that of her sister who had died almost twenty years earlier. And throughout her years in Paris are glimpses of Marie-Victoire's contact with her brother. In one group of Charles' papers there is a note on the origins of the d'Auvergne family which mentions Captain Corbet James' brother, father and uncle by name. Charles jotted down underneath a curious comment in latin: 'The French shouldn't be trusted because they are superficial, deceitful people and immortal God himself considers them impious'.[63] Then he jotted down a short history of Tivoli whence came the name of the fashionable new Paris *quartier* in which his sister was living, centred on the gardens founded in 1798 between the rue St. Lazare and the rue de Clichy.[64] There is also a draft letter to his lawyer after Charles had accused a fraudulent French nobleman of cheating at cards. In it Charles demanded that the latter 'leave Monsieur d'Auvergne alone […] in the disagreeable proceedings he has been so unwise as to institute against Monsieur Stuart'.[65]

Furthermore, Charles went to the trouble of writing down the story of the 'Abbé and the Epée' – a successful comedy playing in Paris at the time. It was the story of a beggar boy brought in from the streets of Paris by a good abbé. After a while it became obvious that 'the child had been ill-treated through some nefarious design'. But the abbé realised 'that the youth was the noble heir of a large fortune […] and had been purposefully lost by his interested guardian […] At last […] his uncle, the usurper, was dispossessed and the youth returned to his estates and honours'. The story's parallels with Charles' nephew Antime are striking. Both he and the beggar boy were the same age. Both were nobles by birth. Both were heirs to large fortunes. Both were living in Paris. The tight purse strings of Antime's uncle and guardian were echoed by the beggar boy's uncle and guardian who tried to keep his estate from him. And, tellingly, the beggar boy was called Theodore, the very name by which Antime was sometimes called by Marie-Victoire. Or perhaps

---

[63] *Ibid.*, letter 14, footnote 35.

[64] Documents of C.E. Roehenstart, Ms Fr b9 13.

[65] *Ibid.*, Ms Fr b9 133 & 134. The fact that there is a letter heading from the writing paper of Charles' lawyer, Monsieur Lelouche of the *Tribunal Civil de Première Instance* with the date January 7th, 1825 and that d'Auvergne died on or before February 5th, 1825 suggests that Charles was warning the cheat (who called himself the 'Marquis' or 'Baron' Hercules) off d'Auvergne because of the illness from which the latter was dying. The most likely date for this letter is October-December 1824; See also G. Sherburn, *op. cit.*, pp.84–85.

Charles adopted that name for his nephew because of the play's parallels?[66]

There is another glimpse of Marie-Victoire's brother in one of her letters. In 1824 she asked Louis de Rohan to provide a reference for someone who was evidently important to her: 'In a matter of this type, the testimony of a statesman is indispensible in the eyes of the law. Please reply that you will agree to give your signature [...] for a young man who finds himself in the same situation of birth as I do'. One person who was both close to her, of natural birth and in need of testimonies to support claims was her brother Charles.[67]

After d'Auvergne's burial in Paris on February 5th, 1825 Marie-Victoire travelled to London, presumably in search of the '2,000 francs in England' which her late husband had claimed to possess there. However, though the sole heir under the terms of his will of February 8th, 1824, when probate was granted on May 14th, 1825 Marie-Victoire inherited less than £100. During her stay she lived at 28, Soho Square – literally around the corner from her brother's address at 63, Frith Street.[68]

With this unhappy episode finally closed, Marie-Victoire found herself a homeless widow of forty-six, soon to lose her co-guardian's allowance because her son was about to come into his inheritance. Moreover, since at least 1823, Antime had been far away from his mother, serving as a cadet with the Austrian Imperial 4th Cuirassiers of Crown Prince Ferdinand, a commission probably arranged for him by Louis, an Austrian general.[69] Marie-Victoire's plans are hinted at in one of her final letters to Louis in which she spoke of the de Rohans as 'this noble family which so generously gave shelter to our brothers in exile' – in other words, Austria. It seems her thoughts returned to the 'Chevalier from amongst the Veterans of the Army of de Condé' whom she had hoped to marry five years earlier, though her letter did not mention whether he was living in Paris or in Austrian exile where so many royalist veterans remained. By then his 'five years of the strictest mourning' must certainly have ended. Whatever her reasons,

---

[66] Documents of C.E. Roehenstart, Ms Fr b9 160; See appendix, Letters of Marie Victoire ..., footnote 6.

[67] *Ibid.*, letter 18.

[68] Family Records Centre, Clerkenwell, Prerogative Court of Canterbury Wills, Probate 11/1699/255, d'Auvergne; *Ibid.*, Indexes to Estate Duty Wills and the Death Duty Registers, IR27/192, IR26/1304 1825 C-D f.257–455, IR26/1304/422, d'Auvergne; Documents of C.E. Roehenstart, Ms Fr 44 81.

[69] Kriegsarchiv, Vienna, Military Records for Anthim, Ritter von Nikorowicz 1823–1829.

Marie-Victoire returned to the capital of Austria's largest province, Galicia, and her son's neighbouring estate.

The first evidence of her return to Lwów was from nearly two years later. In late 1826 Count Louis Jabłonowski was only just sixteen. Decades later he wrote his memoirs. In them he recalled his schooldays in Lwów:

> From under the care of three tutors I was released like a bird from the cage and placed in the house of the de Pauws. The lady of the house, a very respectable woman formerly known for her beauty, was from the noble family of de Thorigny, but unsatisfied with this she used to relate that she was the daughter of the famous Cardinal Louis, Prince de Rohan, the unfortunate lover of Marie-Antoinette. Monsieur de Pauw, a decent old soul, having left his home country with the Austrian Army, took part in several campaigns in the hussars, and was administering Krzywczyce, the estate of Antime Nikorowicz, the son of his wife from her first marriage, whilst living in their beautiful town house. They lived pretty slendidly, surrounded by Frenchmen serving in the Army. The commanding officer Fresnel, General Piret, Picard, the Marquis Boquen, the Abbé Parmentier, A.Morris, Charles de Brzezie Lanckoroński, Stadion – the Knight of Malta and General Steininger with his delightful daughter (of sad history) were everyday guests [as well as] Miss Geisruk, daughter of the former Governor.[70]

Jabłonowski wildly exaggerated in describing Cardinal Louis as Marie-Antoinette's lover. He is likewise mistaken in referring to him later as de Rohan-Chabot instead of de Rohan-Guéméné. Jabłonowski must have assumed that Marie-Victoire was referring to the famous cardinal when in his mid-teens he heard her talking about a Prince Louis de Rohan as her 'father', not realising that she only meant 'second father' and not the cardinal but his little-known great-nephew and namesake. To further confuse the issue, both were popularly referred to by their respective contemporaries as simply: 'Prince Louis'.[71]

---

[70] PSB, pp.229–230, see Jabłonowski Ludwik hr. (1810–1887); L. Jabłonowski, *Pamiętniki*, Cracow 1962, pp.95–96.

[71] This mistaken identity has been mentioned above. See also Appendix, Letters of Marie-Victoire ..., footnote 30. In letter 10 Marie-Victoire reveals she has been persuaded that it was

The 'beautiful town house' in which Marie-Victoire lived with her third husband was undoubtedly the family property which Antime had inherited in the oldest part of Lwów. Appropriately, it stood on Ormiańska Street.[72] And the man she had married was the emigré French nobleman, Jean de Pauw who precisely fitted Marie-Victoire's description in her letter to Louis de Rohan. He had indeed fought as a royalist cavalry officer alongside the Austrian army under the Prince de Condé. His name appears several times in the records of that counter revolutionary force but not even once in the Austrian military records which it would have done had he been directly under their command.[73] Furthermore de Pauw had every reason to have been in 'five years of

footnote 71 (*cont.*)

neither Jules-Hercule (who on her baptismal certificate referred to her as his daughter), nor Ferdinand, but the second oldest brother, Admiral Armand, Prince de Montbazon, who was her father. His full Christian name was Louis-Armand, so it is just possible that Jabłonowski heard Marie-Victoire referring to him. But this is unlikely because the four de Rohan brothers were universally known as: Jules-Hercule, Armand, Louis and Ferdinand, whilst all Europe had heard of the famous 'Prince Louis'. Jabłonowski is also inaccurate in recalling that Abbé Parmentier described Louis as 'de Rohan-Chabot'. The latter family, whilst holding the title of 'Duke de Rohan', inherited through a de Rohan heiress, is in fact that of Chabot and descended only on the distaff line from the de Rohans. Louis' family was 'de Rohan-Guéméné', the senior line of the de Rohans of unbroken male descent. Had Parmentier really said this Marie-Victoire would have loudly protested as the de Rohans regarded the Chabots as usurpers of their name, title and birthright. It may seem surprising that Marie-Victoire mentioned the de Rohan name in society but not the more illustrious one of Stuart. However, she was only referring to Louis de Rohan as her 'second father' and 'father of the family' (see appendix, Letters of Marie-Victoire ..., footnote 2), not as her own father. Even had she spoken of herself as a de Rohan by birth she would not have revealed her 'secret'. To have mentioned her Stuart maternity would have been to do the reverse, cause a sensation or disbelief, both of which would have caused unpleasant public repercussions. Neither is it strange Marie-Victoire should have remained silent about her 'secret' so many years after Charlotte Stuart's death in 1789. Firstly, she had given her word of honour not to do so. Secondly, the de Rohans remained at the very apex of European Society, whereas Prince Charles' alchoholism after 1745 had badly damaged the late Stuarts' reputation – not yet repaired by the era of romanticism. Thirdly, Marie-Victoire's feelings concerning the Stuarts must have been mixed because of the negative propaganda heard during her childhood from her grandmother, Clementina Walkinshaw, concerning the latter's bad treatment by both Charles and Henry, the latter of whom she suspected of being somehow responsible for her daughter's premature death as well as mean regarding the implementation of Charlotte's will.

[72] 'Armenian Street' – still its name today.

[73] Archives de l'Armée de Terre au Château de Vincennes, Paris, Fonds pour l'Armée de Condé, Table Alphabétique XV 1797–1801, de Pauw; ibid., XU3, Table Alphabétique des Certificats del.par M.le Prince de Condé, 1801, de Pauw; Piniński Archive in Warsaw, the absence of de Pauw's name for the period 1740–1820 is confirmed in the letter (ref: GZ 5652/O-KA/97 of October 9th, 1997) to the author from Dr Christopher Tepperberg, director of the Kriegsarchiv, 1030 Vienna, Nottendorfer Gasse 2.

the strictest mourning', as his wife had died early leaving him a widower with a young son.[74]

Much as Marie-Victoire had gravitated in Paris towards the merito-cratic, legal and political family of Berryer, so too was that the descrip-tion of her Lwów-based circle. Its members stood at the apex of Galicia's Austrian administration and included high ranking former French royalist officers such as General Piret and Count Ferdinand Pierre Hennequin de Fresnel et Curel who, after fighting against Napoleon, had become an Austrian general in 1817. There was also Field Marshal Jean Piccard von Grünthal and General Carl Steininger, whilst the snuff-taking Abbé Parmentier belonged to the more worldly of the priesthood. The aristocracy was represented by the Marquis Boquen as well as Count Charles Lanckoroński and politics by the Governor of Galicia and future Imperial Minister of the Interior, Count Franz Stadion. Two things are noticeable. Marie-Victoire appeared to have little to do with either Antime's family or the indige-nous Polish nobility. For although Lanckoroński was a Pole, he was also a pre-eminent member of the Habsburg court where he became first chamberlain then director of the court theatres and was later dec-orated with the order of the Golden Fleece. This was untypical. Polish antipathy towards the Austrians and their supporters was strong during the first half of the nineteenth century.[75]

[74] See appendix, Letters of Marie-Victoire ..., footnote 16. The graveyard in Grzymałów where both father and son de Pauw were buried was levelled on the orders of the Ukrainian commu-nists during the 1970's and is today a meadow. All that remains of the former graveyard are broken pieces of memorial stones heaped into a pile in one corner. Nevertheless the graves of both Jean de Pauw and his son, Zenon, are clearly remembered by Count George Wolański who was brought up at Grzymałów until late 1939 by the estate's last owner, his mother, Countess Julia Pinińska (1885–1976). The latter recalled not only their graves but also Zenon de Pauw's employment by her grandfather, Count Leonard Piniński (1824–1886), in the great steam mill at Grzymałów.

[75] L. Jabłonowski, *op. cit.*, pp.391–427; J. Dunin-Borkowski, *Almanach Błękitny*, Lwów 1908, p.552; *Słownik geograficzny ...*, *op. cit.*, vol.4, see Krzywczyce (de Pauw is wrongly given as the owner of Krzywczyce's lucrative sugar refinery – he was only its director); F.K.Prek, *Czasy i Ludzie*, Wrocław 1959, p.32; R. Aftanazy, *Materiały do dziejów rezydencji*, Warsaw 1990, vol.7a, pp.336–343 & 349–351. Count de Fresnel, like de Pauw, also ended up managing an estate. In this case it was the property of Suzannah Strzembosz (1803–1892), a rich heiress whom he finally succeeded in marrying despite the opposition of her pathologically violent father, Thomas, an ex-officer of Prince Joseph Poniatowski and the owner of the Galician estates of Olszanica, Lackie and Laszki Murowane. The legendarily powerful Strzembosz, who had killed men with his bare hands just for annoying him, even came to armed blows with his daughter's suitor, so much did the latter's Austrian affiliation antagonise him. De Fresnel managed his wife's estate of Laszki near Lwów where one of the farms became known as 'Frenelówka'.

Marie-Victoire did not remain tied to Lwów for, apart from her visits to Vienna, she returned at least once more to Paris where in the early 1830's she saw her and her sister's old friends, the Berryers. She wrote to them of 'whist evenings' and that 'some of your friends are coming to see me this evening'. Then later: 'I was very sorry, Monsieur, to find your visiting card [...] I had written two days earlier to one of our friends prior to which we had decided to meet on Wednesday [...] to put back this little intimate dinner until Thursday'.[76]

From this period comes further evidence of Marie-Victoire's contacts with her brother. On December 31st, 1833 Charles wrote to his wife from Castellamare in Sicily that 'Count Alexander Potocki has lost 25 millions in landed property'. What possible relevance could this have had for Constance who was in Paris at the time?

Potocki was the owner of several landed estates as well as the magnificent palace of Wilanów near Warsaw, formerly the summer residence of King John Sobieski. Furthermore, he was the son of Count Stanislas Kostka Potocki, Fergusson-Tepper's fellow freemason and co-investor in the Black Sea Company. But how might Charles have heard, or who might have written to him, in his tiny Sicilian holiday resort about a far-away Polish sequestration at the other end of Europe?

At the end of 1833 news of Alexander Potocki's forfeiture was still fresh. It was an act of Russian vengeance for his sons' participation in the 1831 Uprising despite the fact that their father had spent the time living discreetly on his estates in East Galicia. Feeling that he was being treated unfairly, Potocki appealed against the judgement during the years 1832–34 and eventually managed to reverse the decision – though only after Charles had sent his letter to Constance. The sequestered estate was Satanów. It ran from that town many kilometres north up to Kokoszyńce along the east bank of the River Zbrucz which divided Austria's Polish Galicia from the Russian-held Polish-Lithuanian provinces upon which the uprising had taken place. Facing Satanów, on the other side of the river, was the Castle of Grzymałów. Satanów was so close that you could see it easily from the Grzymałów's large forest above Wolica. Not long before, Grzymałów had even belonged to the family of Potocki's grandmother, Princess Elizabeth Lubomirska who had fled Paris at the beginning of the Revolution with Count Adalbert Mier. Yet the castle and estate of Grzymałów had been

---

[76] Archives Nationales, Paris, Archives Privées, Berryer papers, 223 AP 34 & 40, Countess de la Morlière & Countess de Thorigny; See also part 2, ch.2.

sold almost three years earlier, on March 15th, 1831. Its new owner was none other than Marie-Victoire's son, Antime.

As Antime was an active participant in the Uprising it, like Krzywczyce, was almost certainly managed at the time by Charles' new brother-in-law, Jean de Pauw – indeed, both he and his son, Zenon, were buried at Grzymałów. The castle became Antime's principal residence and it was there that Marie-Victoire's letters from Louis de Rohan were kept. Charles may have been half a continent away from his sister in late December 1833, but for her the sequestration of Satanów was major local news and all the more relevant as the Potocki family had featured in Marie-Victoire and Charles' youth as core members of the Fergusson-Tepper clique.[77]

Contact between Marie-Victoire and her brother is further indicated by the following. Charles' passport for 1834 is stamped with visas given in Paris for travelling through Bavaria and Austria.[78] On February 13th, 1835 he received an account from M.S. Bing of Frankfurt for the sale of the 'grand and magnificent palace, number 70 in Vienna'.[79] This begs investigation, for the property did not belong to Charles. House number 70 in Vienna was the palace of the Counts d'Harnoncourt. It was created out of houses 70 and 71. The earlier history of 70 is that in 1796 it had been bought by Countess Johanna von Unverzagt and inherited in 1814 by Countess Leopoldine d'Harnoncourt who bequeathed it in 1835 to Count Hubert Ludwig d'Harnoncourt. As it was not sold in 1835

---

[77] J. Dunin-Borkowski, *op. cit.*, pp.497, 754–755; PSB, vol.27, pp.756–760; Documents of C.E. Roehenstart, Ms Fr b7 229 & Ms Fr 44 223; Central Historical State Archive of the Ukraine in Lwów, Archive of the former Court of Nobility, documents from 1845 concerning the dispute arising out of the purchase of the Grzymałów Estate from Leopold Elkan de Elkanberg by Antime, Chevalier de Nikorowicz on March 15th, 1831, C 48900. It should be noted that a second Count Alexander Potocki, born in Tulczyn, suffered a large sequestration at about this time. He was a close friend of the eminent romantic poet, Sigismund Krasiński and, as there is a note in Charles' papers with the Italian addresses of an Alexander Potocki and a Count Krasiński and son, one might imagine that this is the Alexander Potocki to whom Charles is referring. However, Charles' addresses were amongst his papers for the year 1815 at which time the poet Krasiński was only four. Nor was the Count Krasiński called Sigismund but Joseph. The only Count Joseph Krasiński with one son alive in 1815 was an Austrian major-general who was the owner of the Galician estate of Rohatyn, not far from the estate of Brzeżany which belonged to Alexander Potocki of Satanów and Wilanów. Also, in Charles' letter of 1833 he adds: '... the sister's daughter, nearly forty, married to one of my people'. This eliminates Potocki from Tulczyn (1798–1868) as opposed to Potocki of Satanów (1776–1845). Lastly, Potocki from Tulczyn's forfeiture had taken place immediately after the collapse of the 1831 Uprising and was no longer news in late 1833.

[78] Documents of C.E. Roehenstart, *op. cit.*, Ms Fr 44 236.

[79] *Ibid.*, Ms Fr 44 240; G. Sherburn, *op. cit.*, p.122.

Charles' account must refer to the other half, formerly 71. It was bought in 1798 by Anton von Bianchi, then sold to Magdalena von Gintow in 1815 from whom it was inherited in 1835 by Theresa von Giuliani who, allowing for land registry delays, straight away sold it to Count Hubert Ludwig d'Harnoncourt. He then joined the two halves to form the palace which remained in his family's hands until 1873.[80] What link, therefore, existed between the von Giuliani family and Charles?

Once again the family has a strangely familiar profile. Francesco Giuliani was of bourgeois Neapolitan origin. He became a doctor and orientalist who opened a shop in Constantinople. In 1736 he was appointed official translator to the Polish Embassy there and rapidly became a prominent, even ostentatious member of it. He also maintained close contacts with Poles trading between Turkey and Poland. In 1758 he was ennobled by the king for his long service and retired to Warsaw in 1761 leaving two of his sons to be educated in Lwów. In Warsaw, despite Giuliani's contacts at the highest level, his salary was reduced and so, to supplement his income, he started his own trading activities with Constantinople. He spoke Turkish, Tatar, French, Latin, Italian, Greek as well as some Arab and Hebrew and had pretensions to being a poet. His son, Peter, was also a linguist who, with his brother Henry, had studied at the Royal Polish Oriental School in Constantinople. Peter became an official translator for the Polish diplomatic service and was based in Kamieniec Podolski. He was also engaged in Polish trade with the Black Sea and Polish espionage directed towards Turkey and Moldavia. In 1775 he was ennobled and in 1776 parliament granted him the right to acquire land in Poland. Throughout this period the family corresponded with the Stuarts' cousin, Prince Charles Radziwiłł. Peter's younger brother, Henry, became translator for the Spanish Embassy in Constantinople whilst another became doctor to the Grand Vizier himself. Finally, Michael Giuliani became a Polish freemason in 1821. To summarise: the von Giuliani family was intimately connected with Polish diplomatic and trading activities on the Warsaw-Lwów-Constantinople axis; had direct

---

[80] P. Harrer-Lucienfeld, *Wien – seine Häuser*, Menschen und Kultur, Bd 7, Vienna, pp.166–168, manuscript at the Viennese Stadt und Landesarchiv. As there is no record of any Austrian noble family called von Gintow, this must refer to the Polish noble family of Gintowt or Gintowt-Dziewiałtowski, arms *Trąby*, who were landowners in Austrian Galicia – *Poczet szlachty galicyjskiej i bukowińskiej*, Lwów 1857, p.65. Theresa von Giuliani inherited the house and therefore must have been in some way related to the Gintowts. Apart from the Giulianis mentioned in the main text there is no record of any other noble family of that name being related to, or members of, the Polish nobility of the old Polish-Lithuanian Commonwealth or the Austrian Empire.

links with the elite of both Poland and Turkey; were in correspondence with Fergusson-Tepper and Nikorowicz's client, Radziwiłł; had first-class knowledge of oriental languages and were associated with Polish freemasonry. The extraordinary overlap with the family of Marie-Victoire's first husband and son meant that the two families could not have avoided each other. Nor did they. Their names of Giuliani and Nikorowicz even appear together on the same documents. Therefore, whilst it is not clear why Charles received an account for the sale of the house in Vienna, it was obviously somehow connected with the relationship between the von Giuliani's and the in-laws of Charles' sister.[81]

The final trace of contact between Charles and Marie-Victoire is in a letter dated August 1st, 1836 which he sent from Naples to 'Madame Stuart, 4 rue du Harlay, au Marais, Paris'. As described earlier, Charles kept Marie-Victoire's existence secret, even from Constance, his second wife. In this context it is perhaps not so odd after all that he devoted no less than twelve lines in grief at an apparently irrelevant piece of news from Austria. Charles began with the words: 'I am sorry to hear the Cholera is raging in Vienna'.[82] It probably took a few weeks for the news to reach Charles, again abroad on his solitary peregrinations, that at five o'clock in the morning of April 27th his sister had died – at no 1132 Untere Bräunerstrasse, in Vienna. The cause of death was, of course, cholera. Two days later Marie-Victoire was buried in the Maria Hietzing cemetery just outside the Austrian capital – in grave 55. Alongside was grave 56. – that of Baroness Marie-Anne de Bourguignon who had died in 1817, the wife of Prince Radziwiłł's protégé, Joseph de Nikorowicz. Next was grave 57. Since 1816 it had been that of Anna Leiner von Negelfürst, Antime's mother-in-law.

Marie-Victoire was not old when she died. Her death certificate from St. Michael's Parish in Vienna states simply:

The high and noble born Madame Marie de Pauw, née de Thorigny, originating from Tours [...] fifty six years old.[83]

---

[81] PSB, vol.8, pp.11–13; AGAD, Archiwum Radziwiłłów, dz.5, 4214; S. Małachowski-Łempicki, *op. cit.*; Biblioteka Narodowa, Biblioteka Czartoryskich, sygn.617, Akta dotyczące stosunków z Turcją 1699–1756. Francesco Giuliani (+1765) & Peter Giuliani (born c.1749).

[82] Documents of C.E. Roehenstart, *op. cit.*, Ms Fr 44 263.

[83] Records of the Parish of St. Michael, 1010 Vienna, Habsburgerg.12, Death Protocols May 1824 – December 1844, p.142; Piniński Archive in Lwów, fond 79, nr 1–2, Nikorowicz; Piniński Archive in Warsaw, documentation concerning the death of Marie-Victoire, 3 documents & correspondence; Archive of the Maria Hietzing Cemetery, Vienna, group 4, graves 55, 56 & 57 – today none of these three graves exist, having been granted to new occupants decades ago.

For exactly that number of years had passed since June 19th, 1779 when the head of the de Rohans, the old Duke de Montbazon, had brought the infant daughter of his brother Ferdinand and cousin, Charlotte Stuart, to the chapel of the Château de Couzières and legitimised her with the title of 'the demoiselle de Thorigny'. One wonders what the good Jules-Hercule thought as he watched the water of baptism roll from his little niece's innocent brow.

The last of the Duchess of Albany's three flowers was gone. There was only one member of the next generation, Antime, whom his mother had once called: 'God's gift'.

CHAPTER SIXTEEN

The Tartars' Way

A very attractive girl of Armenian origin,
but what was peculiar was that she was
an Armenian blonde.

Casimir Chłędowski
Memoirs, Vienna 1881–1901

Antime was three when his father died. His mother was his only family, and she kept him away from both the de Rohans and his half-brothers and sisters. Yet whatever influence Marie-Victoire had on him, one thing he did inherit was her bright blue eyes which came straight from Charlotte Stuart. His childhood was almost certainly spent at his mother's side during the early part of her ten years' travelling after her first husband's death in 1810. Then, up to at least 1818, Antime was educated at the Royal College in Versailles[1] and afterwards in Austria. There, from 1823 until 1828, he rose from the rank of cadet to lieutenant in the Imperial 4th Cuirassiers of Crown Prince Ferdinand based at St. Georgen near Pressburg[2] under the command of Colonel Count Carl Clam-Martinitz. Antime's military papers record that he was a nobleman with significant private income who had not bought his military title but earned it; that he spoke fluent French, German and Polish; and was impulsive as well as brave, honourable, dynamic and good natured. General Wybranowski described him as 'a very kind person, and extremely polite in manner',[3] whilst Count Louis Jabłonowski spoke of him as 'the most decent and most noble of men'.[4]

---

[1] Today the Lycée Hoche.
[2] Now called Bratislava, in Slovakia.
[3] R. Wybranowski, *Pamiętniki*, Lwów 1882.
[4] L. Jabłonowski, *op. cit.*, p.274.

When he left the 4th Cuirassiers Antime registered the continued right to his military rank in Lwów's Imperial Court of Nobility on October 21st, 1828. His career had come to an end because he was to marry Anna, the daughter of Captain August Leiner von Negelfürst, a retired officer of the Austrian Army. It appears Antime met his wife through the Viennese-based circle of exiled French nobles who had fought with de Condé. For over a decade earlier his paternal aunt, Baroness Marie-Anne de Bourgignon and his mother-in-law had both been buried side by side in Vienna. Antime was in his early twenties when he married and already a wealthy man as the owner of a mansion in Lwów and the palace, estate and sugar refinery at Krzywczyce. To this Anna added her rich dowry with which the young couple bought the estate of Grzymałów on March 15th, 1831 comprising its sixteenth century castle, town, extensive arable land, forestry to the south-east as well as five villages.[5] The castle was a massive, four-bastioned quadrangle built by the Ludzicki family in 1590 and situated on a small hill overlooking the River Gniła which formed a lake beneath the escarpment when in flood. Underneath ran subterranean passages which led to the town from the castle's huge cellars. Such escape routes were more than useful in times such as 1651 and 1675 when the castle had been besieged by Cossacks and then by a Turkish army under Ibrahim Shishman Pasha. After those onslaughts the ruined property was acquired by Field-Marshal Adam Sieniawski.[6] By 1731 the castle, town, Greek-Catholic Uniate Church and baroque synagogue had all been restored, though the Roman Catholic Church of the Holy Trinity was not finished until 1752. Sieniawski's grand-daughter was the same Princess Elizabeth Lubomirska who fled the French Revolution with Count Mier. Reputedly Europe's richest private woman, she owned sixteen towns and 232 villages, several castles, Sobieski's magnificent palace of Wilanów near Warsaw, two others there, more in Lwów and Vienna, as well as priceless collections of art. However, it was Grzymałów's rich forests and black earth which produced her largest single source of income.

In Elizabeth's day the estate comprised 3 towns and 37 villages. It also embraced a strange formation of hills known as the *Miodobory*[7] which ran in an arc from the north down to the Potocki estate of

[5] The five villages were: Zamurze, Mazurówka, Bucyki Podlesie and Eleonorówka.
[6] (+1726).
[7] 'The Honey Woods'.

Satanów on the River Zbrucz in the south-east. Their name came from the extraordinary quantity of bees which lived there, whose produce was gratefully harvested by the locals. The area was also sometimes called 'Swiss Podolia'. Here were ancient tombs over a thousand years old and the whole area was formed of raised land made of pre-historic coral reefs which sometimes pierced the soil, standing over thirty metres tall. Besides the bees the peculiar micro-climate also produced many rare plants which nestled amongst queer rock formations such as the *Okniny*.[8] They were four small round lakes whose waters were extremely deep. In summer they were bitterly cold yet in winter never froze. Such were the landscapes of Podolia's high river-cut plateau traversed by the 'Tartars' Way' upon which stood the Castle of Grzymałów.

In 1818 Elizabeth's daughter, Countess Constance Rzewuska, inherited the estate. However, she went bankrupt. Five years later the castle, town, forestry and five villages were bought at auction by the Viennese banker, Leopold Elkan de Elkanberg. It was from him that Antime and his wife acquired the property in early 1831 – later enlarging it by adding the neighbouring estates of Zielona and Pajówka.

1831 was also the year of the 'November Rising' aimed at regaining Poland's liberty. It was fought on the Russian-occupied territories of the old Polish-Lithuanian Commonwealth. But Galicia was used as a base and many Poles who were Austrian citizens crossed the border to take up arms and fight. One of those idealistic young patriots who rode off to join the rising was the ex-officer of Crown Prince Ferdinand's 4th Cuirassiers. Antime's description as impulsive, brave, honourable and dynamic recall those of his great-grandfather who, at exactly the same age, had ridden off from Rome in 1744 to an earlier rising, no less heroic, no less doomed.

Amongst the several political activists whom the Russians exiled to Voronezh as a preventive measure was the ex-marshal of the Vilnius Nobility, Michael Römer, together with his sixteen-year-old son, Severin. Römer was the grandson of a Radziwiłł and closely associated with that family. Since 1813 he had also been a pre-eminent Polish freemason intimately connected with the movement's Warsaw elite. However, as a reform-oriented Polish patriot, he had been arrested by the Russians and held in Warsaw without trial from 1826 until February 1830 whereupon he was released. But he was re-arrested in

---

[8] 'The Little Windows'.

December as an 'unsure element' and sent into exile. On May 1st, 1831 his diary from Voronezh records: 'More Polish officers have arrived here – Apolinary Grabowski, a captain of the 3rd Rifle Brigade, and Nikorowicz, a lieutenant of the cavalry [...] Nikorowicz was sick with fever [...] There was also Marcinkiewicz and Krasiński [...] They are all going on to Ufa'. Antime had fought with the Polish 1st Lancers and been taken prisoner. However, as an Austrian citizen with no property in Russia for them to sequestrate he was already on his way home on January 6th, 1832 when, still suffering the last effects of the severe fever which had already lasted seven months, he wrote to Römer: 'We are in Kursk and tomorrow press on further'. Antime told him of the terrible condition of the roads, of having not yet seen either the colonel's wife or Krasiński but passed the time with Ossoliński and Tarnowski. Finally, thanking Römer for making his imprisonment in the remoteness of Russia one in which he had made so many deep friendships, he asked him to 'embrace dear Severin warmly and ask him if he could find out if there were any letters or money forwarded, as promised, via the post-master at Żytomierz'. Afterwards, though the rising was crushed, those who still dreamed of freedom continued to plot and Antime became president of his district's clandestine association which used to hold its secret meetings in a back room of Grzymałów's inn.

Just before riding off to fight, Antime and Anna had started a family. On November 5th, 1830 he became a father. Two days later his child was baptised in Lwów's Armenian-Catholic Cathedral. The godparents were 'Marie de Pauw' and 'Captain Jean de Pauw'. One wonders whether the infant's name was not chosen by Marie-Victoire. For it had never been used before in the Nikorowicz family. Inevitably, that name was Charles. Without doubt she was the only one present who knew its 'Secret'. Marie-Victoire had two more grandchildren: Julia Thérèse who was born on May 21st, 1833 and six years later, Stanislas.

During his children's early years Antime concentrated on his home and family. About the year 1840 he converted the austere fortress of Grzymałów into a palace. Retaining the main body of the building with its two rear towers, he added a large, galleried portico as well as a gothic clock-tower containing a spiral staircase. The defensive ramparts were then pulled down and an 'English' park laid out which included the seventeenth century avenue of lime trees planted by Field-Marshal Sieniawski. To decorate the castle Antime began to collect works of art including a very fine collection of engravings by Vernet.

Antime was not only amongst the very first to emancipate his peasants but by writing numerous articles in the press he was also one of the most vociferous advocates of reform. In addition he founded a greek-catholic church for the local population at Krzywczyce. However, life in the Galician countryside began to be dangerous. In 1846 the Austrian authorities tried to stamp out the nationalistic ambitions of their Polish province by promoting a policy of setting the peasantry against the landowners. Given a completely free hand and in a number of cases open assistance by local Austrian bureaucrats, groups of peasants committed appalling atrocities on hundreds of gentry, irrespective of wealth or 'guilt'. Antime therefore rented out Grzymałów for nine years to the lawyer John Fedorowicz[9] and based himself and his family in Lwów.

Two years later the European-wide series of uprisings known as 'The Spring of the Nations' broke out. Again Antime was amongst the first to join. Again his hopes were dashed. Though events in Lwów were serious, nevertheless the minor armed clashes did not flare up into large scale revolution. This was due to the iron hand of the Austrian governor of Galicia, Count Franz Stadion, Marie-Victoire's former courtier. It was he who was the probable author of the Austrian-inspired butchery of the Polish landowners – and it was that action which successfully destroyed any chance for unity between the Polish elite and rural population. In 1848 Stadion also managed to split the political unity within the revolutionary movement itself. Patriotic aspirations had crystallized into four main power centres. One was the parallel Polish government called the 'National Council' of which Antime was a member. Another was the Lwów-based chapter of the secret pan-European 'Carbonari' movement which had strong links with international freemasonry. Having originated in Italy its Central-European incarnation was dedicated to the overthrow of Austrian rule. Then

---

[9] John Fedorowicz later served under Antime's command as one of his ADC's during the Spring of the Nations in 1848 whilst in June 1940, during the Second World War, his direct descendant, Father Thadée Fedorowicz, having obtained permission from Archbishop Twardowski of Lwów, volutarily boarded one of the Soviet cattle trucks taking Polish deportees to Siberia. Posing as a lawyer he smuggled aboard a chalice and as many communion wafers as possible. He was sent to labour in the forests of the Ural Mountains but when the Molotov-Ribbentrop Pact fell apart in 1941 with the Nazi attack on the Soviet Union he joined the Polish army being formed there by General Ladislas Anders, gaining from him permission to travel throughout Kazachstan working as a priest. Arrested by the Soviets and imprisoned in Semipalatynsk he was released and became chaplain of the Polish 4th Division. Ultimately he became Pope John Paul II's confessor.

there were the two military formations. One was the 'National Guard' and the other was the 'Academic Legion' which comprised a force of 1200 armed students organised into six companies of two hundred men. At the beginning of 1848 they voted on who would be their commanding officer. The man they unanimously elected was Antime. On March 23rd, 1848 he addressed them with the words:

> Comrades in Arms!
> You have honoured me with your confidence in choosing me as your commander. I feel it and I am grateful! [...] Today all Europe demands the rights that belong to her [...] In you rests the hope of our land. Give of yourselves an example to others! And may you convince the whole Nation that you are worthy to carry the arms which the Country has placed in your hands – in the name of Peace, Order and the Safety of the People!
>
> Nikorowicz

His words are barely worth recording. But it was curious they were those of the heir of the man to whom much the same number had rallied at Glenfinnan a century before – and whose fateful name was borne by his eldest son.

Of all the Polish military formations active in Galicia during the Spring of the Nations, General Wybranowski described the cavalry force under Antime's command as 'the best maintained and organised; [...] this formation was kept in perfect military order'. However, at the end of 1848 Stadion ordered his artillery to bombard Lwów into submission. It was something no-one expected and was therefore all the more effective. As elsewhere in Europe, the Spring of the Nations in Lwów proved a premature flowering whose fruits would ripen only later.

1848 was also the year Antime's wife died. Within three years he too was dead. He had gone to the spa at Carlsbad to try and improve his health but died there on February 16th, 1852 at the age of forty-five. In 1870 his remains were brought back and reinterred in Grzymałów's cemetery at the end of the great Lime Avenue on the high plateau of Sobieski's native Podolia. After Antime's death his property was divided. His eldest son Charles received the castle, town and estate of Grzymałów as well as the palace, estate and sugar refinery at Krzywczyce. Julia inherited that part of Grzymałów called Eleonorówka, together with a share of Charles' income. Stanislas got Zielona, Pajówka and the

mansion in Lwów – but the latter's descendants died out two generations later.

Charles, like his father, though only seventeen, had also rallied to the
Spring of the Nations becoming a junior officer in the Polish National
Guard. Similarly, he too promoted the emancipation of the peasantry.
In 1853 he married Aniela, the daughter of Baron Joseph Eder, vice-
president of the Galician Court of Appeal. And at Krzywczyce, on
September 15th, 1854 Charles became a father. He called his son
Antime. In 1857 a daughter, Michalina, was born.

Fate continued its persecution of all bearing the name Charles or
Charlotte. In 1858 Charles quarrelled with a friend. Poland's most
famous nineteenth century horse painter, Julius Kossak, was his second
when the dispute was settled by way of an 'American Duel'. Two bullets
were placed in a bag. Charles drew the black one. He had one year in
which to commit suicide. During this time he arranged for his two children to be looked after by his sister Julia at the Castle of Grzymałów,
having exchanged that estate for Rokietnica near Jarosław which
belonged to Julia's husband. He then travelled to Paris. Exactly one
year after the duel Charles killed himself at Versailles. It was where
Marie-Victoire had lived upon her return to France and his father had
studied at the Royal College. One can only speculate as to why he chose
that place. Charles was twenty-eight. Not long after, a plaque appeared
on the wall of the church at Rokietnica. Its text is still legible:

> To the late Charles Nikorowicz
> who died an unnatural death at Versailles in France
> on August 31st, 1859
> To the deceased
> from a true friend who as proof of his immortal memory
> has placed this stone here, asking Divine Grace for his soul

No-one knows who put it there.

Charles' daughter died childless. However, Young Antime completed his education at the Higher School of Economics in Paris and
married Sophie, the daughter of landowner James Wiktor. Somehow
the great landed wealth of Young Antime's family had slipped away and
he became the owner of the minor estates of Wola Baraniecka near
Sambor and Szelpaki near Zbaraż as well as the lease-holder of Zubrze
near Lwów. Nevertheless, he was highly thought of as a financier,
became director of the bank in Tarnopol at the age of thirty-three and

then, in 1898, when the Galician Savings Bank crashed, was appointed its chairman and nursed it back to health. Young Antime died in the mountain resort of Zakopane in 1908 at the age of fifty-three and was buried in Lwów – the last of the Chevaliers de Nikorowicz, for he left only daughters and they in turn left only daughters – except for one son who died childless.

One last footnote remains. Young Antime's eldest daughter bore the ill-fated name of Charlotte. On September 17th, 1939 Stalin's Red Army invaded Poland. The NKVD knocked on her door at four o'clock in the morning of April 13th, 1940. Without any explanation as to why or what would happen to her, completely innocent of any crime, she was given an hour to pack a single bag, forced into an over-crowded, fetid rail-truck whose conditions were barely fit for animals, then sent by rail to the wastelands of Soviet Kazakhstan. Winter temperatures varied from minus 20 to minus 40 degrees. The weak perished. Charlotte's husband was amongst them. He died in Gieorgiewki on August 23rd, 1943. Yet Charlotte was relatively lucky, for it was summer and the ground was soft. In winter the soil became hard as granite and corpses could only be covered with frozen chunks of loose earth and rocks. Six years later, on May 25th, 1946 with over four hundred others packed twenty to a truck, the destitute Charlotte began the long journey back to what remained of Poland after Lwów and the eastern half of the country had been annexed by the Soviet Union. On June 10th she reached Voronezh where Marie-Victoire's son had been during his own exile after the November Rising. A week later the trucks rolled slowly across the border into communist-occupied Poland where Charlotte died in 1951 at the height of the Stalinist Terror.

Though the male line died out with Young Antime's death in 1908, there still remained direct descendants of Charlotte Stuart. But of those girls only one bore her husband a son whose line survives unbroken to the present day. She was Marie-Victoire's grand-daughter Julia who succeeded her brother Charles at the Castle of Grzymałów. At the end of the 19th century the diarist Casimir Chłędowski described her thus:

A very attractive girl of Armenian origin, but what was peculiar was that she was an Armenian blonde.

CHAPTER SEVENTEEN

Through Europe's Tapestry

It passed long since – I've accepted fate
That what's buried does not return
Why then the echo strange
Of songs for ever broken off?

Alexander August Piniński

Marie-Victoire's grand-daughter Julia Thérèse[1] married Count Leonard Francis Xavier Piniński[2] in Lwów on June 8th, 1853. To judge by his elder brother's comments, the family may have been old, but it was also a bit long in the tooth, for Eustace answered the letters of genealogist Count Alexander Krasicki by rambling on about how much better the tea was in Vienna than Lwów. When pressed for something more directly related to family history, Eustace told Krasicki that 'all members of the Piniński family are mad'. This enlightening correspondence was sent from Eustace's home in Vienna where he spent his time conducting experiments with explosive materials.

The family took its name from the estate of Pinino in the province of Dobrzyń, north-west of Warsaw, which their ancestor, Andrew 'Ramrod' Dołęga of Wierzbick and Cebryszewo, Judge of Dobrzyń[3] added to his adjoining estate of Kobrzyniec. Pinino's purchase was signed in Lipno on November 26th, 1379 by Margaret, Princess of

---

[1] (1833–1893).
[2] (1824–1886).
[3] (1364–1413).

Dobrzyń and witnessed by the province's premier nobles, Andrew Ogończyk, castellan of Dobrzyń and Peter Świnka, castellan of Rypin. On April 7th, 1380 a further confirmation was signed in Płock by Ladislas, Duke of Opole, Wieluń and Kujavia. Pinino was later inherited by Andrew's grandson, Nicholas, castellan of Dobrzyń[4]. But his son, Nicholas, grand standard bearer of Dobrzyń[5] left no male heir, so the estate of Pinino passed through the female line to his grandson and namesake, Nicholas Boleszczyc. The latter bought out his brother John's half-share in 1518 after which Nicholas' descendants began to use the surname Piniński.[6]

The older line died out in the early nineteenth century with Joseph, chamberlain of Kowel who was also a chamberlain of King Stanislas August Poniatowski and who reached such old age and respect that he became popularly known as 'the Patriarch of Volhynia'. The younger line continued with a second Joseph[7] who acquired a number of estates, the principal one being the neo-classical palace adorned with fine baroque statuary at Babica. Schneider's 'Encyclopedia of Galicia' records that in the mid-eighteenth century 'the beautiful palace [...] was famous for the splendour of its interiors' and its owners 'regularly hosted grand hunting parties' as the surrounding hills and forests teemed with some of Europe's finest game.

Joseph's two sons were called Stanislas[8] and George[9]. They belonged to the generation which saw the first partition of Poland in 1772. By that time the majority of their estates were in the old commonwealth's southern swathe which had been annexed by Austria. Since 1744 Stanislas had been district governor of Pilzno which rank, according to Empress Maria-Theresa's law of 1776, qualified him for the hereditary title of count.[10] By

---

[4] The dates of his castellanship were 1435–1454. The highest ranks in Poland, bringing with them seats in the Senate, were those of Provincial Governor (*Wojewoda*) and Castellan (*Kasztelan*).

[5] Appointed in 1480.

[6] Grammatically identical with 'of' or 'de Pinino'. The surname '*Boleszczyc*' was the name of the heraldic clan (al.*Jastrzębiec*) to which the Pinińskis had belonged since before the earliest surviving records.

[7] (1689–1735).

[8] (+after March 7th, 1800).

[9] (+ March 28th, 1793).

[10] Titles of nobility were almost unknown in the old Polish-Lithuanian Commonwealth where noble status with its wide political rights and privileges was inherited by all sons. As nobility could be endlessly divided, whereas wealth could not, almost 10% of the population became politically enfranchised. Taken together with the elective monarchy this resulted in a degree of democracy unequalled in contemporary Europe. To become king, candidates had to make

his wife, Marianne,[11] daughter of Joseph Drohojowski, castellan of Przemyśl, he had one son, Anthony,[12] who left only a daughter by Countess Josephine Ankwicz.

George was also granted the title of count in 1778. His wealth was as considerable as his career was dull. His sole achievements were to be created a knight of the Order of St. Stanislas in 1791 as well as build and furnish a beautiful late-baroque church on his estate of Babice-upon-San. The massive portraits of the founder and his second wife Catherine[13] still hang on either side of the main altar. Resplendent in full armour, George had himself portrayed as the saint of the same name. No less immodest were his landed properties which comprised the palace of Babica, a number of neo-classical manor houses, two towns and some twenty villages. The centrepiece was the Castle of Krasiczyn built at the end of the sixteenth century under the supervision of the Italian architect Galeazzo Appiani from Lugano. Apart from the Royal Castle of Wawel in Cracow it is Poland's most magnificent renaissance residence and is spoken of as the 'pearl of Polish architecture'. In an 1811 inventory of their new province the Austrians described it as 'the oldest and best maintained magnatial castle' in the district of Przemyśl. Then, in 1832, the Lwów periodical *Rozmaitości* wrote: 'As regards the ancient castles of Galicia the best preserved is unquestionably that of Krasiczyn'. George died in 1793 and his second wife in 1827. Thereafter his estates were divided between his eight children. The eldest, another Joseph,[14] sold the castle with eight villages to Prince Leon Sapieha on October 20th, 1836 whilst of his brothers the only one to have sons was the youngest, Francis Xavier.[15]

---

footnote 10 (*cont.*)

electoral promises resulting in ever more power passing into the hands of the noble electorate and out of the hands of the central executive, thus weakening the state at a time when neighbouring powers were highly autocratic and militarily expansive. This and the comparatively small number of nobles of magnatial wealth meant that the lesser and impoverished nobility could and did veto the creation of a two-tier peerage-gentry system out of fear of losing the theoretical equality between all of noble birth. This changed as a result of the three late eighteenth-century partitions of the commonwealth when the country was divided between Russia, Prussia and Austria, each of whom had titled aristocracies. The first few titles of nobility bestowed upon Polish nobles by the Habsburgs between 1776 and 1784 were not for services rendered to that partitioning power but, as in the case of the Pinińskis, related specifically to the respective peer's rank in the old Polish-Lithuanian Commonwealth.

[11] (+c.1794).
[12] (+March 7th, 1800).
[13] Née Woszczyńska, (+March 3rd, 1827).
[14] (1775–1853).
[15] (1783–1835).

He inherited Babice-upon-San, took part in the November Rising of 1831, never recovered from his wounds and died four years later. Of Francis' four sons the eldest was Eustace,[16] the Viennese-based tea taster and bomb enthusiast who considered his entire family mad; and the youngest two were Anthony[17] and Victor,[18] officers in the Austrian 8th Hussars and 2nd Cuirassiers respectively. None had children.

There remained the second oldest, Leonard. Besides his share of Babice-upon-San he also inherited Rokietnica, having bought out his eccentric brother's half. Leonard was one of those patriots who joined the Spring of the Nations in 1848, serving as a cavalry officer of the National Guard in Lwów. There, on June 8th, 1853 he married Marie-Victoire's grand-daughter, Julia. Her dowry had been that part of Grzymałów called Eleonorówka plus a share of the income from the rest. However, in 1855, shortly before his ill-fated duel, her brother Charles exchanged Rokietnica for Grzymałów. A little later Julia's younger brother sold Leonard his two neighbouring properties thus reuniting the original Grzymałów estate. Leonard then went on to enlarge it by buying Soroka and half of neighbouring Iwanówka from Alexander Giziński, before inheriting another share of it in 1870 from a family friend, Tytus Sozański.[19] Finally Leonard bought the estates of Suszczyn and Koszyłowce with their neo-classical palaces. In addition he renovated and industrialised Grzymałów's sugar refinery, ordering large steam-powered turbines from Vienna, the final leg of whose journey to rural Podolia were the hundred plus horse-drawn kilometres from Lwów. The investment was completed by 1864, becoming East Galicia's largest private flour mill. Later the 'Steam Mill' even generated electricity for the town. And it was here that a management position was found for Zenon, the son of Marie-Victoire's third husband, Jean de Pauw.

Leonard's business acumen was reflected in his membership of the committee of the Galician Economic Society, his election as delegate of the Galician Land Credit Society and his membership of the supervisory board of the Galician Credit Bank. But by the age of sixty he was already suffering from a progressive, sclerotic depression which provoked fits of rage, weird demands and constant attempts to escape from the care of his son Leon and long-suffering butler Jamie. The

---

[16] (1822–1901).

[17] (1826–1902).

[18] (1830–1897).

[19] Antime's lawyer was a Sozański – almost certainly Tytus or possibly his father.

demented man would wander the streets of Lwów and engage strangers in mad conversation. He died on July 18th, 1886 and two days later was buried alongside his father-in-law Antime and de Pauw in the graveyard at Grzymałów.

Six years after her husband's death Julia died of a gynaecological cancer which she had been too shy to admit to her doctor. Three days later her body was taken to Grzymałów and on February 26th, 1893 took its place alongside those of her husband, father and step-grandfather. To his puzzled observation that Julia was an Armenian blonde, the diarist Chłędowski added: 'In any case she stood higher with regard to the nobility of her feelings than her husband'. Another diarist, Marian Bogdanowicz, described Julia as a 'refined and witty lady, [...] always immeasurably warm, friendly and kind'. The leading Lwów journalist and editor, Adam Krechowiecki, wrote that Leonard's:

> ... hard work, high sense of public duty and energy combined most curiously with the refined, artistic nature of his wife and together created a specific atmosphere in the ancient Castle of Grzymałów, at once serious yet loving, warm but creative, in which the intellects of the younger generation grew and matured, instilling in them a truly high level of culture.

Of that culture the eminent historian Michael Bobrzyński commented that it 'soared high above the level of the Podolian nobility'. As for the castle which was open to the public the art historian Alexander Czołowski described it as 'exquisitely decorated and carefully maintained by the Counts Pininski'. Edward Chwalewik's compendium of Polish collections said that 'the palace, converted from a castle, possesses many historical objects, family portraits, paintings of the old school and other works of art of a similar nature'. Those were the collections which included the pastel portrait of Marie-Victoire which she had asked to leave at Louis de Rohan's Parisian mansion in 1825. Yet half a century later no-one any longer knew that it portrayed one of the Duchess of Albany's 'three flowers'.

Leonard and Julia had four fair-haired, blue-eyed boys. Once again it fell to the youngest, Alexander August,[20] to continue the male line. But his elder brother, Leon,[21] the co-heir of Grzymałów, not only played a

[20] (1864–1902).
[21] (1857–1938).

key role in the curious story of the Stuarts' later descendants, but of all of them was the most distinguished. In 1938 Professor Stanislas Łempicki compared Leon's vast knowledge to that of the great men of the Renaissance. Later, in the 1990s, Professor Waldemar Łazuga described Leon as 'an astonishingly erudite man of vast humanistic interests'. His career had three distinct strands. He became an internationally recognised professor of law who chaired that faculty at Lwów University before becoming its chancellor in 1928 and a 'Professor of Honour' in 1935. He was also an eminent statesman who played a dominant role in the highly effective Polish Circle of the Austrian parliament in Vienna, gaining the reputation of a brilliant orator. Then, in March 1898, Emperor Franz Joseph appointed Leon imperial Viceroy of Galicia which for Poles was the highest position in the Austro-Hungarian Empire apart from that of prime minister.

Leon was also a music and literary critic, composer, art historian, collector and benefactor. He not only amassed a vast collection of art in his mansion and private museum on Lwów's Matejko Street but also organised the conservation and restoration of art and architecture throughout Galicia. As referee of the parliamentary Budget Committee he negotiated the terms of the Austrian Army's removal from the devastated Royal Castle of Wawel in Cracow. Having published his own restoration and refurbishment project in 1905 he then publicly announced that he would donate all his existing art collections as well as future purchases to the Wawel. He did not buy for himself but to provide representative works from each of the main schools as a framework for a national gallery which he foresaw housed at the royal castle. In 1931 he gave nearly four hundred paintings, sculptures and altarpieces as well as Italian renaissance furniture to the Wawel. In 1935 the art historian Dr Stanislas Świerz-Zaleski said: 'In first place, both in terms of quantity and value, the Wawel Foundation of Count Leon Piniński stands out, [...] the result of effort and sacrifice throughout this great benefactor's life, a collection gathered together from youth with the single thought of decorating the restored interiors of the Wawel Castle.'

In addition he left his library, seven hundred graphic works and about a hundred old master drawings to the National Institute in Lwów.[22] And apart from a number of individual bequests to other public galleries he left his mansion with over seven hundred paintings

---

[22] Known as the Ossolineum after its founders, the Counts Ossoliński.

and altarpieces as well as his collections of porcelain, glass and furniture to the Polish State Collections of Art in Lwów. Leon's British paintings were not amongst his most important, nevertheless to this day they remain the largest and best group of that school in Poland. When they were exhibited in Cracow in 1993 it was ironic that the person who, by opening the exhibition should unwittingly pay tribute to the most eminent descendant of the Stuarts, was none other than the Hanoverians' heir, the present Prince of Wales.

Doctor *honoris causa* of three universities, Leon's published works exceeded one hundred and forty. He received the 'Gold Laurels' of the Polish Academy of Literature, was made an honorary citizen of dozens of towns throughout Galicia, a life member of the Austrian House of Lords and was decorated with Poland's highest contemporary civilian honour, the Order of Polonia Restituta. It was awarded in its 2nd class, the highest for non-heads of state. As for his character Professor Łazuga wrote: 'Piniński was a far better political analyst than psychologist. He always attached too much importance to logic (and the formal appearance of things) and too little to emotion, posturing, gestures and that whole area of imponderabilia.'

Of Leon, Professor Łempicki asked, 'whence so much energy, so much spiritual and intellectual power in so slight, almost, frail, a man?' Yet Roman Dybowski concluded from an analysis of Leon's literary criticism that he had 'a pessimistic attitude to the world'. Nevertheless, when the Russians invaded East Galicia in 1914 and occupied Lwów he did not flee, like so many others. Instead, he joined the Citizens' Guard and Defence Committee, tried to restart Polish education, stood at the head of the Red Cross and supported all initiatives to help war victims and their families. He also tried to soften tsarist repression against the captured Polish soldiers of Piłsudski's Legions.[23] When the military situation was reversed in 1916 Leon returned to the leadership of the Central National Committee, whose aim was full autonomy for Galicia, and in the Viennese House of Lords fought against Count Czernin and Seidler's anti-Polish policies. In 1917 he openly criticed Austrian repression in Galicia and, in early 1918, co-led negotiations with Hungary on behalf of the Viennese Polish Circle aimed at winning their support for Polish policies towards the Ukraine. A decade and a half later the Polish Inland

---

[23] Though Poland had not yet regained her statehood during the First World War, nevertheless Marshal Joseph Piłsudski created purely Polish legions which fought as an independent national force.

Revenue foolishly tried to impose taxes on Leon's bequest to the Wawel. He ordered the immediate removal of forty-six paintings including all thirty-two of the British ones and deposited them in a bank in London. The authorities caved in and the paintings returned to the Wawel two years later. Leon also stood unflinchingly against the growing anti-Semitism of inter-war Poland, categorically refusing to limit the number of Jewish pupils at university. He was equally strong in his support of women in academic life and it was thanks to his determination that Caroline Lanckorońska became Poland's first female professor.[24]

Criticised by his wife as mean for believing that every penny not spent on art was wasted, the caricaturist Casimir Sichulski once portrayed the tattily dressed, bearded, wispy-haired count nurturing Polish culture from a watering can connected by a hose to his brain. 1903's 'Parliamentary Sketches' described him as the 'deputy-King of Galicia' and declared that 'the Lord of Grzymałów is entirely happy – you can see it from his smile, from his animated expression, from his every movement!' The reason was marriage. The blond intellectual, with eyes either tired and depressed or twinkling with mischief had enjoyed remarkable success with the fairer sex. His career included a passionate romance with Countess Cecile Mier, the last of a polonised family of Scottish origin whose surname was a corruption of Muir. Unfortunately at the time she was married to Count Stanislas Badeni, marshal of the Galician parliament and brother of the Austro-Hungarian prime minister. This led to a degree of somewhat understandable friction. Badeni was obliged to come one day to the Castle of Grzymałów during Leon's viceroyship but became irritated when another guest thought it sweet Leon's dog should wag his tail at his master so enthusiastically. 'So would I', the marshal growled, 'if only I saw him that seldom'. On June 15th, 1903, in the private chapel of the archbishop of Lwów, Leon married Maria, the daughter of Count Alphonse Mniszech. Hers was the family whence the historical figure of Marina, the wife of the 'false Tsar Dmitri' of Mussorgsky's opera 'Boris Godunov'. Forty-four when she married, Maria was childless when she died in February 1922. Leon lived on until April 1938. One night the sound of music being quietly played was heard from a room in his Lwów mansion. Then it stopped. A few minutes later the old man was

---

[24] Her academic title was *docent* – junior professor.

found dead on the couch. Beethoven's death march lay open on the piano.

And so it was Leon's youngest brother, Alexander August, who continued the male line. In September 1898, Countess Anne Kwilecka wrote to her sister-in-law about a dinner party at a Podolian estate:

> Sunday dinner was trumpetted in our honour. I appeared with an emerald beneath my chin and, for my further glorification, was led to the table by Huyn[25] [...] He is already a Lt. Colonel and in Spring hopes for still further promotion. On my other side was Alexander Piniński, his wife is a Wolańska (her father died suddenly at her coming-out ball in Lwów!) [...] It was great fun, because the Piniński brothers were brilliant at mimicking all sorts of Galician notables and characters!

Alexander inherited the eighteenth-century neo-classical manor house and estate at Suszczyn together with four others near Tarnopol, whilst his wife's dowry brought four more. But he had an incurable heart problem and his personality expressed itself in poetry. Some of his works were edited by Adam Krechowiecki and Alexander badly wanted them to be published before his death. The modest volume was printed in October 1902. But he died in mid-May, aged only thirty-seven. It was not his poetry which was great, it was the reflection in it of his deep love of country, strong faith and personal simplicity. He knew he was dying and once said: 'He only fears death who has wrong on his conscience'. In his foreword Krechowiecki commented that Alexander:

> ... was not only free from evil, but from every trace of it [...] In his family relations he was the best of sons and brothers, in his home life a loving husband and father, a good citizen and the kindest of neighbours [...] But this sketch would not be complete if it omitted to say how faithful, sensitive and sincere he was towards friends [...] Writing this it seems to me I hear his words, ever generous, always wishing to give me pleasure or produce a smile with some elegant and delicate joke.

The Lwów Gazette wrote:

[25] Count Carl Huyn.

May 16th. With unspeakable grief we place a cross by the name of Count Alexander Piniński who passed away today in our city in the prime of life, defeated by a serious, untreatable disease of the heart. Of quiet and modest nature, he never pushed himself forward, though possessed of rare talents and marked by the extraordinary qualities of unequalled serenity and gentlemanliness [...] By his marriage to Countess Irena Wolańska he leaves two young boys – may their tears for the best of fathers be comforted by the universal sympathy felt for them.

Four days later the newspaper continued:

The funeral procession was led by Archbishops Bilczewski and Teodorowicz[26] accompanied by their clergy. Behind the coffin, surmounted on a carriage drawn by four horses, walked his widow and beside her, his brothers, His Excellency the Viceroy Count Leon Piniński, then Stanislas and Mieczyslas with his wife, the Marshal of Parliament Count Potocki and his wife, the Minister His Excellency Monsieur Zaleski, the President of the High Court His Excellency Dr Alexander Mniszek-Tchórznicki ... etc.

The coffin was then placed in a special train which left at midnight for Grzymałów accompanied by 'the family of the deceased and several tens of people. Amongst them, the Marshal Count Andrew Potocki, Prince Andrew Lubomirski, Count Starzeński, Count Michael Baworowski ... etc.'. The train arrived at eight o'clock the next morning and was met by the clergy of both the Roman Catholic and Greek Catholic rites, the sheriffs of the area, banner-carrying members of the guilds as well as crowds of country people. Mass according to both rites began at 11 o'clock after which the coffin was carried by representatives of the peasantry to the cemetery where it was interred at three in the afternoon alongside the other family graves. There then followed a reception at Grzymałów Castle after which the train took the guests back to Lwów.

After her period of mourning ended, Alexander's widow, Irena, married the Austro-Hungarian and, after 1918, Polish general, Count Robert Lamezan Salins.[27] She also bought the fifteenth century castle

---

[26] Respectively the Roman-Catholic and Armenian-Catholic archbishops of Lwów.
[27] (1869–1930).

of Świrz which had been remodelled in the renaissance period. With Robert she put her heart into its restoration which had not long been completed when on September 2nd, 1914 it was plundered and burnt by the retreating Russian Army. Only its walls remained. Its works of art, rich library and ancient frescoes were all destroyed. Irena's three children were Ladislas,[28] Mieczyslas[29] and their sister, Renia.[30] Only eight and six respectively when Alexander died, the two boys were educated at Vienna's elite Collegium Kalksburg from 1907–1912 during their step-father's term as Austro-Hungarian military attaché in Brussels and Paris. After completing their studies both entered the Imperial Cavalry Cadet School in Vienna, spending their holidays either in Lwów, Suszczyn or at the Castle of Świrz. There, when supervising the re-roofing of the old fortress by Russian prisoners of war in 1918, Mieczyslas found a long sealed-up dungeon in the lowest of three underground levels beneath the right hand front bastion. When its door was forced open he found a human skeleton chained to the wall, all that was left of some prisoner from the unsuccessful Cossack siege of 1648 or perhaps from 1675 when the Turks were repelled and the castle provided shelter for refugees from Sobieski's neighbouring castle at Pomorzany.

Mieczyslas' elder brother, Ladislas, inherited the Suszczyn estate and became a cavalry major who at the Battle of Komarów on August 31st, 1920 led the final charge of the greatest and last major cavalry battle of the twentieth century.[31] His Polish 8th Lancers destroyed the sixfold greater forces of Bolshevik General Budyonny's legendary 'Horse Army'. Dr Bohdan Skaradziński described the charge as 'no longer a scene from Napoleon, but from Grunwald itself'.[32]

Like his elder brother, Mieczyslas possessed an intense warmth which even strangers noticed immediately. However, unlike him, he was neither gregarious nor vivacious but pensive and serious. He married a nineteen-year-old ballerina – tiny and beautiful, with an easy laugh, modest and deeply religious. Her name was Janina Maria Helena. She came from a Viennese family which three generations

---

[28] (1893–1945).

[29] (1895–1945).

[30] (1904–1968).

[31] The charge was led together with Kornel Krzeczunowicz. Cavalry charges occurred later, however Komarów was the last full-scale battle in history in which only cavalry took part.

[32] As King Robert the Bruce's Bannockburn of 1314 is to Scots, so King Ladislas Jagiełło's Grunwald of 1410 (when the Teutonic Knights were decisively defeated by a combined Polish-Lithuanian army) is to Poles.

before had moved to the Żywiec estate of the Habsburgs as adminis-
trators. Her grandfather married a girl from the local gentry, become
polonised, adopted the Polish name of Żywiak and retired to Lwów.
And it was in that city's Opera that Mieczyslas met 'Janusia' whom he
married in December 1922. The next year was spent in Lwów – but
then life began to take a series of unpredictable turns.

Mieczyslas managed his fortune with great success. Having inherited
the Grzymałów properties of Zielona and Pajówka he then bought the
large forest estates of Rozłucz near Turka and Michalin near Kosów.
Rozłucz was connected by rail to Lwów, next to which station he built a
timber processing factory for large scale finished products. Michalin also
had big timber yards. In addition he oversaw the management of Leon's
estates. When his uncle argued with the Polish tax authorities it was
Mieczyslas who took Leon's paintings to London and deposited them in
the bank. And when Leon died, Mieczyslas was his sole heir and inherited the estates of Iwanówka as well as Grzymałów Forest[33] overlooking
the old Potocki estate of Satanów. However, upon the renaissance of
Polish statehood after the First World War, Lwów became a provincial
Polish city. No longer was it the modern, thriving, cosmopolitan capital
of the Austro-Hungarian Empire's largest province whose population
was over half as big again as that of present day Scotland. Nor was
Vienna any more the seat of imperial power. Perhaps that was why
Mieczyslas turned to Paris and acquired an apartment on the rue St.
Didier in the sixteenth *arrondissement* near the Bois de Boulogne where
he kept a horse called Gradiska. Later he bought the antique-filled Villa
Brunicki, a three-storied, frescoed house overlooking a terraced garden
of bamboo and its own private bay at Abbazia on the Istrian Peninsula.
Abbazia had formerly been Austro-Hungary's premier Adriatic resort
and near the Villa Brunicki stood the Habsburgs' Villa Amalia. Winters
were spent ski-ing in the Alps at Mégève or Chamonix, summers on the
French Riviera, in Normandy, Brittany or on the Polish estates. It was a
life of unquestioned wealth and privilege.

Thus, during the inter-war period, Mieczyslas' base became the
Paris whence his ancestress Marie-Victoire had returned to Lwów
almost exactly a century before. Throughout the twenties and thirties
he commuted between Paris and Lwów to oversee his properties and
businesses there. In the latter decade, when exchange controls were
introduced by the Polish government, Mieczyslas managed to pay for

---

[33] Which he named Werbyczna.

his family's life in Paris by filling a hollowed-out walking stick with dia-
monds which he bought in Lwów or Warsaw and sold in France. In
February 1925 his only child was born, a son called Stanislas Alexander
– 'Stash'. He was the only member of his generation. His father said
that he didn't want his son 'brought up a provincial Polish snob' and
therefore sent him to the cosmopolitan Ecole Gerson and then to the
Lycée Janson de Sailly on Paris' rue de la Pompe. It was intended that
Stash should complete his education at a modern French agricultural
college before returning permanently to Poland upon graduation; for
he was to inherit not only his father and great-uncle Leon's combined
estates but also those of his childless uncle Ladislas. And amongst
Stash's colleagues at school were two boys whose name had once meant
so much to his forebears. They were Guy and Charles de Rohan. But
neither family any longer knew about their Stuart secret from one
hundred years before.

Events had shifted the family to Paris. But a chance meeting added
a further twist. Just after the turn of the century Leon's interest in
Shakespeare[34] led him to invite a young Scottish graduate of English
literature to lecture at Lwów University. His name was William
Robertson-Butler. Leon ensured that he was warmly received by the
Polish nobility and invited him to take part in their charity plays at
which William would sing old Scottish ballads, many of them Jacobite.
At the same time a young Scottish graduate of medicine from Glasgow
University turned down her father's proposal of a holiday on the
French Riviera and instead asked to spend a post-graduate year at
Lwów University. She was Elizabeth Fraser, the sister of Lord
Strathalmond who became chairman of British Petroleum. Not
knowing how to arrange a place at the university Elizabeth turned to
the British Foreign Office which got in touch with the polyglot Viceroy
of Galicia. Leon then introduced the two Scottish graduates to one
another and they fell in love, married and became close friends with
both him and his nephew, Mieczyslas. The couple returned to Britain
where William worked in the headquarters of British Petroleum in
London before retiring to the fashionable resort of Eastbourne on the
south coast. Between the wars they would travel to Europe and during
Leon's constant journeys all over the Continent and Middle East the
three of them would arrange to meet in various capitals. Similarly,

[34] Leon wrote an authoritative two volume monograph on Shakespeare – L. Piniński, *Shakespeare
– wrażenia i szkice z twórczości poety*, 2 vol's, Lwów 1924.

William and Elizabeth would also stay in Paris with Mieczyslas and his family en route to the Mediterranean, inviting them in turn to take their summer holidays in Eastbourne in 1937 and 1938. Finally, as the clouds of war gathered in the beautiful summer of 1939, Mieczyslas sent Janina and Stash on holiday to the Robertson-Butlers once more whilst he went to look after the family estates and businesses in south-east Poland.

Mieczyslas' mother had died in 1929 and his step-father a year later. Both were buried in the crypt of the chapel at the Castle of Świrz. Between their deaths Mieczyslas' sister had married in Vienna. Renia's husband was Count Thadée Komorowski,[35] the commanding officer of the 9th Lancers and a superb show-jumper who had represented Poland in the 1924 Olympics and captained the silver medal-winning team in the 1936 Berlin Games. When the Germans unleashed their *blitzkrieg* on Poland on September 1st, 1939 Renia was in Grudziądz in western Poland where her husband was commanding the Central Cavalry School. From there she drove all the way to Świrz which she had inherited in 1930 and offered the castle as a military hospital. Afterwards she travelled east to her brother's estate of Suszczyn near Grzymałów. But Ladislas was fighting with the 22nd Lancers. When the Red Army attacked Poland from the east on September 17th the local Ukrainian peasants protected Renia and her sister-in-law, putting guards around the estate's park. From there they could hear the Soviet tanks as they crossed the border into Polish territory. Soon after, a communist commissar informed them that everything had been nationalised. Both women became penniless refugees.

Renia's husband also fought in the 1939 September Campaign. But his subsequent career was to have a decisive impact on the fate of his brothers-in-law and their families, for he co-founded the 'Home Army'[36] and became its Commander in 1943. Hitler then put a price of £400,000 on his head. But they never caught the apolitical man whose principal code name was 'General Bór'[37] and who commanded the heroic Warsaw Uprising of 1944. The capital had food for six days, fought for sixty-three and suffered 84% total destruction. Having negotiated the surrender 'Bór' was taken into captivity and held with his senior officers at Colditz together with the Earl of Hopetoun, Earl

---

[35] (1895–1966).

[36] '*Armia Krajowa*' – Europe's largest, best organised and most effective resistance movement of the Second World War.

[37] *Bór* means forest.

Haig, Viscount Lascelles, the Master of Elphinstone, the nephews of Field Marshal Alexander and Winston Churchill as well as the son of the US ambassador to London. At Colditz they were known the *Die Prominenten*, to be used as a bargaining counter for Hitler's life. Released as the war drew to a close, Renia's husband flew to London and took up his position as commander-in-chief of the Polish armed forces[38] and afterwards became prime minister of the Polish government-in-exile[39] as well as a member of the most senior exiled political body, the Council of Three.[40] Decorated during his lifetime with the Cross of Valour, Virtuti Militari (5th, 4th, 3rd & 2nd class) and Polonia Restituta (4th & 2nd class) he was also posthumously decorated with the American Legion of Merit by President Ronald Reagan and the Order of the White Eagle by President Lech Wałęsa. In 1994, after the fall of communism, on the fiftieth anniversary of the Warsaw Uprising, Renia and her husband's ashes were brought back to Poland and buried in Warsaw with full State honours.

Renia's eldest brother, Ladislas, was captured by the Germans on September 23rd, 1939 at the Battle of Jacnia but later released. He then re-formed his old regiment, the 8th Lancers, as an underground regiment within the Home Army and was appointed its commanding officer. Until mid-1944 he lived with his wife in Cracow. But the Gestapo knew who his brother-in-law was and arrested Ladislas and his wife just prior to the Warsaw Uprising. He was taken to the Montelupi Prison in Cracow and from there to Gross Rosen concentration camp where he arrived on July 29th, 1944. After some time he was sent to the even more dreadful conditions of Camp Dora in Saxony. How he died or where his body lies no-one knows. Some say he died at, or just after, the moment of liberation by the Americans and that his emaciated body was buried by a railway track in today's Czech Republic. Others believe he was executed after a failed escape attempt a little earlier. After her arrest, Ladislas' wife was taken to Ravensbrück concentration camp which she survived along with Leon Piniński's protégée, Caroline Lanckorońska.

In 1939, after Mieczyslas' return to Lwów, he avoided arrest by the Soviet NKVD because his administrator, Mr Kaufmann, took over his flat and hid him there – being Jewish the latter was not under threat. Then the situation was reversed. Nazi Germany attacked

---

[38] (1944–1947).
[39] (1947–1949).
[40] (1955–1966).

their Soviet ally in 1941 and became Lwów's new occupier. Jews became their prime target. However, the impeccably dressed, dark haired Mieczyslas spoke flawless, refined German and his presence gave him an authority over the class-concious Germans. He needed it. For he now had to protect his Jewish friends. The Kaufmann family remained hidden in the flat for several months but by 1942 could take no more and decided to go out into the fresh air. They were arrested. As soon as Mieczyslas heard, he requested their release but was predictably refused. He then placed a Berlin telegraph number on the Nazi officer's desk and told him to report his refusal to the general whose name he had written down and await the consequences. Aware that the well-known aristocrat might easily have high ranking friends, the German decided it was not worth risking anything for the sake of one Jewish family. It was a bluff. There was no such general. Mieczyslas left as soon as he could for his villa in Abbazia, helped by a letter of recommendation from King Victor Emanuel of Italy. For had he been discovered the punishment for any Pole caught even trying to help a Jew was death not only for the accused but his entire family. What happened to the Kaufmanns is not known. And how much of this is true is hard to say. But it was certainly in Mieczyslas' style. He loathed anti-Semitism and Nazis in equal measure. Before the war, when travelling by train through Germany on his way to Lwów, a member of the railway police ordered him to show him what he had in his suitcases. Furious at their constant checks and insolence Mieczyslas fixed him in the eye and through clenched teeth enunciated the words: 'Here I have anti-German propaganda, here pistols, here bombs and I am a Jew'. Four post-cards to his elder brother survived the war. They contain the following encoded messages:

Lwów. January 30th, 1942.
... I am sending her the picture of Edward. I have been very worried that you are again suffering with your liver. Stanislas Komor. told me about it, but I haven't been able to find out anything about the doctor we both know. Please write to me if you are better. Concerning myself, I have had bad flu lately but it's passed. So far I have managed to arrange everything with the authorities. Amongst other things I now have a letter from the Director of Police that Kauf. and his family can stay in my flat until 1.4.1942 [...] In your letter of 18.12 in which you mentioned

the furniture and the new 'injection', you told me to let you know when such an injection will be necessary. Well … [*rest missing*].

Later, Mieczyslas wrote whilst en route to Abbazia:

Vienna. October 1st, 1942.
Here all are well. Nothing has changed. I've delivered the sweets. Both little dogs are well. The journey went as smoothly as in peacetime. Kiss Maniusia[41] – I embrace you very sincerely,

Your Miko[42]

Those were his last known words. Mieczyslas made it to the Villa Brunicki, for local people remember him being there. However it seems that in early 1945 Tito's partisans tried to kill him and injured him so badly that he died anyway, for in late 1945 a British Red Cross doctor told the family that someone answering his description had died in a field hospital near Abbazia in February or March. As with his brother, no-one knows exactly how or when Mieczyslas died. Nor where, nor even if, he was buried.

With his father's death Stash became the sole descendant in the male line of Charlotte Stuart's great grand-daughter, Julia. He had been sent on holiday with his mother in 1939 to be near Elizabeth and William Robertson-Butler. With his mother he stayed at the Kingsdown Hotel in Eastbourne from mid-July and they were to have remained there until early September. But when Stash heard the announcement of the Molotov-Ribbentrop Pact on August 23rd he refused to return to Paris. He was not yet fifteen but already knew that war usually began when the harvest was in. He also remembered the words of Captain Fournier who had won the *croix de guerre* in the First World War. During peacetime Fournier had been in the reserves and run a shop on the rue de la Pompe. In November 1938 he had been recalled to his regiment. He was shocked by the mess. His unit was not where it was supposed to be, the bullets didn't fit the rifles and the iron rations contained tins of sardines dated '1917'. 'If it comes to war', he told the Polish teenager, 'this time France will be beaten'. So mother and son remained in Eastbourne. Hitler attacked Poland on September 1st.

After that date the Roberton-Butlers arranged that Stash and his

---

[41] Maria née Traczewska (1890–1963), Ladislas' wife.
[42] This was Mieczyslas' familiar name.

mother should live in the large house of their wealthy friend, Mr Douglas, a retired jute merchant from Dundee. They also found a place for Stash at Eastbourne College and paid the fees for his first two terms. The English public school was very different from the Ecole Gerson and Lycée Janson in Paris. And the false status of unwanted guest with the Douglas family was a strain. Nevertheless life maintained some semblance of its pre-war appearance with breakfasts served from covered silver dishes in a hushed atmosphere full of servants. Then things began to change. By January 1940 Mr Douglas felt he had done his bit. Taking the hint, Janina accepted an offer to move in with the Falkus family whose son David was also at Eastbourne College. In March Stash again insisted that he and his mother remain in England when a scientist called Dr Suckling offered to pay their fares back to Paris. Once more the decision was right. On May 10th, whilst buying valves for a crystal radio, Stash and David heard the radio crackle out the news that Nazi Germany had invaded Holland. Captain Fournier's prediction proved correct. France fell within weeks. Shortly afterwards the Gestapo came to the rue St. Didier apartment to arrest the family – it transpired that they had discovered where the immediate relatives lived of all those they considered might be potential resistance leaders.[43]

As England prepared for invasion the south coast became a danger zone. The Robertson-Butlers left hastily for a house they'd bought in Glasgow. The Falkus family moved to Reigate in Surrey. And Eastbourne College began its evacuation to Radley School near Oxford. With the remains of their holiday money from 1939 and the proceeds from selling their leather suitcases at Mappin and Webb in London Janina moved in to a couple of rooms she had rented on the outskirts of Eastbourne. She had no money for her son's education. But neither did the school offer to evacuate him to Radley with the other pupils. So before he left for Reigate Mr Falkus found Stash a job as a labourer on a farm high up on the South Downs where he worked throughout the Battle of Britain and until the end of 1940. That autumn his mother had to leave her rooms and move again, this time to a tiny cottage at Heathfield in Sussex. A week later her previous

---

[43] Before the war the politically important relative the Nazis had identified was probably not Komorowski but Leon Piniński – the former's importance emerged only later. Gestapo officers then occupied the apartment during the German occupation of France and, incredibly, when vacating it left on the kitchen table an amount of money equal to the unpaid rent for the whole period of the war! The apartment was rented by Mieczyslas and so that money was intended not for him but for the French landlords.

lodgings were destroyed by a bomb. Janina contacted the Polish Relief Fund who sent second-hand clothes for Stash who had grown out of those he had brought from France. The charity also contacted the Polish government-in-exile in London who sent some money. More importantly, Miss Dunfield of the Polish Relief Agency persuaded Eastbourne College to give Stash a free place. So he rejoined the school as a boarder in February 1941, managing to pass his School Certificate exam in December that year despite his disruptions and having to do so in his third language.

No longer able to afford the rent for the little cottage, Janina lived from mid-1941 as a guest of the Belgian de Pré family who had a farm at Heathfield. Mrs de Pré was the wealthy daughter of a professor from Louvain and her piano teacher was a Miss Edna Randle who had moved from Hastings and was living nearby with her elderly mother. When Janina had to leave the de Pré family at the end of 1943 she was taken in by Edna with whom she lived for three years after which they went to live in a cramped flat in Hastings. A year later Janina found a bedsit of her own in the same Parish, to which she became devoted, moving twice more before she died in 1976 but remaining close to her most loyal friend until the end.

After he left Eastbourne College at Radley in mid-1943 Stash joined the Polish Air Force in Britain. His basic training took him to Bridge of Allan near Stirling. It was his first contact with Scotland. In 1945 he gained his wings as a fighter pilot just as the war was grinding to a halt which brought only the hollowest of victories for Poland. And though they had nothing, his mother insisted that he complete his education at university.

Stash was twenty-one when he was given a place at St. Andrews University. There he studied economics which he rightly thought would be useful in post-war Britain. It was clearly out of the question to return to a Poland in the grip of Stalin's communist puppet-government which was sentencing his uncle's soldiers to death, causing countless others to 'disappear' or just gunning them down in the street. Any close relation of General Bór ran the risk of being used to force the 'accused' back to face execution, just as Bór's successor, General Okulicki, had been murdered in 1946 after a Moscow show-trial.

There was nowhere and no-one in Europe for Stash and his mother to return to. The rue St. Didier apartment had only been rented. After the war some Poles associated with the embassy lived there and organised the sale of its remaining antiques for Janina. There were oil paintings of dramatic cavalry scenes by Adalbert Kossak,[44] a collection of Copenhagen porcelain and the apartment's gilded Louis XV furniture. But the prices fetched in the aftermath of the war were a fraction of their true value. The only thing Janina couldn't bring herself to part with was the jewellery she had taken with her on holiday in the summer of 1939. Later she never wore any. No-one even knew it existed until after her death when it was found locked away in her small flat. As far as the Polish estates and businesses were concerned, they were lost forever in what had become the Ukrainian and Bielorussian provinces of the Soviet Union. The mansion which had once housed the Piniński Museum was now the headquarters of the Lwów KGB. Even the Villa Brunicki with its rich collection of antiques was nationalised without compensation for Polish citizens, for it was on the Istrian Peninsula, annexed by communist Yugoslavia.

Stash always remained grateful for the safety of England after the chilling atmosphere of the Continent's final pre-war months. But in Scotland he 'felt comfortable – even the cold expanse of the Forth felt homely'. Some time after he arrived at St. Andrews he fell in love with a fellow student who had spent the latter part of the war working in the Admiralty. Her name was Jean Graham.[45] She introduced him to the Isle of Arran which her family had known for generations and where she had sheltered during the war after the fall of France. Thus began annual migrations to the island which continue to this day. Stash asked Jean to

---

[44] Son of Julius Kossak who was Charles Nikorowicz's second in his American duel.

[45] This cadet branch of Graham of Montrose descends from: William Graham (+1571), 2nd Earl of Montrose and Lady Janet Keith, d.of the 3rd Earl Marischal, whose fourth son was William, 1st of Killearn (+1597). His descendant, Robert Graham, was granted the feu of Wood of Ledlewan (also known as the Quinloch) in 1642 by James Graham, 1st Marquis of Montrose. Robert's fifth son was Archibald in Auchenmill of Kilmannan whose second son was Walter (b.1736) and youngest son was James (b.1750). Walter became a Burgess of Glasgow which office passed to James in 1773. On March 10th, 1777 at Killearn, James married Jean, d.of James Provan, 1st of Ledlewan (who purchased that estate in 1736 from Archibald Edmonstone of Duntreath and John Williamson, tenanted at that time by John Graham in Wood of Ledlewan. Ledlewan had previously been the property of Captain Henry Graham of Killearn). James Graham's third son was John (b.1789) who gained an M.A. at Glasgow University and an M.D. at the Royal College of Surgeons in London. John's third son by Isabella McMillan of Rothesay was Daniel (1835–1910), a lawyer, who had the following children by Isabella Main of Glasgow: (a) John (1879–1958), major RAMC 1914–1918, professor and dean of Anderson College of Medicine, x Isabella Fraser, d.of William Fraser J.P., sis.of 1st Baron Strathalmond; (b) Isabella; (c) Wilhelmina, x John Paul of Long Court, Randwick & Park House, Stroud, Gloucestershire; (d) Daniel + young; (e) James (1889–1974), captain RADC 1916–1918, OBE (mil.), x Jessie Cameron Paul (sister of John Paul) – *these latter being Jean's parents*; (f) Robert (b.1891), 2nd lt., 10th Duke of Wellington's Rgt., killed in action Oct.4th, 1916.

marry him, so she introduced him to her aunts and uncles. Her father's sister, Bella Graham, asked how Stash had come to be in Britain, so he recounted the story. When he mentioned the Robertson-Butlers she cried out in astonishment. She showed him a published piano composition. At the top was a dedication to her from its composer – William Robertson-Butler. She then showed him a picture of a boy aged thirteen – it was a photo of himself! For Elizabeth Robertson-Butler was Bella's cousin and her close friend since childhood. The Fraser and Graham girls had spent holidays golfing together on Arran's Blackwaterfoot course in long Edwardian skirts and cumbersome bonnets in the years before the First World War. Elizabeth's sister, Isabella, had even married Jean's uncle, Professor John Graham. And Elizabeth had given Stash's photo to Bella because she had arranged for her nephew, Kenneth Fraser, to become Stash's pen-pal in the late thirties.

But it was not the only coincidence. Amongst the names Jean's mother gave her first born was one of which her family had long been proud. That name was Cameron. For Jessie Cameron Graham was the granddaughter of Jessie Cameron of Glenhurich by Loch Shiel, three of whose four grandparents were Camerons. In particular her mother was Margaret Cameron of Goirtean Eorna, south of Moidart. She in turn was the daughter of Mary Cameron in Ranachanmor. And Mary's father was the same John Cameron of Fassiefern who had been imprisoned by the Hanoverians in 1746, 1751 and 1753, who had helped his brothers during the 'Forty-Five, taken part in the Elibank Plot and seen his younger brother, Dr Archie, hung, drawn and quartered at Tyburn without trial in 1753 – the last man to be executed for his part in the 'Forty Five.[46]

---

[46] The Cameron descent is: Jean Graham (1926–1999) d.of Jessie Cameron Paul (1886–1974), d.of Jessie Cameron Todd (1853–1914, x William Henry Paul of Long Court, Randwick & Park House, Stroud), d.of Jessie Cameron (1821–1875, x John Todd of Glenhurich House, in Glenhurich. All of Jessie's siblings emigrated to Australia), the d.of Margaret Cameron (1801–1871, x Alexander Cameron of Gorton House, tacksman of Goirtean Eorna by Acharacle. Of Margaret's siblings two sisters emigrated to Australia, two to America, whilst her brother, John Cameron, entered the army with a commission bought by his uncle, Sir Allan Cameron of Erracht, founder of the 79th Cameron Highlanders. After John's death in Gibralter in 1798 as a captain in the Black Watch Sir Duncan Cameron of Fassiefern travelled there to collect his personal belongings), d.of Mary Cameron (x Samuel Allan Cameron in Ranachanmor, Sunart, s.of Allan Cameron, Younger of Erracht, by Margaret, d.of Allan Cameron of Glendessary. Mary Cameron was the youngest sister of Sir Ewen Cameron Bt., 2nd of Fassiefern, the father of Colonel John Cameron commanding officer of the 92nd Gordon Highlanders, 1771–1815, and Sir Duncan Cameron Bt.,3rd of Fassiefern, 1775–1863), d.of John Cameron, 1st of Fassiefern (+1786), s.of John Cameron, 18th of Lochiel, Lord Lochiel in the Jacobite peerage.

The names of Cameron, Lochiel and Fassiefern had echoed through Jean Graham's childhood. After moving from Glenhurich to Glasgow her great-uncle's family had named their new home, Fassiefern. And throughout Jean's closest family were distributed various objects which had belonged to Colonel John Cameron, Younger of Fassiefern, who had been killed whilst leading the 92nd Gordon Highlanders at the Battle of Quatre Bras on the eve of Waterloo. More than three thousand highlanders followed his coffin when Colonel John's remains returned to Lochaber. And the epitaph on his tomb at Kilmallie Churchyard by Loch Eil was written by Sir Walter Scott. Those heirlooms included three swords, one of which was a captured French sabre, a powder horn, walnut knife box and a crystal water glass. There was also the colonel's hide-covered travelling-chest which stood in Jean's nursery throughout her childhood as well as a copy of his memoirs with a dedication from his younger brother, Sir Duncan Cameron Bt., 3rd of Fassiefern. But in particular there was a decanter and four wine goblets said to have been those used when Prince Charles dined at Fassiefern House on August 23rd, 1745 whilst the Highland army, billetted outside, picked roses from the bushes in the gardens and pinned them to their bonnets as the campaign badge of the 'Forty Five, symbolic of the Stuarts' white rose. A century later two generations of Jean's gaelic-speaking ancestors lived at Glenhurich House by Loch Shiel where Lochiel and Fassiefern's first cousin, Alexander Cameron of Dungallon, had earlier lived. He had been the standard bearer in Prince Charles' army and his sister had married Dr Archie. It was at Glenhurich House that Lochiel, Dr Archie with his pregnant wife and John Murray of Broughton with his, together with other Jacobite fugitives, had hidden after 'Butcher' Cumberland's men had burned Lochiel's Achnacarry to the ground in May 1746.

Two centuries later and years before anyone would even begin to try and discover who Marie-Victoire was, it happened that a young Polish refugee who had no idea he was the senior male descendant of the last of the Stuarts, chose for his bride a Scottish girl who by strict female descent was the offspring of the arch-Jacobite Camerons of Lochiel.

Six generations separate Stanislas Alexander from his brilliant but flawed ancestor of the 'Forty Five. Likewise six separate his late wife Jean from the Camerons of Lochiel. During the intervening time the blood of their forbears had threaded its way through much of Europe's unhappy tapestry to re-unite at the altar on May 12th, 1951 – a union whose genesis lay in a chance encounter some fifty years before between two Scots and a Pole in the very shadow of King John Sobieski's old mansion in Lwów.

Here ends my story. Not one of glory. Nor neat and tidy. Not always does the line pass through some convenient succession of first-born sons. But then it never did. And anyway, isn't that what happens in the real world? Just six people stand between my father and Charles Edward Stuart. Barely enough to fill a dinner table. I wonder, what would we talk about if we sat down together? Of faults and mistakes? Of how things might have been if only one could only re-live History once again? Or would the unspeakable horror of the past hang over us all in silent shame?

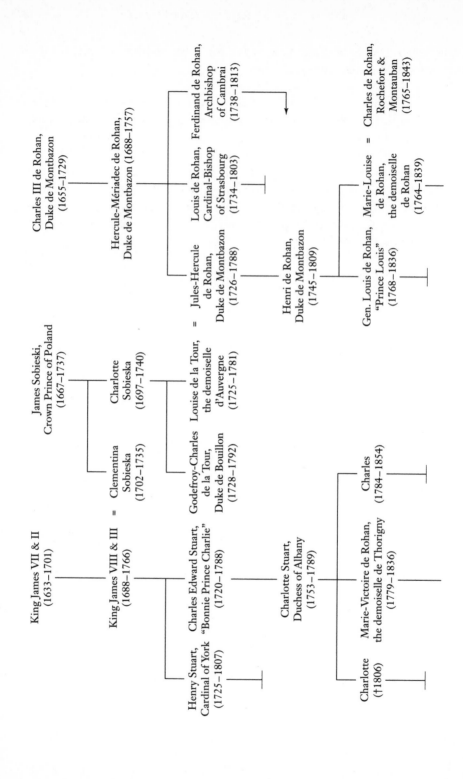

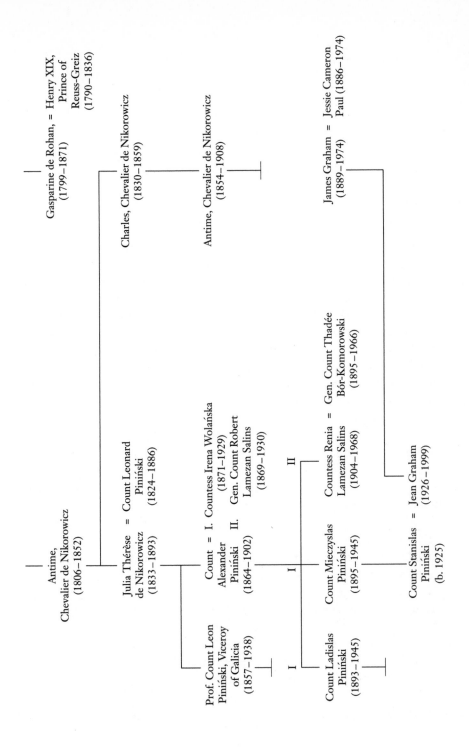

Postscript

Entering the field of the history of the last Stuarts, in particular that of Prince Charles, is to invite controversy. However, until now only the life of his grandson has been known about. And that only since Professor Sherburn discovered his letters in 1935 and published his biography in 1960. Histories concerning the last Stuarts have hitherto related that Charlotte Stuart's two daughters disappeared without trace. Having found the documents and letters described in this book, which had remained undiscovered or unrecognised for almost two centuries, there seemed an obligation to write about them, though the subject is barely a footnote of history.

This book does not give sources for well-known historical facts. They are available in the books listed in the bibliography and elsewhere. This applies to Polish and Scottish history as well as to the Nikorowicz and Pinínski families whose genealogies have been published many times during the nineteenth and twentieth centuries. The bibliography does, however, include additional sources for both of those families, indicating where further material is located. But where the text is concerned with previously unpublished information concerning the generation of Charlotte Stuart's children, precise references have been given and footnotes added indicating exactly where the original source documents are located. In certain cases the archive is not within easy reach, for example the Pinínski Archive in the W. Stefanyk Scientific Library of the Ukrainian Academy of Science and other documents concerning the Nikorowicz family in the Central State Historical Archive of the Ukraine – both in the former Polish city of Lwów. Likewise Marie-Victoire's letters are in the de Rohan Sychrov Archive in the State Archives at Děčin in the Czech Republic. Similarly, the letters and documents of Charlotte Stuart's son which are at the Bodleian Library in

Oxford were not microfilmed at the time of research whilst Ludovic Vieira's *History of the Château de Thorigny* was only published privately. Consequently copies of all the original documents, a microfilm of the Bodleian documents and a significant amount of supplementary material have been deposited at the Royal Castle in Warsaw in the *Gabinet Genealogiczny* under the name, the Piniński Archive.

There survive numerous descendants of the last of the Stuarts, the senior of whom is Count Stanislas Piniński, then his son (the present author) and grandson, Alexander. Since Charlotte Stuart only theirs has passed twice through the female line. With three passes follow Counts George and Andrew Wolański, Father Stanislas Malec, Andrew Ramsay and James, Charles, Thomas and Adam Wells. With four passes are Christopher and Stephen Komornicki and their respective sons, Fernando and Marcello Monticelli, as well as Anthony, John, Stanislas and Ignatius Kraiński. The remaining Stuart descendants are the respective children of Elizabeth Olechowska, Marie Księżopolska and Rose Christie. Where the number of passes through the female line is equal, seniority is by proximity of the Stuart quartering to the respective male line, then by order of birth.

Though the present book deals with the descendants of the *de jure* Kings of Scotland, England and Ireland it should in no way way be construed as constituting any legal claim of any sort whatsoever. Charlotte Stuart, Duchess of Albany, was legitimised, created Her Royal Highness and granted the right of Royal Succession by Prince Charles Edward as *de jure* King Charles III which acts were confirmed by the Vatican as well as the King and parliament of France. The authority of such institutions is beyond question and her status clear. Her only child to leave descendants was Marie-Victoire, the demoiselle de Thorigny, who was legitimised at baptism in 1779 by the head of the de Rohans, Prince Jules-Hercule, Duke de Montbazon and sovereign Prince de Guéméné. In so doing she became a legitimate princess of the House of de Rohan with full legal rights. However, Marie-Victoire's natural father and mother were unable personally to recognise her without completely destroying what little was left of the Stuart Cause, their own positions and, by extension, their children's as well as Clementina Walkinshaw's.

Yet Charlotte Stuart's situation was more complex still. On the one hand she adored her children, as is evident from her twice weekly letters to her mother, kept at the Bodleian Library. On the other hand, she was the victim of her father's order in 1775 never to marry nor take the veil, as well as other uniquely impossible political and social circumstances. But irrespective of those considerations and no matter how much Charlotte loved her children, she could not have legitimised them with regard to their Stuart parentage before she herself was belatedly legitimised by Prince Charles in 1783, of which fact she was not informed until 1784. Subsequently Stuart legitimisation for her children was ruled out during the lifetime of Charlotte's uncle, Cardinal Henry Stuart, for obvious reasons. But instead of surviving him, Charlotte died prematurely from cancer in 1789, predeceasing Henry by almost two decades.

These extraordinary circumstances, as well as general and political ones affecting the last Stuarts, scarcely rendered Marie-Victoire's some ordinary royal illegitimacy. Nevertheless the fact remains that Charlotte Stuart did not legitimise Marie-Victoire with regard to her Stuart parentage. Therefore, whilst Marie-Victoire was a legitimate member of the de Rohan family with full rights of inheritance, neither she nor any of her descendants have any formal legal rights whatsoever relating to the Stuarts.

That an evil star hung over the House of Stuart has long been recognised. However, in examining the succession of generations from Prince Charles down to the present day, it is not a little curious to compare the fates of each who bore the name Charles or Charlotte. Charles' life was an almost constant stream of bad luck and failure, from the military ill fortune of 1744–1746 and after, through to Louise von Stolberg-Gedern proving barren. His son, Charles, by Louise de Rohan, died aged only five months; whilst his daughter, Charlotte, suffered a traumatic childhood, appalling treatment at the hands of her father and a premature death in her mid-thirties after an agonising illness. Her own daughter, Charlotte, after no less unhappy a childhood, died in childbirth in her mid-twenties. The latter's brother, Charles, lost all he had as a result of no less than three separate financial disasters, was deeply unhappy in love, failed in nearly all his endeavours and, though twice married, never had a child. Marie-Victoire's grandson, Charles, lost an American duel and had to commit suicide at the age of twenty-eight. And his grand-daughter, Charlotte, was deported to the Soviet nightmare of Kazachstan for six years in 1940, which killed her husband. It is noticeable that none of the siblings of these successive Charles' and Charlottes suffered fates as unhappy.

Apart from Professor Sherburn's biography of Charlotte Stuart's son, there has hitherto never been any serious evidence to substantiate the many claims of would-be Stuart 'descendants'. The phenomenon is by no means limited to Britain or the Stuarts. In almost all european countries there exist fantastic claims to thrones or titles. However, in the case of the Stuarts the matter is complicated by the proliferation of myth and legend based on untruths or half-truths generated by the Jacobites themselves who, as their cause grew desperate, became ever more ready to grasp at straws. Even before the 'Forty-Five Charles wrote to his father in exasperation about many of them. No less a Stuart sympathiser than Francis Skeet, in his 1932 biography entitled *H.R.H. Charlotte Stuart, Duchess of Albany* draws the reader's attention to Charles' solemn declaration that 'except Miss Walkinshaw's daughter he had no child'. And it was Charlotte whom Charles apointed his sole heir and who remained his devoted nurse and faithful companion up to the very moment of her father's death. One might imagine those facts alone would be convincing. Yet the Summer 1957 edition of *The Royalist* (the journal of the Royal Stuart Society), wrote of some fifteen Stuart 'claimants'. According to *The Royalist* only the subject of Professor Sherburn's biography, Charlotte's son Charles, 'emerges as a convincing, authentic Stuart'. In that same edition is the statement made at the turn of the century by Alice Shield in her life of Cardinal Henry that 'one constantly hears up and down Italy of this and that insignificant person claiming to be the "last of the Stuarts"'. Nor is it just Italy. Again in that edition C.L. Berry wrote:

> Father Brun suggests that 'Clementina Stuart d'Albanie' may have been one of the royal Stuarts reported to have turned up in Belgium. The Dictionary of National Biography XIX 107, under 'Sobieski-Stuart', mentions a letter in the *Journal de la Belgique* sometime in April 1816, which refers to the presence of several 'royal Stuarts' in Belgium at that time. This, it should be remembered, was propaganda for the 'Sobieski-Stuart' fable [...] etc.

It was these colourful brothers who were the most exotic of all Stuart frauds. However, though they took in quite a few people at the time, they are today described by the Dictionary of National Biography as: 'demonstrably false'.

One recent, heroically unsubstantiated claim is that Prince Charles married in 1785 and fathered a legitimate child. This 'fact', (which has escaped the notice of every historian for over two hundred years!), is particularly imaginative considering the prince was married at the time, being only separated from Louise von Stolberg-Gedern after April 3rd, 1784, who remained under the protection of the Pope. Nor was eighteenth century Rome the best of cities for an internationally known Roman Catholic prince to commit bigamy. It also ignores Charles' wretchedly infirm condition from before that date until his death three years later. Likewise does it ignore the presence (and insult the memory) of Charles' daughter and sole heir, Charlotte, who was daily at her father's side, nursing him right up to the moment of his death despite her own cancer. Professing direct descent on the female line from this 'marriage' the same claimant equally fails to provide any evidence, proper references or verifiable source documents for his additional assertion of descent on the male line from not one, but both daughters of Charlotte Stuart. Professor Lenman describes all of this as: 'The industry of Stuart charlatanism'.

APPENDIX 1

The Letters of Marie-Victoire to Louis de Rohan

The twenty-three letters written in French cover the period from c.1816 to 1825. Previous documentary evidence of Marie-Victoire dates from 1810, namely the court documents relating to the death intestate of her first husband, Paul Anthony, Chevalier de Nikorowicz, the originals of which are in the Piniński Archive in Lwów. The first material subsequent to these letters dates from late 1826–early 1827 when Marie-Victoire was back in Lwów, married to the emigré widower, Jean de Pauw, a veteran of the French royalist counter-revolutionary army of the Prince de Condé which had fought alongside the Austrian Army. She is described in the memoirs of Count Louis Jabłonowski who lived in Lwów with her for some months as a sixteen-year-old and later became a friend of her only child, Antime.[1]

These letters are the only half of this correspondence to survive – as described in the main text. Louis' replies to Marie-Victoire were kept at the Castle of Grzymałów amongst the oldest and most important Nikorowicz and Piniński family papers. That these letters, of no great age or intrinsic value, were kept with such documents (for example from 1379 and 1380 relating to the purchase of the Pinino estate) must indicate the significance they once had. But all were destroyed during the First World War when the Russians devastated the interior of the castle during their occupation of it in 1914 when the front was nearby. The existence of the letters is known about because Grzymałów's last owner, Countess Julia Pinińska, recalled being shown them by her

[1] L. Jabłonowski, *Pamiętniki, op. cit.,* pp.95–96.

father, Count Stanislas Piniński. She described them to her youngest son who is still alive and remembers it clearly. That ancient documents were kept at the castle is proved by the fact that details of them having been sent there (including the fourteenth-century ones) are recorded in the Adelsarchiv of the Austrian State Archives to whom they had been sent by the earlier Count Stanislas Piniński in 1776 (Allgemeines Verwaltungsarchiv, Adelsarchiv, Proofs of Nobility for Counts Stanislas and George Piniński, 1776–1778).

Marie-Victoire wrote to Louis de Rohan as her 'father' and described herself as his 'daughter' revealing only occasionally that she meant 'second father' and 'father of the family'. This metaphorical 'paternity' is echoed in Jabłonowski's memoirs. No doubt Marie-Victoire returned to the capital of Austrian Galicia because of the triple reason of having lost her second husband in early 1825; wanting to be near her only child, Antime who from 1823 had been a cavalry officer in the Imperial 4th Cuirassiers of Crown Prince Ferdinand;[2] and having to choose between further insecurity on a tight budget in expensive Paris, or Lwów where her son had come into his estate of Krzywczyce which hitherto had been subject to the joint guardianship of his uncle (see part 2, ch.15).

Louis' full name was Prince Jules-Armand-Louis de Rohan (1768–1836). He was a general in the Austrian Army and would certainly have known his elder brother's friend, Field Marshal Prince Ferdinand of Württemberg (see part 2, ch.13). Louis was one of the four children of the bankrupt Henri who succeeded Jules-Hercule as Duke de Montbazon. Louis was therefore a generation younger than Marie-Victoire. But owing to the great difference in age between Henri and Marie-Victoire, Louis was in fact eleven years older than his aunt.

These letters came from the de Rohan family archive formerly at their estate of Sychrov in Bohemia which, upon nationalisation by the communists after the Second World War, was transferred to the Czech State Archives at Děčin (Teschen) where they remain (Státni Oblastí Archiv Litoméřice, Pobočka Děčin, Rodinny Archiv Rohanové, Inventař Děčin 1973, Inv.č.562, k.č.193 II). They are all undated. However, two bear post-marks and the internal evidence of the others allows them to be dated and placed in chronological order as below. Photo-copies of the originals are in the Piniński Archive at the Royal Castle in Warsaw.

---

[2] Kriegsarchiv, Vienna, Military Records for Anthim, Ritter von Nikorowicz, 1823–1829.

Some letters and envelopes bear wax seals. Three display Marie-Victoire's monogram 'M.R.'. Another three display a field azure semé of fleur-de-lys or, with a tower argent masonned sable – namely that of the Counts d'Auvergne but surmounted with a ducal coronet, the escutcheon surrounded by a belt with the motto: 'Nous ne Changerons …' – the last part of which is damaged and illegible. Those arms were evidently used by her second husband in consequence of his family's pretensions to the rights of succession to the Duchy of Bouillon which had passed instead to the de Rohan Dukes de Montbazon.

This correspondence allows one to compare the handwriting of Marie-Victoire's letters sent to Louis and those she sent to the Berryer family. The former group date from c.1816–1825 and the latter from c.1835. They are not only separated by a gap of several years but were written under different psychological conditions and to people with whom she had very different relationships. The background to the earlier de Rohan letters was stress, worry, anger, part inferiority part superiority complex as well as emotional and financial insecurity. In the later Berryer ones she was settled and happy, free from ambition and both socially and financially secure. With Louis and the closest de Rohan family circle Marie-Victoire's was a covert, guilty relationship affected by her complexes of birth and childhood. But with the bourgeois and intellectual Berryers her relationship was relaxed, confident and based on friendship.

Of the French Queen Marie-Antoinette's handwriting after her psychological crisis of 1776 her biographer Vincent Cronin comments:

> She was able to ride the crisis and by late autumn was again her happy self. The attacks in fact helped to mature her. The evidence lies not only in the more assured tone of her letters but in her handwriting. Formerly a childish sprawl, in 1776 quite suddenly it becomes neater, better formed and much more confident, with a strong backward flourish to the d's.[3]

The significance of psychology upon handwriting and the fact that we don't know whether Marie-Victoire suffered from any progressive condition such as arthritis or rheumatism renders all the more impressive the fact that a Criminal Court handwriting analyst could detect only one minor modification to Marie-Victoire's handwriting between

[3] V. Cronin, *Louis and Antoinette*, London 1974, pp.139–140.

the earlier de Rohan letters and the Berryer ones written over a decade later. The change is to the small letter 'z' – (report in the Piniński Archive in Warsaw). Moreover the grammatical and psychological construction of the texts remains identical. The report states that the qualities which in both sets of letters were identical are: the type/degree of contruction; the dynamic/speed of formation and degree of horizontal stretch; the size of distances between lines; the size of distances between words; the usage of the sheet/positioning of the text on the empty page; the uneven quality of margins; the tendency for lines to 'sink' in the middle; the size variations of characters with regard to their placement both above and below the line and on either side of the notional mid-line. In addition both sets of letters display identical idiosynchratic graphical elements. For example: the upper right hand side commencement of the drawing of the oval of the letter 'a'; the exagerrated lines crossing the tops of the letter 't' with a characteristic upper 'hook' as one of the variants; the method of completing the letter 'e' when that letter ends a word; the presence in each set of texts of two variants for both the letter 'd' and the letter 'r'; the method of crossing the letter 't'; the shaping of 'M', 'P' and '9' or '5' as one of the variants; and the usage of decorative finial elaboration completing signatures. As for her grammar, Marie-Victoire's eccentric style in both sets remains woefully unchanged. She constructs sentences of sometimes ridiculous length, communicating a rushed series of ideas in which there are extraordinarily few full stops, and uses instead commas (mainly), colons and dashes. Interpretation requires care so as to identify where one thought stops and another begins, or if a given thought refers to the one preceding or succeeding.

1.

Fearing to be too indiscreet in asking you to help both Mother and Son, I have already told you of the wish I have of trying to enter my son into one of the Paris Colleges, his father having died in the service of the King, he has been educated at the Royal College in Versailles[4] but being unable to go often and stimulate his enthusiasm for his lessons, I am unhappy with him since I myself left Versailles, this Winter I shall only seldom be able to

---

[4] See part 2, ch.13 regarding dying in the service of the king. Today this school is called the Lycée Hoche, but its records for 1812–1830 no longer exist.

make the journey for reasons of economy,[5] and I shall be very worried about Theodore's progress who will find himself isolated and without any encouragement.[6] I would be very happy, if through your protection, my son could be brought back to Paris, the Minister of the Interior is your neighbour and I doubt not but that he would be happy to acquiesce to your request; […] that despite all your benevolence, you might not prior to your departure leave a small portion of happiness for this poor widow, which

[5] Part 2, ch's 13 & 15 describe the Chevalier de Nikorowicz's intestate death in 1810; that Marie-Victoire was not a beneficiary; why, as joint guardian of her son, she could not access income from her son's inheritance, but was dependant upon her joint guardian's allowance. Also described are the reasons why that co-guardian, John de Nikorowicz, as a benefactor of the poor, was probably intolerant of indulgent spending – indeed may even have been antagonistic towards his brother's apparently arranged marriage to a much younger fourth wife of mysterious origin.

[6] Marie-Victoire's use of the name 'Theodore' for Antime seems at first enigmatic. Yet her relationship (and her brother's) with her own name was unusual. She used the monogram 'M.R.' though calling herself 'Victoire', 'Victory' and 'Virginie' – the latter perhaps to emphasize the moral rectitude she professes in her letters to Louis. Below is described a significant note from amongst the papers of her brother at the Bodleian Library (Ms Fr b9 160) – when considering it the following points should be taken into consideration: (a) Marie-Victoire's co-guardianship was restrictive or worse; (b) 'Theodore' (or its Polish translation) was a Nikorowicz name – that of Antime's great uncle who baptised his father. It may have been one of his christian names. His baptismal entry gives only his first name and confirmation name, which does not preclude his having had others as would have been likely; (c) 'Theodore' is traditionally associated with Eastern European and Armenian culture; (d) Of Charlotte Stuart's three children, Charles had no offspring whilst Young Charlotte's was still-born and she died in childbirth just two years prior to Antime's birth – 'Theodore' means 'God's gift'; (e) Polish tradition attached great importance to saints' days. Often a child would take the name of the saint upon whose feast day it was born. We do not know Antime's birthday, only his date of baptism. He was baptised on April 20th, 1806. The feast of St. Theodore is April 15th – which may well have been Antime's date of birth. The note written by Marie-Victoire's brother was written in Paris. He commences by emphasizing the great contemporary interest in humanity and goes on to write down the story of a successful comedy playing at that time in the French capital – the 'Abbé and the Epée': 'One evening the patrol of Paris brought to the Abbé's house a boy of about ten years of age, who was deaf and dumb and covered with rags […] But a man of the Abbé's penetration was not long in discovering that the child had been ill-treated through some nefarious design, he adopted him and placed him in his school. He, the little Theodore, for so his patron called him, gave proof of mental powers unlimited; and in the process of time disputed the poetry prize of the Lycées of Paris and won it. In the meantime the Abbé gained from him such information as convinced him that the youth was the noble heir of a large fortune […] and had been purposefully lost by his interested guardians […] At last Theodore recollected the place of his nativity; […] his uncle, the usurper, was dispossessed and the youth returned to his estates and honours'. Theodore's parallels with Charles' nephew, Antime are obvious and described in part 2, ch.15. whilst the fact that Charles took the trouble to write down this transcript and then keep it signifies its relevance for him. The conclusion would be if that Theodore was not already Antime's saint's day of birth or second name then perhaps the 'Abbé and the Epée' was the inspiration behind its adoption.

is what has made me speak of my son, a request for whom is much easier insofar as he was born in Paris,[7] and this is a requirement for being admitted into a College here.[8] I know that everyone is keen to have his child in Paris, but not everyone has a Prince de Rohan as protector. I am sending you a book which was written in 1785, during the author's trip to Florence, I was only able to find this new edition, the letter which you see and which I beg you to read, has often served to keep up my courage during my misfortunes, and I have kept this copy very carefully, and the reading of these great historical memoirs was like a talisman uplifting my soul.[9] I am enclosing a small memorandum for the Minister even before you have had the goodness to tell me if you would undertake the matter [...] On Thursday I am going to Versailles to see my son[10] about whom I am concerned; his health is fine, but it is his learning which is not going well.

Roehenstart[11]

---

[7] Regarding Marie-Victoire's assertion that Antime was been born in Paris: (a) this might not have been true but been a mother's white lie told in her son's interest to facilitate his getting a place – Louis evidently didn't know where Antime had been born or Marie-Victoire would not have told him; or (b) it might have been true. Antime's military records in the Kriegsarchiv in Vienna state he was born at Krzywczyce in 1804. One would have expected the year, if not the location, to have been accurate. As only his baptismal entry survives it is uncertain where and when he was born. It is possible he might have been born in Paris but baptised in Lwów so the ceremony could take place in the Armenian-Catholic Cathedral there with which Antime's family was so closely connected. There exists a later baptismal certificate (Pinínski Archive in Warsaw) which was transcribed on March 6th, 1906 from the 1806 original. The later copy states Antime was *born* on April 20th, 1806 – but this is inaccurate as the original refers solely to his baptism on that day.

[8] Marie-Victoire reveals herself as a widow with one son (Antime was born in 1806; his father died in 1810) and the letter must date from 1816–1820. Although a widow Marie-Victoire does not use her married name nor 'de Thorigny' title but signs herself 'Roehenstart' (see footnote 11). The Versailles/Paris association continues into the generations of Antime's son and grandson – the former travelling all the way from Lwów to Versailles in 1859 to commit suicide, the latter being sent to school in the early 1870's, neither in Lwów nor Vienna as was usual at the time, but in Paris (Fundacja-Zakład Narodowy im.Ossolińskich, Wrocław, sygn.rkp.nr 15.971).

[9] This passage refers to the year 1785, Charlotte Stuart's first full year in Florence with Prince Charles.

[10] In later letters Marie-Victoire no longer mentions her son who evidently was not living with her in Paris. Either he remained at Versailles or he may have been sent to Austria where he reappeared in 1823 as a cadet of the Imperial 4th Cuirassiers of Crown Prince Ferdinand. His military records confirm he spoke fluent French, German and Polish at that time.

[11] Marie-Victoire's use of the 'maiden' name 'Roehenstart', though a widow, may reflect some or all of the following: (a) the name Nikorowicz is difficult for foreigners to pronounce; (b) it would have had no social cachet in Paris (Marie-Victoire proves her need to assert status during her second marriage to Corbet d'Auvergne by occasionally using the arms of the Counts

*This letter serves as an example of Marie-Victoire's idiosynchratic grammar.
The following have been corrected.)*

2.

I have presented myself twice yesterday at your residence without
having the pleasure of seeing you [*after Louis'*] long voyages. I
wanted you to name a day when I could have the pleasure of
hearing about the Princesses whom I have always loved. It would
perhaps be very advantageous for your interests that I tell you of
a matter of major importance. From my side I have something to
say to you which could prepare my future happiness.

Virginie R.

*(She mentions in the text that she is Louis' neighbour. As his mansion was at
99, rue de Grenelle she must have been writing from her flat in that street,
to which she refers in letter 23.)*

3.

Each day I have been praying for your happy return. I have something of great importance to tell you relating to your interests.
[*She refers to his*] long journeys which always worry me. I will send
someone before 8 am to get your news and find out when you
might receive me – that is if you would not prefer to come and
visit me. I will always be flattered by the visit of my second father.
A thousand affectionate respects,

Virginie de R.

footnote 11 (*cont.*)

d'Auvergne surmounted by a ducal coronet as well as by her use of the assumed title 'Countess
de Thorigny' during her third marriage to Jean de Pauw; (c) the name Roehenstart identified
her with her dead sister and brother; (d) it also emphasized kinship with the de Rohans without
actually risking annoying them by publicly using that name (her letters show her sometimes
identifying with the de Rohans, sometimes not); (e) it equally allowed Marie-Victoire to identify with her secret Stuart side which she had promised never to reveal (it may be significant
that she never used the name Roehenstart outside the inner de Rohan family circle – in public
she used the title/name de Thorigny in Paris, Vienna and Lwów); (f) for Marie-Victoire,
Nikorowicz was the foreign name of a husband over a generation older than herself with whom
she was probably never in love – the product of an arranged marriage; (g) the use of
'Roehenstart' rather than the 'de Rohan' to which she was legally entitled suggests she was
unaware of her 1779 baptismal legitimisation by the head of the family; (h) it also implies that
not all her siblings were successfully legitimised – once could scarcely call one child 'de Rohan'
and the others 'Roehenstart'.

4.

In prolonging the discussion by my disinterest in better serving my brother, I forgot to ask you [...] to obtain an audience for me with the British Ambassador [...] During your absence I could ask him to keep me informed as to where my brother is, and who could better know his place of residence than Lord Stuart?[12] My health which suffers by all these worries needs a rest. I have neglected the business of my lessons with my English ladies[13] ever since your kind attempts on my behalf [...].

5.

Please can you tell me all you can about the success of the case relating to the Duchy of Bouillon [*the papers of which she*] often asked to be able to put under the eyes of my friends[14] so that they might, in case of need, defend your legitimate rights having full knowledge of the matter. Please therefore, good Prince, send me prior to your departure the précis of the case and the defence of the judgement. All the material will be read with the greatest interest, and will help crystallise my ideas on new claims that one might assert (which will, I pray to God, preserve your illustrious house). [*Marie-Victoire also advises Louis on matters of the heart, instructing him that if a certain lady*] presents herself to you during your voyage, tell her pitilessly that you want nothing to do with her [...] I must thank you for your kind visit. The pleasure of your conversation so captivated me that I completely forgot to tell you something very important. When you are free after your return I will ask you for a second meeting for my response. The fulfillment of my wishes[15] is approaching. It will perhaps be given to me to

---

[12] Sir Charles Stuart (1779–1845), British ambassador in Paris (1815–1824 & 1828–1831), created Baron Stuart de Rothesay (1828) (see part 2, ch.14 & ch.15; also G. Sherburn, *op. cit.*, p.70 regarding the year 1817). Marie-Victoire's use of the title 'lord' does not mean the date of this letter is after 1828. Previous to his peerage Sir Charles was a baronet, a title frequently misunderstood by foreigners to mean its holder is a lord.

[13] C.L. Berry's legend that one of Charlotte Stuart's daughters was a teacher in Paris is described in part 2, ch.11.

[14] Here Marie-Victoire demonstrates her friendship with high ranking lawyers, consistent with the letters to the pre-eminent legal family of Berryer sent by her sister and herself, signed 'Countess de la Morlière' and 'Countess V.de Thorigny' (see part 2, ch.12).

[15] In the original she uses the word '*expiration*' of her wishes, by which she must mean that the period of wishing or hoping is coming to an end.

choose a Chevalier from amongst the Veterans of the Army of de Condé, waiting for the end of five years of the strictest mourning.[16] I shall continue to keep myself far from Society so as to avoid hearing those insults which have been numerous, of being 'stand-offish', 'un Clou de Charette' – I will never forget this last phrase which was given me by a very kind 'Grand Seigneur'. I did not see why I should explain my complete indifference to Society by telling him my Secret [...].[17] How many volumes are full of the romances and loves of the Stuarts and Rohans. This Breton blood which runs in my veins has not been very comforting. It was necessary, therefore, to take an extreme course so as to moderate one's conduct. And that was in running around the world throughout the ten years during which I have conserved my liberty.[18] Let others judge if there wasn't more merit in resisting so as to triumph – Well, I could tell them in a low voice, that not believing myself any better than the next person, I saw no other course than being done with this disaster at precisely the point when I could no longer stand the perfidious and seductive child.[19] [...] There is nothing left, therefore, other than the reasonable choice of becoming united with an old Veteran of the Glory. [*She apologises for her frankness, again describing Louis as ...*] my second father.

(*This letter has the post-mark:* '1820'.)[20]

---

[16] Marie-Victoire's third husband, Jean de Pauw, was a veteran of the army of the Prince de Condé and de Pauw's wife died prematurely leaving him with a young child which would have justified 'five years of the strictest mourning' (see part 2, ch.15). It appears that de Pauw was eclipsed by d'Auvergne who died unexpectedly in early 1825, after which Marie-Victoire returned to her 'reasonable choice' who by then had finished his five years of mourning – this letter being post-marked 1820. It is clear that d'Auvergne aroused Marie-Victoire's passion, whereas de Pauw was more a companion.

[17] Compare G. Sherburn's biography of her brother for references to his 'Secret', as well as Charles' letters at the Bodleian Library, for example: 'I had taken the engagement never to break the silence which I have so strictly observed' (Ms Fr b7 182); or: 'Had I not lost my brig [...] I should have religiously kept my word, and never said a thing about my claims' (Ms Fr 44 18).

[18] 'Ten years of liberty' was precisely the period of time since the death of her first husband. The Chevalier de Nikorowicz died in 1810 – this letter is post-marked 1820.

[19] This curious last passage must have been intelligble to Louis de Rohan, but its meaning is now obscure.

[20] My thanks to Monsieur Raymond Poulain, administrator of the Société des Amis du Musée de la Poste in Paris for deciphering the two post marks in Marie-Victoire's de Rohan letters as well as those on her Berryer letters.

6.

In looking this morning for a small apartment I met a very rec-
ommendable person who has the honour of knowing your niece.
She said to me, 'Ah! If the Princess Berthe[21] who is so good and
so religious knew that her relation hasn't returned you the money
received from you, she would do everything to pull you out of
your trouble. I advise you strongly to write to her [...]'. Dare I,
for the first time in my life, ask of my Protector a financial favour?
Delicacy and pride have made me endure the greatest unhappi-
nesses without becoming troublesome to you. For more than
three years I have made all manner of sacrifice, relying on the
promise of the Princess Charles;[22] since the news of the marriage
of Princess Gasparine,[23] and having been living with her mother
(and not having had to buy an apartment) I have used a large
amount to settle old debtors.[24] I have also used up a lot of money
for a marriage trousseau worthy of the august person whom I had
the honour of accompanying. Princess Charles, having removed
all hope for the joy of remaining with her, and as your very good
and kind self has not succeeded in finding me (in so short a space
of time) a suitable position, I shall soon find myself in a very
awkward position. I need a small apartment in order to leave the
filled-up hotels which I detest. The unhappiness of being
enslaved with foreigners is still so recent that I would far prefer to
give lessons in my own place than be subjected once more to this
burden. [*She then goes on to tell Louis of her*] strong desire to re-
establish an honest independence [*and asks him to support her
request to Princess Berthe to lend her 2,000 francs*].

Roehenstart

---

[21] Princess Berthe (1782–1841), the daughter of Prince Charles de Rohan, Duke de Montbazon
(1764–1836), who married her uncle, Prince Victor de Rohan (1766–1846; Charles and Louis'
brother) on July 23rd, 1800.

[22] Princess Marie-Louise de Rohan (1765–1839), the daughter of Jules-Hercule's son, Henri de
Rohan, Duke de Montbazon (1745–1809), (and therefore the sister of Charles, Victor and
Louis). She married her cousin from a younger branch, Prince Charles de Rohan-Rochefort
and Montauban (1765–1843) on July 12th, 1780.

[23] Princess Gasparine (1799–1871), the daughter of Princes Charles de Rohan, Rochefort and
Montauban, who married Henry XIX, the reigning Prince of Reuss-Greiz (1790–1836) on
January 7th, 1822.

[24] The implication is that Marie-Victoire was indeed irresponsible with money or that these are
creditors of her brother (whom his papers show existed; see also G. Sherburn, *op. cit.*, chapter
on Charles' finances) for whom Marie-Victoire appears to have been financier of last resort.

(News of Gasparine's marriage in January and the July rental period for flats dates the letter as mid-1822.)

7.

[*Marie-Victoire asks if she can appeal to the*] honesty of the father of the family on behalf of Pierre Cazeaux who has lost his place through a great injustice as guard of the Forest of Saumur. [*She asks that he be reinstated as he is*] worthy of your confidence and has a perfect acquaintance of your properties in the Midi [...] I am utterly devoted to the interests of your illustrious house. [*Louis has been taking the waters at Carlsbad and*] I would be very pleased if you would give me your news and those of the Princesses.[25] [...] I would be very interested to know if the pregnancy of Princess Gasparine is not causing any worry.

Roehenstart
Rue des Saint Pères, nr 67

(PS: Please pass on my respects to the Princess Charles and Princess Berthe. I sincerely hope to hear that their health is good and likewise that of the Princes.)[26]

(This letter dates from mid-1822 as Gasparine's child was born in December that year.)

8.

[...] if I have the pleasure of seeing my second father twice in one day! Flattering myself that you will honour the promise that you made to come and take tea this evening I have already invited the respected foreigner.

Virginie R.

(Sealed with her monogram: 'M.R.')

---

[25] Presumably the daughters of Charles and Marie-Louise de Rohan-Rochefort and Montauban: Hermine (1784–1843), Armande (1787–1864) and Gasparine (1799–1871).
[26] Presumably the sons and brothers of the above princesses, namely: Camille (1800–1843) and Benjamin (1804–1846).

9.

My respected and good Father, [...] please choose between Thursday, Friday and Saturday for giving me the honour of taking tea with the noble and honest Englishman. He told me it was impossible for him to come today. [*She offers Louis punch saying she*] will be well pleased that my good Father tries it; this being in my capacity of a little doctor that I urge you to make use, with all confidence, of the little flask that I permit myself to offer you purely as a sample.

Virginie de Roehenstart

(*On the back of the envelope is written:* 'Rohan Stuard d'Overgne'.)[27]

10.

I know that there is no need to stimulate your kindness in doing justice to a poor orphan <u>of the pure blood of the R.'s and the S.'s,</u>[28] but I beg you not to lose courage [...] that would be to give up when everything is going so well. Christian charity will maintain your benevolence, at least up until the time of the marriage!! These are services that are worth more than gold!! I have reflected that yesterday, in revealing to you my disquiet (that a certain phrase mischievously spoken is not going to affect your feelings) you were able to see that I had not spoken very frankly of the natural birth.[29] He is as aware of the above as much as we are. Nor has he overlooked the fact that the brave Admiral Prince de M.[30] never married the

---

[27] These names on the back of the envelope are significant. In Marie-Victoire's letters she openly speaks of her Stuart and de Rohan parentage. But this is the only example of her actually using the surnames 'Rohan' and 'Stuart' – the use of the letter 'd' instead of 't' occurs in old French and Italian documents. For example the San Bagio necrology gives 'Stuardo'; the marble slab over her grave read in Latin 'Stuarda'; whilst the old Bologna guide of c. 1793 describes 'il mausoleo di Carlotta Stuarda'. D'Overgne is curious – the phonetic spelling of d'Auvergne suggesting a still early acquaintance. It appears that Marie-Victoire is emphasizing her identification with d'Auvergne and that the invitation is from both of them – thus from: 'Rohan Stuard' and 'd'Overgne'.

[28] In the original 'orphan' is used in the feminine case and clearly refers to Marie-Victoire. The 'R's' and 'S's' are obviously the Rohans and Stuarts. This author prefers to use 'de Rohan' in English though the French speak of the 'House of Rohan', for example in the family motto: 'Rohan suis'.

[29] The phrase 'natural birth' does not clarify whether or not Marie-Victoire knew of her baptismal legitimisation. Her birth was 'natural', but upon legitimisation by the Duke de Montbazon she was no longer 'illegitimate'.

[30] Admiral Louis-Armand de Rohan (known as Armand), Prince de Montbazon (1731– guillotined 1794), the second of the four brothers: Prince Jules-Hercule, Duke de Montbazon,

Duchess.[31] I believed it necessary, all the same, to warn Monsieur d'A. that he could perhaps hear repeated in Society the terrible lie that hangs over the head of my respected uncle and guardian, the Prince F.[32] As soon as Monsieur d'A. spoke to me of his hopes for a union[33] I told him about everything quite frankly. He knows that the Prince F., nominated guardian after the death of the Prince de M., only supervised my education and that by having appeared to be interested in me, has fallen victim to this lie. I have always the honour of asking you once again to be my generous Chevalier in life, and if it is necessary then I shall promise never to dishonour the illustrious family from which I come. Monsieur d'A. has often said to me that he loves the nobility of our feelings (I am not modest enough not to repeat this compliment!) and that he fully knows that I lack certain documents to prove other titles of nobility, but that it is all the same to him, and that I was always in his eyes an R.and an S. Right now I doubly regret that the Princess Charles is not in Paris, who could have told me who has the right and that if I don't have any fortune, at least I possess a spotless reputation. I defy my greatest enemy to say that I have had even a single lover. You will laugh at me for having such bourgeois morality, and I believe I can see my friendly and gallant Prince smile at my lack of sociability. But for myself I don't regret it, for it has made me worthy of a gentleman who is giving me his name […] but once again, I beg you to maintain this fervour of benevolence (which is so precious to me); the words that you utter to me are like an article of faith; and in bearing witness to the truth you consolidate my happiness. In the midst of my anti-social attitude and estrangement from Society I have kept up relations with a few people of note (once or twice a year). For example I know the person whose name you have quoted and to whom you are going on Sunday. If by design or by chance he should speak to you of me, I would invoke your deepest paternal feelings not to deny me […]

Prince de Guémené (head of the de Rohans) (1726–1788); Prince Armand; Prince Louis, Cardinal-Bishop of Strasbourg (1734–1803); & Prince Ferdinand, Archbishop of Cambrai, Count of the Empire (Napoleonic) (1738–1819). Marie-Victoire reveals that either she was aware of her 1779 baptismal legitimisation by Jules-Hercule but realised he was not her father, or that her legitimisation had been hidden from her and she had been deceived into believing that her childless uncle Armand was her natural father.

[31] Charlotte Stuart, Duchess of Albany (1753–1789).

[32] Prince Ferdinand de Rohan.

[33] In other words, when d'Auvergne proposed to her.

11.

(Marie-Victoire asks if she and her new husband can come and see Prince Louis, signing: …)

Monsieur and Madame d'Auvergne

12.

(Similar, but signed only by Marie-Victoire: …)

Madame d'Auvergne.

13.

My good and honest friend, whom I would like to avoid even the smallest sorrow, had this morning a very unpleasant visit from a creditor set upon tormenting Monsieur d'Auvergne because of his former business people. Since Monsieur d'Auvergne withdrew his proxy they are so enraged that they try to do him all the harm possible. You know, my Prince, that to satisfy my heart, and to give proof of the devotion and respect towards the august family which I cherish, that I have always preached peace (before and after my marriage). To be perfectly sure that no court case would be begun, I have had nothing to do with business people. I am thus the cause of new sorrows for Monsieur d'Auvergne. He said to me this morning (in his gentlest tone of voice), 'Victory, you ought not to have demanded of me that I withdraw my proxy before these creditors were paid'. I would therefore ask you, more insistently than yesterday, to plead my cause with the good Princess. She would surely agree to heal the several wounds caused by two years spent in Paris. Monsieur d'Auvergne gave me his word that he arrived here, happy, in good health with four thousand louis d'or in order to await the justice that is owing to him! […] Respect forbids me any reflection […][34]

Victory

[34] The similarity between d'Auvergne's finances and those of Marie-Victoire's brother, Charles, as well as the fact that both were pursued by creditors at the same time and place is striking. Perhaps they were or became connected by business. What is clear, however, is the way in which d'Auvergne uses Marie-Victoire's relationship with the de Rohans to pursue his own interests, regardless of the damage this might do his wife. He must have been aware of the psy-

14.

Monsieur d'Auvergne[35] has the honour of requesting that the Count de Silly prepare a legal declaration which affirms that

chological importance her cousins had for her. Nor does Marie-Victoire's devotion to her second husband obscure his instrumental treatment of her.

[35] The d'Auvergne family of Jersey had pretensions to the title of 'Prince of Bouillon'. As mentioned above (see part 2, ch.15) this title belonged to the family of Jules-Hercule de Rohan's wife – de la Tour d'Auvergne. After that family died out with the death of Jules-Hercule's nephew the duchy passed to Jules-Hercule's grandson in 1816 after the Bourbon restoration, having been contested by the d'Auvergnes and Bourbons. The genealogy of d'Auvergne is as follows: (1) Philip d'Auvergne of Jersey, claimed descent from the last reigning Duke of Bouillon. His son: (2) Edward (1660–1737), military historian, chaplain of the Scots Guards with whom he served in Flanders, King William III's domestic chaplain and his regiment's historian. His son: (3) Philip, left numerous offspring including: (3a) James (1726–1799), commissioned whilst at Greenwich Academy, equerry to the king, retired with the rank of major-general, mayor of Southampton 1795, died 12.1799, buried 1.1.1800 at All Saints Church, Southampton; (3b) Charles, commissioned whilst at Greenwich Academy, twice took part in the expedition of 1758 on the coast of France with the Duke of Marlborough, resigned on health grounds, married twice, firstly Elizabeth, daughter of Philip le Geyt, chief civil magistrate of the Royal Court and president of the States of Jersey, secondly Bandinel, daughter of the seigneur de Meleschés. His sons: (4a) Philip (1754–1816), fourth and surviving son of his father's first marriage, claimant to the title 'Prince of Bouillon', 2nd lt. 2.6.1777, captain 22.1.1784, rear-admiral 9.11.1805, vice-admiral 31.7.1810, committed suicide 18.9.1816 having ruined himself by contesting the rights of succession to the Duchy of Bouillon, buried at St. Margaret's Church, Westminster. (4b) Edward (1757–1820), first son of his father's second marriage, burgess of Southampton 31.1.1800, married Mary Mester (1759–1828), buried 12.8.1820 at All Saints Church, Southampton where his wife was later also buried. (4c) Corbet James (1764/5–1825), second son of his father's second marriage, adopted by his elder half-brother Philip as successor and heir to his claims to the title 'Prince de Bouillon', lt. 20.1.1794, commander 17.10.1804, captain 12.8.1812, appointed acting governor of Heligoland by Vice-Admiral Thomas MacNamara Russel 1807, burgess of Southampton 5.12.1800, reputedly died 2.2.1825 at Le Havre but town archives have no such record, British Embassy (Paris) Consular Records state that he was buried 5.2.1825 in Paris – (sources: *Dictionary of National Biography*; A. Temple-Patterson, *A History of Southampton*, vol.1, 1700–1835; *The Naval Chronicle*, vol.13, 1805, pp.190–199; ibid., vol.36, 1816, p.264; *The Army List* 1792 & 1795; *Commissioned Sea Officers of the Royal Navy 1660–1815*, Navy Records Society, vol.1, 1954; J. Marshall, *Royal Navy Biography*, 1823, pp.414–415; *Parish Registers*, All Saints Church, Southampton). Significant is the note amongst Marie-Victoire's brother's papers (Documents of C.E. Roehenstart, Ms Fr b9 7): 'Charles d'Auvergne esq., and his brother, James, Major-General, who died in December 1799 at Southampton, Mayor of the Corporation, both were acknowledged by letters patent from the sovereign Duke de Bouillon as his relations, their common ancestor being the ancient Counts of Auvergne. The formal documents were recorded in the College of Arms by His Majesty's most gracious license, as was the Duke's adoption of Captain Philip d'Auvergne, his cousin, for his son and successor. This branch of the family came over in the year 1232 under the King. Philip d'Auvergne, Duke of Bouillon, Rear-Admiral. 'Gallis fidem non habendam, hominibus levibus, perfidis et ipsos Deos immortalis impiis'. ' (trans: *The French should not be trusted because they are superficial, deceitful people and immortal God himself considers them impious.*) This note of Marie-Victoire's brother precedes one on the history of Tivoli (Ms Fr b9 13) –

Monsieur the Duke de Montbazon acknowledges that he saw in favour of the late Admiral d'Auvergne the sum of 3,000 pounds sterling which was made out to him as a receipt, that this same receipt has been presented to you intact and without any other signature other than that of the Prince de Rohan, that by this reason the recognition of three thousand pounds was perhaps lost. The Admiral, not having passed the succession to anyone else, his sole heir, the Captain d'Auvergne, has a right to be reimbursed which the Duke de Montbazon cannot refuse. If the Prince Louis didn't know of anyone from the Paris Bar, I would ask a lawyer for a model of the declaration that Monsieur d'Auvergne claims by the justice of the Prince, but I prefer to confide in the loyalty of my natural protector in order to have drawn up this declaration in a manner most advantageous to the legitimate heir of the Admiral. I need this document now and would ask you to tell me on which day I can come and get it. Monsieur d'Auvergne returned yesterday quite ill. It was repeated to him that all the misfortunes which he has experienced are caused by the illustrious house which ought to give him every manner of assistance. It is said to Monsieur d'Auvergne, 'These are the Princes de Rohan who have the estate of your brother, the Admiral, far from persecuting you they should agree to your just complaint.[36] If respect did not hold back my pen I would add many other commentaries, but I prefer to appeal to the good heart of Prince Louis. For he has contributed to giving me as a husband the best of men, and so I feel for him the most sincere affection. I beseech you not to persecute my good and fair benefactor who deserves all the tenderness of his 'Victory'. Monsieur d'Auvergne said that he never knew misfortune (to have debts) other than since he has been involved in a just claim ['*réclamation*'] with Prince Louis. We beseech you to give us a proof as to whether you are our friend or our enemy. The declaration, frank and fair, that we ask of the good Prince, will show us his true intentions with regard to us. You know how disinterested I am and without ambition. Likewise is Monsieur d'Auvergne. But I cannot

---

footnote 35 (*cont.*)

Marie-Victoire and d'Auvergne were living on the rue St. Lazare in new and fashionable Parisian district of Tivoli which took its name from the Tivoli Gardens created in 1798 located between the rue St. Lazare and the rue de Clichy.

[36] The word in the French original is 'réclamation'. This was the word universally applied by Marie-Victoire's brother when writing in English about his claims.

resist sorrow when I see my fair friend deceived in all his just hopes [...]

15.

My Prince, I am in the carriage awaiting the reply that you would well like to give M. ... Time presses, my dear Prince. Your refusal of yesterday stopped me from closing my eyes all last night. I am sure that you would not have the courage to cut off the livelihood of the noble Englishman who has nursed for twenty five years all your Breton [*illegible*]. It is awful that a man of honour is tormented for 200 louis when he possesses more than 2,000 francs in England. We are making with M. all the arrangements that he would like and before a month is out he will be reimbursed to the extent of 4,000 francs with all the interest that will be determined.

16.

Do not fear that I dare to be so indiscreet as to insist on the object of Thursday's request. Your point blank refusal is engraved on my memory. The point of this note is to discover if I could on Tuesday morning send for the declaration that you have promised me? I doubt not that your intention is anything other than to entirely conform to the justice due to the Admiral. With regard to the receipt signed by the Duke de Montbazon I hope (after the word of the Prince) that the Count de Silly will make tomorrow, that is Tuesday, the declaration.

Victoire d'Auvergne

(*Post mark:* 'July 7th, 1824'. *Sealed with the arms of the Counts d'Auvergne under a ducal coronet.*)

17.

Madame d'Auvergne presents her respectful affection to Monsieur and wishes very much to learn if the case of Liège has been won. Madame Victoire wishes to have the honour of seeing the Prince today [...] As Monsieur d'Auvergne is ill, it is more prudent not to speak of business in front of him.[37]

---

[37] The authority with which Marie-Victoire speaks about legal matters as well as her references to the Paris Bar in letter 14 are further reflections of her friendship with the Berryer family.

18.

I was hoping to wish you a happy voyage yesterday, but my duty as an affectionate wife kept me at the side of Monsieur d'Auvergne. His doctor ordered the application of leeches [...] Since your last visit the oppression on the chest of my dear patient became extreme and it is for this reason that the doctor judged that he should be bled. Despite your kindly disposed conversation the feelings of Monsieur d'Auvergne are extremely animated when he thinks that the judgement which a beloved brother has taken from him was perhaps going to prevent the advantage of the adversary of the unfortunate Prince Philip [...]. Please be sure of my desire that all your legal cases turn out in the happiest way for you. I hope with all my heart that all the claims [*réclamations*] of Monsieur d'Auvergne end amiably with all the parties concerned. I have no ambition other than that of seeing my benefactor happy in a modest situation and I sincerely wish not to find myself at war with the family that I respect. Permit me, my Prince, to entrust myself to your indulgence so as to be sure that the testimony of Princess Charles (of which I am sending you a word for word copy) will be done as legally as possible and that you will be so good as to add there also your signature. I recall all your grounds that you have alleged to me (for this project which is of so great an interest to me) when I permit myself to tell you that in a matter of this type, the testimony of a Statesman is indispensible in the eyes of the law. Please reply to me that you will agree to give your signature, motivated by the same manner that you have done for a young man who finds himself in the same situation of birth as I do.[38] I hope, my Prince, that after having served me as a father, you will consolidate the happiness of your daughter by giving true

---

[38] Again Marie-Victoire speaks with authority on legal matters. The phrase 'as legally as possible' does not imply that something illegal is being considered, but that the testimony should be prepared as professionally as possible. Though she earlier in this letter spoke of d'Auvergne, she is not referring to him here but to a 'young man [...] in the same situation of birth' as herself – ie of natural birth. Aged sixty, d'Auvergne was neither young nor was he of natural birth. On the other hand her brother Charles was still in his thirties, a generation younger than Louis de Rohan and obviously 'in the same situation of birth' as his sister. In this letter she is clearly doing a major favour in asking for Louis' help. In letter 4 she wanted to 'better serve my brother' whose dogged pursuit of his 'reclamations' would surely have included soliciting his elder sister's help through her close contacts with their de Rohan relations. It therefore seems very probable that Marie-Victoire is here trying to help Charles.

witness to the justice which is synonymous with your family. I have the honour of asking that after your return to Prague you pass to me the testimony via Monsieur de Clerke [...] Monsieur d'Auvergne asks me to pass on to you his regrets that he couldn't come and wish you a happy voyage, but he is suffering too much to go out.

19.

(This letter is written on black-edged paper indicating she was in mourning.)

(After revealing that she is living at Tivoli she continues) I have waited six weeks for your return to Paris (in order to write to the King) and that since your arrival I was obliged to suspend again my request to His Majesty. I have the honour of asking you to inform me as to your intentions with regard to the Duke [...] that it was not a pension of pure favour that was asked for. You know in part how much the venerable friend for whom I mourn had the right to a benefaction from the Bourbons. I admit to you, at the risk of displeasing you, that I believe in your intention of honouring the memory of the English Prince who was so unhappy in France.

Your respectful daughter, Victory

PS: I have had the honour of going to see the Princess de Reuss-Greiz this morning [...][39]

20.

(On black-edged paper.)

He, Monsieur Voizot, told me this morning of the happiness of your visit and I respectfully waited in all day for my very honoured father. [*But she had to go out for pressing reasons. She refers to Louis coming to her in Tivoli and also to the courier*] for letters to England.

Your very distressed daughter, Victory d'Auvergne

---

[39] Marie-Victoire's second husband died on or about February 2nd, 1825. See footnote 35 regarding her usage of the title prince.

21.

(*On black-edged paper.*)

Presuming that you haven't yet been able to see the Duke, I have the honour of asking you to re-read the list of services so as to erase all those that you don't find suitable and to tell me what would be more useful to mention [...] It is very tiresome at present to be forced to work on matters of business, but the idea of doing all I can to honour the memory of the best of men excites my courage. I fully recognise that Your Highness has the good-ness to wish to interest himself on behalf of your unhappy daugh-ter, and I place all my hope in your persuasive eloquence and count on your paternal sentiments [...] my attachment for you has increased still more in view of the suffering which you have borne with great courage for a year;[40] I confess that it is more than affec-tion I have for you. I feel a sort of veneration for the head of this noble family which so generously gave shelter to our brothers in exile.[41] I never seemed able to sufficiently show my devotion for my unhappy friend – he used to say that he didn't want to regain his health other than to bring happiness to his 'Victory' [...] Forgive me, my Prince, I am forgetting myself in speaking of him who merits my regret!

With the affectionate respect of your daughter,
Victory d'Auvergne

22.

(*On black-edged paper.*)

Madame d'Auvergne presents her respects to her very honoured father and lord [*requesting that he receive her*].

rue St. Lazare nr 88, Tivoli

---

[40] The year-long suffering almost certainly refers to the legal battles conducted by d'Auvergne, the brunt of which seem to have been borne by Louis – hence her apology for mentioning 'him who merits my regret'.

[41] 'Our brothers in exile' were the French royalist officers, including Marie-Victoire's third husband, who fought alongside the Austrian army with the army of the Prince de Condé and remained in exile in Austria.

23.

(On black-edged paper.)

Your Highness will find with reason that two letters in one day is far too much. My excuse lies in the necessity of asking a small service of you – it is to give your permission that the family pictures which were always in the Gros Caillou might momentarily be placed in your mansion. I have been told that the new tenants of the apartment I was occupying on the rue de Grenelle cannot keep them as they themselves have a lot of engravings to hang [...] Not knowing yet which apartment I will be occupying when I leave Tivoli I would ask you not to refuse my request. There are only two big paintings, the others are busts of an ordinary dimension. The little 'genre' pictures were never taken to the Gros Caillou, there are only those of the family. I am going to put a list of them in with this letter so you can judge that they do not need a big room in which to be kept. The bearer of this letter is the daughter of de Carr, (an old servant of the Princes de Rohan) [...] This is a real service that you do for me in my sad personal situation [...] you know, my Prince, that I don't have my own place.

Your respectful daughter, Victory[42]

---

[42] See the section on the portrait of her sister in part 2, ch.12.

APPENDIX 2

Marie-Victoire's Identity

Because Charlotte Stuart's son often used combinations of two of the three names Korff, Roehenstart and Stuart over a long period of time, overlaps occur between all three leaving no doubt that this is one and the same person. And though his handwriting is sometimes inconsistent and even deliberately disguised it is usually obvious which of the letters and documents amongst his papers at the Bodleian Library are by his hand.

His sister, Marie-Victoire, was baptised as the daughter of the eldest of the four de Rohan brothers, Jules-Hercule, told that she was the daughter of the second, Armand, but was in fact the daughter of the fourth, Ferdinand, whom she was told was her guardian. Her situation was complicated by the fact that she did not use double-barrelled combinations of surnames like her brother. In addition she had three married names. Altogether the names she used or was described by in official documents were de Thorigny (as both name and title, both before and after she was married), Roehenstart (both before and after she was married), de Nikorowicz, d'Auvergne and de Pauw.

Overlaps occur. For example, Marie-Victoire's baptismal entry links de Rohan and de Thorigny. In documents of the Imperial Court of Nobility in Lwów as well as in Austrian baptismal and death certificates, the names de Thorigny, de Nikorowicz and de Pauw appear together. Jabłonowski's memoirs mention de Rohan, de Thorigny, de Nikorowicz and de Pauw. Marie-Victoire's letters to Louis de Rohan group together de Rohan, Stuart, Roehenstart and d'Auvergne. The Berryer letters link de Thorigny and de la Morlière. And de la Morlière, de Rohan and Roehenstart appear together in the extracts from Young Charlotte's marriage contract. Therefore, all the groups of

286

names overlap with one another and each name is connected with each other either directly or indirectly.

As regards Marie-Victoire's christian names of Marie (formal) and Victoire (familiar), the only exception to these (or their equivalents in English, Polish or German) being the universal reference to her is her own choice of Virginie as a signature for a few of her early letters to Louis de Rohan.[1] However, it is clear from the handwriting, content, surname and signature that Virginie and Victoire are one and the same person.

Apart from comparisons and cross checks between all the available pieces of evidence (for example: handwriting, page usage, grammar, psychological content, consistency of internally derived information with all other external sources etc), Marie-Victoire's identity may be double-checked by testing the hypothesis as to whether it is credible that there might have been two Marie-Victoires. According to this, one Marie-Victoire would have been baptised as the daughter of Jules-Hercule (who was in a position to legitimise a child), then married the son of Fergusson-Tepper's colleague and the Stuarts' closest Polish cousin's banker, de Nikorowicz, then become widowed in 1810 with one son, then married de Pauw in 1826, and been an intimate friend of the Berryers like Ferdinand's daughter, Charlotte. The second Marie-Victoire would be the daughter of Ferdinand (who was not in a position to legitimise a child), and would have had some unknown first marriage, become widowed in 1810 with one son, then married d'Auvergne in 1823 and after his death in February 1825 disappeared without trace.

To make this possible, the following would have to be coincidences:

1. The ageing Jules-Hercule and Ferdinand both simultaneously fathered two natural daughters.
2. Jules-Hercule and Ferdinand then decided to call both daughters by identical Christian names.
3. Five years later both Jules-Hercule and Ferdinand simultaneously fathered two natural sons.
4. In 1810 Jules-Hercule's Marie-Victoire and Ferdinand's Marie-Victoire both became widowed.
5. Both widowed Marie-Victoires were left with only one child, a son – both apparently the same age.

[1] See letters of Marie-Victoire, footnote 6.

6. Both Marie-Victoires then became engaged or married to retired officers of the emigré army of de Condé.
7. Both those veterans had reasons to be in deep mourning.
8. Both Marie-Victoires had intimate contacts with the Paris legal world.
9. The handwriting of both Marie-Victoires, despite being written in different circumstances and periods, possesses a wide range of identical and unusual idiosyncracies and other characteristics as well as exactly the same grammatical style, page and line usage and rushed way of expressing ideas.
10. Both Marie-Victoires reveal the same psychological complex in their assumption of titles.
11. Jules-Hercule's Marie-Victoire appears to have used an escutcheon with a fess, reminiscent of the Stuarts' fess, yet it would have been Ferdinand's Marie-Victoire who was the daughter of a Stuart.
12. When Jules-Hercule's Marie-Victoire appears in source documents Ferdinand's Marie-Victoire disappears. And when the latter appears then the former disappears. Not once do the two appear in different places at the same time. Nor is there even the implication of this in any letter, memoir or other document. A source document date comparison would be:

Jules-Hercules' Marie-Victoire: 1779   1806–11   1826–36
Ferdinand's Marie-Victoire: 1804   1816–25

Furthermore, the 'double Marie-Victoire hypothesis' requires an explanation for each of the following:

13. Why, as he approached the age of sixty, did Jules-Hercule turn from being (according to Professor L.L.Bongie) a 'dutiful and tender' man 'whose style almost drips with family sentimentality' into someone who suddenly betrayed his wife?
14. What was so important as to convince Jules-Hercule to legitimise Marie-Victoire in 1779, with all the legal consequences of so doing, making her the only girl to have ever been legitimised by the head of the de Rohans and a Duke de Montbazon, despite being, in theory, only the daughter of a humble member of Jules-Hercule's household at Couzières and Ussé?
15. Despite Marie-Victoire being so important as to warrant this unique legitimisation, why did Jules-Hercule so furtively legit-

imise her in the exclusive company of people completely sub-servient to him, in the remote rural retreat of the Château de Couzières at Veigné?

16. Having legitimised Marie-Victoire, why did Jules-Hercule not obtain the confirmation of the King of France as the de Rohans had done in the three previous cases of legitimising natural sons, given that Jules-Hercule's position at court in 1779 was such that the matter would have been a mere formality and there would have been no reason not to if he really was Marie-Victoire's natural father?

17. Having been legitimised, why is there no mention of Marie-Victoire in any genealogical almanach, despite the fact that other legitimised children are included?

18. If Marie-Victoire remained with Jules-Hercule after her baptism, why is there no evidence of this?

19. Why is there (a) no general mention whatsoever of Marie-Victoire in the extensive corespondence from the 1780's between Jules-Hercule and his son, Henri? After all, Marie-Victoire was sup-posed to be the 'daughter' of the former and 'sister' of the latter; and (b) why, in that same correspondence, if Marie-Victoire was the *de facto* daughter of Jules-Hercule, is she completely unmen-tioned despite the family's extremely serious financial problems even though she was the *de jure* co-heir of Jules-Hercule as a con-sequence of her legitimisation?

20. If, on the other hand, Jules-Hercule's Marie-Victoire remained with Miss Grosset after her baptism, why did Jules-Hercule grant the latter a life annuity, the notarial act of which contains not a single word about Marie-Victoire and the legal consequences of which would have left Marie-Victoire destitute in the event of something happening to Miss Grosset?

21. What were the 'services rendered' to which that act explicitly referred and for which Miss Grosset was being 'rewarded'?

22. What was so special about Jules-Hercule's 'son' as to warrant his attempted legitimisation, despite the fact that only three natural boys had ever been legitimised by heads of the de Rohans and Dukes de Montbazon?

23. If that boy was not Ferdinand and Charlotte's son, Charles, then who was he and what happened to him? Why is there not a single trace anywhere of either a legitimised or an illegitimate son of Jules-Hercule?

24. Why was it Jules-Hercule's Marie-Victoire, not Ferdinand's, who was found a home through the Fergusson-Tepper clique together with Ferdinand and Charlotte's son, Charles?

25. Why was it Jules Hercule's Marie-Victoire, not Ferdinand's, who was intimate with the Berryer family together with Ferdinand and Charlotte's daughter, Charlotte?

26. Whilst it was natural for Ferdinand's Charles to have been in regular contact with Ferdinand's Marie-Victoire, why was he also in regular contact with Jules-Hercule's Marie-Victoire?

27. The set of correspondence addressed to Louis de Rohan and kept at the de Rohan Palace of Sychrov was from Ferdinand's Marie-Victoire. Why then was there a set of correspondence from Louis kept at the Nikorowicz-Piniński Castle of Grzymałów, addressed to Jules-Hercule's Marie-Victoire?

28. And why, in all the letters and memoirs relating to both Marie-Victoires, is Jules-Hercule not even once spoken of as her father, despite appearing in that role at Veigné in 1779?

The considerable body of other circumstantial evidence in the present work (for example, the wide range of fits, links and absence of contradiction between the biographical data for Marie-Victoire and both her sister, Young Charlotte, and brother, Charles), the 'names overlap' described above, the neglible statistical probability of points 1–12 all being coincidences and the difficulty of providing convincing explanations for each of points 13–28 would seem to rule out a double Marie-Victoire hypothesis.

Besides, given their extraordinary circumstances, in particular those of the Duchess of Albany, was it not in fact eminently reasonable for Ferdinand de Rohan and Charlotte Stuart to have their daughter, Marie-Victoire, legitimised at baptism on their behalf by Jules-Hercule, the 'dutiful' head of the family whom his brothers considered they had 'in the pocket'?

Bibliography

PRIMARY SOURCES

Allgemeines Verwaltungsarchiv, Vienna,
  Hofkanzley, Adelsarchiv.
  Pinino-Piniński 1780 (E).
Archives de l'Armée de Terre au Château de Vincennes, Paris,
  Acts of the Army of de Condé (de Pauw).
Archives de Paris,
  Registers of Baptisms, Marriages and Deaths (Roehenstart).
  Registers of Property Ownership.
Archives Départementales d'Indre-et-Loire, Chambray-les-Tours,
  Commune de Veigné, N.M.D. 1779 (Marie de Thorigny).
Archives Départementales d'Indre-et-Loire, Tours,
  Centre des Archives Historiques, Insinuations et Donations,
    Généralité de Tours 1782 (Jules-Hercule de Rohan).
Archives Générales de Royaume et Archives de l'Etat dans les
    Provinces,
  Registers of Death (Cousin de la Morlière).
Archives Nationales, Paris,
  Archives Privées, Archive Berryer.
            Archive de Rohan.
Archiwum Archidiecezjalne obrządku łacińskiego w Przemyślu,
  Ksiegi parafialne z Babic nad Sanem.
  Spis kolatorów kościoła w Krasiczynie XVIII-XIX w.
Archive of the Maria Hietzing Cemetary, Vienna,
  Group 4, nrs 55–57 (de Nikorowicz, Leiner & de Thorigny/de
    Pauw).

Archiwum Główne Akt Dawnych, Warsaw,
  Archiwum Królestwa Polskiego, Etats des Débiteurs et Créanciers
  de Fergusson-Tepper et Charles Schultz.
Archiwum Masońskie.
Archiwum Radziwiłłów, dz.5.
Metryki Koronne nr 105, 213.
Archiwum Państwowe w Przemyślu,
  Acta Castrensis Premislensis, liber 156, XVIIIw.
  Archiwum b.Sądu Okręgowego w Przemyślu, Księgi hipoteczne dla
  wielkiej własności – materiały dotyczące dóbr krasiczyńskich
  1834–1836.
Biblioteka Narodowa, Warsaw,
  Biblioteka Czartoryskich, Akta dotyczące stosunków z Turcją
  1699–1756.
  Römer M., Korespondencja, sygn.8701, vol.3.
  Zbiór Aleksandra Czołowskiego, Notaty do genealogii różnych
  rodzin XVIIIw. z akt archiwalnych we Lwowie.
Biblioteka Uniwersytetu Warszawskiego, Warsaw,
  Ikonnikov N., La Noblesse de la Russie, vol.46 (Korff).
  Katalog Rękopisów Synodu Ewangelistów Reformowanych, vol.3.
Bibliothèque de la Société Archéologique de Tourraine, Tours,
  Vieira L., Le Château de Thorigny, Tours 1997.
Bobrzyński M., Z moich pamiętników, Wrocław 1957.
Bodleian Library, Oxford,
  Department of Western Manuscripts, Documents & Letters of
                                     Charles Edward
                                     Roehenstart.
                                     Letters of Charlotte Stuart
                                     to Clementina
                                     Walkinshaw.
Bogdanowicz M.Rosco-, Wspomnienia, Cracow 1958.
Central State Historical Archive of the Ukraine in Lwów,
  Archive of the Armenian-Catholic Cathedral of Lwów.
  Archive of the former Imperial Court of Nobility.
Chłędowski K., Pamiętniki, Cracow 1951.
College of Heralds, London,
  W.L.Chester MSS, Bigland's Pedigrees.
Family Records Centre, Clerkenwell,
  Prerogative Court of Canterbury Wills, Misc.Marriages & Burials
  in Consular Records, Paris.

Fundacja-Zakład Narodowy im.Ossolińskich, Wrocław,
  Dział Rekopisów, Mańkowska S. z Nikorowiczów, sygn.15.971.
Guides to the National Register of Archives 4, HMSO London, The
  Royal Commission on Historical Manuscripts, Private Papers of
  British Diplomats 1782–1900.
Jabłonowski L., *Pamiętniki*, Cracow 1962.
Kodeks dyplomatyczny Polski, ed.J.Bartoszewicz, J.Helcel, J.Muczkowski,
  L.Rzyszczewski, vols 1–3, Warsaw 1847–1852 (Pinino).
Kriegsarchiv, Vienna,
  Military Records for Anthim, Ritter von Nikorowicz, 1823–1829.
National Register of Archives, Chancery Lane, London, (Charles
  Stuart, Baron Stuart de Rothesay),
  http://www.hmc.gov.uk/nra/Pidocs.asp/P-2759.
Sobieski J., *Listy do Marysieńki*, ed.L.Kukulski, Warsaw 1962.
Státni Oblastní Archiv Litoméřice, Pobočka Děčin,
  Archiv Rohanové.
Teki Włodzimierza Dworzaczka, Materiały historyczno-genealogiczne
  do dziejów szlachty wielkopolskiej 1995, nr 1, CD-rom.
W. Stefanyk Scientific Library of the Ukrainian Academy of Science in
  Lwów, Piniński Archive.
Wybranowski R., *Pamiętniki*, Lwów 1882.
Zamek Królewski, Warsaw,
  Gabinet Genealogiczny, Archiwum Pinińskich.

SECONDARY SOURCES

A Jacobite Echo, 'The Oban Times', 24 VI 1939.
Aftanazy R., *Materiały do dziejów rezydencji*, Warsaw 1986–1993.
Almanach National 1879, Paris 1879.
Almanach Royal 1784, ed.L.d'Houry, Paris 1784.
Archiwa rodzinno-majatkowe w zbiorach państwowych we Lwowie,
  ed.S.Pijaj, Warsaw 1995.
Baloche C., *Eglise Saint Merry de Paris*, Paris 1912.
Bär M., *Der Adel in Polnisch-Preussen*, Leipzig 1911.
Barącz S., *Żywoty sławnych Ormian w Polsce*, Lwów 1856.
Baron Roehenstart, 'The Oban Times', 5 VIII 1939.
Bartoszewicz K., *Radziwiłłowie*, Warsaw & Cracow 1928.
Berry C.L., *The Young Pretender's Mistress*, London 1977.
Bieniak J., *Elita Ziemi Dobrzyńskiej w późnym średiowieczu; stolica i region*

Włocławek i jego dzieje na tle przemian Kujaw i Ziemi Dobrzyńskiej, Włocławek 1995.

Bihan A.le, *Franc-Maçons et Ateliers Parisiens de la Grande Loge de France au XVIIIe siècle (1760–1795)*, Paris 1973.

Biliński A., *Szlachta Ziemi Dobrzyńskiej*, Warsaw 1932.

Bongie L.L., *The Love of a Prince*, Vancouver 1986.

Boniecki A., *Herbarz polski*, vols 1–16, Warsaw 1899–1913.

Bord G., *La Franc-Maçonnerie en France des Origines à 1815*, Paris 1908.

Borkowski J. Dunin-, *Almanach błękitny*, Lwów 1908.

Borkowski J. Dunin-, *Genealogie zyjących utytułowanych rodów polskich*, Lwów 1914.

Borkowski J. Dunin-, *Rocznik szlachty polskiej*, vols 1 & 2, Lwów 1881 & 1883.

Bouilly C.-L., *Les Récapitulations*, Paris 1840.

Broglie J., *Le Secret du Roi*, Paris 1878.

Busserolle J.X.Carré de, *Dictionnaire Géographique d'Indre-et-Loire*, 1883.

Cassavetti E., *The Lion and the Lilies*, London 1977.

Charewiczowa Ł., *Czarna Kamienica i jej mieszkańcy*, Lwów 1935.

Chevalier P., *Histoire de la Franc-Maçonnerie*, Paris 1992.

Chwalewik E., *Zbiory polskie*, Warsaw 1926 – (Grzymałów & Lwów-Piniński Hr.Leon).

Correspondence de Benoît XIV, ed.E.Heeckeren, Paris 1912.

Correspondence Secrète de Louis XV, ed.M.E.Boutaric, Paris 1866.

Correspondence Secrète du Comte de Broglie avec Louis XV, ed. D. Ozanum & M.Antoine, Paris 1961.

Cronin V., *Louis & Marie-Antoinette*, London 1974.

Czołowski A., *Jan III i zamek w Olesku*, Lwów 1935.

Czołowski A. & Bohdan J., *Przeszłość i zabytki woj.tarnopolskiego*, Tarnopol 1926.

Daiches D., *Charles Edward Stuart*, London 1975.

Demeulenaere-Douyère C., *Guide des Sources de l'Etat Civil Parisien*, Paris.

Deyon P.& S., *Henri de Rohan – Huguenot de Plume et d'Epée*, Paris 2000.

Dictionnaire de la Noblesse, Paris 1872 – (de Rohan).

Douglas H., *The Private Passions of Bonnie Prince Charlie*, Stroud 1998.

Drohojowski J., *Kronika Drohojowskich*, Cracow 1904.

Epsztein T. & Górzyński S., *Spis ziemian Rzeczypospolitej Polskiej w roku 1930, woj. stanisławowskie i tarnopolskie*, Warsaw 1991.

Epsztein T. & Górzyński S., *Spis ziemian Rzeczypospolitej Polskiej w roku 1930, woj. poleskie i wołyńskie*, Warsaw 1996.

Forster M., *The Rash Adventurer*, London 1973.

Frąckiewicz A., *Polish Students at St. Andrews University*, Edinburgh 1994.

Frank K.F.von, *Standeserhebungen und Gnadenakte für das Deutsche Reich und die österreichischen Erblande bis 1806 sowie kaiserlich österreichische bis 1823 mit einingen Nachträgen zum „Alt Österreichischen Adels-Lexicon' 1823–1918*, bd.1–5, Senftenegg 1974.

Gawroński F.R., *Rodzina Hurków*, Cracow 1895.

Genealogisches Handbuch des Adels, Gräfliche Häuser, bd.9 & 15, Limburg an der Lahn 1979 & 1997.

Gibson J.S., *Lochiel of The '45*, Edinburgh 1994.

Gilbert J., *Narratives of the Detention, Liberation and Marriage of Maria Clementina Stuart, styled Queen of Great Britain and Ireland*, Dublin 1894.

Górzyński S., *Nobilitacje w Galicji w latach 1772–1918*, Warsaw 1997.

Gostwicka J., *Włoskie meble renensansowe w zbiorach wawelskich*, Warsaw 1954.

Gothaisches Genealogisches Taschenbuch der Gräflichen Häuser, Gotha 1862–1920.

Graeme L., *A Book of the Graemes and Grahams*, Edinburgh 1924.

Guthrie-Smith J., *Strathendrick and its Inhabitants from Early Times*, 1896.

Harrer-Lucienfeld P., *Wien – seine Häuser*, Menschen und Kultur, bd.7, Vienna.

Hass L., *La Franc-Maçonnerie et les Sciences Occultes au XVII-XVIIIe Siècle: Jean Luc-Louis de Toux de Salvert*, Warsaw 1986.

Hass L., *Loża i Polityka – masoneria rosyjska 1822–1995*, Warsaw 1998.

Hass L., *Wolnomularstwo w Europie Środkowo-Wschodniej w XVIII i XIX w.*, Wrocław 1982.

Hass L., *Ze studiów nad wolnomularstwem polskim ostatniej ćwierci XVIII w.*, Warsaw 1973.

Haynin E.de, *Louis de Rohan – le Cardinal 'Collier'*, Paris 1997.

'Héraldique et Généalogique', 1981, July-August, vol.XIII D.4927.

Huart S.d', *Archives Rohan-Bouillon*, Paris 1970.

Kervella A., *La Franc-Maçonnerie Ecossaise dans l'Ancien Régime*, Paris 1999.

Konarski S., *Armorial de la Noblesse Polonaise Titrée*, Paris 1958.

Konarski S., *O heraldyce i 'heraldycznym snobiźmie'*, Paris 1967.

Konarski S., *Szlachta kalwińska w Polsce*, Warsaw 1936.

Kornatowski W., *Kryzys bankowy w Polsce 1793 r. – upadłość Teppera, Szulca, Kabryta, Prota Potockiego, Łyszkiewicza i Heyzlera*, Warsaw 1937.

Korwin L., *Ormiańskie rody szlacheckie*, Cracow 1934.

Korzon T., *Wewnętrzne dzieje Polski za Stanisława Augusta*, Cracow 1897–1898.

Krasiczyn, ed.L.Majewski, Rzeszów 2000.

Krasiczyn, 'Rozmaitości', nr 39, Lwów 1832.

Kriegseisen W., *Ewangelicy polscy i litewscy w epoce saskiej*, Warsaw 1996.

Kruczkowski S.Korwin, *Poczet Polaków wyniesionych do godności szlacheckiej przez monarchów austrjackich 1773–1918*, Lwów 1935.

Kryciński S., *Krasiczyn*, Warsaw 1990.

Krzeczunowicz K., *Historia jednego rodu*, London 1973.

Krzeczunowicz K., *Księga 200–lecia ułanów ks.Józefa*, London 1984.

Krzeczunwicz K., *Ułani księcia Józefa*, London 1960.

Książęca wizyta w królewskim miejście, 'Czas Krakowski', 20 V 1993.

Land A., *Prince Charles Edward*, London 1990.

Lasocki Z., Dołęga czy do Łęgia?, Cieszyn 1932.

Lees-Milne J., *The Last Stuarts*, London 1983.

Lenczewski T., *Genealogie rodów utytułowanych w Polsce*, Warsaw 1995–1996.

Lenman B., *The Jacobite Cause*, Glasgow 1986.

Lenman B., *The Jacobite Clans of the Great Glen 1650–1784*, London 1984.

Lenman B., *The Jacobite Risings in Britain 1689–1746*, London 1980.

Linklater E., *The Prince in the Heather*, London 1965.

Livre d'Or des Souverains, Tours 1907.

Lynch M., *Scotland – A New History*, London 1991.

Łazuga W., *Ostatni Stańczyk*, Poznań 1995.

Łazuga W., *'Rządy polskie' w Austrii 1895–1897*, Poznań 1991.

Mackiewicz S., *Dom Radziwiłłów*, Warsaw 1990.

MacLagan M., *Lines of Succession*, London 1981.

MacLean F., *Bonnie Prince Charlie*, London 1988.

Macleod J., *Highlanders*, London 1996.

Mądzik M., *Powstanie i pierwsze lata działalności Kompanii Czarnomorskiej 1782–1785*, 'Rocznik Lubelski', vol.21, 1979.

Magier A., *Estetyka miasta stołecznego Warszawy*, Wrocław 1963.

Małachowski-Łempicki S., *Wykaz członków polskich lóż wolnomularskich w latach 1738–1821*, Cracow 1930.

Mańkowski , T., *Pasy Polskie*, Cracow 1938.

Mańkowski, T. *Szłuka Islamu w Polsce w XVII i XVIII wieku*, Crackow 1935.

Martin G., *Histoire et Généalogie de la Maison de Rohan*, Lyon 1998.

Martin G., *Histoire et Généalogie des Maisons de Rohan, Chabot et Rohan-Chabot*, Lyon 1977.

Matwijów M., *Walka o lwowskie dobra kultury w latach 1945–1948*, Wrocław 1996.

McLaren M., *Bonnie Prince Charlie*, London 1992.

McLynn F., *France and the Jacobite Risings of 1745*, Edinburgh 1981.

McLynn F., *The Jacobites*, London 1985.

Miller P., *A Wife for the Pretender*, London 1965.

Morgan J.de, *The History of the Armenian People*, Boston 1965.

Morton J., *Sobieski*, London 1932.

Murdoch S., *Soldiers, Sailors, Jacobite Spy: Russo-Jacobite Relations 1688–1750*, 'Slavonica', vol.3, nr 1, 1996–1997.

Nanke C., *Szlachta wołyńska wobec Konstytucji Trzeciego Maja*, Lwów 1907.

Niemojowska M., *Ostatni Stuartowie*, Warsaw 1992.

Niesiecki K., *Herbarz*, vols 1–10, Leipzig 1839–1845.

Nomenclature des Voies Publiques et Privées, 7th ed., Paris 1951.

Nouvelle Biographie Générale, Paris 1863.

Ormianie polscy, Cracow 1999.

Ostrowski J.K., *Kresy bliskie i dalekie*, Cracow 1998.

Osuchowski W., *Bibliografja prac Leona Pinińskiego.*, *Księga pamiątkowa ku czci Leona Pinińskiego*, Lwów 1936.

Partacz C., *Od Badeniego do Potockiego*, Toruń 1996.

Payne R., *The Crusades*, London 1994.

Perrault G., *Le Secret du Roi, l'Ombre de la Bastille*, Paris 1993.

Perrault G., *Le Secret du Roi, la Passion Polonaise*, Paris 1992.

Petrie C., *The Jacobite Movement*, London 1959.

Piniński A., *Poezye*, Cracow 1903.

Piniński L., *Zamek na Wawelu*, Lwów 1905.

Poczet szlachty galicyjskiej i bukowińskiej, Lwów 1857.

Polski słownik biograficzny, vols 1–36, Warsaw 1935–1997.

Prebble J., *Culloden*, London 1961.

Prek F.K., *Czasy i ludzie*, Wrocław 1959.

Protokoły Rady Narodowej Centralnej we Lwowie (14 IV – 29 X 1848 r.), ed.S.Kiniewicz & F.Ramotowska, Warsaw 1996.

Pułaski K., *Kronika polskich rodów szlacheckich Podola, Wołynia i Ukrainy*, vol.1 Brody 1911, vol.2 Warsaw 1991.

Rabowicz E., *Poezje zebrane Wojciecha Miera*, Wrocław 1991.

Raemy T.de, *L'Emigration Française dans le Canton de Fribourg (1789–1798)*, Fribourg 1935.

Randwick 1893–1993, Randwick Historical Society, Stroud 1995, (Paul/Cameron Todd).

Raunié E., *Epitaphier du Vieux Paris*, Paris 1890, (Parish of St. Benoît).

Rietstap J., *Armorial Général*, vol.1, Lyon, (Barbieri).

Sage H., *Une République de Trois Mois: le Prince de Rohan-Guéméné*, Verviers 1909.

Schneider A., *Encyklopedia do krajoznawstwa Galicji*, vols 1–2, Lwów 1868–1874.

Schuchard M.K., *The Young Pretender and Jacobite Freemasonry: New Light from Sweden on his role as 'Hidden Grand Master'*, (revised), *The Consortium on Revolutionary Europe, 1750–1850, Selected Papers*, Florida State University 1994.

Sherburn G., *Roehenstart – a Late Stuart Pretender*, Edinburgh & London 1960.

Siebmacher J., *Galizischer Adel*, Nuremberg 1905.

Sire H.J.A., *The Knights of Malta*, New Haven & London 1949.

Skeet F.J.A., *H.R.H. Charlotte Stuart, Duchess of Albany*, London 1932.

Skubiszewska M., *Malarstwo włoskie w zbiorach wawelskich*, Cracow 1973.

Słownik geograficzny Królestwa Polskiego i innych krajów słowiańskich, vols 1–15, Warsaw 1880–1902.

Smoleński W., *Mieszczaństwo warszawskie w końcu wieku XVIII*, Warsaw 1976.

Speck W., *The Butcher*, Oxford 1981.

Spisok dworjan podolskoj gubernii, Kamieniec Podolski 1913.

Spisok dworjan wolyn.gubernii, Żytomierz 1900.

Spisok dworjan wnessenych w dworjanskuju rodoslownuju knigu podolskoj gubernii, Kamieniec Podolski 1897.

Stewart of Ardvorlich J., *The Camerons – A History of Clan Cameron*, Glasgow 1974.

Stopka K., *Ormianie w Polsce dawnej i dziesiejszej*, Cracow 2000.

Straka G., *The Revolution of 1688: Whig Triumph or Palace Revolution?*, Boston 1963.

Stuart M., *Scottish Family History*, Edinburgh 1930.

Szulc E., *Cmentarz Ewangelicko-Augsburski w Warszawie*, Warsaw 1989.

Szulcowie J.& E., *Cmentarz Ewangelicko-Reformowany w Warszawie*, Warsaw 1989.

Świerz-Zaleski S., *Zbiory Zamku Królewskiego na Wawelu w Krakowie*, Cracow 1935.

Taylor A.& H., *1745 and After*, London 1938.

Taylor H., *Prince Charlie's Daughter*, London 1950.

Temple-Patterson A., *A History of Southampton 1700–1914*, vol.1, Southampton 1975.

The Army List 1792 & 1795.

The Heather Grave on Campbell Island – a Stuart legend, 'The Oban Times', 15 IV 1939.

The Incorporation of Bakers of Glasgow, Glasgow 1937, (Graham).

The Naval Chronicle, vol.13, 1805.

The Parish of Killearn, Killearn Trust, Glasgow 1988, (Graham).

'The Royalist', Journal of the Royal Stuart Society, vol.VI, nr 31, 1957.

'The Scottish Genealogist', vol.XVIII/4, 1971; vol.XIX/2, 1972.

Tynna J.de la, *Dictionnaire Topographique, Historique et Etymologique des Rues de Paris*, Paris 1817, (Parish of St. Benoît).

Uruski S., *Rodzina. Herbarz szlachty polskiej*, vols 1–15, Warsaw 1904–1938.

Velde F., *History of the Duchy of Bouillon*, (http://www.heraldica.org/topics/france/bouillon.htm).

Waliszewski K., *Marysieńka*, London 1898.

Winiewicz J. & Kozak S., *Anglicy – malarstwo i grafika XVII–XIXw. Dary Leona hr.Pinińskiego dla Wawelu i Ossolineum*, Wrocław 1999.

Winiewicz J. & Kuczman K., *Malarstwo angielskie w zbiorach wawelskich – Fundacja Leona hr.Pinińskiego*, Cracow 1993.

Wizerunki Sejmowe, Lwów 1903.

Z dziejów Römerów na Litwie, ed. A. Rosner & D. Kamolowa, Warsaw 1992.

Zamoyski A., *The Last King of Poland*, London 1992.

Ziemianie polscy XX w., vols 1–3, Warsaw 1992–1996.

Zlat M., *Zamek w Krasiczynie*, Studia renesansowe, Wrocław 1963.

Żychliński T., *Złota księga szlachty polskiej*, Poznań 1879–1908, (vol.23).

Index

Baworowski, Count Michael 244
de Beauchaine, Charles-François Radet 69
Beaufort, Duke of *see* Somerset
Beauvallet 133
Benedict XIII, Pope 17
Benedict XIV, Pope 179
de la Bérarde, Henriette Sarra, née Gauné de Cazau 152
de la Bérarde, Louis Sarra 152
Bernatowicz, family 170
Bernatowicz, Christopher 170
Bernatowicz, James 178
Bernatowicz, Lawrence 178
Berry, C.L. 126, 156, 206, 211
Berryer, family 154, 208, 221, 222
Berryer, Antoine-Pierre 154
Berryer, Hippolyte-Nicolas 156
Berryer, Pierre-Nicolas 154, 156
Berwick, Duke of *see* FitzJames
Besson, Claude-Marie 152
de Béthune, Maximilien, Duke de Sully 106
von Bianchi, Anton 224
Bilczewski, Archbishop Joseph 244
Bing, M. 223
de Biron, Duke 59
de Biron, Peter, Duke of Courland 141
Blairfelty 75
Blandford, Lord *see* Churchill
Blank, Peter 64, 161
Blondin, Marie 128
Bobrzyński, Michael 239
Boffrand, Germain 62
Bogdanowicz, Marian Rosco- 239
Boleszczyc, John *see* Piniński
Boleszczyc, Nicholas *see* Piniński
Bongie, Prof. L.L. 60, 128
Boquen, Marquis 219, 221
Borgia, Cardinal 120
Bouchier Smith, family 198
Bouchier Smith, Joseph 198

de Bouillon, Baldwin, King of Jerusalem 167
de Bouillon, Duke *see* de la Tour
de Bouillon, Eustace 167
de Bouillon, Godfrey 167
Bouilly, C.-L. 135, 136
Bourbon, Kings of France 62, 68, 106, 132, 143, 154, 180, 211, 215
Bourbon, Charlotte, Princess de Condé, née Princess de Rohan-Soubise 72, 143, 145
Bourbon, Princess Louise, de Condé 72, 145
Bourbon, Prince Louis, Dauphin of France 59
Bourbon, Louis-François, Prince de Conti 68
Bourbon, Louis, Prince de Condé 67, 143, 181, 208, 209, 211, 218, 220, 228
Bourbon, Prince Louis, Duke d'Enghien 143, 146
Bourbon, Prince Louis Philippe I, Duke of Orléans 69
Bourbon, Prince Philippe II, Duke of Orléans 14, 16
de Bourgignon, Prof. Jean, Baron von Baumberg 180, 193
Boyd, William, 4th Earl of Kilmarnock 30
Boyle, Charles, 4th Earl of Orrery 14
Bradstreet, Dudley 33
Branicka, Catherine, née Princess Radziwiłł 68
Branicka, Izabela, née Poniatowska 67, 68
Branicki, John Clemence 68
Breadalbane, Lord *see* Campbell
Brittany, Dukes of 106
de Broglie, Count Charles-François 68
Bruce, Kings of Scots 6

Forbes, Alexander 30
Forbes, Alexander, 4th Lord Forbes
  of Pitsligo 30, 39, 45
Forbes, Duncan 42
Forbes of Skellater, George 75
Forbes, John 187, 188, 194
Fournier, Alain 251, 252
Francis I of Lorraine, Holy Roman
  Emperor 101
Francis I von Habsburg-Lorraine,
  Emperor of Austria 172
Franz Joseph I von Habsburg-
  Lorraine, Emperor of Austria 240
Fraser, clan 39, 40, 43
Frasers of Aird 45
Frasers of Stratherrick 45
Fraser of Inverallochy, Charles 38
Fraser, Kenneth 255
Fraser, Simon, 11th Lord Lovat 19,
  45
Fraser, Simon, Master of Lovat, 38
Fraser, William, 1st Lord
  Strathalmond 247
Frederick II the Great, King of
  Prussia 57, 75
Frederick William II, King of
  Prussia 139
Frederick I, King of Würrtemberg
  165
de Fresnel et Curel, Count
  Ferdinand Hennequin 219, 221
Fryczyński, James 178

Gasparine de Rohan, Princess of
  Reuss-Greiz 208, 209
Gaydon, Richard 9
Gehegan 96
Geisruk 219
George I, King of Great Britain
  8–10, 13, 15, 16, 35, 90
George II, King of Great Britain,
  13, 16, 22, 25, 31, 32, 39, 49, 59,
  75, 76, 90, 179

George III, King of Great Britain
  85, 121, 195, 197
George, Prince Regent, George IV,
  King of Great Britain (1820) 159,
  188, 193, 195
von Gintowt, Magdalena
  Dziewałtowska 224
Giovanetti, Cardinal-Archbishop
  Andrea 119
von Giuliani, Theresa 224, 225
Giuliani, Francesco 224
Giuliani, Henry 224
Giuliani, Michael 224
Giuliani, Peter 224
Giziński, Alexander 238
Glen, William 40
Golovkin, Count 187
Gordon, clan 30, 40
Gordon of Aberlour 30
Gordon, Iain 158, 159
Gordon, Abbé John 86, 104
Gordon of Glenbucket, John 25, 30,
  39, 45
Gordon, Lord Lewis 30, 34, 39, 41,
  45
Gordon of Park, Sir William 33
Goring, Sir Charles 74
Goring, Sir Henry 14, 60, 73, 75,
  81, 82
Grabowski, Apolinary 230
Graeme, Sir John 57, 83
Graham, Isabella 255
Graham, Isabella, née Fraser
  (Barons Strathalmond) 255
Graham, Jean (wife of Count
  Stanislas Piniński) 254–256
Graham, Jessie, née Cameron Paul
  255
Graham 20
Graham of Claverhouse, James,
  Viscount Dundee 3
Graham, James 255
Graham, Prof. John 255